THE COMPLETE JOSEPH SMITH TRANSLATION OF THE NEW TESTAMENT

THE COMPLETE JOSEPH SMITH TRANSLATION OF THE NEW TESTAMENT

A SIDE-BY-SIDE COMPARISON WITH THE KING JAMES VERSION

EDITED BY THOMAS A. WAYMENT

Text from the original Joseph Smith Translation used by permission of the Community of Christ.

Introduction and Compilation © 2005 Thomas A. Wayment

All rights reserved. No part of this book may be reproduced in any form or by any means without permission in writing from the publisher, Deseret Book Company, at permissions@deseretbook.com or P. O. Box 30178, Salt Lake City, Utah 84130. This work is not an official publication of The Church of Jesus Christ of Latter-day Saints. The views expressed herein are the responsibility of the author and do not necessarily represent the position of the Church or of Deseret Book Company.

DESERET BOOK is a registered trademark of Deseret Book Company.

Visit us at DeseretBook.com

Library of Congress Cataloging-in-Publication Data

Bible. N.T. English. Joseph Smith Translation. 2005.
  The complete Joseph Smith Translation of the New Testament : a side-by-side comparison with the King James Version / edited by Thomas A. Wayment.
     p. cm.
  Includes bibliographical references.
  ISBN 978-1-59038-439-8 (hardbound : alk. paper)
  ISBN 978-1-62972-183-5 (paperbound)
  I. Wayment, Thomas A. II. Bible. N.T. English. Authorized. 2005. III. Title.
BX8630.A2 2005
225.5'209—dc22   2005007710

Printed in the United States of America
Alexander's Print Advantage, Lindon, UT

26 25 24 23 22

Contents

Introduction vii
The Testimony of St Matthew 1
The Gospel According to St Mark. 92
The Gospel According to St Luke 144
The Testimony of John. 224
The Acts of the Apostles 248
The Epistle to the Romans 253
The First Epistle to the Corinthians 267
The Second Epistle to the Corinthians 275
The Epistle to the Galatians 278
The Epistle to the Ephesians. 280
The Epistle to the Philippians. 282
The Epistle to the Colossians 284
The First Epistle to the Thessalonians. 286
The Second Epistle to the Thessalonians. 288
The First Epistle to Timothy. 289
The Second Epistle to Timothy 291
The Epistle to Titus 293
The Epistle to the Hebrews. 294
The Epistle of James 301
The First Epistle of Peter. 304
The Second Epistle of Peter 308
The First Epistle General of John 312
The Epistle of Jude 315
The Revelation of John. 316

Introduction

The publication of the text of the New Translation of the New Testament is a momentous occasion for those interested in the Prophet Joseph Smith's inspired changes to the biblical text. Until quite recently, we have relied on the *Inspired Version* published by the Reorganized Church of Jesus Christ of Latter Day Saints (now Community of Christ) for the text of Joseph Smith's translation of the Bible. Some of the longer and more doctrinally significant changes have also been included in the Latter-day Saint edition of the Bible and Pearl of Great Price since 1979. However, not all verses were included. Several previous publications on the JST have presented the complete *Inspired Version,* the text published by the Community of Christ beginning in 1867, but none of them has been based independently on the original JST manuscripts.

In 2004, Scott H. Faulring, Kent P. Jackson, and Robert J. Matthews published for the first time the complete transcribed text of the New Translation manuscripts as well as a facsimile reproduction of the passages in the Prophet's marked Bible.[1] This effort was facilitated by the generosity of the Community of Christ, who allowed the aforementioned scholars access to the manuscripts. Unlike any prior publication on the New Translation, this new text presents all changes made to the biblical text by the Prophet Joseph Smith.

The Manuscripts of the New Translation

In June 1830, Joseph Smith began his work on a new translation of the Bible. He began with Genesis 1, copying out the entire text and making changes as he went. His scribe was Oliver Cowdery, who wrote down the biblical text, with changes, as it was read to him. Work on the Old Testament continued until March 8, 1831, and progressed as far as Genesis 24:42. The scribes for this portion of the manuscript were, in chronological order, Oliver Cowdery, John Whitmer, Emma Smith, John Whitmer, and Sidney Rigdon.

On March 8, 1831, with Sidney Rigdon acting as scribe, the Prophet began translating the New Testament. This work continued until June of that same year, extending to Matthew 26:71 in the manuscript.

Like the work in the Old Testament, the text of the New Testament was initially written out in its entirety, with changes and additions being dictated directly to Sidney Rigdon. The work proved slow and had only progressed partway through Genesis and most of the way through the Gospel of Matthew. While the Prophet continued his work on the New Testament, John Whitmer began copying the text of the Old Testament that had been completed previously. These two texts of the Old Testament are known as OT1 (the first draft) and OT2 (John Whitmer's copy) respectively.

After arriving at Matthew 26:71 in the New Testament, the Prophet changed scribes and continued on through the Gospel of Mark. Sidney Rigdon then returned as scribe, while John Whitmer began copying the initial work done on Matthew 1:1 to Matthew 26:71. These two manuscripts, the first draft and subsequent copy by John Whitmer, are known as NT1 and NT2, with NT2 being a copy nearly duplicating the first draft. During their work on the Gospel of John, the Prophet realized that the work of translation would proceed much more quickly if they marked the points of insertion directly into the Bible and then included in the manuscripts only those changes to the text. Using this new system of notation they were able to finish the translation of the New Testament in July 1832.

Using Sidney Rigdon and Frederick G. Williams as scribes, Joseph Smith made additional changes to NT2. Therefore, NT2 no longer represented a direct copy of NT1. The text of NT2 also included changes to the manuscripts after the text was declared finished by the Prophet on July 20, 1832. These changes may have been made by the Prophet, his scribes, or unknown editors. In comparing these two manuscripts, which directly overlap only for Matthew 1:1 to Matthew 26:71, I found numerous instances where the two manuscripts departed from one another. Resolving the differences was not as simple as it may initially appear. Because the manuscripts are handwritten, there are multiple instances of scribal error and inadvertent changes to the text. In those instances where there are differences, it may be that the Prophet dictated the text as he desired it in NT1, only to have that subsequent change left out of NT2 due to scribal error. Therefore, this publication includes the variant readings and changes made between NT1 and NT2. NT2 is always given preference; however, NT1 readings are included in parentheses below the NT2 text for comparison purposes.

After completing the New Testament, the Prophet returned to his work on the Old Testament, including using the marked Bible to indicate changes. The entire process was declared finished on July 2, 1833. Both the manuscripts and marked Bible are now in the possession of the Community of Christ.[2]

Was the New Translation Finished?

This question has been asked by those interested in the text of the New Translation for nearly two centuries. As a result of the work done on the New Translation in the past decade, it is now possible to speak about this question with some confidence. Joseph Smith worked on every book of the Bible, declaring some books complete as already printed (for example, Ruth, Lamentations, Obadiah, Micah, Nahum, and Malachi), while significantly altering the text of others. After the work had been declared finished, the Prophet did not indicate that he intended to make any more major corrections to the Bible. But the incomplete nature of the New Translation really lies in the fact that it was never fully prepared for publication. Numerous inconsistencies exist that would have rendered it difficult to publish.

For example, spelling in the manuscripts was not consistent, the chapter headings and system of numbering were not consistent, many changes were made that were not consistent throughout the manuscripts—such as "saith" being changed to "said" or "ye" to "you"—and some points of insertion are still unclear and, in a few instances, are left unmarked. Instead of speaking of the New Translation as incomplete, perhaps it would be wiser to speak of the *manuscripts* as incomplete, with those manuscripts needing to be carefully compared and corrected for consistency prior to publication. The issue of verse numbering would need considerable attention, especially in the longer insertions of text that do not contain any verse breaks. Typically the KJV text includes a single sentence as a verse, whereas the New Translation can include a lengthy addition within a single verse. The issue of punctuation would also need consideration, since the punctuation employed by the Prophet's scribes is somewhere between modern punctuation and KJV punctuation.

During the Prophet's lifetime, he sought funds to enable him to publish the New Translation but was never able to make that endeavor a reality. A printer's copy, with consistent spelling, punctuation, versification, titles, and so forth, would have required considerable effort, accuracy, and funding.

Efforts to Print the New Translation

Joseph Smith's earliest statement regarding the publication of the New Translation of the Bible can be dated to February 1833, when he said that the New Translation "was sealed up, no more to be opened until it arrived in Zion."[3] While living in Kirtland, Ohio, the Prophet intended to take the manuscripts and marked Bible to Jackson County, Missouri, where the New Translation would be published using the Church's printing press there. Those hopes were dashed in July 1833, when the press was destroyed by a mob. The manuscript likely never arrived in Jackson County, but instead traveled with the Prophet to Far West when he moved there with his family.

Because of severe persecution in the late 1830s, the manuscripts of the New Translation were taken by Emma Smith to Commerce, Illinois, for safekeeping (Commerce eventually became the city of Nauvoo). Again in 1840 the Prophet sought to publish the manuscripts and asked that the Church procure funding to make it possible. Samuel Bent and George W. Harris were given this assignment to seek funding. Several requests were made for the needed money, but apparently the Prophet never generated enough revenue to make publication of the New Translation a reality.[4] The Prophet was martyred on June 27, 1844. Exactly how much money the Church had raised at that point is unknown, but the Prophet remained frustrated until the end of his life that he had to attend to temporal matters rather than focus on publishing the New Translation, as well as a new hymnal, a new edition of the Doctrine and Covenants, a new edition of the Book of Mormon, and the Book of Abraham.

Because the manuscripts of the New Translation were kept in the Prophet's home, at his death they passed directly into the hands of Emma Smith. Subsequent requests by Willard Richards to obtain the manuscripts were denied by the Prophet's widow. As the Church moved west, the manuscripts remained in Illinois in the hands of Emma Smith and her descendants. On July 1, 1867, the Reorganized Church of Jesus Christ of Latter Day

Saints began work on publishing the New Translation from a new text that had been created over the course of the previous year. The work proceeded in earnest and in December 1868 the publication was finally made available. The first edition of the New Translation was titled *The Holy Scriptures*.

In 1892–93 the Reorganized Church again published the New Translation in a book called *The Two Records*, which contained not only the New Testament but also the Book of Mormon. This printing was aimed at aiding the missionary work of the church and sending the inspired words of the Prophet Joseph Smith to the world. A later edition, published in 1936, was directed at teachers and students and included an index for the first time. This edition was also the first to be titled the *Inspired Version*, a name that would become a standard used until today. The *Inspired Version* was published again in 1944. Intended to be a corrected and revised version, the text was set in linotype and in 1974 was reset using a computer. The *Inspired Version* that is available today is based on the 1944 corrected edition and contains no significant differences from that text. In 1970 the Reorganized Church published a parallel-column version of the New Translation using the text of the 1944 edition.

Reception of the New Translation by The Church of Jesus Christ of Latter-day Saints

Since the publication of the 1979 edition of the scriptures, the New Translation has been known as the Joseph Smith Translation. Because the manuscripts were not in our possession, and because early requests to obtain or purchase the manuscripts were turned down, modern perception of the Joseph Smith Translation has relied on a variety of anecdotes, some helpful and others not. As early as October 8, 1855, Brigham Young expressed his views concerning the accuracy of the King James Version, perhaps in response to the fact that many in the Church had concerns about the accuracy of the KJV text and anticipated the forthcoming publication of the Joseph Smith Translation. Because the Church no longer had direct access to the New Translation, they were obligated to rely on a Bible that they had been taught contained errors and inconsistencies. President Young therefore taught, "The Bible is good enough just as it is, it will answer my purpose, and it used to answer it very well when I was preaching in the world."[5] Although the New Translation would not be published for another thirteen years, the environment of the 1850s and 1860s reveals a consistent concern for the accuracy of the KJV, with an eye on the anticipated publication of the New Translation.

Perhaps the most vocal supporter of the New Translation was Orson Pratt. Given a copy of the book by Joseph Smith III, the leader of the Reorganized Church, when the text was first published in the late 1860s, Elder Pratt taught consistently from it on a number of occasions in general conferences of the Church.[6] President Young, however, exercised considerable caution in accepting the Reorganized Church's publication.

This situation was discussed extensively in the school of the prophets in Salt Lake City, after which they presented an official position on the *Holy Scriptures* in 1868:

1. The Reorganized Church's publication was not authorized and was not to be accepted as the official Bible of the Church.

2. Joseph Smith never completed the revision of the Bible.

3. The Bible corrections made by Joseph Smith were, however, inspired and valuable for study and use.

4. The Authorized Version (i.e., the KJV) was the Bible of the Church.

5. When God desired the Saints to have a different Bible, he would so direct and empower the proper authorities.[7]

Some of the key points of the Church's official position in 1868 are an allusion to the future coming forth of the New Translation under the direction of God, a clear endorsement of the inspiration that the Prophet Joseph had received while working on the Bible, and the belief that the New Translation was not complete.

Regarding points numbers two and five, Elder Charles W. Penrose succinctly clarified the official position, saying,

"But this important work was not fully completed, and it was his intention to give it a careful examination, correcting all errors that might have been made by scribes or other inaccuracies that might have occurred, and preparing it in such a shape that it would be a standard for the Church, before it should be published to the world. The work not being thus completed its publication has not yet been authorized from the proper source."[8]

It was common in the late nineteenth century to voice the belief that the New Translation was incomplete, as well as the hope that it would one day come forth in its purity. Those days have not yet arrived.

The Current Publication

After working on a project that was dependent upon the absolute accuracy of the written text of the Joseph Smith Translation, I became aware that my work could not proceed on the basis of any existing text. For the purposes of my research, I had to have a text that was one hundred percent accurate to the original manuscripts of the New Translation, without interpolation or bias. This publication of the Joseph Smith Translation represents that text.

In the process of completing this text, several issues have been addressed. The spelling in the manuscripts is in many instances different from modern spelling. Rather than indicate modern changes in spelling or misspellings as JST changes to the text, the spelling of the KJV has been retained. In a few instances the spelling of Joseph Smith's Bible, an 1828 H. & E. Phinney Bible published in Cooperstown, New York, differs from our 1979 LDS edition of the Bible. For example, the 1828 Bible used "Judea," whereas the 1979 LDS edition uses "Judaea" (Matthew 2:1). The Phinney translation also commonly used "a" before nouns beginning with "h" such as "a holy calling," whereas our current Bible commonly uses "an" (2 Timothy 1:9). Both of these changes in spelling appear in the manuscripts to be changes to the text, but are in reality differences between the two versions of the King James text. These changes have been included in the JST column, but are not indicated as changes in bold font. This also occurs on a number of other occasions where the Prophet Joseph Smith preferred the spelling "fullness" instead of the KJV's "fulness" and often preferred "diverse" instead of "divers."

In a very few instances, archaic spellings of names, such as Noe to Noah (Matthew 24:37), were updated in the JST manuscripts. These changes are included in this publication, but were not placed in bold because they are issues of spelling rather than text or doctrine.

In compiling the JST text, I also realized that there were several issues of consistency that needed to be addressed. For example, in the Gospel of Matthew, Joseph Smith added and altered chapter headings of his King James Version, but stopped doing so after Matthew 26. The manuscripts also frequently employ different conventions to relay the same idea. For example, the beginning of a chapter may state "Chapter 19th," "Chapter (19th)," or "Chapter XIX." These differences have been harmonized in this publication for readability and because they offer no significant doctrinal change to the text. In the case of the Gospel of Matthew and the Gospel of John (the two Gospel writers who were apostles), the titles were changed to "The Testimony of St Matthew" or "The Testimony of John," according to the New Translation. Throughout, I have used the book titles found in the Joseph Smith Translation, without a King James Version comparative and without comment.

Punctuation was another issue. The JST text used punctuation inconsistently, with NT1 often omitting it entirely. I have typically followed the punctuation used in the King James Version.

The Prophet's Bible also contains numerous instances of verses where words are crossed out, sometimes in pencil and sometimes in ink, but for which there is no corresponding change indicated in the manuscripts. These changes are represented in the present publication, but the manuscripts did not clarify how these deletions were to be understood. The main reason for including them in this publication is that in a few verses where a change in the manuscripts also included a crossed-out word, the crossed-out words are left out of the recorded text. Therefore, it appears that when the text was dictated to the scribe, the Prophet would remove the crossed-out words, indicating that they should be considered as JST changes.

Another issue associated with the text is numbering of verses. In the majority of instances, the verse numbering indicated in the manuscripts corresponds to the verse numbering of our 1979 LDS edition. However, in a few instances the JST manuscripts depart from our verse numbering and alter how verses were to be divided and which verses were to be included in each chapter. This information is critical for understanding how the text was to be structured prior to publication, but it does not significantly alter the doctrine. In all instances, the text of the King James Version and the Joseph Smith Translation text are given in order. In this way, the reader can follow either text continuously to see which words were altered (indicated by strikethrough) or which were added (indicated by bold font).

This publication of the text of the Joseph Smith Translation is one piece of a rich and sacred history. The work of the Prophet Joseph Smith on revising the text of the Bible has never been so readily available to all members of the Church. While it will become evident that the text still needs correction and improvement, for the first time all changes made to the Bible are available for study. Having the full revision available will permit us to see that the Prophet clarified the text of the Bible to make it easier to read, clarified in a number of instances the relationship between the Father and the Son, harmonized certain portions of the Gospels, and presented the mission of the Son in greater clarity and power.

In a few instances, there are minor differences between this printed Joseph Smith Translation and what is included in our modern edition of the scriptures. These differences, while not doctrinally significant, are a result of now having the fully transcribed text and marked Bible available for study. This text of the Joseph Smith Translation is easily accessible, with all changes indicated by strikethrough in the King James Version and with corresponding corrections in the JST indicated in bold. This publication should prove useful for all those who wish to teach and study the inspired changes made by Joseph Smith, the prophet of the Restoration.

Notes

1. Scott H. Faulring, Kent P. Jackson, and Robert J. Matthews, eds., *Joseph Smith's New Translation of the Bible: Original Manuscripts* (BYU Religious Studies Center: Provo, Utah, 2004).

2. For the most comprehensive study of the scribes and dating of the New Translation, see Faulring, Jackson, and Matthews, eds., *Joseph Smith's New Translation of the Bible*, 55–59.

3. Joseph Smith, *History of the Church of Jesus Christ of Latter-day Saints,* 2d ed. rev., 7 vols. (Salt Lake City: Deseret Book, 1957), 1:324.

4. Smith, *History of the Church,* 4:164; 4:187; 5:293.

5. *Journal of Discourses,* 26 vols. (Liverpool: Latter-day Saints' Book Depot, 1854–86), 3:116.

6. For example, see *Journal of Discourses* 1:56–57; 7:176–77; 15:248–49. John Taylor also made consistent use of the JST in his publication *Mediation and Atonement* (Salt Lake City: Deseret News, 1882), 1, 10, 18–19, and throughout.

7. Cited in Reed C. Durham Jr., *A History of Joseph Smith's Revision of the Bible,* Ph.D. dissertation (Brigham Young University: Provo, Utah, 1965), 254–55.

8. Charles W. Penrose, "The Revised Scripture," *Deseret Evening News,* 22 April 1881.

The Testimony of St Matthew

King James Version

Joseph Smith Translation

Matthew 1:6 And Jesse begat David the king; and David the king begat Solomon of her ~~that had been the wife~~ of Urias;

And Jesse begat David the king; and David the king begat Solomon of her **whom David had taken** of Urias;

Matthew 1:16 And Jacob begat Joseph the husband of Mary, of whom was born Jesus, who is called Christ.

And Jacob begat Joseph the husband of Mary, of whom was born Jesus, **as the prophets have written**, who is called Christ.

Matthew 1:17 So all the generations from Abraham to David ~~are~~ fourteen generations; and from David until the carrying away into Babylon ~~are~~ fourteen generations; and from the carrying away into Babylon ~~unto~~ Christ ~~are~~ fourteen generations.

So all the generations from Abraham to David **were** fourteen generations; and from David until the carrying away into Babylon **were** fourteen generations; and from the carrying away into Babylon **until** Christ **were** fourteen generations.

Matthew 1:18 Now the birth of Jesus Christ was on this wise: ~~When as~~ his mother Mary was espoused to Joseph, before they came together, she was found with child of the Holy Ghost.

Now, **as it is written**, the birth of Jesus Christ was on this wise: **After** his mother Mary was espoused to Joseph, before they came together, she was found with child of the Holy Ghost.

(**NTI** Now the birth of Jesus Christ was on this wise: when his mother Mary was espoused to Joseph **as it is written**, before they came together, she was found with child of the Holy Ghost.)

Matthew 1:19 Then Joseph her husband, being a just ~~man~~, and not willing to make her a publick example, was minded to put her away privily.

(**NT1** Then Joseph her husband, being a just **one**, and not willing to make her a publick example, was minded to put her away privily.)

Matthew 1:20 But while he thought on these things, behold, the angel of the Lord appeared unto him in a ~~dream~~,

But while he thought on these things, behold, the angel of the Lord appeared unto him in a **vision**, saying, Joseph, saying, Joseph, thou son of David, fear not to take unto thee Mary thy wife: for that which is conceived in her is of the Holy Ghost.

Matthew 1:22 Now ~~all~~ this ~~was done~~, that ~~it~~ might be fulfilled which was spoken of the Lord by the ~~prophet~~, saying,

Matthew 1:24 Then Joseph ~~being raised from sleep~~ did as the angel of the Lord had bidden him, and took unto him his wife:

Matthew 1:25 And knew her not ~~till~~ she had brought forth her firstborn son: and ~~he~~ called his name JESUS.

Matthew 2:2 Saying, Where is ~~he~~ that is born ~~King~~ of the Jews? for we have seen his star in the east, and ~~are~~ come to worship him.

Matthew 2:3 When Herod the king had heard ~~these things~~, he was troubled, and all Jerusalem with him.

Matthew 2:4 And when he had gathered all the chief priests and scribes of the people together, he demanded of them where Christ should be born.

Matthew 2:5 And they said unto him, In Bethlehem of Judaea: for thus ~~it is written by the prophet~~,

thou son of David, fear not to take unto thee Mary thy wife: for that which is conceived in her is of the Holy Ghost.

Now this **took place**, that **all things** might be fulfilled which was spoken of the Lord by the **prophets**, saying,

Then Joseph, **awaking out of his vision**, did as the angel of the Lord had bidden him, and took unto him his wife:

And knew her not **until** she had brought forth her firstborn son: and **they** called his name JESUS.

Saying, Where is **the child** that is born **the Messiah** of the Jews? for we have seen his star in the east, and **have** come to worship him.

When Herod the king had heard **of the child**, he was troubled, and all Jerusalem with him.

And when he had gathered all the chief priests and scribes of the people together, he demanded of them, **saying**, Where **is the place that is written of by the prophets in which** Christ should be born? **For he greatly feared, yet he believed not the prophets.**

(**NT1** And when he had gathered all the chief priests and scribes of the people together, he demanded of them **saying**, Where **is it written that** Christ should be born. **For he greatly feared, yet he believed not the prophets.**)

And they said unto him, **It is written by the prophets, that he should be born** in Bethlehem of Judea: for thus **have they said,**

The Testimony of St Matthew

	(NT1 And they said unto him, **It is written by the prophet, that he should be born** in Bethlehem of Judea: for thus have they said,)
Matthew 2:6 And thou Bethlehem, *in* the land of Juda, art not the least among the princes of Juda: for out of thee shall come ~~a Governor, that~~ shall ~~rule~~ my people Israel.	**The word of the Lord came unto us, saying,** And thou Bethlehem, **which layeth** in the land of Judea, **in thee shall be born a Prince, which** art not the least among the princes of Judea: for out of thee shall come **the Messiah, who** shall **save** my people Israel.
	(NT1 **The word of the Lord came unto them, saying,** And thou Bethlehem, **which layeth** in the land of Judea, **in thee shall be born a Prince, which** art not the least among the princes of Judea: for out of thee shall come a governor, that shall rule my people Israel.)
Matthew 2:7 Then Herod, when he had ~~privily~~ called the wise men, enquired of them diligently what time the star appeared.	Then Herod, when he had called the wise men **privily**, enquired of them diligently what time the star appeared.
Matthew 2:8 And he sent them to Bethlehem, and said, Go and search diligently for the young child; and when ye have found ~~him~~, bring me word again, that I may come and worship him also.	And he sent them to Bethlehem, and said, Go and search diligently for the young child; and when ye have found **the child**, bring me word again, that I may come and worship him also.
Matthew 2:9 When they had heard the ~~king~~, they departed; and, lo, the star, which they saw in the east, went before them, ~~till~~ it came and stood over where the young ~~child~~ was.	When they had heard the **King**, they departed; and, lo, the star, which they saw in the east, went before them, **until** it came and stood over where the young **Child** was.
	(NT1 When they had heard the **King**, they departed; and, **Lo! Lo!** the star, which they saw in the east, went before them, till it came and stood over where the young child was.)

Matthew 2:13 And when they were departed, behold, the angel of the Lord ~~appeareth~~ to Joseph in a ~~dream~~, saying, Arise, and take the young child and his mother, and flee into Egypt, and ~~be~~ thou there until I bring thee word: for Herod will seek the young child to destroy him.	And when they were departed, behold, the angel of the Lord **appeared** to Joseph in a **vision**, saying, Arise, and take the young child and his mother, and flee into Egypt, and **tarry** thou there until I bring thee word: for Herod will seek the young child to destroy him.
	(**NT1** And when they were departed, behold, the **angel** of the Lord **appeared** to Joseph in a dream, saying, Arise, and take the young child and his mother, and flee into Egypt, and **tarry** thou there until I bring thee word: for Herod will seek the young child to destroy him.)
Matthew 2:14 ~~When~~ he arose, ~~he~~ took the young child and ~~his~~ mother by night, and departed into Egypt:	**And then** he arose, **and** took the young child and **the child's** mother by night, and departed into Egypt:
	(**NT1 And** when he arose, he took the young child and **the child's** mother by night, and departed into Egypt:)
Matthew 2:16 Then Herod, when he saw that he was mocked of the wise men, was exceeding wroth, and sent forth, and slew all the children that were in Bethlehem, and ~~in~~ all the ~~coasts~~ thereof, from two years old and under, according to the time which he had diligently enquired of the wise men.	Then Herod, when he saw that he was mocked of the wise men, was exceeding wroth, and sent forth, and slew all the children that were in Bethlehem, and all the **coast** thereof, from two years old and under, according to the time which he had diligently enquired of the wise men.
Matthew 2:17 Then was fulfilled that which was spoken by ~~Jeremy~~ the prophet, saying,	Then was fulfilled that which was spoken by **Jeremiah** the prophet, saying,
Matthew 2:18 In Rama ~~was there~~ a voice heard, lamentation, and weeping, and great mourning, Rachel weeping *for* her children, and would not be comforted, because they ~~are~~ not.	In Rama **there was** a voice heard, lamentation, and weeping, and great mourning, Rachel weeping for **the loss of** her children, and would not be comforted, because they **were** not.

Matthew 2:19 But when Herod was dead, behold, an angel of the Lord ~~appeareth~~ in a ~~dream~~ to Joseph in Egypt,	But when Herod was dead, behold, an angel of the Lord **appeared** in a **vision** to Joseph in Egypt,
	(NT1 But when Herod was dead, behold, an angel of the Lord **appeared** in a dream to Joseph in Egypt,)
Matthew 2:20 Saying, Arise, and take the young child and his mother, and go into the land of Israel: for they are dead ~~which~~ sought the young child's life.	Saying, Arise, and take the young child and his mother, and go into the land of Israel: for they are dead **who** sought the young child's life.
Matthew 2:21 And he arose, and took the young child and ~~his~~ mother, and came into the land of Israel.	(NT1 And he arose, and took the young child and **the child's** mother, and came into the land of Israel.)
Matthew 2:22 But when he heard that Archelaus did reign in Judaea in the ~~room~~ of his father Herod, he was afraid to go thither: notwithstanding, being warned of God in a ~~dream~~, he ~~turned aside~~ into the parts of Galilee:	But when he heard that Archelaus did reign in Judea in the **stead** of his father Herod, he was afraid to go thither: **but** notwithstanding, being warned of God in a **vision**, he **went** into the **eastern** parts of Galilee:
	(NT1 But when he heard that Archelaus did reign in Judea in the room of his father Herod, he was afraid to go thither: **but** notwithstanding, **having been** warned of God in a dream, he **went** into the **eastern** parts of Galilee:)
Matthew 2:23 And he came and dwelt in a city called Nazareth: that it might be fulfilled which was spoken by the prophets, He shall be called a Nazarene.	And he came and dwelt in a city called Nazareth: that it might be fulfilled which was spoken by the prophets, He shall be called a Nazarene. **And it came to pass, that Jesus grew up with his brethren, and waxed strong, and waited upon the Lord for the time of his ministry to come. And he served under his father, and he spake not as other men, neither could he be taught; for he needed not that any man should teach him. And after many years, the hour of his ministry drew nigh.**

Matthew 3:1 In those days came John the Baptist, preaching in the wilderness of Judaea,

Matthew 3:3 For ~~this is~~ he ~~that~~ was spoken of by the prophet Esaias, saying, The voice of one crying in the wilderness, Prepare ye the way of the Lord, make his paths straight.

Matthew 3:4 And the same John had his raiment of camel's hair, and a leathern girdle about his loins; and his ~~meat~~ was locusts and wild honey.

Matthew 3:6 And were baptized of him in Jordan, confessing their sins.

Matthew 3:8 Bring forth ~~therefore~~ fruits meet for repentance:

Matthew 3:9 And think not to say within yourselves, We ~~have~~ Abraham ~~to~~ our father: for I say unto you, that God is able of these stones to raise up children unto Abraham.

Matthew 3:10 And now also the axe is laid unto the root of the trees: therefore every tree which bringeth not forth good fruit ~~is~~ hewn down, and cast into the fire.

Matthew 3:11 I indeed baptize you with water ~~unto~~ repentance: ~~but~~ he ~~that~~ cometh ~~after me~~ is mightier than I, whose shoes I am not worthy to bear: he

And in those days came John the Baptist, preaching in the wilderness of Judea,

For **I am** he **who** was spoken of by the prophet Esaias, saying, The voice of one crying in the wilderness, Prepare ye the way of the Lord, **and** make his paths straight.

And the same John had his raiment of camel's hair, and a leathern girdle about his loins; and his **food** was locusts and wild honey.

And **many** were baptized of him in Jordan, confessing their sins.

Why is it, that ye receive not the preaching of him whom God hath sent? If ye receive not this in your hearts, ye receive not me; and if ye receive not me, ye receive not him of whom I am sent to bear record; and for your sins ye have no cloak. Repent therefore, and bring forth fruits meet for repentance:

And think not to say within yourselves, We **are the children of** Abraham, **and we only have power to bring seed unto** our father **Abraham**; for I say unto you, that God is able of these stones to raise up children unto Abraham.

And now also the axe is laid unto the root of the trees: therefore every tree which bringeth not forth good fruit **shall be** hewn down, and cast into the fire.

I indeed baptize you with water **upon your** repentance: **and when** he **of whom I bear record** cometh, **who** is mightier than I, whose shoes I am not worthy

~~shall~~ baptize you with the Holy Ghost, and ~~with~~ fire:	to bear, (or whose place I am not able to fill,) as I said, I indeed baptize you before he cometh, that when he cometh he may baptize you with the Holy Ghost, and fire:
	(**NT1** I indeed baptize you with water **upon your** repentance: **and when** he **of whom I bear record** cometh, **who** is mightier than I, whose shoes I am not worthy to bear, (**or whose tracks I am not able to fill**,) as I said, I indeed baptize you before he cometh, that when he cometh he **may** baptize you with the Holy Ghost, and fire:)
Matthew 3:12 Whose fan ~~is~~ in his hand, and he will throughly purge his floor, and gather his wheat into the garner; but ~~he~~ will burn up the chaff with unquenchable fire.	**And it is he of whom I shall bear record**, whose fan **shall be** in his hand, and he will thoroughly purge his floor, and gather his wheat into the garner; but **in the fullness of his own time** will burn up the chaff with unquenchable fire. **Thus came John, preaching and baptizing in the river of Jordan; bearing record, that he who was coming after him, had power to baptize with the Holy Ghost and fire.**
Matthew 3:13 Then cometh Jesus from Galilee to Jordan unto John, to be baptized of him.	**And** then cometh Jesus from Galilee to Jordan unto John, to be baptized of him.
Matthew 3:14 But John ~~forbad~~ him, saying, I have need to be baptized of thee, and comest thou to me?	But John **refused** him, saying, I have need to be baptized of thee, and **why** comest thou to me?
Matthew 3:15 And Jesus answering said unto him, Suffer ~~it to be so now~~: for thus it becometh us to fulfil all righteousness. Then he suffered him.	And Jesus answering said unto him, Suffer **me to be baptized of thee**, for thus it becometh us to fulfil all righteousness. Then he suffered him. **And John went down into the water, and baptized him.**
Matthew 3:16 And Jesus, when he was baptized, went up straightway out of the water: and, ~~lo~~, the heavens were opened	And Jesus, when he was baptized, went up straightway out of the water: **and John saw**, and, **lo!** the heavens were

unto him, and he saw the Spirit of God descending like a dove, and lighting upon ~~him~~:

Matthew 3:17 And ~~lo~~ a voice from heaven, saying, This is my beloved Son, in whom I am well pleased.

Matthew 4:1 Then ~~was~~ Jesus led up of the Spirit into the wilderness to be ~~tempted of the devil~~.

Matthew 4:2 And when he had fasted forty days and forty nights, he was afterward an hungred.

Matthew 4:4 But ~~he~~ answered and said, It is written, Man shall not live by bread alone, but by every word that proceedeth out of the mouth of God.

Matthew 4:5 Then ~~the devil taketh him~~ up into the holy city, and setteth him on ~~a~~ pinnacle of the temple,

Matthew 4:6 And ~~saith unto him~~, If thou be the Son of God, cast thyself down: for it is written, He shall give his angels charge concerning thee: and in *their* hands they shall bear thee up, lest at any time thou dash thy foot against a stone.

opened unto him, and he saw the Spirit of God descending like a dove, and lighting upon **Jesus**:

(NT1 And Jesus, when he was baptized, went up straightway out of the water: **and John saw, and lo!** the heavens were opened unto him (**John**), and he saw the Spirit of God descending like a dove, and lighting upon **Jesus**:)

And **lo! he heard** a voice from heaven, saying, This is my beloved Son, in whom I am well pleased; **hear ye him.**

Then Jesus **was** led up of the Spirit into the wilderness to be **with God.**

And when he had fasted forty days and forty nights, **and had communed with God,** he was afterwards an hungred **and was left to be tempted of the devil.**

But **Jesus** answered and said, It is written, Man shall not live by bread alone, but by every word that proceedeth out of the mouth of God.

Then **Jesus was taken** up into the holy city, and **the Spirit** setteth him on **the** pinnacle of the temple.

Then the devil came unto him and **said,** If thou be the Son of God, cast thyself down: for it is written, He shall give his angels charge concerning thee: and in their hands they shall bear thee up, lest at any time thou dash thy foot against a stone.

(NT1 **Then the devil came unto him** and saith, If thou be **a** Son of God, cast thyself down: for it is written, He shall give his angels charge concerning thee: and in **thy** hands they shall bear thee

	up, lest at any time thou dash thy foot against a stone.)
Matthew 4:8 Again, ~~the devil~~ taketh him up into an exceeding high mountain, and sheweth him all the kingdoms of the world, and the glory of them;	And again, **Jesus was in the spirit and it** taketh him up into an exceeding high mountain, and sheweth him all the kingdoms of the world, and the glory of them;
	(NT1 And again, **Jesus was taken in the spirit and it** taketh him up into an exceeding high mountain, and sheweth him all the kingdoms of the world, and the glory of them;)
Matthew 4:9 And ~~saith unto him~~, All these things will I give thee, if thou wilt fall down and worship me.	**And the devil came unto him again,** and **said**, All these things will I give **unto** thee, if thou wilt fall down and worship me.
	(NT1 **And the devil came unto him again,** and saith, All these things will I give thee, if thou wilt fall down and worship me.)
Matthew 4:10 Then ~~saith~~ Jesus unto him, Get thee hence, Satan: for it is written, Thou shalt worship the Lord thy God, and him only shalt thou serve.	Then **said** Jesus unto him, Get thee hence, Satan: for it is written, Thou shalt worship the Lord thy God, and him only shalt thou serve.
Matthew 4:11 Then the devil leaveth him, ~~and, behold, angels came and ministered unto him~~.	Then the devil leaveth him.
Matthew 4:12 Now ~~when~~ Jesus ~~had heard~~ that John was cast into prison, ~~he~~ departed into Galilee;	**And now** Jesus **knew** that John was cast into prison, **and he sent angels, and behold, they came and ministered unto him. And Jesus** departed into Galilee;
	(NT1 **And now** Jesus **knew** that John was cast into prison, **and he sent angels, and behold, they came and ministered unto him (John). And Jesus** departed into Galilee;
Matthew 4:13 And leaving Nazareth, he came and dwelt in Capernaum,	And leaving Nazareth, **in Zebulon,** he came and dwelt in Capernaum, which

which is upon the sea coast, in the borders of ~~Zabulon and~~ Nephthalim:

Matthew 4:15 The land of ~~Zabulon~~, and the land of Nephthalim, ~~by~~ the way of the sea, beyond Jordan, Galilee of the Gentiles;

Matthew 4:16 The people which sat in darkness saw great light; and ~~to~~ them ~~which~~ sat in the region and shadow of death light is sprung up.

Matthew 4:19 And he ~~saith~~ unto them, Follow me, and I will make you fishers of men.

Matthew 4:20 And they ~~straightway~~ left *their* ~~nets~~, and followed him.

Matthew 4:21 And going on from thence, he saw other two brethren, James ~~the son of Zebedee~~, and John his brother, in a ship with Zebedee their father, mending their ~~nets~~; and he called them.

Matthew 4:22 And they immediately left the ship ~~and their father~~, and followed him.

Matthew 4:23 And Jesus went about all Galilee, teaching in their synagogues, and preaching the gospel of the kingdom, and healing all manner of sickness and all manner of ~~disease~~ among the people.

Matthew 4:24 And his fame went throughout all Syria: and they brought unto him all sick people that were taken with divers diseases and torments, and those ~~which~~ were possessed with devils, and those ~~which~~ were lunatick, and those that had the palsy; and he healed them.

is upon the sea coast, in the borders of Nephthalim:

The land of **Zebulon**, and the land of Nephthalim, **in** the way of the sea, beyond Jordan, Galilee of the Gentiles;

The people which sat in darkness saw **a** great light; and **unto** them **that** sat in the region and shadow of death light is sprung up.

And he **said** unto them, **I am he of whom it is written by the prophets**; follow me, and I will make you fishers of men.

And they, **believing on his words**, left their **net** and **straightway** followed him.

And going on from thence, he saw other two brethren, James, and John his brother, **the sons of Zebedee**, in a ship with Zebedee their father, mending their **net**; and he called them.

And they immediately left **their father in** the ship, and followed him.

And Jesus went about all Galilee, teaching in their synagogues, and preaching the gospel of the kingdom, and healing all manner of sickness and all manner of **diseases** among the people **which believed on his name**.

And his fame went throughout all Syria: and they brought unto him all sick people that were taken with diverse diseases and torments, and those **who** were possessed with devils, and those **who** were lunatic, and those that had the palsy; and he healed them.

The Testimony of St Matthew

Matthew 4:25 And there followed him great multitudes of people from Galilee, and ~~from~~ Decapolis, and ~~from~~ Jerusalem, and ~~from~~ Judaea, and ~~from~~ beyond Jordan.

Matthew 5:1 And seeing the multitudes, ~~he~~ went up into a mountain: and when he was set, his disciples came unto him:

Matthew 5:2 And he opened his mouth, and taught them, saying,

And there followed him great multitudes of people from Galilee, and Decapolis, and Jerusalem, and Judea, and beyond Jordan.

And **Jesus** seeing the multitudes, went up into a mountain: and when he was set **down**, his disciples came unto him:

And he opened his mouth, and taught them, saying, **Blessed are they who shall believe on me; and again, more blessed are they who shall believe on your words when ye shall testify that ye have seen me and that I am. Yea, blessed are they who shall believe on your words and come down into the depth of humility and be baptized in my name; for they shall be visited with fire and the Holy Ghost, and shall receive a remission of their sins.**

(**NT1** And he opened his mouth, and taught them, saying, **Blessed are they who shall believe on me; and again, more blessed are they who shall believe on your words when ye shall testify that ye have seen me and that I am. Yea, blessed are they that shall believe on your words and come down into the depths of humility and be baptized in my name; for they shall be visited with fire and with the Holy Ghost, and shall receive a remission of their sins.**

Matthew 5:3 Blessed *are* the poor in spirit: for theirs is the kingdom of heaven.

Matthew 5:4 Blessed *are* they that mourn: for they shall be comforted.

Matthew 5:5 Blessed *are* the meek: for they shall inherit the earth.

Yea, blessed are the poor in spirit, **which cometh unto me;** for theirs is the kingdom of heaven.

And again, blessed are **all** they that mourn: for they shall be comforted.

And blessed are the meek: for they shall inherit the earth.

Matthew 5:6 Blessed *are* they ~~which~~ do hunger and thirst after righteousness: for they shall be filled.

Matthew 5:7 Blessed *are* the merciful: for they shall obtain mercy.

Matthew 5:8 Blessed *are* the pure in heart: for they shall see God.

Matthew 5:9 Blessed *are* the peacemakers: for they shall be called the children of God.

Matthew 5:10 Blessed *are* they ~~which~~ are persecuted for ~~righteousness~~' sake: for theirs is the kingdom of heaven.

Matthew 5:11 Blessed are ye, when *men* shall revile you, and persecute *you,* and shall say all manner of evil against you falsely, for my sake.

Matthew 5:12 ~~Rejoice~~, and be ~~exceeding~~ glad: for great *is* your reward in heaven: for so persecuted they the prophets ~~which~~ were before you.

Matthew 5:13 ~~Ye are~~ the salt of the earth: but if the salt ~~have lost his~~ savour, wherewith shall ~~it~~ be salted? ~~it is~~ thenceforth good for nothing, but to be cast out, and to be trodden under foot of men.

Matthew 5:14 ~~Ye are~~ the light of the world. A city that is set on an hill cannot be hid.

Matthew 5:15 ~~Neither~~ do men light a candle, and put it under a bushel, but on a candlestick; and it giveth light ~~unto~~ all that are in the house.

Matthew 5:16 Let your ~~light~~ so shine before ~~men~~, that they may see your

And blessed are **all** they **that** do hunger and thirst after righteousness: for they shall be filled **with the Holy Ghost**.

And blessed are the merciful: for they shall obtain mercy.

And blessed are **all** the pure in heart: for they shall see God.

And blessed are **all** the peacemakers: for they shall be called the children of God.

And blessed are **all** they **that** are persecuted for **my name's** sake: for theirs is the kingdom of heaven.

And blessed are ye, when men shall revile you, and persecute you, and shall say all manner of evil against you falsely, for my sake.

For ye shall have great joy, and be **exceedingly** glad: for great **shall be** your reward in heaven: for so persecuted they the prophets **who** were before you.

Verily, verily, I say unto you, I give unto you to be the salt of the earth: but if the salt **shall lose its** savour, wherewith shall **the earth** be salted? **The salt shall be** thenceforth good for nothing, but to be cast out, and to be trodden under foot of men.

Verily, verily, I say unto you, I give unto you to be the light of the world. A city that is set on a hill cannot be hid.

Behold, do men light a candle, and put it under a bushel? **Nay**, but on a candlestick; and it giveth light **to** all that are in the house.

Therefore let your **lights** so shine before **this world**, that they may see your good

good works, and glorify your Father ~~which~~ is in heaven.

Matthew 5:18 For verily I say unto you, ~~Till~~ heaven and earth pass, one jot or one tittle shall in no wise pass from the law, ~~till~~ all be fulfilled.

Matthew 5:19 Whosoever therefore shall break one of these least commandments, and shall teach men so, he shall ~~be called the least~~ in the kingdom of heaven: but whosoever shall do and teach ~~them~~, the same shall be called great in the kingdom of heaven.

Matthew 5:20 For I say unto you, ~~That~~ except your righteousness shall exceed ~~the righteousness~~ of the scribes and Pharisees, ye shall in no case enter into the kingdom of heaven.

Matthew 5:21 Ye have heard that it ~~was~~ said by them of old time, Thou shalt not kill; and whosoever shall kill shall be in danger of the judgment:

Matthew 5:22 But I say unto you, That whosoever is angry with his brother ~~without a cause~~ shall be in danger of ~~the~~ judgment: and whosoever shall say to his brother, Raca, shall be in danger of the council: ~~but~~ whosoever shall say, Thou fool, shall be in danger of hell fire.

Matthew 5:23 Therefore if thou bring thy gift to the altar, and there rememberest that thy brother hath ought against thee;

Matthew 5:24 Leave ~~there~~ thy gift before the altar, and go thy way; first

works, and glorify your Father **who** is in heaven.

For verily I say unto you, heaven and earth **must** pass **away, but** one jot or one tittle shall in no wise pass from the law, **until** all be fulfilled.

Whosoever therefore shall break one of these least commandments, and shall teach men so **to do**, he shall **in no wise be saved** in the kingdom of heaven: but whosoever shall do and teach **these commandments of the law until it be fulfilled**, the same shall be called great **and shall be saved** in the kingdom of heaven.

For I say unto you, except your righteousness shall exceed **that** of the scribes and Pharisees, ye shall in no case enter into the kingdom of heaven.

Ye have heard that it **hath been** said by them of old time, **that,** Thou shalt not kill; and whosoever shall kill shall be in danger of the judgment **of God.**

But I say unto you, That whosoever is angry with his brother shall be in danger of **his** judgment: and whosoever shall say to his brother, Raca, **or Rabcha,** shall be in danger of the council: **and** whosoever shall say **to his brother**, Thou fool, shall be in danger of hell fire.

Therefore, **if ye shall come unto me, or shall desire to come unto me, or** if thou bring thy gift to the altar, and there rememberest that thy brother hath aught against thee;

Leave **thou** thy gift before the altar, and go thy way **unto thy brother, and** first be reconciled to thy brother, and then come and offer thy gift.

Matthew 5:25 Agree with thine adversary quickly, whiles thou art in the way with him; lest at any time ~~the~~ adversary deliver thee to the judge, and the judge deliver thee to the officer, and thou be cast into prison.

Matthew 5:26 Verily I say unto thee, Thou shalt by no means come out thence, ~~till~~ thou hast paid the uttermost farthing.

Matthew 5:27 ~~Ye have heard that~~ it ~~was said~~ by them of old time, Thou shalt not commit adultery:

Matthew 5:28 But I say unto you, That whosoever looketh on a woman to lust after her hath committed adultery with her ~~already~~ in his heart.

Matthew 5:29 ~~And~~ if thy right eye offend thee, pluck it out, and cast *it* from thee: for it is profitable for thee that one of thy members should perish, and not *that* thy whole body should be cast into hell.

Matthew 5:30 ~~And~~ if thy right hand offend thee, cut it off, and cast *it* from thee: for it is profitable for thee that one of thy members should perish, and not *that* thy whole body should be cast into hell.

be reconciled to thy brother, and then come and offer thy gift.

Agree with thine adversary quickly, while thou art in the way with him; lest at any time **thine** adversary deliver thee to the judge, and the judge deliver thee to the officer, and thou be cast into prison.

Verily I say unto thee, Thou shalt by no means come out thence, **until** thou hast paid the uttermost farthing.

Behold it **is written** by them of old time, **that,** Thou shalt not commit adultery:

But I say unto you, That whosoever looketh on a woman to lust after her hath committed adultery with her **already. Behold, I give unto you a commandment, that ye suffer none of these things to enter into your heart, for it is better that ye should deny yourselves of these things, wherein ye will take up your cross, than that ye should be cast into hell.**

Wherefore, if thy right eye offend thee, pluck it out, and cast it from thee: for it is profitable for thee that one of thy members should perish, and not that thy whole body should be cast into hell.

Or if thy right hand offend thee, cut it off, and cast it from thee: for it is profitable for thee that one of thy members should perish, and not that thy whole body should be cast into hell. **And now this I speak, a parable concerning your sins; wherefore, cast them from you, that ye may not be hewn down and cast into the fire.**

Matthew 5:31 It hath been ~~said~~, Whosoever shall put away his wife, let him give her a writing of divorcement:

It hath been **written, that,** Whosoever shall put away his wife, let him give her a writing of divorcement.

Matthew 5:32 ~~But~~ I say unto you, *That* whosoever shall put away his wife, saving for the cause of fornication, causeth her to commit adultery: and whosoever shall marry her that is divorced committeth adultery.

Verily, verily, I say unto you, That whosoever shall put away his wife, saving for the cause of fornication, causeth her to commit adultery: and whosoever shall marry her that is divorced committeth adultery.

Matthew 5:33 Again, ~~ye have heard that~~ it hath been ~~said~~ by them of old time, Thou shalt not forswear thyself, but shalt perform unto the Lord thine oaths:

Again, it hath been **written** by them of old time, Thou shalt not forswear thyself, but shalt perform unto the Lord thine oaths:

Matthew 5:38 ~~Ye~~ have heard that it hath been said, An eye for an eye, and a tooth for a tooth:

You have heard that it hath been said, An eye for an eye, and a tooth for a tooth:

Matthew 5:40 And if any man will sue thee at the law, and take away thy coat, let him have *thy* cloke also.

And if any man will sue thee at the law, and take away thy coat, let him have **it; and if he sue thee again, let him have** thy cloke also.

Matthew 5:41 And whosoever shall compel thee to go a mile, go with him twain.

And whosoever shall compel thee to go a mile, **go with him a mile; and whosoever shall compel thee to go with him twain, thou shalt** go with him twain.

Matthew 5:45 That ye may be the children of your Father ~~which~~ is in heaven: for he maketh his sun to rise on the evil and on the good, and sendeth rain on the just and on the unjust.

That ye may be the children of your Father **who** is in heaven: for he maketh his sun to rise on the evil and on the good, and sendeth rain on the just and on the unjust.

Matthew 5:46 For if ye love them which love you, what reward have ~~ye~~? do not even the publicans the same?

For if ye love **only** them which love you, what reward have **you**? do not even the publicans the same?

Matthew 5:47 And if ye salute your brethren only, what do ~~ye~~ more *than others*? do not even the publicans ~~so~~?

And if ye salute your brethren only, what do **you** more than others? Do not even the publicans **the same**?

Matthew 5:48 ~~Be~~ ye therefore perfect, even as your Father ~~which~~ is in heaven is perfect.

Matthew 6:1 Take heed that ~~ye~~ do not your alms before men, to be seen of them: otherwise ye have no reward of your Father ~~which~~ is in heaven.

Matthew 6:2 Therefore when thou doest ~~thine~~ alms, do not sound a trumpet before ~~thee~~, as the hypocrites do in the synagogues and in the streets, that they may have glory of men. Verily I say unto you, They have their reward.

Matthew 6:3 But when thou doest alms, let ~~not~~ thy left hand ~~know~~ what thy right hand doeth:

Matthew 6:4 That thine alms may be in secret: and thy Father ~~which~~ seeth in secret himself shall reward thee openly.

Matthew 6:5 And when thou prayest, thou shalt not be as the ~~hypocrites are~~: for they love to pray standing in the ~~synagogues~~ and in the corners of the streets, that they may be seen of men. Verily I say unto you, They have their reward.

Matthew 6:6 But thou, when thou prayest, enter into thy closet, and when thou hast shut ~~thy~~ door, pray to thy Father ~~which~~ is in secret; and thy Father

Ye **are** therefore **commanded to be** perfect, even as your Father **who** is in heaven is perfect.

And it came to pass, as Jesus taught his disciples, he said unto them, Take heed that **you** do not your alms before men, to be seen of them: otherwise ye have no reward of your Father **who** is in heaven.

Therefore when thou doest alms, do not sound a trumpet before **you**, as the hypocrites do in the synagogues and in the streets, that they may have glory of men. Verily I say unto you, They have their reward.

(**NT1** Therefore when thou doest alms, do not sound a trumpet before thee, as the hypocrites do in the synagogues and in the streets, that they may have glory of men. Verily I say unto you, They have their reward.)

But when thou doest alms, let **it be unto thee as** thy left hand **not knowing** what thy right hand doeth:

That thine alms may be in secret: and thy Father **who** seeth in secret himself shall reward thee openly.

And when thou prayest, thou shalt not be as the **hypocrite**: for they love to pray standing in the **synagogue** and in the corners of the streets, that they may be seen of men. **For** verily I say unto you, They have their reward.

But thou, when thou prayest, enter into thy closet, and when thou hast shut **the** door, pray to thy Father **who** is in secret; and thy Father **who**

The Testimony of St Matthew

~~which~~ seeth in secret shall reward thee openly.

Matthew 6:7 But when ye pray, use not vain ~~repetitions~~, as the ~~heathen do~~: for they think that they shall be heard for their much speaking.

Matthew 6:8 Be not ~~ye therefore~~ like unto them: for your Father knoweth what things ye have need of, before ye ask him.

Matthew 6:9 After this manner ~~therefore~~ pray ~~ye~~: Our Father ~~which~~ art in heaven, Hallowed be thy name.

Matthew 6:10 Thy kingdom come. Thy will be done ~~in~~ earth, as *it is* in heaven.

Matthew 6:12 And forgive us our ~~debts~~, as we forgive ~~our debtors~~.

Matthew 6:13 And ~~lead~~ us not into temptation, but deliver us from evil: For thine is the kingdom, and the power, and the glory, for ever. Amen.

Matthew 6:14 For if ye forgive men their trespasses, your heavenly Father will also forgive you:

Matthew 6:15 But if ye forgive not men their trespasses, neither will your Father forgive your trespasses.

Matthew 6:16 Moreover when ~~ye~~ fast, be not, as the hypocrites, of a sad countenance: for they disfigure their faces,

---

seeth in secret shall reward thee openly.

But when ye pray, use not vain **repetition**, as the **hypocrites**: for they think that they shall be heard for their much speaking.

Therefore be **ye** not like unto them: for your Father knoweth what things ye have need of, before ye ask him

Therefore after this manner **ye shall** pray, **saying**, Our Father **who** art in heaven, Hallowed be thy name.

Thy kingdom come. Thy will be done **on** earth, as it is **done** in heaven.

And forgive us our **trespasses**, as we forgive **them who trespass against us.**

And **suffer** us not **to be led** into temptation, but deliver us from evil: For thine is the kingdom, and the power, and the glory, forever **and ever.** Amen.

(NT1 And **suffer** us not **to be led** into temptation, but deliver us from evil: For thine is the kingdom, and the power, and the glory, forever **and forever.** Amen.)

For if ye forgive men their trespasses, **who trespass against you,** your heavenly Father will also forgive you:

But if ye forgive not men their trespasses, neither will your **heavenly** Father forgive **you** your trespasses.

Moreover when **you** fast, be not, as the hypocrites, of a sad countenance: for they disfigure their faces, that they may that they may appear unto men to fast. Verily I say unto you, They have their reward.

Matthew 6:18 That thou appear not unto men to fast, but unto thy Father ~~which~~ is in secret: and thy Father, ~~which~~ seeth in secret, shall reward thee openly.

Matthew 6:22 The light of the body is the eye: if therefore thine eye be single, thy whole body shall be full of light.

Matthew 6:23 But if thine eye be evil, thy whole body shall be full of darkness. If therefore the light ~~that~~ is in thee be darkness, how great ~~is~~ that darkness!

Matthew 6:25 Therefore I say unto you, Take no thought for your life, what ye shall eat, or what ye shall drink; nor yet for your ~~body~~, what ye shall put on. Is not the life more than meat, and the body than raiment?

Matthew 6:26 Behold the fowls of the air: for they sow not, neither do they reap, nor gather into barns; yet your

appear unto men to fast. Verily I say unto you, They have their reward.

That thou appear not unto men to fast, but unto thy Father **who** is in secret: and thy Father, **who** seeth in secret, shall reward thee openly.

The light of the body is the eye: if therefore thine eye be single **to the glory of God**, thy whole body shall be full of light.

But if thine eye be evil, thy whole body shall be full of darkness. If therefore the light **which** is in thee be darkness, how great **shall** that darkness **be**.

(**NT1** But if thine eye be evil, thy whole body shall be full of darkness. If therefore the light **that** is in thee be darkness, how great **shall be** that darkness.)

And again, I say unto you, go ye into the world and care not for the world; for the world will hate you, and will persecute you, and will turn you out of their synagogues; nevertheless, ye shall go forth from house to house, teaching the people; and I will go before you; and your Heavenly Father will provide for you, whatsoever things ye need for food, and what you shall eat; and for raiment, what ye shall wear or put on. Therefore I say unto you, Take no thought for your life, what ye shall eat, or what ye shall drink; nor yet for your **bodies**, what ye shall put on. Is not the life more than meat, and the body than raiment?

Behold the fowls of the air: for they sow not, neither do they reap, nor gather into barns; yet your heavenly Father

The Testimony of St Matthew

heavenly Father feedeth them. Are ye not much better than they?	feedeth them. Are ye not much better than they? **How much more will he not feed you? Wherefore take no thought for these things, but keep my commandments wherewith I have commanded you.**
Matthew 6:27 Which of you by taking thought can add one cubit unto his stature?	**For** which of you by taking thought can add one cubit unto his stature?
Matthew 6:30 Wherefore, if God so clothe the grass of the field, which to day is, and to morrow is cast into the oven, ~~shall he not~~ much more ~~clothe you, O~~ ye ~~of~~ little faith?	Wherefore, if God so clothe the grass of the field, which to day is, and to morrow is cast into the oven, **how** much more **will he not provide for you, if ye are not** of little faith.
Matthew 6:32 ~~(For~~ after all these things do the Gentiles seek:~~)~~ ~~for~~ your heavenly Father knoweth that ye have need of all these things.	**Why is it that ye murmur among yourselves, saying, We cannot obey thy word; because ye have not all these things; and seek to excuse yourselves, saying that,** After all these things do the Gentiles seek? **Behold, I say unto you, that** your heavenly Father knoweth that ye have need of all these things.
Matthew 6:33 But seek ye first the kingdom of God, and his righteousness; and all these things shall be added unto you.	**Wherefore, seek not the things of this world,** but seek ye first **to build up** the kingdom of God, and **to establish** his righteousness; and all these things shall be added unto you.
Matthew 6:34 Take therefore no thought for the morrow: for the morrow shall take thought for the things of itself. Sufficient unto the day ~~is~~ the evil thereof.	Take therefore no thought for the morrow: for the morrow shall take thought for the things of itself. Sufficient unto the day **shall be** the evil thereof.
Matthew 7:1 Judge not, that ye be not judged.	**Now these are the words which Jesus taught his disciples that they should say unto the people.** Judge not **unrighteously,** that ye be not judged; **but judge righteous judgment.**
Matthew 7:2 For with what judgment ye judge, ye shall be judged: and with	For with what judgment ye **shall** judge, ye shall be judged: and with what

what measure ye mete, it shall be measured to you again.

Matthew 7:3 And why beholdest **thou** the mote that is in thy brother's eye, but considerest not the beam that is in thine own eye?

Matthew 7:4 Or how wilt thou say to thy brother, Let me pull out the mote out of thine eye; and, behold, a beam *is* in thine own eye?

Matthew 7:5 ~~Thou hypocrite~~, first cast out the beam out of thine own ~~eye~~; and then shalt thou see clearly to cast out the mote out of thy brother's eye.

measure ye mete, it shall be measured to you again.

And **again, ye shall say unto them,** why **is it that thou** beholdest the mote that is in thy brother's eye, but considerest not the beam that is in thine own eye?

Or how wilt thou say to thy brother, Let me pull out the mote out of thine eye; and **canst not** behold a beam in thine own eye? **And Jesus said unto his disciples, beholdest thou the scribes, and the Pharisees, and the priests, and the Levites? They teach in their synagogues but do not observe the law; nor the commandments, and all have gone out of the way, and are under sin. Go thou and say unto them, Why teach ye men the law and the commandments, when ye yourselves are the children of corruption?**

(**NT1** Or how wilt thou say to thy brother, Let me pull out the mote out of thine eye; and **cannot** behold a beam in thine own eye? **And Jesus said unto his disciples, beholdest thou the scribes, and the Pharisees, and the priests, and the Levites? They teach in their synagogues but do not observe the law nor the commandments, and all have gone out of the way, and are under sin. Go thou and say unto them, Why teach ye men the law and the commandments, when ye yourselves are the children of corruption?**)

Say unto them, Ye hypocrites, first cast out the beam out of thine own **eyes**; and then shalt thou see clearly to cast out the mote out of thy brother's eye.

(**NT1** Say unto them, Thou hypocrites, first cast out the beam out of thine own

	eyes; and then shalt thou see clearly to cast out the mote out of thy brother's eyes.)
Matthew 7:6 Give ~~not~~ that which is holy unto the dogs, neither cast ye your pearls ~~before~~ swine, lest they trample them under their feet, ~~and~~ turn again and rend you.	Go ye into the world, saying unto all, Repent, for the kingdom of heaven has come nigh unto you. And the mysteries of the kingdom ye shall keep within yourselves; for it is not meet to give that which is holy unto the dogs, neither cast ye your pearls **unto** swine, lest they trample them under their feet; **for the world cannot receive that which ye yourselves are not able to bear; wherefore ye shall not give your pearls unto them, lest they** turn again and rend you.
	(NT1 Go ye into the world, saying unto all, Repent, for the kingdom of heaven has come nigh unto you. And the mysteries of the kingdom ye shall keep within yourselves; for it is not meet to give that which is holy unto the dogs, neither cast ye your pearls **unto** swine, lest they trample them under their feet; **for the world cannot receive that which ye yourselves are not able to bear; wherefore ye shall not cast your pearls unto them, lest they** turn again and rend you.)
Matthew 7:7 Ask, and it shall be given you; seek, and ye shall find; knock, and it shall be opened unto you:	**Say unto them, Ask of God**; ask, and it shall be given you; seek, and ye shall find; knock, and it shall be opened unto you:
Matthew 7:8 For every one that asketh receiveth; and he that seeketh findeth; and ~~to~~ him that knocketh it shall be opened.	For every one that asketh receiveth; and he that seeketh findeth; and **unto** him that knocketh it shall be opened
Matthew 7:9 Or what man is there ~~of~~ you, ~~whom~~ if his son ask bread, will he give him a stone?	**And then said his disciples unto him, They will say unto us, We ourselves are righteous and need not that any man**

	should teach us; God, we know, heard Moses, and some [of] the prophets; but us he will not hear. And they will say, We have the law for our salvation, and that is sufficient for us. Then Jesus answered, and said unto his disciples, Thus shall ye say unto them, What man among you, having a son, and he shall be standing out, and shall say, Father, open thy house that I may come in and sup with thee; will he not say, Come in, my son; for mine is thine, and thine is mine? Or what man is there **among** you, **who** if his son ask bread, will he give him a stone?
	(NT1 And then said his disciples unto him, They will say unto us, We ourselves are righteous and need not that any man should teach us; God, we know, heard Moses, and some of the prophets; but us he will not hear. And we have the law for our salvation, and that is sufficient for us. Then Jesus answered, and said unto his disciples, Thus shall ye say unto them, What man among you, having a son, and he shall be a standing out, and shall say, Father, open thy house that I may come in and sup with thee; will he not say, Come in, my son; for mine are thine, and thine are mine? Or what man is there **among** you, whom if his son ask bread, will he give him a stone?)
Matthew 7:11 If ye then, being evil, know how to give good gifts unto your children, how much more shall your Father ~~which~~ is in heaven give good things to them that ask him?	If ye then, being evil, know how to give good gifts unto your children, how much more shall your Father **who** is in heaven give good things to them that ask him?
Matthew 7:13 Enter ye in at the strait gate: for wide *is* the gate, and broad *is*	**Repent therefore, and** enter ye in at the strait gate: for wide is the gate,

The Testimony of St Matthew

the way, that leadeth to destruction, and many there be ~~which~~ go in thereat:

Matthew 7:14 Because strait *is* the gate, and narrow *is* the way, ~~which~~ leadeth unto life, and few there be that find it.

Matthew 7:15 Beware of false prophets, ~~which~~ come to you in sheep's clothing, but inwardly they are ravening wolves.

Matthew 7:16 Ye shall know them by their fruits. Do men gather grapes of thorns, or figs of thistles?

Matthew 7:18 A good tree cannot bring forth evil fruit, neither ~~can~~ a corrupt tree bring forth good fruit.

Matthew 7:21 Not every one that saith unto me, Lord, Lord, shall enter into the kingdom of heaven; but he that doeth the will of my Father ~~which~~ is in heaven.

Matthew 7:22 Many will say ~~to~~ me in that day, Lord, Lord, have we not prophesied in thy name? and in thy name have cast out devils? and in thy name done many wonderful works?

Matthew 7:23 And then will I ~~profess unto them, I~~ never knew ~~you~~: depart from me, ye that work iniquity.

and broad is the way, that leadeth to destruction, and many there be **who** go in thereat:

(**NT1 Repent therefore, and** enter ye in at the strait gate: for wide is the gate, and broad the way, that leadeth to destruction, and many there be **who** go in thereat:)

Because strait is the gate, and narrow the way, **that** leadeth unto life, and few there be that find it.

And again, beware of false prophets, **that** come to you in sheep's clothing, but inwardly they are ravening wolves.

Ye shall know them by their fruits; **for** do men gather grapes of thorns, or figs of thistles?

A good tree cannot bring forth evil fruit, neither a corrupt tree bring forth good fruit.

Verily I say unto you, it is not every one that saith unto me, Lord, Lord, **that** shall enter into the kingdom of heaven; but he that doeth the will of my Father **who** is in heaven.

For the day soon cometh, that men shall come before me to judgment, to be judged according to their works. And many will say **unto** me in that day, Lord, Lord, have we not prophesied in thy name? and in thy name have cast out devils? and in thy name done many wonderful works?

And then will I **say, Ye** never knew **me**: depart from me, ye that work iniquity.

	(**NT1** And then will I **say unto them, Ye** never knew **me**: depart from me, ye that work iniquity.)
Matthew 7:24 Therefore whosoever heareth these sayings of mine, and doeth them, I will liken him unto a wise man, ~~which~~ built his house upon a rock:	Therefore whosoever heareth these sayings of mine, and doeth them, I will liken him unto a wise man, **who** built his house upon a rock:
Matthew 7:26 And every one that heareth these sayings of mine, and doeth them not, shall be likened unto a foolish man, ~~which~~ built his house upon the sand:	And every one that heareth these sayings of mine, and doeth them not, shall be likened unto a foolish man, **who** built his house upon the sand:
Matthew 7:28 And it came to pass, when Jesus had ended these sayings, the people were astonished at his doctrine:	And it came to pass, when Jesus had ended these sayings **with his disciples**, the people were astonished at his doctrine:
Matthew 7:29 For he taught them as *one* having authority, and not as the scribes.	For he taught them as one having authority **from God**, and not as **having authority from** the scribes.
Matthew 8:1 When ~~he~~ was come down from the mountain, great multitudes followed him.	**And** when **Jesus** was come down from the mountain, great multitudes followed him.
Matthew 8:2 And, behold, there came a leper ~~and worshipped~~ him, saying, Lord, if thou wilt, thou canst make me clean.	And, behold, there came a leper **worshipping** him, saying, Lord, if thou wilt, thou canst make me clean.
Matthew 8:4 And Jesus ~~saith~~ unto him, See thou tell no man; but go thy way, shew thyself to the ~~priest~~, and offer the gift that Moses commanded, for a testimony unto them.	And Jesus **said** unto him, See thou tell no man; but go thy way, **and** shew thyself to the **priests**, and offer the gift that Moses commanded, for a testimony unto them.
Matthew 8:7 And Jesus ~~saith~~ unto him, I will come and heal him.	And Jesus **said** unto him, I will come and heal him.
Matthew 8:10 When Jesus heard ~~it~~, he ~~marvelled, and~~ said ~~to~~ them that followed, Verily I say unto you, I have not found so great faith, no, not in Israel.	**And when they that followed him heard this they marveled. And** when Jesus heard **this**, he said **unto** them that followed, Verily I say unto you, I have

The Testimony of St Matthew

Matthew 8:11 And I say unto you, That many shall come from the east and west, and shall sit down with Abraham, and Isaac, and Jacob, in the kingdom of heaven.

Matthew 8:12 But the children of the ~~kingdom~~ shall be cast out into outer darkness: there shall be weeping and gnashing of teeth.

Matthew 8:13 And Jesus said unto the centurion, Go thy way; and as thou hast believed, ~~so~~ be it done unto thee. And his servant was healed in the selfsame hour.

Matthew 8:16 When the ~~even~~ was come, they brought unto him many that were possessed with devils: and he cast out the spirits with ~~his~~ word, and healed all that were sick:

Matthew 8:18 Now when Jesus saw great multitudes about him, he gave commandment to depart unto the other side.

Matthew 8:19 And a certain scribe came, and said ~~unto him~~, Master, I will follow thee whithersoever thou goest.

Matthew 8:20 And Jesus ~~saith~~ unto him, The foxes have holes, and the birds of the air *have* nests; but the Son of man hath not where to lay *his* head.

Matthew 8:23 And when he was entered into a ship, his disciples ~~followed~~ him.

not found so great faith, no, not in Israel.

And I say unto you, That many shall come from the east and **the** west, and shall sit down with Abraham, and Isaac, and Jacob, in the kingdom of heaven.

But the children of the **wicked one** shall be cast out into outer darkness: there shall be weeping and gnashing of teeth.

(**NT1** And Jesus said unto the centurion, Go thy way; and as thou hast believed, be it done unto thee. And his servant was healed in the selfsame hour.)

Now when the **evening** was come, they brought unto him many that were possessed with devils: and he cast out the **evil** spirits with **the** word, and healed all that were sick:

Now when Jesus saw great multitudes about him, he gave commandment to depart unto the other side **of the sea**.

And a certain scribe came **unto him** and said, Master, I will follow thee whithersoever thou goest.

And Jesus **said** unto him, The foxes have holes, and the birds of the air have nests; but the Son of man hath not where to lay his head.

(**NT1** And Jesus saith unto him, The foxes have holes, and the birds of the air nests; but the Son of man hath not where to lay his head.)

And when he was entered into a ship, his disciples **came unto** him.

Matthew 8:25 And his disciples came ~~to~~ *him,* and awoke him, saying, Lord, save us: we perish.

Matthew 8:26 And he ~~saith~~ unto them, Why are ye fearful, O ye of little faith? Then he arose, and rebuked the winds and the sea; and there was a great calm.

Matthew 8:28 And when he was come to the other side into the country of the Gergesenes, there met him ~~two~~ possessed with devils, coming out of the tombs, exceeding fierce, so that no man ~~might~~ pass ~~by~~ that way.

Matthew 8:29 And, behold, ~~they~~ cried out, saying, What have we to do with thee, Jesus, thou Son of God? art thou come hither to torment us before the time?

Matthew 8:31 So the devils besought him, saying, If thou cast us out, suffer us to go ~~away~~ into the herd of swine.

Matthew 8:33 And they that kept them fled, and went their ways into the city, and told every thing, and what was befallen ~~to~~ the possessed of the devils.

Matthew 8:34 And, behold, the whole city came out to meet Jesus: and when they saw him, they besought *him* that he would depart out of their ~~coasts~~.

Matthew 9:1 And ~~he~~ entered into a ship, and passed over, and came into his own city.

And his disciples came **unto** him, and awoke him, saying, Lord, save us: **else** we perish.

And he **said** unto them, Why are ye fearful, O ye of little faith? Then he arose, and rebuked the winds and the sea; and there was a great calm.

And when he was come to the other side into the country of the Gergesenes, there met him **a man** possessed with devils, coming out of the tombs, exceeding fierce, so that no man **could** pass that way.

(**NT1** And when he was come to the other side into the country of the Gergesenes, there met him two **men** possessed **of** devils, coming out of the tombs, exceeding fierce, so that no man might pass by that way.)

And, behold, **he** cried out, saying, What have we to do with thee, Jesus, thou Son of God? art thou come hither to torment us before the time?

So the devils besought him, saying, If thou cast us out, suffer us to go into the herd of swine.

And they that kept them fled, and went their ways into the city, and told every thing **which took place**, and what was befallen the possessed of the devils.

And, behold, the whole city came out to meet Jesus: and when they saw him, they besought him that he would depart out of their **coast**.

And **Jesus** entered into a ship, and passed over, and came into his own city.

Matthew 9:2 And, behold, they brought to him a man sick of the palsy, lying on a bed: and Jesus ~~seeing~~ their faith said unto the sick of the palsy; Son, be of good cheer; thy sins be forgiven thee.	And, behold, they brought to him a man sick of the palsy, **lying** on a bed: and Jesus **knowing** their faith said unto the sick of the palsy; Son, be of good cheer; thy sins be forgiven thee; **go thy way and sin no more**.
Matthew 9:4 And Jesus knowing their thoughts said, Wherefore think ~~ye~~ evil in your hearts?	And Jesus knowing their thoughts said, Wherefore **is it that ye** think evil in your hearts?
Matthew 9:5 For ~~whether~~ is easier, to say, *Thy* sins be forgiven thee; ~~or~~ to say, Arise, and walk?	For is **it not** easier to say, Thy sins be forgiven thee; **than** to say, Arise, and walk?
Matthew 9:6 But that ye may know that the Son of man hath power on earth to forgive sins, ~~(then~~ ~~saith he to~~ the sick of the palsy,~~)~~ Arise, take up thy bed, and go unto ~~thine~~ house.	But **I said this** that ye may know that the Son of man hath power on earth to forgive sins. Then **Jesus said unto** the sick of the palsy, Arise, take up thy bed, and go unto **thy** house.
Matthew 9:7 And he arose, and departed to his house.	And he **immediately** arose, and departed to his house.
Matthew 9:8 But when the ~~multitudes~~ saw *it,* they marvelled, and glorified God, ~~which~~ had given such power unto men.	But when the **multitude** saw it, they marvelled, and glorified God, **who** had given such power unto men.
Matthew 9:9 And as Jesus passed forth from thence, he saw a man, named Matthew, sitting at the ~~receipt of custom~~: and he ~~saith~~ unto him, Follow me. And he arose, and followed him.	And as Jesus passed forth from thence, he saw a man, named Matthew, sitting at the **place where they received tribute, as was customary in those days**; and he **said** unto him, Follow me. And he arose, and followed him.
Matthew 9:10 And it came to pass, as Jesus sat at meat in the house, behold, many publicans and sinners came and sat down with him and his disciples.	And it came to pass, as Jesus sat at meat in the house, behold, many publicans and sinners came and **sat** down with him and **with** his disciples.
Matthew 9:11 And when the Pharisees saw ~~it~~, they said unto his disciples, Why eateth your Master with publicans and sinners?	And when the Pharisees saw **them**, they said unto his disciples, Why eateth your Master with publicans and sinners?

Matthew 9:12 But when Jesus heard ~~that~~, he said unto them, They that be whole need not a physician, but they that are sick.

Matthew 9:13 But go ye and learn what ~~that~~ meaneth, I will have mercy, and not sacrifice: for I am not come to call the righteous, but sinners to repentance.

Matthew 9:14 ~~Then~~ came to him the disciples of John, saying, Why do we and the Pharisees fast oft, but thy disciples fast not?

Matthew 9:16 No man putteth a piece of new cloth ~~unto~~ an old garment, for that which is put in to fill it up taketh from the garment, and the rent is made worse.

Matthew 9:18 While he spake these things unto them, behold, there came a certain ruler, and worshipped him, saying, My daughter is even now ~~dead~~: but come and lay thy hand upon her, and she shall live.

Matthew 9:19 And Jesus arose, and followed him, and ~~so did~~ his disciples.

Matthew 9:26 And the fame ~~hereof~~ went abroad into all that land.

But when Jesus heard **them**, he said unto them, They that be whole need not a physician, but they that are sick.

But go ye and learn what **this** meaneth, I will have mercy, and not sacrifice: for I am not come to call the righteous, but sinners to repentance.

And while he was thus teaching, there came to him the disciples of John, saying, Why do we and the Pharisees fast oft, but thy disciples fast not?

Then said the Pharisees unto him, Why will ye not receive us with our baptism, seeing we keep the whole law? But Jesus said unto them, Ye keep not the law. If ye had kept the law, ye would have received me; for I am he that gave the law. I receive not you with your baptism, because it profiteth you nothing. For when that which is new is come, the old is ready to be put away. For no man putteth a piece of new cloth **on** an old garment, for that which is put in to fill it up taketh from the garment, and the rent is made worse.

While he spake these things unto them, behold, there came a certain ruler, and worshipped him, saying, My daughter is even now **dying**: but come and lay thy hand upon her, and she shall live.

And Jesus arose, and followed him, and **also** his disciples, **and much people thronged him.**

And the fame **of Jesus** went abroad into all that land.

The Testimony of St Matthew

Matthew 9:27 And when Jesus departed thence, two blind men followed him, crying, and saying, *Thou* Son of David, have mercy on us.	And when Jesus departed thence, two blind men followed him, crying, and saying, **Jesus,** thou Son of David, have mercy on us.
Matthew 9:28 And when he was come into the house, the blind men came to him: and Jesus ~~saith~~ unto them, Believe ye that I am able to do this? They said unto him, Yea, Lord.	And when he was come into the house, the blind men came to him: and Jesus **said** unto them, Believe ye that I am able to do this? They said unto him, Yea, Lord.
Matthew 9:30 And their eyes were opened; and ~~Jesus~~ straitly charged them, saying, See *that* no man know *it.*	And their eyes were opened; and straitly **he** charged them, saying, **Keep my commandments, and** see **thou tell no man in this place** that no man know it.
Matthew 9:32 As they went out, behold, they brought to him a dumb man possessed with a devil.	**And** as they went out, behold, they brought to him a dumb man possessed with a devil.
Matthew 9:33 And when the devil was cast out, the dumb spake: and the ~~multitudes~~ marvelled, saying, It was never so seen in Israel.	And when the devil was cast out, the dumb **man** spake: and the **multitude** marvelled, saying, It was never so seen in Israel.
Matthew 9:34 But the Pharisees said, He casteth out devils through the prince of the devils.	But the Pharisees said, He casteth out **the** devils through the prince of the devils.
Matthew 9:35 And Jesus went about all the cities and villages, teaching in their synagogues, and preaching the gospel of the kingdom, and healing every sickness and every disease among the people.	(NT1 And Jesus went about all the cities and **the** villages, teaching in their synagogues, and preaching the gospel of the kingdom, and healing every sickness and every disease among the people.)
Matthew 9:36 But when he saw the ~~multitudes~~, he was moved with compassion on them, because they fainted, and were scattered abroad, as sheep having no shepherd.	But when he saw the **multitude**, he was moved with compassion on them, because they fainted, and were scattered abroad, as sheep having no shepherd.
Matthew 10:1 And when he had called unto *him* his twelve disciples, he gave them power ~~against~~ unclean spirits, to	And when he had called unto him his twelve disciples, he gave them power **over** unclean spirits, to cast them out,

cast them out, and to heal all manner of sickness and all manner of disease.

Matthew 10:5 These twelve Jesus sent forth, and commanded them, saying, Go not into the way of the Gentiles, and into *any* city of the Samaritans ~~enter ye not~~:

Matthew 10:6 But ~~go rather~~ to the lost sheep of the house of Israel.

Matthew 10:11 And into whatsoever ~~city~~ or ~~town~~ ye shall enter, enquire who in it is worthy; and there abide till ye go thence.

Matthew 10:14 And whosoever shall not receive you, nor hear your words, when ye depart out of that house or city, shake off the dust of your feet.

Matthew 10:15 Verily I say unto you, It shall be more tolerable for the land of Sodom and Gomorrha in the day of judgment, than for that city.

Matthew 10:16 Behold, I send you forth as sheep in the midst of wolves: be ye therefore wise ~~as serpents~~, and harmless as doves.

Matthew 10:22 And ye shall be hated of all ~~men~~ for my name's sake: but he that endureth to the end shall be saved.

Matthew 10:23 But when they persecute you in ~~this~~ city, flee ye into another: for verily I say unto you, Ye shall not have gone over the cities of Israel, till the Son of man ~~be~~ come.

Matthew 10:24 The disciple is not above *his* master, nor the servant above his lord.

and to heal all manner of sickness and all manner of disease.

These twelve Jesus sent forth, and commanded them, saying, Go not into the way of the Gentiles, and **enter ye not** into any city of the Samaritans:

But **rather go** to the lost sheep of the house of Israel.

And into whatsoever **town** or **city** ye shall enter, enquire who in it is worthy; and there abide till ye go thence.

And whosoever shall not receive you, nor hear your words, when ye depart out of that house or city, shake off the dust of your feet **for a testimony against them**.

And verily I say unto you, It shall be more tolerable for the land of Sodom and Gomorrha in the day of judgment, than for that city.

Behold, I send you forth as sheep in the midst of wolves: be ye therefore wise **servants**, and **as** harmless as doves.

And ye shall be hated of all **the world** for my name's sake: but he that endureth to the end shall be saved.

But when they persecute you in **one** city, flee ye into another: for verily I say unto you, Ye shall not have gone over the cities of Israel, till the Son of man come.

Remember, the disciple is not above his master, nor the servant above his lord.

Matthew 10:25 It is enough ~~for~~ the disciple ~~that he~~ be as his master, and the servant as his lord. If they have called the master of the house Beelzebub, how much more *shall they call* them of his household?	It is enough **that** the disciple be as his master, and the servant as his lord. If they have called the master of the house Beelzebub, how much more shall they call them of his household?
Matthew 10:27 What I tell you in darkness, ~~that speak~~ ye in light: and what ye hear in the ear, ~~that~~ preach ye upon the housetops.	What I tell you in darkness, **preach** ye in light: and what ye hear in the ear, preach ye upon the housetops.
Matthew 10:28 And fear not them which kill the body, but are not able to kill the soul: but rather fear him which is able to destroy both soul and body in hell.	And fear not them which **are able to** kill the body, but are not able to kill the soul: but rather fear him which is able to destroy both soul and body in hell.
Matthew 10:29 Are not two sparrows sold for a farthing? and one of them shall not fall on the ground without your Father.	Are not two sparrows sold for a farthing? and one of them shall not fall on the ground without your Father **knoweth it**.
Matthew 10:30 ~~But~~ the very hairs of your head are all numbered.	**And** the very hairs of your head are all numbered.
Matthew 10:32 Whosoever therefore shall confess me before men, him will I confess also before my Father ~~which~~ is in heaven.	Whosoever therefore shall confess me before men, him will I confess also before my Father **who** is in heaven.
Matthew 10:33 But whosoever shall deny me before men, him will I also deny before my Father ~~which~~ is in heaven.	But whosoever shall deny me before men, him will I also deny before my Father **who** is in heaven.
Matthew 10:34 Think not that I am come to send peace on earth: I ~~came~~ not to send peace, but a sword.	Think not that I am come to send peace on earth: I **come** not to send peace, but a sword.
Matthew 10:36 And a man's foes ~~shall be~~ they of his own household.	And a man's foes **will** be they of his own household.
	(**NT1** And a man's foes **are** they of his own household.)

Matthew 10:37 He ~~that~~ loveth father or mother more than me is not worthy of me: and he ~~that~~ loveth son or daughter more than me is not worthy of me.

Matthew 10:38 And he ~~that~~ taketh not his cross, and followeth after me, is not worthy of me.

Matthew 10:39 He ~~that findeth~~ his life shall lose it: and he ~~that~~ loseth his life for my sake shall find it.

Matthew 10:40 He ~~that~~ receiveth you receiveth me, and he ~~that~~ receiveth me receiveth him ~~that~~ sent me.

Matthew 10:41 He that receiveth a prophet in the name of a prophet shall receive a prophet's reward; and he that receiveth a righteous man in the name of a righteous man shall receive a righteous man's reward.

Matthew 11:3 And said unto him, Art thou he that should come, or do we look for another?

Matthew 11:4 Jesus answered and said unto them, Go and ~~shew~~ John again those things which ye do hear and see:

Matthew 11:5 The blind receive their sight, and the lame walk, the lepers are cleansed, and the deaf hear, the dead are raised up, and the poor have the gospel preached ~~to~~ them.

Matthew 11:6 And blessed is ~~he~~, whosoever shall not be offended in me.

He **who** loveth father or mother more than me is not worthy of me: and he **who** loveth son or daughter more than me is not worthy of me.

And he **who** taketh not his cross, and followeth after me, is not worthy of me.

He **who seeketh to save** his life shall lose it: and he **who** loseth his life for my sake shall find it.

He **who** receiveth you receiveth me, and he **who** receiveth me receiveth him **who** sent me.

He that receiveth a prophet in the name of a prophet shall receive a prophet's reward; and he that receiveth a righteous man in the name of a righteous man shall receive a righteous man's reward. **And whosoever shall give to drink unto one of these little ones a cup of cold water only, in the name of a disciple, verily I say unto you, he shall in no wise lose his reward.**

And said unto him, Art thou he **of whom it is written in the prophets** that should come, or do we look for another?

Jesus answered and said unto them, Go and **tell** John again **of** those things which ye do hear and see:

How the blind receive their sight, and the lame walk, **and** the lepers are cleansed, and the deaf hear, **and** the dead are raised up, and the poor have the gospel preached **unto** them.

And blessed is **John, and** whosoever shall not be offended in me.

Matthew 11:7 And as they departed, Jesus began to say unto the multitudes concerning John, What went ye out into the wilderness to see? A reed shaken with the wind?	And as they departed, Jesus began to say unto the multitudes concerning John, What went ye out into the wilderness to see? **Was it** a reed shaken with the wind? **And they answered him, No.**
Matthew 11:8 But what went ye out for to see? A man clothed in soft raiment? behold, they that wear soft ~~clothing~~ are in kings' houses.	**And he said,** But what went ye out for to see? **Was it** a man clothed in soft raiment? behold, they that wear soft **raiment** are in kings' houses.
Matthew 11:10 For this is ~~he~~, of whom it is written, Behold, I send my messenger before thy face, which shall prepare thy way before thee.	For this is **the one** of whom it is written, Behold, I send my messenger before thy face, which shall prepare thy way before thee.
Matthew 11:13 For all the prophets and the law prophesied until John.	**But the days will come, when the violent shall have no power;** for all the prophets and the law prophesied, **that it should be thus** until John. **Yea, as many as have prophesied, have foretold of these days.**
Matthew 11:14 And if ye will receive it, ~~this is~~ Elias, ~~which~~ was for to come.	And if ye will receive it, **verily he was** the Elias, **who** was for to come **and prepare all things.**
	(**NT1** And if ye will receive **me,** I am Elias, which was for to come.)
Matthew 11:17 And saying, We have piped unto you, and ye have not danced; we have mourned ~~unto~~ you, and ye have not lamented.	And saying, We have piped unto you, and ye have not danced; we have mourned **for** you, and ye have not lamented.
Matthew 11:19 The Son of man came eating and drinking, and they say, Behold a ~~man gluttonous~~, and a winebibber, a friend of publicans and sinners. But wisdom is justified of her children.	The Son of man came eating and drinking, and they say, Behold a **gluttonous man**, and a winebibber, a friend of publicans and sinners. But **I say unto you,** wisdom is justified of her children.
Matthew 11:21 Woe unto thee, Chorazin! woe unto thee, Bethsaida! for if the mighty works, which were done in you, had been done in Tyre and	Woe unto thee, Chorazin! woe unto thee, Bethsaida! for if the mighty works, which were done in you, had been done in Tyre and Sidon, they would have

Sidon, they would have repented long ~~ago~~ in sackcloth and ashes.

Matthew 11:25 At that time Jesus answered and said, I thank thee, O Father, Lord of heaven and earth, because thou hast hid these things from the wise and prudent, and hast revealed them unto babes.

Matthew 11:27 All things are delivered unto me of my Father: and no man knoweth the Son, but the Father; neither knoweth any man the Father, save the Son, and ~~he~~ to ~~whomsoever~~ the Son will reveal ~~him~~.

Matthew 11:28 Come unto me, all ~~ye~~ that labour and are heavy laden, and I will give you rest.

Matthew 12:2 But when the Pharisees saw ~~it~~, they said unto him, Behold, thy disciples do that which is not lawful to do upon the sabbath day.

Matthew 12:4 How he entered into the house of God, and did eat the shewbread, which was not lawful for him to eat, neither for them ~~which~~ were with him, but only for the priests?

Matthew 12:5 Or have ye not read in the law, how that on the sabbath days the priests in the temple profane the sabbath, and are blameless?

Matthew 12:8 For the Son of man is Lord even of the sabbath ~~day~~.

Matthew 12:9 And when he was departed thence, he went into their ~~synagogue~~:

Matthew 12:10 And, behold, there was a man which had ~~his hand~~ withered. And they asked him, saying, Is it lawful

repented long **since** in sackcloth and ashes.

And at that time **there came a voice out of heaven; and** Jesus answered and said, I thank thee, O Father, Lord of heaven and earth, because thou hast hid these things from the wise and prudent, and hast revealed them unto babes.

All things are delivered unto me of my Father: and no man knoweth the Son, but the Father; neither knoweth any man the Father, save the Son, and to **whom** the Son will reveal **himself, they shall see the Father also**.

Then spake Jesus, saying, Come unto me, all **you** that labour and are heavy laden, and I will give you rest.

But when the Pharisees saw **them**, they said unto him, Behold, thy disciples do that which is not lawful to do upon the sabbath day.

How he entered into the house of God, and did eat the shewbread, which was not lawful for him to eat, neither for them **that** were with him, but only for the priests?

Or have ye not read in the law, how that on the sabbath days the priests in the temple profane the sabbath, and **ye say they** are blameless?

For the Son of man is Lord even of the sabbath.

And when he was departed thence, he went into their **synagogues**:

And, behold, there was a man which had **a** withered **hand**. And they asked him, saying, Is it lawful to heal on the

THE TESTIMONY OF ST MATTHEW

to heal on the sabbath days? that they might accuse him.

Matthew 12:13 Then ~~saith~~ he to the man, Stretch forth ~~thine~~ hand. And he stretched *it* forth; and it was restored whole, like ~~as~~ the other.

Matthew 12:15 But ~~when~~ Jesus knew ~~it~~, he withdrew himself from thence: and great multitudes followed him, and he healed ~~them all~~;

Matthew 12:17 That it might be fulfilled which was spoken by Esaias ~~the prophet~~, saying,

Matthew 12:23 And all the people were amazed, and said, Is ~~not~~ this the son of David?

Matthew 12:24 But when the Pharisees heard ~~it~~, they said, This ~~fellow~~ doth not cast out devils, but by Beelzebub the prince of ~~the~~ devils.

Matthew 12:26 And if Satan cast out Satan, he is divided against himself; how shall ~~then~~ his kingdom stand?

Matthew 12:27 And if I by Beelzebub cast out devils, by whom do your children cast ~~them~~ out? therefore they shall be your judges.

Matthew 12:28 But if I cast out devils by the Spirit of God, then the kingdom of God is come unto you.

Matthew 12:31 Wherefore I say unto you, All manner of sin and blasphemy shall be forgiven unto men: but the

sabbath days? that they might accuse him.

Then **said** he to the man, Stretch forth **thy** hand. And he stretched it forth; and it was restored whole, like **unto** the other.

But Jesus knew **when they took counsel, and** he withdrew himself from thence: and great multitudes followed him, and he healed **their sick**;

That it might be fulfilled which was spoken by **the prophet** Esaias, saying,

And all the people were amazed, and said, Is this the son of David?

But when the Pharisees heard **that he had cast out the devil**, they said, This **man** doth not cast out devils, but by Beelzebub the prince of devils.

And if Satan cast out Satan, he is divided against himself; how **then** shall his kingdom stand?

And if I by Beelzebub cast out devils, by whom do your children cast out **devils**? therefore they shall be your judges.

But if I cast out devils by the Spirit of God, then the kingdom of God is come unto you, **for they also cast out devils by the Spirit of God, for unto them is given power over devils that they may cast them out.**

Wherefore I say unto you, All manner of sin and blasphemy shall be forgiven unto men **who receive me and repent**:

blasphemy *against* the *Holy* Ghost shall not be forgiven unto men.	but the blasphemy against the Holy Ghost it shall not be forgiven unto men.
	(**NT1** Wherefore I say unto you, All manner of sin and blasphemy shall be forgiven unto men **who receive me and repenteth**: but the blasphemy against the Holy Ghost shall not be forgiven unto men.)
Matthew 12:33 Either make the tree good, and his fruit good; or else make the tree corrupt, and his fruit corrupt: for the tree is known by ~~his~~ fruit.	Either make the tree good, and his fruit good; or else make the tree corrupt, and his fruit corrupt: for the tree is known by **the** fruit.
Matthew 12:34 O ~~generation~~ of vipers, how can ye, being evil, speak good things? for out of the abundance of the heart the mouth speaketh.	**And Jesus said**, O ye **generations** of vipers, how can ye, being evil, speak good things? for out of the abundance of the heart the mouth speaketh.
Matthew 12:36 ~~But~~ I say unto you, That every idle word ~~that~~ men shall speak, they shall give account thereof in the day of judgment.	**And again**, I say unto you, That every idle word men shall speak, they shall give account thereof in the day of judgment.
Matthew 12:41 The men of Nineveh shall rise in judgment with this generation, and shall condemn it: because they repented at the preaching of Jonas; and, behold, a greater than Jonas *is* here.	The men of Nineveh shall rise **up** in judgment with this generation, and shall condemn it: because they repented at the preaching of Jonas; and **ye**, behold, a greater than Jonas is here.
Matthew 12:42 The queen of the south shall rise up in the judgment with this generation, and shall condemn it: for she came from the uttermost parts of the earth to hear the wisdom of Solomon; and, behold, a greater than Solomon *is* here.	The queen of the south shall rise up in the **day of** judgment with this generation, and shall condemn it: for she came from the uttermost parts of the earth to hear the wisdom of Solomon; and **ye**, behold, a greater than Solomon is here.
Matthew 12:43 When the unclean spirit is gone out of a man, he walketh through dry places, seeking rest, and findeth none.	**Then came some of the scribes and said unto him, Master, it is written, that, Every sin shall be forgiven; but ye say, Whosoever speaketh against the Holy Ghost shall not be forgiven. And they asked him, saying, How can these**

The Testimony of St Matthew

Matthew 12:44 Then he saith, I will return into my house from whence I came out; and when he is come, he findeth ~~it~~ empty, swept, and garnished.

Matthew 12:45 Then goeth ~~he~~, and taketh with himself seven other spirits more wicked than himself, and they enter in and dwell there: and the last ~~state~~ of that man is worse than the first. Even so shall it be also unto this wicked generation.

Matthew 12:46 While he yet talked to the people, behold, *his* mother and ~~his~~ brethren stood without, desiring to speak with him.

Matthew 12:48 But he answered and said unto ~~him~~ that told him, Who is my mother? and who are my brethren?

Matthew 12:50 ~~For~~ whosoever shall do the will of my Father which is in heaven, the same is my brother, and sister, and mother.

Matthew 13:1 The same day ~~went~~ Jesus out of the house, and sat by the sea side.

Matthew 13:5 Some fell upon stony places, where they had not much earth: and forthwith they sprung up, ~~because they had no deepness of earth~~:

things be? And he said unto them, When the unclean spirit is gone out of a man, he walketh through dry places, seeking rest, and findeth none; **but when a man speaketh against the Holy Ghost,**

Then he saith, I will return into my house from whence I came out; and when he is come, he findeth **him** empty, swept, and garnished; **for the good spirit leaveth him unto himself.**

Then goeth **the evil spirit**, and taketh with himself seven other spirits more wicked than himself, and they enter in and dwell there: and the last **end** of that man is worse than the first. Even so shall it be also unto this wicked generation.

And while he yet talked to the people, behold, his mother and brethren stood without, desiring to speak with him.

But he answered and said unto **the man** that told him, Who is my mother? and who are my brethren?

And he gave them charge concerning her, saying, I go my way for my father hath sent me, and whosoever shall do the will of my Father which is in heaven, the same is my brother, and sister, and mother.

And it came to pass the same day Jesus **went** out of the house, and sat by the sea side.

Some fell upon stony places, where they had not much earth: and forthwith they sprung up,

Matthew 13:6 And when the sun was up, they were scorched; ~~and~~ because they had no root, they withered away.	And when the sun was up, they were scorched, because they had no **deepness of earth; and because they had no** root, they withered away.
Matthew 13:8 But other fell into good ground, and brought forth fruit, some an hundredfold, some sixtyfold, some thirtyfold.	But **others** fell into good ground, and brought forth fruit, some an hundredfold, some sixtyfold, **and** some thirtyfold.
Matthew 13:10 ~~And~~ the disciples came, and said unto him, Why speakest thou unto them in parables?	**Then** the disciples came, and said unto him, Why speakest thou unto them in parables?
Matthew 13:12 For whosoever ~~hath~~, to him shall be given, and he shall have more abundance: but whosoever ~~hath~~ not, from him shall be taken away even that he hath.	For whosoever **receiveth**, to him shall be given, and he shall have more abundance: but whosoever **continueth** not **to receive**, from him shall be taken away even that he hath.
Matthew 13:13 Therefore ~~speak~~ I to them in parables: because they seeing see not; and hearing they hear not, neither do they understand.	Therefore I **speak** to them in parables: because they seeing see not; and hearing they hear not, neither do they understand.
Matthew 13:14 And in them is fulfilled the prophecy of Esaias, which saith, By hearing ye shall hear, and shall not understand; and seeing ye shall see, and shall not perceive:	And in them is fulfilled the prophecy of Esaias **concerning them**, which saith, By hearing ye shall hear, and shall not understand; and seeing ye shall see, and shall not perceive:
Matthew 13:15 For this people's heart is waxed gross, and *their* ears are dull of hearing, and their eyes they have closed; lest at any time they should see with *their* eyes, and hear with *their* ears, and should understand with *their* ~~heart~~, and should be converted, and I should heal them.	For this people's heart is waxed gross, and their ears are dull of hearing, and their eyes they have closed; lest at any time they should see with their eyes, and hear with their ears, and should understand with their **hearts**, and should be converted, and I should heal them.
Matthew 13:16 But blessed *are* your eyes, for they see: and your ears, for they hear.	But blessed are your eyes, for they see: and your ears, for they hear. **And blessed are you because these things are come unto you, that you might understand them.**

The Testimony of St Matthew

Matthew 13:17 ~~For~~ verily I say unto you, ~~That~~ many prophets ~~and righteous men~~ have desired to see ~~those things~~ which ~~ye~~ see, and have not seen *them;* and to hear ~~those things~~ which ~~ye~~ hear, and have not heard ~~them~~.

Matthew 13:19 When any one heareth the word of the kingdom, and understandeth ~~it~~ not, then cometh the wicked *one,* and catcheth away that which was sown in his heart. This is he ~~which~~ received seed by the way side.

Matthew 13:20 But he that received the seed into stony places, the same is he that heareth the word, and ~~anon~~ with joy receiveth it;

Matthew 13:21 Yet hath ~~he~~ not root in himself, ~~but dureth~~ for a while: for when tribulation or persecution ariseth because of the word, by and by he is offended.

Matthew 13:22 He also ~~that~~ received seed among the thorns is he that heareth the word; and the care of this world, and the deceitfulness of riches, choke the word, and he becometh unfruitful.

Matthew 13:23 But he ~~that~~ received seed into the good ground is he that heareth the word, and understandeth ~~it~~; which also beareth fruit, and bringeth forth, some an hundredfold, some sixty, some thirty.

Matthew 13:24 Another parable put he forth unto them, saying, The kingdom of heaven is likened unto a man ~~which~~ sowed good seed in his field:

And verily I say unto you, many **righteous** prophets have desired to see **these days** which **you** see, and have not seen them; and to hear **that** which **you** hear, and have not heard.

When any one heareth the word of the kingdom, and understandeth not, then cometh the wicked one, and catcheth away that which was sown in his heart. This is he **who** received seed by the way side.

But he that received the seed into stony places, the same is he that heareth the word, and **readily** with joy receiveth it;

Yet **he** hath not root in himself, **and endureth but** for a while: for when tribulation or persecution ariseth because of the word, by and by he is offended.

He also **who** received seed among the thorns is he that heareth the word; and the care of this world, and the deceitfulness of riches, choke the word, and he becometh unfruitful.

But he **who** received seed into the good ground is he that heareth the word, and understandeth **and endureth**; which also beareth fruit, and bringeth forth, some an hundredfold, some sixty, **and** some thirty.

Another parable put he forth unto them, saying, The kingdom of heaven is likened unto a man **who** sowed good seed in his field:

Matthew 13:25 But while ~~men~~ slept, his enemy came and sowed tares among the wheat, and went his way.	But while **he** slept, his enemy came and sowed tares among the wheat, and went his way.
Matthew 13:26 But when the blade ~~was~~ sprung up, and brought forth fruit, then appeared the tares also.	But when the blade sprung up, and brought forth fruit, then appeared the tares also.
Matthew 13:27 So the servants of the householder came and said unto him, Sir, didst not thou sow good seed in thy field? ~~from~~ whence then hath it tares?	So the servants of the householder came and said unto him, Sir, didst not thou sow good seed in thy field? whence then hath it tares?
Matthew 13:28 He said unto them, An enemy hath done this. The servants said unto him, Wilt thou then that we go and gather them up?	He said unto them, An enemy hath done this. **And** the servants said unto him, Wilt thou then that we go and gather them up?
Matthew 13:30 Let both grow together until the harvest: and in the time of harvest I will say to the reapers, Gather ye together first the tares, ~~and bind them~~ in bundles to ~~burn them: but gather the wheat into my barn~~.	Let both grow together until the harvest: and in the time of harvest I will say to the reapers, Gather ye together first the **wheat into my barn, and the** tares **are bound** in bundles to **be burned.**
Matthew 13:34 All these things spake Jesus unto the ~~multitude~~ in parables; and without a parable spake he not unto them:	All these things spake Jesus unto the **multitudes** in parables; and without a parable spake he not unto them:
Matthew 13:35 That it might be fulfilled which was spoken by the ~~prophet~~, saying, I will open my mouth in parables; I will utter things which have been kept secret from the foundation of the world.	That it might be fulfilled which was spoken by the **prophets**, saying, I will open my mouth in parables; I will utter things which have been kept secret from the foundation of the world.
Matthew 13:38 The field is the world; the good seed are the children of the kingdom; but the tares are the children of the wicked ~~one~~;	The field is the world; the good seed are the children of the kingdom; but the tares are the children of the wicked;
Matthew 13:39 The enemy that sowed them is the devil; the harvest is the end of the world; ~~and~~ the reapers are the angels.	The enemy that sowed them is the devil; the harvest is the end of the world, **or the destruction of the**

	wicked; the reapers are the angels, **or the messengers sent of heaven.**
Matthew 13:40 As therefore the tares are gathered and burned in the fire; so shall it be in the end of this world.	As therefore the tares are gathered and burned in the fire; so shall it be in the end of this world, **or the destruction of the wicked.**
Matthew 13:41 The Son of man shall send forth his angels, and they shall gather out of his kingdom all things that offend, and them which do iniquity;	**For in that day, before** the Son of man shall **come, he shall** send forth his angels, **and messengers of heaven,** and they shall gather out of his kingdom all things that offend, and them which do iniquity;
Matthew 13:42 And shall cast them ~~into a furnace of fire~~: there shall be wailing and gnashing of teeth.	And shall cast them **out among the wicked:** and there shall be wailing and gnashing of teeth, **for the world shall be burned with fire.**
Matthew 13:43 Then shall the righteous shine forth as the sun in the kingdom of their Father. Who hath ears to hear, let ~~him~~ hear.	Then shall the righteous shine forth as the sun in the kingdom of their Father. Who hath ears to hear, let **them** hear.
Matthew 13:44 Again, the kingdom of heaven is like unto treasure hid in a field; ~~the which~~ when a man hath found, he ~~hideth~~, and for joy thereof goeth and selleth all that he hath, and buyeth that field.	Again, the kingdom of heaven is like unto **a** treasure hid in a field. **And** when a man hath found **a treasure which is hid,** he **secureth it** and **straightway** for joy thereof goeth and selleth all that he hath, and buyeth that field.
	(**NT1** Again, the kingdom of heaven is like unto **a** treasure hid in a field. **And** when a man hath found **the treasure which is hid,** he **hideth it** and **straightway** for joy thereof goeth and selleth all that he hath, and buyeth that field.)
Matthew 13:46 Who, when he had found one pearl of great price, went and sold all that he had, and bought it.	Who, when he had found one pearl of great price, **he** went and sold all that he had, and bought it.
Matthew 13:49 So shall it be at the end of the world: the angels shall come	So shall it be at the end of the world; **and the world is the children of the**

forth, and sever the wicked from among the just,

Matthew 13:50 And shall cast them into the ~~furnace of fire:~~ there shall be wailing and gnashing of teeth.

Matthew 13:52 Then said he unto them, ~~Therefore every~~ scribe ~~which is~~ instructed ~~unto~~ the kingdom of heaven is like unto a ~~man~~ *~~that is~~* an householder, which bringeth forth out of his treasure ~~things~~ new and old.

Matthew 13:53 And it came to pass, ~~that~~ when Jesus had finished these parables, he departed thence.

Matthew 13:54 And when he was come his own country, he taught them in their ~~synagogue~~, insomuch that they were astonished, and said, Whence hath this ~~man~~ this wisdom, and *these* mighty works?

Matthew 13:57 And they were offended ~~in~~ him. But Jesus said unto them, A prophet is not without honour, save in his own country, and in his own house.

Matthew 14:3 For Herod had laid ~~hold~~ on John, and bound him, and put *him* in prison for Herodias' sake, his brother Philip's wife.

Matthew 14:9 And the king was sorry: nevertheless for the oath's sake, and them ~~which~~ sat with him at meat, he commanded *it* to be given ~~her~~.

wicked. The angels shall come forth, and sever the wicked from among the just,

And shall cast them **out** into the **world to be burned;** there shall be wailing and gnashing of teeth.

Then said he unto them, **Every** scribe **well** instructed **in the things of** the kingdom of heaven is like unto a householder, **a man therefore**, which bringeth forth out of his treasure **that which is** new and old.

And it came to pass, when Jesus had finished these parables, he departed thence.

And when he was come **unto** his own country, he taught them in their **synagogues**, insomuch that they were astonished, and said, Whence hath this **Jesus** this wisdom, and these mighty works?

(**NT1** And when he was come into his own country, he taught them in their synagogue, insomuch that they were astonished, and said, Whence hath this **Jesus** this wisdom and mighty works?)

And they were offended **at** him. But Jesus said unto them, A prophet is not without honour, save in his own country, and in his own house.

For Herod had laid **hands** on John, and bound him, and put him in prison for Herodias' sake, his brother Philip's wife.

And the king was sorry: nevertheless for the oath's sake, and them **that** sat with him at meat, he commanded it to be given.

The Testimony of St Matthew

Matthew 14:13 When Jesus heard ~~of it~~, he departed thence by ship into a desert place apart: and when the people had heard ~~thereof~~, they followed him on foot out of the cities.

Matthew 14:17 And they ~~say~~ unto him, We have here but five loaves, and two fishes.

Matthew 14:19 And he commanded the multitude to sit down on the grass, and took the five loaves, and the two fishes, and looking up to heaven, he blessed, and brake, and gave the loaves to ~~his~~ disciples, and the disciples to the multitude.

Matthew 14:24 But the ship was now in the midst of the sea, tossed with waves: for the wind was contrary.

Matthew 15:4 For God commanded, saying, Honour thy father and mother: and, He that curseth father or mother, let him die the death.

Matthew 15:5 But ye say, Whosoever shall say to ~~his~~ father or ~~his~~ mother, ~~It is a gift~~, by whatsoever thou mightest be profited by me;

Matthew 15:6 And honour not his father or ~~his~~ mother, ~~he shall be free~~. Thus have ye made the commandment of God of none effect by your tradition.

Matthew 15:7 ~~Ye~~ hypocrites, well did Esaias prophesy of you, saying,

Matthew 15:8 This people ~~draweth~~ nigh unto me with their mouth, and honoureth me with ~~their~~ lips; but their heart is far from me.

When Jesus heard **that John was beheaded**, he departed thence by ship into a desert place apart: and when the people had heard **of him**, they followed him on foot out of the cities.

And they **said** unto him, We have here but five loaves, and two fishes.

And he commanded the multitude to sit down on the grass, and **he** took the five loaves, and the two fishes, and looking up to heaven, he blessed, and brake, and gave the loaves to **the** disciples, and the disciples to the multitude.

But the ship was now in the midst of the sea, tossed with **the** waves: for the wind was contrary.

For God commanded, saying, Honour thy father and mother: and, He that curseth father or mother, let him die the death **which Moses shall appoint.**

But ye say, Whosoever shall say to father or mother, by whatsoever thou mightest be profited by me **it is a gift from me;**

And honour not his father or mother, **it is well**. Thus have ye made the commandment of God of none effect by your tradition.

O! ye hypocrites, well did Esaias prophesy of you, saying,

This people **draw** nigh unto me with their mouth, and honoureth me with lips; but their heart is far from me.

Matthew 15:9 But in vain ~~they~~ do worship me, teaching ~~for~~ doctrines the commandments of men.

Matthew 15:11 Not that which goeth into the mouth defileth ~~a~~ man; but that which cometh out of the mouth, this defileth ~~a~~ man.

Matthew 15:17 Do not ~~ye~~ yet understand, that whatsoever entereth in at the mouth goeth into the belly, and is cast out into the draught?

Matthew 15:19 For out of the heart proceed evil thoughts, murders, ~~adulteries, fornications~~, thefts, false witness, ~~blasphemies~~:

Matthew 15:20 These are ~~the~~ *things* which defile a man: but to eat with unwashen hands defileth not a man.

Matthew 15:24 ~~But~~ he answered ~~and said~~, I am not sent but unto the lost sheep of the house of Israel.

Matthew 15:27 And she said, Truth, Lord: yet the dogs eat ~~of~~ the crumbs ~~which~~ fall from ~~their~~ masters' table.

Matthew 15:30 And great multitudes came unto him, having with them ~~those that were~~ lame, blind, dumb, maimed, and many others, and cast them down at Jesus' feet; and he healed them:

Matthew 15:31 Insomuch that the multitude wondered, when they saw the dumb to speak, the maimed to be whole, the lame to walk, and the blind to see: and they glorified the God of Israel.

But in vain do **they** worship me, teaching **the** doctrines **and** the commandments of men.

Not that which goeth into the mouth defileth **the** man; but that which cometh out of the mouth, this defileth **the** man.

Do **you** not yet understand, that whatsoever entereth in at the mouth goeth into the belly, and is cast out into the draught?

(**NT1** Do **ye** not yet understand, that whatsoever entereth in at the mouth goeth into the belly, and is cast out into the draught?)

For out of the heart proceed evil thoughts, murders, **adultery**, **fornication**, thefts, false witness, **blasphemy**:

These are things which defile a man: but to eat with unwashen hands defileth not a man.

He answered, I am not sent but unto the lost sheep of the house of Israel.

And she said, Truth, Lord: yet the dogs eat the crumbs **that** fall from **the** master's table.

And great multitudes came unto him, having with them **some** lame, blind, dumb, maimed, and many others, and cast them down at Jesus' feet; and he healed them:

Insomuch that the multitude wondered, when they saw the dumb to speak, **and** the maimed to be whole, the lame to walk, and the blind to see: and they glorified the God of Israel.

The Testimony of St Matthew

Matthew 15:32 Then Jesus called his disciples ~~unto him~~, and said, I have compassion on the multitude, because they continue with me now three days, and have nothing to eat: and I will not send them away fasting, lest they faint in the way.

Matthew 15:36 And he took the seven loaves and the fishes, and gave thanks, and brake ~~them~~, and gave to his disciples, and the disciples to the multitude.

Matthew 15:37 And they did all eat, and were filled: and they took up of the broken *meat* ~~that was left~~ seven baskets full.

Matthew 15:39 And he sent away the multitude, and took ship, and came into the ~~coasts~~ of Magdala.

Matthew 16:1 The Pharisees also with the Sadducees came, and tempting desired him that he would shew them a sign from heaven.

Matthew 16:2 He answered and said unto them, When it is evening, ye say, ~~It will be~~ fair weather~~: for the sky is red~~.

Matthew 16:3 And in the morning, ~~It will be~~ foul ~~weather~~ to day: for the sky is red and lowring. O ~~ye~~ hypocrites, ~~ye~~ can discern the face of the sky; but ~~can~~ ye ~~not discern~~ the signs of the times?

Matthew 16:7 And they reasoned among themselves, saying, ~~It is~~ because we have taken no bread.

Matthew 16:8 ~~Which~~ when Jesus perceived, he said unto them, O ye of little

Then Jesus called his disciples and said, I have compassion on the multitude, because they continue with me now three days, and have nothing to eat: and I will not send them away fasting, lest they faint in the way.

And he took the seven loaves and the fishes, and gave thanks, and brake **the bread**, and gave to his disciples, and the disciples to the multitude.

And they did all eat, and were filled: and they took up of the broken meat seven baskets full.

And he sent away the multitude, and took ship, and came into the **coast** of Magdala.

The Pharisees also with the Sadducees came, and tempting **Jesus**, desired him that he would shew them a sign from heaven.

And he answered and said unto them, When it is evening, ye say, **The** weather **is fair;**

(**NT1 And** he answered and said unto them, When it is evening, ye say, **The** weather **is fair** for the sky is red.)

And in the morning, **ye say, The** weather **is** foul to day: for the sky is red and lowering. O hypocrites, **you** can discern the face of the sky; but ye **cannot tell** the signs of the times.

And they reasoned among themselves, saying, **He said this** because we have taken no bread.

And when **they reasoned among themselves,** Jesus perceived **it; and** he said

faith, why reason ye among yourselves, because ye have brought no bread?

Matthew 16:11 How is it that ye do not understand that I spake ~~it~~ not ~~to~~ you concerning bread, that ye should beware of the leaven of the Pharisees and of the Sadducees?

Matthew 16:13 When Jesus came into the coasts of Caesarea Philippi, he asked his disciples, saying, Whom do men say that I the Son of man am?

Matthew 16:14 And they said, Some say ~~that thou art~~ John the Baptist: some, Elias; and others, Jeremias, or one of the prophets.

Matthew 16:15 He ~~saith~~ unto them, But whom say ye that I am?

Matthew 16:17 And Jesus answered and said unto him, Blessed art thou, Simon Bar-jona: for flesh and blood hath not revealed ~~it~~ unto thee, but my Father ~~which~~ is in heaven.

Matthew 16:21 From that time forth began Jesus to shew unto his disciples, how that he must go ~~unto~~ Jerusalem, and suffer many things of the elders and chief priests and scribes, and be killed, and be raised again the third day.

Matthew 16:22 Then Peter took him, and began to rebuke him, saying, Be it far from thee, Lord: this shall not be unto thee.

Matthew 16:24 Then said Jesus unto his disciples, If any ~~man~~ will come after me, let him deny himself, and take up his cross, and follow me.

unto them, O ye of little faith, why reason ye among yourselves, because ye have brought no bread?

How is it that ye do not understand that I spake not **unto** you concerning bread, that ye should beware of the leaven of the Pharisees and of the Sadducees?

And when Jesus came into the coasts of Caesarea Philippi, he asked his disciples, saying, Whom do men say that I the Son of man am?

And they said, Some say John the Baptist: some, Elias; and others, Jeremias, or one of the prophets.

He **said** unto them, But whom say ye that I am?

And Jesus answered and said unto him, Blessed art thou, Simon Bar-jona: for flesh and blood hath not revealed **this** unto thee, but my Father **who** is in heaven.

From that time forth began Jesus to shew unto his disciples, how that he must go **to** Jerusalem, and suffer many things of the elders and chief priests and scribes, and be killed, and be raised again the third day.

Then Peter took him, and began to rebuke him, saying, Be it far from thee, Lord: this shall not be **done** unto thee.

Then said Jesus unto his disciples, If any will come after me, let him deny himself, and take up his cross, and follow me.

The Testimony of St Matthew

Matthew 16:25 For whosoever will save his life shall lose it: and whosoever will lose his life for my sake shall find it.	And now for a man to take up his cross, is to deny himself from all ungodliness, and from every worldly lust, and keep my commandments. Break not my commandments, for to save your lives; for whosoever will save his life **in this world**, shall lose it **in the world to come**; and whosoever will lose his life **in this world** for my sake shall find it **in the world to come**.
Matthew 16:26 For what is a man profited, if he shall gain the whole world, and lose his own soul? or what shall a man give in exchange for his soul?	**Therefore, forsake the world, and save your souls;** for what is a man profited, if he shall gain the whole world, and lose his own soul? or what shall a man give in exchange for his soul?
Matthew 17:4 Then answered Peter, and said unto Jesus, Lord, it is good for us to be here: if thou wilt, let us make here three tabernacles; one for thee, ~~and~~ one for Moses, and one for Elias.	Then answered Peter, and said unto Jesus, Lord, it is good for us to be here: if thou wilt, let us make here three tabernacles; one for thee, one for Moses, and one for Elias.
Matthew 17:5 While he yet spake, behold, a ~~bright~~ cloud overshadowed them: and behold a voice out of the cloud, which said, This is my beloved Son, in whom I am well pleased; hear ye him.	While he yet spake, behold, a **light** cloud overshadowed them: and behold a voice out of the cloud, which said, This is my beloved Son, in whom I am well pleased; hear ye him.
Matthew 17:6 And when the disciples heard ~~it~~, they fell on their ~~face~~, and were sore afraid.	And when the disciples heard **the voice**, they fell on their **faces**, and were sore afraid.
Matthew 17:11 And Jesus answered and said unto them, Elias truly shall first come, and restore all things.	And Jesus answered and said unto them, Elias truly shall first come, and restore all things **as the prophets have written**.
Matthew 17:12 ~~But~~ I say unto you, That Elias ~~is~~ come already, and they knew him not, ~~but~~ have done unto him whatsoever they listed. Likewise shall also the Son of man suffer of them.	**And again** I say unto you, That Elias **has** come already, **concerning whom it is written, Behold I will send my messenger and he shall prepare the way before me**; and they knew him not, **and** have done unto him whatsoever they listed. Likewise shall also the Son of man suffer of them.

Matthew 17:13 Then the disciples understood that he spake unto them of John the Baptist.	But I say unto you, Who is Elias? Behold, this is Elias whom I send to prepare the way before me. Then the disciples understood that he spake unto them of John the Baptist **and also of another which should come and restore all things, as it is written by the prophets.**
	(NT1 But I say unto you, Who is Elias? Behold, this is Elias who I send to prepare the way before me. Then the disciples understood that he spake unto them of John the Baptist **and also of another which should come and restore all things as they were written by the prophets.**)
Matthew 17:14 And when they were come to the multitude, there came to him a ~~certain~~ man, kneeling down to him, and saying,	And when they were come to the multitude, there came to him a man, kneeling down to him, and saying,
Matthew 17:20 And Jesus said unto them, Because of your unbelief: for verily I say unto you, If ye have faith as a grain of mustard seed, ye shall say unto this mountain, Remove ~~hence~~ to yonder place; and it shall ~~remove~~; and nothing shall be impossible unto you.	And Jesus said unto them, Because of your unbelief: for verily I say unto you, If ye have faith as a grain of mustard seed, ye shall say unto this mountain, Remove to yonder place; and it shall **move**; and nothing shall be impossible unto you.
Matthew 17:24 And when they were come to Capernaum, they that received tribute ~~money~~ came to Peter, and said, Doth not your master pay tribute?	And when they were come to Capernaum, they that received tribute came to Peter, and said, Doth not your master pay tribute?
Matthew 17:25 He ~~saith~~, ~~Yes~~. And when he was come into the house, Jesus ~~prevented~~ him, saying, What thinkest thou, Simon? of whom do the kings of the earth take custom or tribute? of their own children, or of strangers?	He **said**, Yea. And when he was come into the house, Jesus **rebuked** him, saying, What thinkest thou, Simon? of whom do the kings of the earth take custom or tribute? of their own children, or of strangers?
Matthew 17:26 Peter ~~saith~~ unto him, Of strangers. Jesus ~~saith~~ unto him, Then are the children free.	Peter **said** unto him, Of strangers. Jesus **said** unto him, Then are the children free.

The Testimony of St Matthew

Matthew 18:3 And said, Verily I say unto you, Except ~~ye~~ be converted, and become as little children, ye shall not enter into the kingdom of heaven.	And said, Verily I say unto you, Except **you** be converted, and become as little children, ye shall not enter into the kingdom of heaven.
Matthew 18:6 But whoso shall offend one of these little ones which believe in me, it were better for him that a millstone were hanged about his neck, and ~~that~~ he were drowned in the depth of the sea.	But whoso shall offend one of these little ones which believe in me, it were better for him that a millstone were hanged about his neck, and he were drowned in the depth of the sea.
	(**NT1** But whoso shall offend one of these little ones which believe in me, it were better for him that a millstone **was** hanged about his neck, and he **was** drowned in the depth of the sea.)
Matthew 18:8 Wherefore if thy hand or thy foot offend thee, cut ~~them~~ off, and cast ~~them~~ from thee: it is better for thee to enter into life halt or maimed, rather than having two hands or two feet to be cast into everlasting fire.	Wherefore if thy hand or thy foot offend thee, cut **it** off, and cast **it** from thee: **for** it is better for thee to enter into life halt or maimed, rather than having two hands or two feet to be cast into everlasting fire.
Matthew 18:9 And if thine eye offend thee, pluck it out, and cast *it* from thee: it is better for thee to enter into life with one eye, rather than having two eyes to be cast into hell fire.	And if thine eye offend thee, pluck it out, and cast it from thee: it is better for thee to enter into life with one eye, rather than having two eyes to be cast into hell fire. **And a man's hand is his friend, and his foot also; and a man's eye, are they of his own household.**
	(**NT1** And if thine eye offend thee, pluck it out, and cast it from thee: it is better for thee to enter into life with one eye, rather than having two eyes to be cast into hell fire. **And a man's hand is his friend, and his feet also; and a man's eye, are they of his own household.**)
Matthew 18:10 Take heed that ye despise not one of these little ones; for I say unto you, That in heaven their angels do always behold the face of my Father ~~which~~ is in heaven.	Take heed that ye despise not one of these little ones; for I say unto you, That in heaven their angels do always behold the face of my Father **who** is in heaven.

Matthew 18:11 For the Son of man is come to save that which was lost.	For the Son of man is come to save that which was lost, **and to call sinners to repentance; but those little ones have no need of repentance, and I will save them.**
Matthew 18:13 And if so be that he find it, verily I say unto you, he rejoiceth more ~~of~~ that ~~sheep~~, than ~~of~~ the ninety and nine which went not astray.	And if **it** so be that he find it, verily I say unto you, he rejoiceth more **over** that **which was lost**, than **over** the ninety and nine which went not astray.
Matthew 18:17 And if he shall neglect to hear them, tell *it* unto the church: but if he neglect to hear the church, let him be unto ~~thee~~ as an heathen man and a publican.	And if he shall neglect to hear them, tell it unto the church: but if he neglect to hear the church, let him be unto **you** as a heathen man and a publican.
Matthew 18:19 Again I say unto you, That if two of you shall agree on earth as touching any thing that they shall ask, it shall be done for them of my Father which is in heaven.	Again I say unto you, That if two of you shall agree on earth as touching any thing that they shall ask, **that they may not ask amiss,** it shall be done for them of my Father which is in heaven.
Matthew 18:22 Jesus ~~saith~~ unto him, I say not unto thee, Until seven times: but, Until seventy times seven.	Jesus **said** unto him, I say not unto thee, Until seven times: but, Until seventy times seven.
Matthew 18:23 Therefore is the kingdom of heaven likened unto a certain king, ~~which~~ would take account of his servants.	Therefore is the kingdom of heaven likened unto a certain king, **who** would take account of his servants.
Matthew 18:24 And when he had begun to reckon, one was brought unto him, ~~which~~ owed him ten thousand talents.	And when he had begun to reckon, one was brought unto him, **who** owed him ten thousand talents.
Matthew 18:26 The servant ~~therefore fell down, and worshipped~~ him, saying, Lord, have patience with me, and I will pay thee all.	**And** the servant **besought** him, saying, Lord, have patience with me, and I will pay thee all.
Matthew 18:27 Then the lord of that servant was moved with compassion, and loosed him, and forgave him the debt.	Then the lord of that servant was moved with compassion, and loosed him, and forgave him the debt. **The servant, therefore, fell down and worshipped him.**

The Testimony of St Matthew

Matthew 19:1 And it came to pass, ~~that~~ when Jesus had finished these sayings, he departed from Galilee, and came into the ~~coasts~~ of Judaea beyond Jordan;	And it came to pass, when Jesus had finished these sayings, he departed from Galilee, and came into the **coast** of Judea beyond Jordan;
Matthew 19:2 And great multitudes followed him; and he healed them there.	And great multitudes followed him; **and many believed on him** and he healed them there.
Matthew 19:3 The Pharisees also came unto him, tempting him, and saying unto him, Is it lawful for a man to put away his wife for every cause?	The Pharisees **came** also unto him, tempting him, and saying unto him, Is it lawful for a man to put away his wife for every cause?
Matthew 19:4 And he answered and said unto them, Have ye not read, that he ~~which~~ made ~~them~~ at the beginning made ~~them~~ male and female,	And he answered and said unto them, Have ye not read, that he **who** made **man** at the beginning made **him** male and female,
Matthew 19:8 He ~~saith~~ unto them, Moses because of the hardness of your hearts suffered you to put away your wives: but from the beginning it was not so.	He **said** unto them, Moses because of the hardness of your hearts suffered you to put away your wives: but from the beginning it was not so.
Matthew 19:9 And I say unto you, Whosoever shall put away his wife, except ~~it be~~ for fornication, and shall marry another, committeth adultery: and whoso marrieth her ~~which~~ is put away doth commit adultery.	And I say unto you, Whosoever shall put away his wife, except for fornication, and shall marry another, committeth adultery: and whoso marrieth her **that** is put away doth commit adultery.
Matthew 19:10 His disciples say unto him, If the case of the man be so with ~~his~~ wife, it is not good to marry.	His disciples say unto him, If the case of the man be so with **a** wife, it is not good to marry.
Matthew 19:11 But he said unto them, All ~~men~~ cannot receive this saying, save ~~they~~ to whom it is given.	But he said unto them, All cannot receive this saying. **It is not for them** save to whom it is given.
Matthew 19:12 For there are some eunuchs, which were so born from *their* mother's womb: and there are some eunuchs, which were made eunuchs of men: and there be eunuchs, which have made themselves eunuchs for the	For there are some eunuchs, which were so born from their mother's womb: and there are some eunuchs, which were made eunuchs of men: and there be eunuchs, which have made themselves eunuchs for the kingdom of heaven's

kingdom of heaven's sake. He that is able to receive ~~it~~, let him receive ~~it~~.

Matthew 19:13 Then were there brought unto him little children, that he should put ~~his~~ hands on them, and pray: and the disciples rebuked them.

Matthew 19:14 But Jesus said, Suffer little children, and forbid them not, ~~to come unto me~~: for of such is the kingdom of heaven.

Matthew 19:15 And he laid ~~his~~ hands on them, and departed thence.

Matthew 19:16 And, behold, one came and said ~~unto him~~, Good Master, what good thing shall I do, that I may have eternal life?

Matthew 19:18 He saith unto him, Which? Jesus said, Thou shalt ~~do no murder~~, Thou shalt not commit adultery, Thou shalt not steal, Thou shalt not bear false witness,

Matthew 19:19 Honour thy father and ~~thy~~ mother: and, Thou shalt love thy neighbour as thyself.

Matthew 19:21 Jesus said unto him, If thou wilt be perfect, go ~~and~~ sell that thou hast, and give to the poor, and thou shalt have treasure in heaven: and come *and* follow me.

Matthew 19:25 When his disciples heard ~~it~~, they were exceedingly amazed, saying, Who then can be saved?

Matthew 19:26 But Jesus beheld ~~them~~, and said unto them, With men this is

sake. He that is able to receive, let him receive **my sayings**.

Then were there brought unto him little children, that he should put hands on them, and pray. And the disciples rebuked them, **saying, There is no need, for Jesus hath said such shall be saved.**

But Jesus said, Suffer little children **to come unto me**, and forbid them not, for of such is the kingdom of heaven.

And he laid hands on them, and departed thence.

And, behold, one came and said, Good Master, what good thing shall I do, that I may have eternal life?

He saith unto him, Which? Jesus said, Thou shalt **not kill**, Thou shalt not commit adultery, Thou shalt not steal, Thou shalt not bear false witness,

Honour thy father and mother: and, Thou shalt love thy neighbour as thyself.

Jesus said unto him, If thou wilt be perfect, go sell that thou hast, and give to the poor, and thou shalt have treasure in heaven: and come and follow me.

When his disciples heard **this**, they were exceedingly amazed, saying, Who then can be saved?

But Jesus beheld **their thoughts**, and said unto them, With men this is

The Testimony of St Matthew

impossible; but with God ~~all~~ things are possible.	impossible; but **if they will forsake all things for my sake,** with God **whatsoever** things **I speak** are possible.
Matthew 19:28 And Jesus said unto them, Verily I say unto you, That ye ~~which~~ have followed me, in the ~~regeneration~~ when the Son of man shall ~~sit in~~ the throne of his glory, ye also shall sit upon twelve thrones, judging the twelve tribes of Israel.	And Jesus said unto them, Verily I say unto you, That ye **who** have followed me, **shall,** in the **resurrection,** when the Son of man shall **come sitting on** the throne of his glory, ye also shall sit upon twelve thrones, judging the twelve tribes of Israel.
Matthew 19:29 And every one that ~~hath~~ forsaken houses, or brethren, or sisters, or father, or mother, or wife, or children, or lands, for my name's sake, shall receive an hundredfold, and shall inherit everlasting life.	And every one that **have** forsaken houses, or brethren, or sisters, or father, or mother, or wife, or children, or lands, for my name's sake, shall receive a hundredfold, and shall inherit everlasting life.
Matthew 19:30 But many ~~that are~~ first shall be last; and the last ~~shall be~~ first.	But many **of the** first shall be last; and the last first.
Matthew 20:1 For the kingdom of heaven is like unto a man ~~that is~~ an householder, ~~which~~ went out early in the morning to hire labourers into his vineyard.	For the kingdom of heaven is like unto a man, an householder, **who** went out early in the morning to hire labourers into his vineyard.
Matthew 20:3 And he went out about the third hour, and ~~saw~~ others standing idle in the marketplace,	And he went out about the third hour, and **found** others standing idle in the marketplace,
Matthew 20:5 Again he went out about the sixth and ninth hour, and did likewise.	**And** again he went out about the sixth and ninth hour, and did likewise.
Matthew 20:6 And about the eleventh hour he went out, and found others standing idle, and ~~saith~~ unto them, Why stand ye here all the day idle?	And about the eleventh hour he went out, and found others standing idle, and **said** unto them, Why stand ye here all the day idle?
Matthew 20:7 They say unto him, Because no man hath hired us. He ~~saith~~ unto them, Go ye also into the vineyard; and whatsoever is right, ~~that~~ shall ~~ye~~ receive.	They say unto him, Because no man hath hired us. He **said** unto them, Go ye also into the vineyard; and whatsoever is right, **ye** shall receive.

Matthew 20:8 So when even was come, the lord of the vineyard ~~saith~~ unto his steward, Call the labourers, and give them *their* hire, beginning from the last unto the first.	So when even was come, the lord of the vineyard **said** unto his steward, Call the labourers, and give them their hire, beginning from the last unto the first.
Matthew 20:9 And when they came that ~~were hired~~ about the eleventh hour, they received every man a penny.	And when they came that **began** about the eleventh hour, they received every man a penny.
Matthew 20:11 And when they had received ~~it~~, they murmured against the goodman of the house,	And when they had received **a penny**, they murmured against the goodman of the house,
Matthew 20:12 Saying, These last have wrought ~~but~~ one hour, and thou hast made them equal unto us, ~~which~~ have borne the burden and heat of the day.	Saying, These last have wrought one hour **only**, and thou hast made them equal unto us, **who** have borne the burden and **the** heat of the day.
Matthew 20:14 Take ~~that~~ thine ~~is~~, and go thy way: I will give unto this last, even as unto thee.	Take thine, and go thy way: I will give unto this last, even as unto thee.
Matthew 20:16 So the last shall be first, and the first last: ~~for~~ many ~~be~~ called, but few chosen.	So the last shall be first, and the first last: **and** many called, but few chosen.
	(**NT1** So the last shall be first, and the first last: for many **are** called, but few chosen.)
Matthew 20:19 And shall deliver him to the Gentiles to mock, and to scourge, and to crucify ~~him~~: and the third day he shall rise again.	And shall deliver him to the Gentiles to mock, and to scourge, and to crucify: and the third day he shall rise again.
Matthew 20:20 Then came to him the mother of Zebedee's children with her sons, worshipping ~~him~~, and desiring a certain thing of him.	Then came to him the mother of Zebedee's children with her sons, worshipping **Jesus**, and desiring a certain thing of him.
Matthew 20:21 And he said unto her, What wilt thou? She ~~saith~~ unto him, Grant that these my two sons may sit, the one on thy right hand, and the other on ~~the~~ left, in thy kingdom.	And he said unto her, What wilt thou **that I should do? And** she **said** unto him, Grant that these my two sons may sit, the one on thy right hand, and the other on **thy** left, in thy kingdom.

The Testimony of St Matthew

Matthew 20:23 And he ~~saith~~ unto them, Ye shall drink indeed of my cup, and be baptized with the baptism that I am baptized with: but to sit on my right hand, and on my left, is not mine to give, but ~~it shall be given to them~~ for whom it is prepared of my Father.

Matthew 20:24 And when the ten heard ~~it~~, they were moved with indignation against the two brethren.

Matthew 20:25 But Jesus called them ~~unto him~~, and said, Ye know that the princes of the Gentiles exercise dominion over them, and they that are great exercise authority upon them.

Matthew 20:30 And, behold, two blind men sitting by the way side, when they heard that Jesus passed by, cried out, saying, Have mercy on us, O Lord, ~~thou~~ Son of David.

Matthew 20:31 And the multitude rebuked them, ~~because~~ they should hold their peace: but they cried the more, saying, Have mercy on us, O Lord, ~~thou~~ Son of David.

Matthew 20:34 So Jesus had compassion ~~on them~~, and touched their eyes: and immediately their eyes received sight, and they followed him.

Matthew 21:1 And when ~~they~~ drew nigh unto Jerusalem, and were come to Bethphage, ~~unto~~ the mount of Olives, then sent ~~Jesus~~ two disciples,

Matthew 21:2 Saying unto them, Go into the village over against you, and straightway ~~ye~~ shall find ~~an ass~~ tied, and a colt with her: loose ~~them~~, and bring ~~them~~ unto me.

And he **said** unto them, Ye shall drink indeed of my cup, and be baptized with the baptism that I am baptized with: but to sit on my right hand, and on my left, is **for whom it is prepared of my father,** but not mine to give.

And when the ten heard **this**, they were moved with indignation against the two brethren.

But Jesus called them, and said, Ye know that the princes of the Gentiles exercise dominion over them, and they that are great exercise authority upon them.

And, behold, two blind men sitting by the way side, when they heard that Jesus passed by, cried out, saying, Have mercy on us, O Lord, Son of David.

And the multitude rebuked them, **saying**, They should hold their peace: but they cried the more, saying, Have mercy on us, O Lord, Son of David.

So Jesus had compassion and touched their eyes: and immediately their eyes received sight, and they followed him.

And when **Jesus** drew nigh unto Jerusalem, and **they** were come to Bethphage, **on** the mount of Olives, then **Jesus** sent two disciples,

Saying unto them, Go into the village over against you, and straightway **you** shall find **a colt** tied; loose **it**, and bring **it** unto me.

| | (NT1 Saying unto them, Go into the village over against you, and straightway **you** shall find an ass tied, and a colt with her: loose **the ass and the colt**, and bring them unto me) |

Matthew 21:3 And if any ~~man~~ say ought unto you, ye shall say, The Lord hath need of ~~them~~; and straightway he will send ~~them~~.

And if any **shall** say ought unto you, ye shall say, The Lord hath need of **it**; and straightway he will send **it**.

Matthew 21:4 All this was done, that it might be fulfilled which was spoken by the ~~prophet~~, saying,

All this was done, that it might be fulfilled which was spoken by the **prophets**, saying,

Matthew 21:5 Tell ye the daughter of Sion, Behold, thy King cometh unto thee, meek, and sitting upon an ass, and a colt the foal of an ass.

Tell ye the daughter of Zion, Behold, thy King cometh unto thee, **and he is** meek, and **he is** sitting upon an ass, and a colt the foal of an ass.

Matthew 21:7 And brought the ~~ass, and the~~ colt, and put on ~~them~~ their clothes, and ~~they set him~~ thereon.

And brought the colt, and put on **it** their clothes, and **Jesus took the colt and sat** thereon; **and they followed him.**

Matthew 21:8 And a very great multitude spread their garments in the way; others cut down branches from the trees, and ~~strawed them~~ in the way.

And a very great multitude spread their garments in the way; others cut down branches from the trees, and **strewed** in the way.

Matthew 21:9 And the multitudes that went before, and that followed, cried, saying, Hosanna to the Son of David: Blessed *is* he ~~that~~ cometh in the name of the Lord; Hosanna in the highest.

And the multitudes that went before, and **also** that followed **after**, cried, saying, Hosanna to the Son of David: Blessed is he **who** cometh in the name of the Lord; Hosanna in the highest.

Matthew 21:11 And the multitude said, This is Jesus the prophet ~~of Nazareth~~ of Galilee.

And the multitude said, This is Jesus **of Nazareth**, the prophet of Galilee.

Matthew 21:15 And when the chief priests and scribes saw the wonderful things that he did, and the children crying in the temple, and saying, Hosanna to the Son of David; they were sore displeased,

And when the chief priests and scribes saw the wonderful things that he did, and the children **of the kingdom** crying in the temple, and saying, Hosanna to the Son of David; they were sore displeased,

The Testimony of St Matthew

Matthew 21:16 And said unto him, Hearest thou what these say? And Jesus ~~saith~~ unto them, Yea; have ye never read, Out of the ~~mouth~~ of babes and sucklings thou hast perfected praise?	And said unto him, Hearest thou what these say? And Jesus **said** unto them, Yea; have ye never read **the scriptures which saith**, Out of the **mouths** of babes and sucklings, **O Lord,** thou hast perfected praise?
Matthew 21:19 And when he saw a fig tree in the way, he came to it, and ~~found nothing thereon~~, but leaves only, and said unto it, Let no fruit grow on thee henceforward for ever. And presently the fig tree withered away.	And when he saw a fig tree in the way, he came to it, and **there was not any fruit on it**, but leaves only, and **he** said unto it, Let no fruit grow on thee henceforward for ever. And presently the fig tree withered away.
Matthew 21:20 And when the disciples saw ~~it~~, they marvelled, ~~saying~~, How soon is the fig tree withered away!	And when the disciples saw **this**, they marvelled, **and said**, How soon is the fig tree withered away!
Matthew 21:21 Jesus answered and said unto them, Verily I say unto you, If ye have faith, and doubt not, ye shall not only do this ~~which is done~~ to the fig tree, but also if ye shall say unto this mountain, Be thou removed, and be thou cast into the sea; it shall be done.	Jesus answered and said unto them, Verily I say unto you, If ye have faith, and doubt not, ye shall not only do this to the fig tree, but also if ye shall say unto this mountain, Be thou removed, and be thou cast into the sea; it shall be done.
Matthew 21:22 And all things, whatsoever ye shall ask in prayer, believing, ye shall receive.	And all things, whatsoever ye shall ask in prayer, **in faith** believing, ye shall receive.
Matthew 21:24 And Jesus answered and said unto them, I also will ask you one thing, which if ye tell me, I ~~in~~ like wise will tell you by what authority I do these things.	And Jesus answered and said unto them, I also will ask you one thing, which if ye tell me, I likewise will tell you by what authority I do these things.
Matthew 21:26 But if we shall say, Of men; we fear the people; for all hold John as a prophet.	But if we shall say, Of men; we fear the people; for all **people** hold John as a prophet.
Matthew 21:27 And they answered Jesus, and said, We cannot tell. And he said ~~unto them~~, Neither tell I you by what authority I do these things.	And they answered Jesus, and said, We cannot tell. And he said, Neither tell I you by what authority I do these things.

Matthew 21:28 But what think ye? A ~~certain~~ man had two sons; and he came to the first, ~~and said~~, Son, go work to day in my vineyard.

Matthew 21:29 He answered and said, I will not: but ~~afterward~~ he repented, and went.

Matthew 21:30 And he came to the second, and said likewise. And he answered and said, I ~~go, sir~~: and went not.

Matthew 21:31 Whether of ~~them~~ twain did the will of ~~his~~ father? They say unto him, The first. Jesus ~~saith~~ unto them, Verily I say unto you, That the publicans and the harlots go into the kingdom of God before you.

Matthew 21:32 For John came unto you in the way of righteousness, and ye believed him not: but the publicans and the harlots believed him: and ye, when ye had seen ~~it~~, repented not ~~afterward~~, that ye might believe him.

Matthew 21:33 Hear another parable: There was a certain householder, ~~which~~ planted a vineyard, and hedged it round about, and digged a winepress in it, and built a tower, and let it out to husbandmen, and went into a far country:

But what think ye? A man had two sons; and he came to the first, **saying**, Son, go work to day in my vineyard.

He answered and said, I will not: but **afterwards** he repented, and went.

And he came to the second, and said likewise. And he answered and said, I **will serve**; and went not.

Whether of **these** twain did the will of **their** father? They say unto him, The first. Jesus **said** unto them, Verily I say unto you, That the publicans and the harlots **shall** go into the kingdom of God before you.

(**NT1** Whether of **those** twain did the will of **their** father? They say unto him, The first. Jesus saith unto them, Verily I say unto you, That the publicans and the harlots **shall** go into the kingdom of God before you.)

For John came unto you in the way of righteousness **and bore record of me**, and ye believed him not: but the publicans and the harlots believed him: and ye, **afterward**, when ye had seen **me**, repented not, that ye might believe him; **for he that believed not John concerning me, cannot believe me, except he first repent; and except ye repent, the preaching of John shall condemn you in the day of judgment.**

And again, hear another parable: **for unto you that believe not, I speak in parables, that your unrighteousness may be rewarded unto you. Behold,** there was a certain householder, **who** planted a vineyard, and hedged it round

The Testimony of St Matthew

	about, and digged a winepress in it, and built a tower, and let it out to husbandmen, and went into a far country:
Matthew 21:40 When the lord therefore of the vineyard cometh, what will he do unto those husbandmen?	**And Jesus said unto them,** When the lord therefore of the vineyard cometh, what will he do unto those husbandmen?
Matthew 21:41 They say unto him, He will ~~miserably~~ destroy those wicked men, and will let out ~~his~~ vineyard unto other husbandmen, ~~which~~ shall render him the fruits in their seasons.	They say unto him, He will destroy those **miserable** wicked men, and will let out **the** vineyard unto other husbandmen, **who** shall render him the fruits in their seasons.
Matthew 21:42 Jesus ~~saith~~ unto them, Did ye never read in the scriptures, The stone which the ~~builders~~ rejected, the same is become the head of the corner: this is the Lord's ~~doing~~, and it is marvellous in our eyes?	Jesus **said** unto them, Did ye never read in the scriptures, The stone which the **builder** rejected, the same is **to** become the head of the corner: this is the Lord's **doings**, and it is marvellous in our eyes?
Matthew 21:44 ~~And~~ whosoever shall fall on this stone shall be broken: but on whomsoever it shall fall, it will grind him to powder.	**For** whosoever shall fall on this stone shall be broken: but on whomsoever it shall fall, it will grind him to powder.
Matthew 21:45 And when the chief priests and Pharisees had heard his parables, they perceived that he spake of them.	And when the chief priests and Pharisees had heard his parables, they perceived that he spake of them. **And they said among themselves, Shall this man think that he alone can spoil this great kingdom? And they were angry with him.**
Matthew 21:46 But when they sought to lay hands on him, they feared the multitude, because they took him for a prophet.	But when they sought to lay hands on him, they feared the multitude, because **that** they **learned that the multitude** took him for a prophet. **And now his disciples came to him, and Jesus said unto them, Marvel ye at the words or the parable which I spake unto them? Verily, I say unto you, I am the stone, and those wicked ones reject me. I am the head of the corner. These Jews shall fall upon me, and shall be broken;**

and the kingdom of God shall be taken from them, and shall be given to a nation bringing forth the fruits thereof (meaning the Gentiles). Wherefore, on whomsoever this stone shall fall, it shall grind him to powder. And when the Lord therefore of the vineyard cometh, he will destroy those miserable, wicked men, and will let again his vineyard unto other husbandmen; even in the last days, which shall render him the fruits in their seasons. And then understood they the parable which he spake unto them, that the Gentiles should be destroyed also, when the Lord should descend out of heaven to reign in his vineyard, which is the earth and the inhabitants thereof.

Matthew 22:1 And Jesus answered and spake unto them ~~again by~~ parables, and said,	And Jesus answered **the people again** and spake unto them **in** parables, and said,
Matthew 22:2 The kingdom of heaven is like unto a certain king, ~~which~~ made a marriage for his son,	The kingdom of heaven is like unto a certain king, **who** made a marriage for his son,
Matthew 22:3 And sent forth his servants to call them that were bidden to the wedding: and they would not come.	And **when the marriage was ready, he** sent forth his servants to call them that were bidden to the wedding: and they would not come.
Matthew 22:4 Again, he sent forth other servants, saying, Tell them ~~which~~ are bidden, Behold, I have prepared ~~my dinner~~: my oxen and *my* fatlings ~~are~~ killed, and ~~all things are~~ ready: come unto the marriage.	Again, he sent forth other servants, saying, Tell them **that** are bidden, Behold, I have prepared my oxen, and my fatlings **have been** killed, and **my dinner is ready, and all things are prepared; therefore** come unto the marriage.
Matthew 22:5 But they made light of ~~it~~, and went their ways, one to his farm, another to his merchandise:	But they made light of **the servants**, and went their ways, one to his farm, **and** another to his merchandise:
Matthew 22:7 But when the king heard ~~thereof,~~ he was wroth: and he sent forth	But when the king heard **that his servants were dead,** he was wroth: and

his armies, and destroyed those murderers, and burned up their city.

Matthew 22:8 Then ~~saith~~ he to his servants, The wedding is ready, but they ~~which~~ were bidden were not worthy.

Matthew 22:11 ~~And~~ when the king came in to see the guests, he saw there a man ~~which~~ had not ~~on~~ a wedding garment:

Matthew 22:12 And he ~~saith~~ unto him, Friend, how camest thou in hither not having a wedding garment? And he was speechless.

Matthew 22:13 Then said the king ~~to the~~ servants, Bind him hand and foot, and take ~~him away~~, and cast *him* into outer darkness; there shall be weeping and gnashing of teeth.

Matthew 22:14 For many are called, but few ~~are~~ chosen.

Matthew 22:15 Then went the Pharisees, and took counsel how they might entangle him in ~~his~~ talk.

Matthew 22:16 And they sent out unto him their disciples with the Herodians, saying, Master, we know that thou art true, and teachest the way of God in truth, neither carest thou for any ~~man~~: for thou regardest not the person of men.

Matthew 22:18 But Jesus perceived their wickedness, and said, Why tempt ye me, ~~ye hypocrites~~?

he sent forth his armies, and destroyed those murderers, and burned up their city.

Then **said** he to his servants, The wedding is ready, but they **who** were bidden were not worthy.

But when the king came in to see the guests, he saw there a man **who** had not a wedding garment:

(**NT1 But** when the king came in to see the guests, he saw there a man **who** had not **on** a wedding garment:)

And he **said** unto him, Friend, how camest thou in hither not having a wedding garment? And he was speechless.

Then said the king **unto his** servants, Bind him hand and foot, and take and cast him **away** into outer darkness; there shall be weeping and gnashing of teeth.

For many are called, but few chosen; **wherefore all do not have on the wedding garment.**

Then went the Pharisees, and took counsel how they might entangle him in talk.

And they sent out unto him their disciples with the Herodians, saying, Master, we know that thou art true, and teachest the way of God in truth, neither carest thou for any: for thou regardest not the person of men.

But Jesus perceived their wickedness, and said, **Ye hypocrites**, Why tempt ye me?

Matthew 22:20 ~~And~~ he ~~saith~~ unto them, Whose *is* this ~~image~~ and superscription?

Matthew 22:21 They ~~say~~ unto him, Caesar's. Then ~~saith~~ he unto them, Render therefore unto Caesar the things which are Caesar's; and unto God the things ~~that~~ are God's.

Matthew 22:22 When they had heard *these words,* they marvelled, and left him, and went their way.

Matthew 22:23 The same day came ~~to him~~ the Sadducees, ~~which~~ say that there is no resurrection, and asked him,

Matthew 22:25 Now there were with us seven brethren: and the first, when he had married a wife, deceased, and, having no issue, left his wife unto his brother:

Matthew 22:26 Likewise the second also, and the third, unto the seventh.

Matthew 22:31 But as touching the resurrection of the dead, have ye not read that which was spoken unto you ~~by~~ God, saying,

Matthew 22:33 And when the multitude heard ~~this~~, they were astonished at his doctrine.

Matthew 22:34 But when the Pharisees ~~had~~ heard that he had put the Sadducees to silence, they were gathered together.

Matthew 22:35 Then one of them, ~~which was~~ a lawyer, ~~asked him a question~~, tempting him, ~~and~~ saying,

Matthew 22:43 He ~~saith~~ unto them, How then doth David in spirit call him Lord, saying,

---

He **said** unto them, Whose **image** is this and superscription?

They **said** unto him, Caesar's. Then **said** he unto them, Render therefore unto Caesar the things which are Caesar's; and unto God the things **which** are God's.

And when they had heard **him say** these words, they marvelled, and left him, and went their way.

The same day came the Sadducees **to him**, **who** say that there is no resurrection, and asked him,

Now there were with us seven brethren: and the first, when he had married a wife, deceased, and, having no issue, **he** left his wife unto his brother:

Likewise the second also, and the third, **and even** unto the seventh.

But as touching the resurrection of the dead, have ye not read that which was spoken unto you **of** God, saying,

And when the multitude heard **him**, they were astonished at his doctrine.

But when the Pharisees heard that he had put the Sadducees to silence, they were gathered together.

Then one of them, a lawyer, tempting him, **asked**, saying,

He **said** unto them, How then doth David in spirit call him Lord, saying,

The Testimony of St Matthew

Matthew 22:45 If David then ~~call~~ him Lord, how is he his son?	If David then **called** him Lord, how is he his son?
Matthew 23:3 All therefore whatsoever they bid you observe, ~~that~~ observe and do; but do not ye after their works: for they say, and do not.	All therefore whatsoever they bid you observe, **they will make you** observe and do; **for they are ministers of the law, and they make themselves your judges,** but do not ye after their works: for they say, and do not.
Matthew 23:4 For they bind heavy burdens and grievous to be borne, ~~and lay them on men's shoulders~~; but they ~~themselves~~ will not move them with one of their fingers.	For they bind heavy burdens and **lay on men's shoulders, and they are** grievous to be borne; but they will not move them with one of their fingers.
Matthew 23:5 ~~But~~ all their works they do ~~for~~ to be seen of men: they make broad their phylacteries, and enlarge the borders of their garments,	**And** all their works they do to be seen of men: they make broad their phylacteries, and enlarge the borders of their garments,
Matthew 23:7 And greetings in the markets, and to be called of men, Rabbi, Rabbi.	And greetings in the markets, and to be called of men, Rabbi, Rabbi **(which is master)**.
Matthew 23:8 But be not ye called Rabbi: for one is your Master, ~~even~~ Christ; and all ye are brethren.	But be not ye called Rabbi: for one is your Master, **which is** Christ; and all ye are brethren.
Matthew 23:9 And call no ~~man~~ your ~~father~~ upon the earth: for one is your Father, ~~which~~ is in heaven.	And call no **one** your **creator** upon the earth **or your Heavenly Father**; for one is your **creator and Heavenly** Father, **even he who** is in heaven.
	(**NT1** And call no **one** your **creator** upon the earth **or your Heavenly Father**; for one is your **creator and Heavenly** Father, **even him who** is in heaven.)
Matthew 23:10 Neither be ye called ~~masters~~: for one is your Master, *even* Christ.	Neither be ye called **master**: for one is your Master, even **he whom your Heavenly Father sent, which is** Christ; **for he hath sent him among you, that ye might have life.**

	(**NT1** Neither be ye called **masters**: for one is your Master, even **him whom your Heavenly Father sent, which is** Christ; **for he hath sent him among you, that ye might have life.**)
Matthew 23:12 And whosoever shall exalt himself shall be abased; and he that shall humble himself shall be exalted.	And whosoever shall exalt himself shall be abased **of him**; and he that shall humble himself shall be exalted **of him**.
Matthew 23:14 Woe unto you, scribes and Pharisees, hypocrites! ~~for~~ ye devour widows' houses, and for a pretence make long ~~prayer~~: therefore ~~ye~~ shall receive the greater ~~damnation~~.	Woe unto you, scribes and Pharisees, **for ye are** hypocrites! Ye devour widows' houses, and for a pretence make long **prayers**: therefore **you** shall receive the greater **punishment**.
	(**NT1** Woe unto you, scribes and Pharisees, **for you are** hypocrites! Ye devour widows' houses, and for a pretence make long **prayers**: therefore **you** shall receive the greater damnation.)
Matthew 23:15 Woe unto you, scribes and Pharisees, hypocrites! for ~~ye~~ compass sea and land to make one proselyte, and when he is made, ye make him twofold more the child of hell than yourselves.	Woe unto you, scribes and Pharisees, hypocrites! for **you** compass sea and land to make one proselyte, and when he is made, **you** make him twofold more the child of hell than **he was before, like unto** yourselves.
Matthew 23:16 Woe unto you, ~~ye~~ blind guides, ~~which~~ say, Whosoever shall swear by the temple, it is nothing; but whosoever shall swear by the gold of the temple, he is a debtor!	Woe unto you, blind guides, **who** say, Whosoever shall swear by the temple, it is nothing; but whosoever shall swear by the gold of the temple, he **committeth sin, and** is a debtor!
	(**NT1** Woe unto you, blind guides, **who** say, Whosoever shall swear by the temple, it is nothing; but whosoever shall swear by the gold of the temple, he **hath committed sin, and** is a debtor!)
Matthew 23:17 ~~Ye~~ fools and blind: for ~~whether~~ is ~~greater~~, the gold, or the temple that sanctifieth the gold?	**You are** fools and blind: for **which** is **the greatest**, the gold, or the temple that sanctifieth the gold?

The Testimony of St Matthew

Matthew 23:18 And, Whosoever ~~shall swear~~ by the altar, it is nothing; but whosoever sweareth by the gift that is upon it, he is guilty.	And, **ye say,** Whosoever **sweareth** by the altar, it is nothing; but whosoever sweareth by the gift that is upon it, he is guilty.
Matthew 23:19 ~~Ye~~ fools and blind: for ~~whether~~ *is* ~~greater~~, the gift, or the altar that sanctifieth the gift?	O fools and blind: for **which is the greatest**, the gift, or the altar that sanctifieth the gift?
Matthew 23:20 Whoso therefore ~~shall swear by the altar~~, sweareth by it, and by all things thereon.	**Verily I say unto you,** whoso therefore sweareth by it, **sweareth by the altar**, and by all things thereon.
Matthew 23:21 And whoso shall swear by the temple, sweareth by it, and by him ~~that~~ dwelleth therein.	And whoso shall swear by the temple, sweareth by it, and by him **who** dwelleth therein.
Matthew 23:22 And he that shall swear by heaven, sweareth by the throne of God, and by him ~~that~~ sitteth thereon.	And he that shall swear by heaven, sweareth by the throne of God, and by him **who** sitteth thereon.
Matthew 23:23 Woe unto you, scribes and Pharisees, hypocrites! for ~~ye~~ pay tithe of mint and anise and cummin, and have omitted the weightier ~~matters~~ of the law, judgment, mercy, and faith: these ought ye to have done, and not to leave the other undone.	Woe unto you, scribes and Pharisees, hypocrites! for **you** pay tithe of mint and anise and cummin, and have omitted the weightier **things** of the law, judgment, mercy, and faith: these ought ye to have done, and not to leave the other undone.
	(NT1 Woe unto you, scribes and Pharisees, hypocrites! for **you** pay tithe of mint and anise and cummin, and have omitted the weightier **things** of the law, **and of** judgment, mercy, and faith: these ought ye to have done, and not to leave the **others** undone.)
Matthew 23:24 ~~Ye~~ blind guides, ~~which~~ strain at a gnat, and swallow a camel.	**You** blind guides, **who** strain at a gnat, and swallow a camel; **who make yourselves appear unto men that you would not commit the least sin, and yet you yourselves transgress the whole law.**
Matthew 23:25 Woe unto you, scribes and Pharisees, hypocrites! for ~~ye~~ make clean the outside of the cup and of the	Woe unto you, scribes and Pharisees, hypocrites! for **you** make clean the outside of the cup and of the platter, but

platter, but within they are full of extortion and excess.

Matthew 23:26 ~~Thou~~ blind ~~Pharisee~~, cleanse first ~~that which is within~~ the cup and platter, that the outside of them may be clean also.

Matthew 23:27 Woe unto you, scribes and Pharisees, hypocrites! for ~~ye~~ are like unto whited sepulchres, which indeed appear beautiful ~~outward~~, but are within full of ~~dead men's~~ bones, and of all uncleanness.

Matthew 23:28 Even so ~~ye~~ also outwardly appear righteous unto men, but within ~~ye~~ are full of hypocrisy and iniquity.

Matthew 23:29 Woe unto you, scribes and Pharisees, hypocrites! because ~~ye~~ build the tombs of the prophets, and garnish the sepulchres of the righteous,

Matthew 23:31 Wherefore ~~ye be~~ witnesses unto yourselves, ~~that ye~~ are the children of them ~~which~~ killed the prophets.

Matthew 23:32 Fill ~~ye~~ up ~~then~~ the measure of your fathers.

Matthew 23:33 ~~Ye~~ serpents, ~~ye~~ generation of vipers, how can ~~ye~~ escape the damnation of hell?

Matthew 23:34 Wherefore, behold, I send unto you prophets, and wise men, and scribes: and ~~some~~ of them ~~ye~~ shall kill and crucify; and ~~some~~ of them shall

within they are full of extortion and excess.

You blind **Pharisees**, cleanse first the cup and platter **within**, that the outside of them may be clean also.

Woe unto you, scribes and Pharisees, hypocrites! for **you** are like unto whited sepulchres, which indeed appear beautiful **outwardly**, but are within full of **the** bones **of the dead**, and of all uncleanness.

Even so **you** also outwardly appear righteous unto men, but within **you** are full of hypocrisy and iniquity.

Woe unto you, scribes and Pharisees, hypocrites! because **you** build the tombs of the prophets, and garnish the sepulchres of the righteous,

Wherefore **you are** witnesses unto yourselves, **of your own wickedness; and you** are the children of them **who** killed the prophets.

And will fill up the measure **then** of your fathers; **for you yourselves kill the prophets like unto your fathers.**

You serpents, **and** generation of vipers, how can **you** escape the damnation of hell?

(**NT1 You** serpents, **a** generation of vipers, how can **you** escape the damnation of hell?)

Wherefore, behold, I send unto you prophets, and wise men, and scribes: and of them **you** shall kill and crucify; and of them **you** shall scourge in your

~~ye~~ scourge in your synagogues, and persecute ~~them~~ from city to city:	synagogues, and persecute from city to city:
Matthew 23:35 That upon you may come all the righteous blood shed upon the earth, from the blood of righteous Abel unto the blood of Zacharias son of Barachias, whom ~~ye~~ slew between the temple and the altar.	(NT1 That upon you may come all the righteous blood shed upon the earth, from the blood of righteous Abel unto the blood of Zacharias son of Barachias, whom **you** slew between the temple and the altar.)
Matthew 23:36 Verily I say unto you, All these things shall come upon this generation.	Verily I say unto you, All these things shall come upon this generation. **You bear testimony against your fathers, when you yourselves are partakers of the same wickedness. Behold your fathers did it through ignorance, but you do not; wherefore their sins shall be upon your heads.**
Matthew 23:37 O Jerusalem, Jerusalem, ~~thou that killest~~ the prophets, and ~~stonest~~ them ~~which~~ are sent unto ~~thee~~, how often would I have gathered ~~thy~~ children together, even as a hen ~~gathereth~~ her chickens under *her* wings, and ~~ye~~ would not!	**Then Jesus began to weep over Jerusalem, saying,** O Jerusalem! Jerusalem! **You who will kill** the prophets, and **will stone** them **who** are sent unto **you**, how often would I have gathered **your** children together, even as a hen **gathers** her chickens under her wings, and **you** would not!
Matthew 23:39 For I say unto you, ~~Ye~~ shall not see me henceforth, ~~till ye~~ shall say, Blessed *is* he ~~that~~ cometh in the name of the Lord.	For I say unto you, **that you** shall not see me henceforth, **and know that I am he of whom it is written by the prophets,** until **you** shall say, Blessed is he **who** cometh in the name of the Lord, **in the clouds of heaven, and all the holy angels with him. Then understood his disciples that he should come again on the earth, after that he was glorified and crowned on the right hand of God.**
Matthew 24:1 And Jesus went out, and departed from the temple: and his disciples came to *him* for to ~~shew~~ him the buildings of the temple.	And Jesus went out, and departed from the temple: and his disciples came to him for to **hear** him, **saying, Master,** shew us concerning the buildings of the temple; **as thou hast said, They shall**

	be thrown down and left unto you desolate.
Matthew 24:2 And Jesus said unto them, See ~~ye~~ not all these things? verily I say unto you, There shall not be left here one stone upon another, that shall not be thrown down.	And Jesus said unto them, See **you** not all these things? **And do you not understand them?** Verily I say unto you, There shall not be left here **upon this temple,** one stone upon another, that shall not be thrown down.
	(NT1 And Jesus said unto them, See **you** not all these things? **And do ye not understand them?** Verily I say unto you, There shall not be left here **upon this temple** one stone upon another, that shall not be thrown down.)
Matthew 24:3 And as he sat upon the mount of Olives, the disciples came unto him privately, saying, Tell us, when shall these things be? and what ~~shall be~~ the sign of thy coming, and of the end of the world?	**And Jesus left them and went upon the mount of Olives.** And as he sat upon the mount of Olives, the disciples came unto him privately, saying, Tell us, when shall these things be **which thou hast said concerning the destruction of the Temple and the Jews**; and what is the sign of thy coming, and of the end of the world (**or the destruction of the wicked, which is the end of the world**)?
Matthew 24:6 ~~And ye shall hear of wars and rumours of wars: see that ye be not troubled: for all *these things* must come to pass, but the end is not yet.~~	
Matthew 24:7 ~~For nation shall rise against nation, and kingdom against kingdom: and there shall be famines, and pestilences, and earthquakes, in divers places.~~	
Matthew 24:8 ~~All these *are* the beginning of sorrows.~~	
Matthew 24:9 Then shall they deliver you up to be afflicted, and shall kill you: and ~~ye~~ shall be hated of all nations for my name's sake.	Then shall they deliver you up to be afflicted, and shall kill you: and **you** shall be hated of all nations for my name's sake.

Matthew 24:10 And then shall many be offended, and shall betray one another, ~~and shall hate one another~~.	And then shall many be offended, and shall betray one another.
Matthew 24:11 And many false prophets shall ~~rise~~, and shall deceive many.	And many false prophets shall **arise**, and shall deceive many.
Matthew 24:13 But he that ~~shall endure unto the end~~, the same shall be saved.	But he that **remaineth steadfast, and is not overcome**, the same shall be saved.
Matthew 24:14 ~~And this gospel of the kingdom shall be preached in all the world for a witness unto all nations; and then shall the end come~~.	
Matthew 24:15 When ~~ye~~ therefore shall see the ~~abomination~~ of desolation, spoken of by Daniel the prophet, stand in the holy place, (whoso readeth, let him understand:)	When **you** therefore shall see the **abominations** of desolation, spoken of by Daniel the prophet, **concerning the destruction of Jerusalem, then you shall** stand in the holy place, (whoso readeth, let him understand:)
Matthew 24:16 Then let them ~~which be~~ in Judaea flee into the mountains:	Then let them **who are** in Judea flee into the mountains:
Matthew 24:17 Let him ~~which~~ is on the housetop ~~not come down~~ to take any thing out of his house:	Let him **who** is on the housetop **flee and not return** to take any thing out of his house:
Matthew 24:18 Neither let him ~~which~~ is in the field return back to take his clothes.	Neither let him **who** is in the field return back to take his clothes.
Matthew 24:19 And woe unto them that are with child, and ~~to~~ them that give suck in those days!	And woe unto them that are with child, and **unto** them that give suck in those days!
Matthew 24:20 ~~But~~ pray ye that your flight be not in the winter, neither on the sabbath day:	**Therefore**, pray ye **the Lord** that your flight be not in the winter, neither on the sabbath day:
	(NT1 **Therefore**, pray **you the Lord** that your flight be not in the winter, neither on the sabbath day:)

Matthew 24:21 For then shall be great ~~tribulation~~, such as was not since the beginning of ~~the world to~~ this time, no, nor ever shall be.	For then, **in those days**, shall be great **tribulations on the Jews and upon the inhabitants of Jerusalem;** such as was not **before sent upon Israel of God,** since the beginning of **their kingdom till** this time, no, nor ever shall be **sent again upon Israel. All things which have befallen them are only the beginning of the sorrows which shall come upon them.**
	(NT1 For then, **in those days,** shall be great tribulation **on the Jews and upon the inhabitants of Jerusalem;** such as was not **before sent upon Israel of the world,** since the beginning of **their reign till** this time, no, nor ever shall be **sent again upon Israel. All these things are the beginnings of sorrows.**)
Matthew 24:22 And except those days should be shortened, there should ~~no~~ flesh be saved: but for the elect's sake those days shall be shortened.	And except those days should be shortened, there should **none of their** flesh be saved: but for the elect's sake, **according to the covenant,** those days shall be shortened.
Matthew 24:23 ~~Then~~ if any man shall say unto you, Lo, here *is* Christ, or there; believe ~~it~~ not.	**Behold those things I have spoken unto you concerning the Jews, and again, after the tribulation of those days which shall come upon Jerusalem,** if any man shall say unto you, Lo! here is Christ, or there; believe **him** not;
	(NT1 **Behold these things I have spoken unto you concerning the Jews, and then immediately after the tribulation of those days which shall come upon Jerusalem,** if any man shall say unto you, Lo, here is Christ, or there; believe **him** not;)
Matthew 24:24 For there shall arise false Christs, and false prophets, and shall shew great signs and wonders;	For **in those days** there shall **also** arise false Christs, and false prophets, and shall shew great signs and wonders;

The Testimony of St Matthew

insomuch that, if ~~it were~~ possible, they shall deceive the very elect.

insomuch that, if possible, they shall deceive the very elect, **who are the elect according to the covenant. Behold, I speak these things unto you for the elect's sake. And you also shall hear of wars, and rumours of wars; see that ye be not troubled; for all I have told you must come to pass, but the end is not yet.**

Matthew 24:27 For as the ~~lightning~~ cometh out of the east, and shineth even unto the west; so shall also the coming of the Son of man be.

For as the **light of the morning** cometh out of the east, and shineth even unto the west, **and covereth the whole earth;** so shall also the coming of the Son of man be.

Matthew 24:28 ~~For~~ wheresoever the carcase is, there will the eagles be gathered together.

And now I shew unto you a parable. Behold, wheresoever the carcase is, there will the eagles be gathered together. **So likewise shall mine elect be gathered from the four quarters of the earth. And they shall hear of wars, and rumours of wars. Behold, I speak unto you for mine elect's sake. For nation shall rise against nation, and kingdom against kingdom; there shall be famine and pestilences and earthquakes in diverse places. And again, because iniquity shall abound, the love of men shall wax cold; but he that shall not be overcome, the same shall be saved. And again, this gospel of the Kingdom shall be preached in all the world, for a witness unto all nations, and then shall the end come, or the destruction of the wicked. And again shall the abomination of desolation, spoken of by Daniel the prophet, be fulfilled.**

(NT1 **And now I shew unto you a parable. Behold,** wheresoever the carcase is, there will the eagles be gathered together. **So likewise shall mine elect be gathered from the four quarters of** the earth. And they shall hear of wars, and rumours of wars. Behold, I speak unto you for mine elect's sake. For nation shall rise against nation, and kingdom against kingdom; there shall be famines and pestilences and earthquakes in diverse places. And again, because iniquity shall abound, the love of men shall wax cold; but he that shall endure unto the end, the same shall be saved. And again, this gospel of the kingdom shall be preached in all the world, for a witness unto all nations, and then shall the end come, or the destruction of the wicked. And again shall the abomination of desolation, spoken of by Daniel the prophet, be fulfilled.)

Matthew 24:29 Immediately after the tribulation of those days ~~shall~~ the sun be darkened, and the moon shall not give her light, and the stars shall fall from heaven, and the powers of ~~the heavens~~ shall be shaken:

And immediately after the tribulation of those days the sun **shall** be darkened, and the moon shall not give her light, and the stars shall fall from heaven, and the powers of **heaven** shall be shaken. Verily I say unto you, this generation in the which these things shall be shewn forth, shall not pass away till all I have told you shall be fulfilled. Although the days will come that heaven and earth shall pass away, yet my words shall not pass away; but all shall be fulfilled.

(**NT1 And** immediately after the tribulation of those days the sun **shall** be darkened, and the moon shall not give her light, and the stars shall fall from heaven, and the powers of **heaven** shall be shaken. Verily I say unto you, this generation in the which these things shall be shewn forth, shall not pass away till all these things be fulfilled. Although the days will come that heaven and earth shall pass away, but

The Testimony of St Matthew

Matthew 24:30 And then shall appear the sign of the Son of man in heaven: and then shall all the tribes of the earth mourn, and they shall see the Son of man coming in the clouds of heaven with power and great glory.

Matthew 24:31 And he shall send his angels with ~~a~~ great sound of a trumpet, and they shall gather together his elect from the four winds, from one end of heaven to the other.

Matthew 24:32 Now learn a parable of the fig tree; When ~~his branch is~~ yet tender, and ~~putteth~~ forth leaves, ~~ye~~ know that summer *is* nigh:

Matthew 24:33 So likewise ~~ye~~, when ~~ye~~ shall see all these things, know that ~~it~~ is near, *even* at the doors.

Matthew 24:34 ~~Verily I say unto you, This generation shall not pass, till all these things be fulfilled~~.

Matthew 24:35 ~~Heaven and earth shall pass away, but my words shall not pass away~~.

Matthew 24:36 But of that day and hour knoweth ~~no man~~, no, not the angels of heaven, but my Father only.

my words shall not pass away; but all shall be fulfilled.)

And **as I said before, after the tribulation of those days, and the powers of the heavens shall be shaken,** then shall appear the sign of the Son of man in heaven: and then shall all the tribes of the earth mourn, and they shall see the Son of man coming in the clouds of heaven with power and great glory.

And whoso treasureth up my words, shall not be deceived; for the Son of man shall come, and he shall send his angels **before him** with the great sound of a trumpet, and they shall gather together **the remainder of** his elect from the four winds, from one end of heaven to the other.

Now learn a parable of the fig tree; When **its branches are** yet tender, and **it begins to put** forth leaves, **you** know that summer is nigh **at hand**.

So likewise, **mine elect,** when **they** shall see all these things, **they shall** know that he is near, even at the doors.

(**NT1** So likewise, **mine elect,** when **they** shall see all these things, **shall** know that **he** is near, even at the doors.)

But of that day and hour **no one** knoweth; no, not the angels of **God in** heaven, but my Father only.

Matthew 24:37 But as the days of Noe ~~were~~, so shall also the coming of the Son of man ~~be~~.	But as **it was in** the days of Noah, so **it** shall **be** also **at** the coming of the Son of man,
Matthew 24:38 For as in the days ~~that~~ were before the flood they were eating and drinking, marrying and giving in marriage, ~~until the day that Noe entered into the ark~~,	For **it shall be with them** as **it was** in the days **which** were before the flood; **for until the day that Noah entered into the ark**, they were eating and drinking, marrying and giving in marriage,
Matthew 24:40 Then shall two be in the field; the one shall be taken, and the other left.	Then shall **be fulfilled that which is written, that in the last days,** two **shall** be in the field; the one shall be taken, and the other left.
Matthew 24:41 Two ~~women~~ shall be grinding at the mill; the one ~~shall be~~ taken, and the other left.	Two shall be grinding at the mill; the one taken, and the other left.
Matthew 24:42 Watch therefore: for ye know not what hour your Lord doth come.	**And what I say unto one, I say unto all men.** Watch therefore: for ye know not **at** what hour your Lord doth come.
Matthew 24:43 But know this, ~~that~~ if the goodman of the house had known in what watch the thief would come, he would have watched, and would not have suffered his house to ~~be~~ broken up.	But know this, if the goodman of the house had known in what watch the thief would come, he would have watched, and would not have suffered his house to **have been** broken up; **but would have been ready**.
Matthew 24:44 Therefore be ye also ready: for in such an hour as ~~ye~~ think not the Son of man cometh.	Therefore be ye also ready: for in such an hour as **you** think not the Son of man cometh.
Matthew 24:47 Verily I say unto you, ~~That~~ he shall make him ruler over all his goods.	**And** verily I say unto you, he shall make him ruler over all his goods.
Matthew 24:48 But ~~and~~ if that evil servant shall say in his heart, My lord delayeth his coming;	But if that evil servant shall say in his heart, My lord delayeth his coming;
Matthew 24:51 And shall cut him asunder, and appoint *him* his portion with the hypocrites: there shall be weeping and gnashing of teeth.	And shall cut him asunder, and **shall** appoint him his portion with the hypocrites: there shall be weeping and gnashing of teeth. **And thus cometh**

	the end of the wicked according to the prophecy of Moses, saying, They should be cut off from among the people; but the end of the earth is not yet, **but by and by.**
Matthew 25:1 Then ~~shall~~ the kingdom of heaven be likened unto ten virgins, ~~which~~ took their lamps, and went forth to meet the bridegroom.	**And** then **at that day, before the Son of man comes,** the kingdom of heaven **shall** be likened unto ten virgins, **who** took their lamps, and went forth to meet the bridegroom.
	(**NT1 And** then **at that day, when the Son of man shall come,** the kingdom of heaven **shall** be likened unto ten virgins, which took their lamps, and went forth to meet the bridegroom.)
Matthew 25:2 And five of them were wise, and five *were* foolish.	And five of them were wise, and five **of them** were foolish.
Matthew 25:6 And at midnight there was a cry made, Behold, the bridegroom cometh; go ~~ye~~ out to meet him.	And at midnight there was a cry made, Behold, the bridegroom cometh; go **you** out to meet him.
Matthew 25:9 But the wise answered, saying, ~~Not so~~; lest there be not enough for us and you: ~~but~~ go ~~ye~~ rather to them that sell, and buy for yourselves.	But the wise answered, saying, Lest there be not enough for us and you: go **you** rather to them that sell, and buy for yourselves.
Matthew 25:11 Afterward came also the other virgins, saying, Lord, Lord, open ~~to~~ us.	Afterward came also the other virgins, saying, Lord, Lord, open **unto** us.
Matthew 25:12 But he answered and said, Verily I say unto you, ~~I~~ know ~~you~~ not.	But he answered and said, Verily I say unto you, **you** know **me** not.
Matthew 25:13 Watch therefore, for ~~ye~~ know neither the day nor the hour wherein the Son of man cometh.	Watch therefore, for **you** know neither the day nor the hour wherein the Son of man cometh.
Matthew 25:14 For ~~the kingdom of heaven~~ *is* as a man travelling into a far country, *who* called his own servants, and delivered unto them his goods.	**Now I will liken these things unto a parable.** For **it is like** as a man travelling into a far country, who called his own servants, and delivered unto them his goods.

Matthew 25:15 And unto one he gave five talents, to another two, and to another one; to every man according to his several ability; and straightway ~~took~~ his journey.	And unto one he gave five talents, to another two, and to another one; to every man according to his several ability; and straightway **went on** his journey.
Matthew 25:16 Then he that had received the five talents went and traded with the same, and ~~made them~~ other five talents.	Then he that had received the five talents went and traded with the same, and **gained** other five talents.
Matthew 25:17 And likewise he ~~that had received~~ two, he also gained other two.	And likewise he **who** had received two **talents**, he also gained other two.
Matthew 25:18 But he that ~~had~~ received one went and digged in the earth, and hid his lord's money.	(**NT1** But he that received one went and digged in the earth, and hid his lord's money.)
Matthew 25:20 And so he that had received five talents came and brought other five talents, saying, Lord, thou deliveredst unto me five talents: behold, I have gained ~~beside~~ them five talents more.	And so he that had received **the** five talents came and brought other five talents, saying, Lord, thou deliveredst unto me five talents: behold, I have gained **besides** them five talents more.
Matthew 25:21 His lord said unto him, Well done, ~~thou~~ good and faithful servant: thou hast been faithful over a few things, I will make thee ruler over many things: enter thou into the joy of thy lord.	His lord said unto him, Well done, good and faithful servant: thou hast been faithful over a few things, I will make thee ruler over many things: enter thou into the joy of thy lord.
Matthew 25:22 He also that had received two talents came and said, Lord, thou deliveredst unto me two talents: behold, I have gained two ~~other~~ talents beside them.	He also that had received two talents came and said, Lord, thou deliveredst unto me two talents: behold, I have gained two talents beside them.
Matthew 25:24 Then he ~~which~~ had received the one talent came and said, Lord, I knew thee that thou art an hard man, reaping where thou hast not sown, and ~~gathering~~ where thou hast not ~~strawed~~:	Then he **who** had received the one talent came and said, Lord, I knew thee that thou art a hard man, reaping where thou hast not sown, and **gathered** where thou hast not **scattered**:

Matthew 25:25 And I was afraid, and went and hid thy talent in the earth: lo, ~~there~~ thou hast ~~that is~~ thine.

Matthew 25:26 His lord answered and said unto him, ~~Thou~~ wicked and slothful servant, thou knewest that I reap where I sowed not, and ~~gather~~ where I have not ~~strawed~~:

Matthew 25:27 Thou oughtest ~~therefore~~ to have put my money to the exchangers, and ~~then~~ at my coming I should have received mine own with usury.

Matthew 25:28 Take therefore the talent from ~~him~~, and give *it* unto him ~~which~~ hath ten talents.

Matthew 25:29 For unto every one ~~that~~ hath shall be given, and he shall have abundance: but from him that hath not shall be taken away even that which he hath.

Matthew 25:30 And cast ye the unprofitable servant into outer darkness: there shall be weeping and gnashing of teeth.

Matthew 25:31 When the Son of man shall come in his glory, and all the holy angels with him, then ~~shall~~ he sit upon the throne of his glory:

Matthew 25:32 And before him shall be gathered all nations: and he shall separate them one from another, as a shepherd divideth ~~his~~ sheep from the goats~~:~~

And I was afraid, and went and hid thy talent in the earth: **and** lo, **here is thy talent; take it from me as** thou hast **from** thine **other servants, for it is thine.**

His lord answered and said unto him, O wicked and slothful servant, thou knewest that I reap where I sowed not, and **gathered** where I have not **scattered**:

Having known this therefore, thou oughtest to have put my money to the exchangers, and at my coming I should have received mine own with usury.

I will take therefore the talent from **you**, and give it unto him **who** hath ten talents.

For unto every one **who** hath **obtained other talents**, shall be given, and he shall have in abundance: but from him that hath not **obtained other talents**, shall be taken away even that which he hath **received**.

And **his lord shall say unto his servants,** Cast ye the unprofitable servant into outer darkness: there shall be weeping and gnashing of teeth.

When the Son of man shall come in his glory, and all the holy angels with him, then he **shall** sit upon the throne of his glory:

And before him shall be gathered all nations: and he shall separate them one from another, as a shepherd divideth sheep from the goats,

Matthew 25:33 ~~And he shall set~~ the sheep on his right hand, but the goats on ~~the~~ left.	The sheep on his right hand, but the goats on **his** left.
Matthew 25:34 Then shall the King say unto them on his right hand, Come, ye blessed of my Father, inherit the kingdom prepared for you from the foundation of the world:	**And he shall sit upon his throne, and the twelve apostles with him. And** then shall the king say unto them on his right hand, Come, ye blessed of my Father, inherit the kingdom prepared for you from the foundation of the world:
Matthew 25:35 For I was an hungred, and ~~ye~~ gave me meat: I was thirsty, and ~~ye~~ gave me drink: I was a stranger, and ~~ye~~ took me in:	For I was an hungred, and **you** gave me meat: I was thirsty, and **you** gave me drink: I was a stranger, and **you** took me in:
Matthew 25:42 For I was an hungred, and ~~ye~~ gave me no meat: I was thirsty, and ~~ye~~ gave me no drink:	For I was an hungred, and **you** gave me no meat: I was thirsty, and **you** gave me no drink:
Matthew 25:43 I was a stranger, and ~~ye~~ took me not in: naked, and ~~ye~~ clothed me not: sick, and in prison, and ~~ye~~ visited me not.	I was a stranger, and **you** took me not in: naked, and **you** clothed me not: sick, and in prison, and **you** visited me not.
Matthew 25:45 Then shall he answer them, saying, Verily I say unto you, Inasmuch as ~~ye~~ did *it* not to one of the least of these, ~~ye~~ did *it* not ~~to~~ me.	Then shall he answer them, saying, Verily I say unto you, Inasmuch as **you** did it not to one of the least of these **my brethren**, **you** did it not **unto** me.
Matthew 25:46 And these shall go away into everlasting punishment: but the righteous ~~into~~ life eternal.	(**NT1** And these shall go away into everlasting punishment: but the righteous **unto** life eternal.)
Matthew 26:2 Ye know that after two days is ~~the feast of~~ the passover, and the Son of man is betrayed to be crucified.	Ye know that after two days is the passover, and **then** the Son of man is betrayed to be crucified.
	(**NT1 You** know that after two days is the passover, and the Son is **to be** betrayed **and** crucified.)
Matthew 26:3 Then assembled together the chief priests, and the scribes, and the elders of the people, unto the palace	(**NT1 And** then assembled together the chief priests, and the scribes, and the

of the high priest, who ~~was~~ called Caiaphas,

Matthew 26:4 And consulted that they might take Jesus by subtilty, and kill *him*.

Matthew 26:5 But they said, Not on the feast *day,* lest there be an uproar among the people.

Matthew 26:7 There came unto him a woman having an alabaster box of very precious ointment, and poured it on his head, as he sat ~~at meat~~.

Matthew 26:8 But when ~~his disciples~~ saw ~~it~~, they had indignation, saying, ~~To~~ what purpose *is* this waste?

Matthew 26:10 When Jesus understood ~~it~~, he said unto them, Why trouble ye the woman? for she hath wrought a good work upon me.

Matthew 26:11 For ye have the poor always with you; but me ye have not always.

Matthew 26:12 For ~~in that~~ she hath poured this ointment on my body, ~~she did it~~ for my burial.

elders of the people, unto the palace of the high priest, who **is** called Caiaphas,)

(NT1 And consulted that they might take Jesus by subtilty, and kill him **that they might put an end to his work**.)

(NT1 But they said, lest there be an uproar among the people, **let us not do it on the feast day**.)

There came unto him a woman having an alabaster box of very precious ointment, and poured it on his head, as he sat **in the house**.

But when **some** saw **this**, they had indignation, saying, **Unto** what purpose is this waste?

(NT1 But when his disciples saw **her**, they had indignation **against her**, saying, To what purpose is this waste?)

When **they had said thus**, Jesus understood **them**, **and** he said unto them, Why trouble ye the woman? for she hath wrought a good work upon me.

(NT1 And when **they had thus reasoned among themselves, and understood not, Jesus knowing their hearts**, he said unto them, Why trouble **you** the woman **and from whence is this evil in your hearts**? for **verily I say unto you**, she hath wrought a good work upon me.)

(NT1 For the poor **you have** always with you; but me **you** have not always.)

For she hath poured this ointment on my body, for my burial.

(NT1 **This woman** hath poured this ointment on my body, for my burial.)

Matthew 26:13 Verily I say unto you, Wheresoever this gospel shall be preached in the whole world, ~~there shall also~~ this, that this woman hath done, be told for a memorial of her.	**And in this thing that she hath done, she shall be blessed; for** verily I say unto you, Wheresoever this gospel shall be preached in the whole world, this **thing** that this woman hath done, **shall also** be told for a memorial of her.

(**NT1** Verily I say unto you, Wheresoever this gospel shall be preached in the whole world, shall this, that this woman hath done, be told for a memorial of her, **for in that she hath done for me, she hath obtained a blessing of my father.**) |
| **Matthew 26:15** And said ~~unto them~~, What will ye give me, and I will deliver him unto you? And they covenanted with him for thirty pieces of silver. | And said, What will ye give me, and I will deliver him unto you? And they covenanted with him for thirty pieces of silver.

(**NT1** And said, What will **you** give me, and I will deliver him unto you? And they covenanted with him for thirty pieces of silver.) |
| **Matthew 26:16** And from that time he sought opportunity to betray ~~him~~. | And from that time he sought opportunity to betray **Jesus**. |
| **Matthew 26:17** Now the first *day* of the *feast of* unleavened bread the disciples came ~~to~~ Jesus, saying unto him, Where wilt thou that we prepare for thee to eat the passover? | Now **on** the first day of the feast of unleavened bread the disciples came **unto** Jesus, saying unto him, Where wilt thou that we prepare for thee to eat the passover?

(**NT1** Now **on** the first day of the unleavened bread the disciples came to Jesus, saying unto him, Where wilt thou that we prepare for thee to eat the passover?) |
| **Matthew 26:19** And the disciples did as Jesus ~~had~~ appointed them; and they made ready the passover. | And the disciples did as Jesus appointed them; and they made ready the passover. |

The Testimony of St Matthew

| | (NT1 And the disciples did as Jesus **commanded** them; and they made ready the passover.) |

Matthew 26:20 Now when the ~~even~~ was come, he sat down with the twelve.

Now when the **evening** was come, he sat down with the twelve.

Matthew 26:24 The Son of man goeth as it is written of him: but woe unto that man by whom the Son of man is betrayed! it had been good for that man if he had not been born.

But the Son of man goeth as it is written of him: but woe unto that man by whom the Son of man is betrayed! it had been good for that man if he had not been born.

Matthew 26:25 Then Judas, ~~which~~ betrayed him, answered and said, Master, is it I? He said unto him, Thou hast said.

Then Judas, **who** betrayed him, answered and said, Master, is it I? He said unto him, Thou hast said.

(NT1 Then Judas, which betrayed him, answered and said, Master, is it I? He said unto him, Thou hast said **truly; for thou art the man.**)

Matthew 26:26 And as they were eating, Jesus took bread, and blessed *it*, ~~and brake it~~, and gave *it* to ~~the~~ disciples, and said, Take, eat; this is my body.

And as they were eating, Jesus took bread, **and break it**, and blessed it, and gave to **his** disciples, and said, Take, eat; this is **in remembrance of** my body, **which I gave a ransom for you.**

(NT1 And as they were eating, Jesus took bread, and blessed it, and brake it, and gave it to the disciples, and said, Take, eat **of it; and a commandment I give unto you, and this is the commandment which I give unto you, that as you see me do, you shall do likewise in remembrance of** my body.)

Matthew 26:27 And he took the cup, and gave thanks, and gave *it* to them, saying, Drink ye all of it;

(NT1 And he took the cup, and gave thanks, **and blessed the cup,** and gave to them, saying, Drink **of it** all of **you**;)

Matthew 26:28 For this is my blood of the new testament, which is shed for many for the remission of sins.

For this is **in remembrance of** my blood of the new testament, which is shed for **as many as shall believe on my name,** for the remission of **their** sins.

	(**NT1** For this **you shall do in remembrance of** my blood—**this is** the new **testimony, which you shall** [give] **unto all men of my blood,** which is shed for as many **as shall believe on my name,** for the remission of **their** sins.)
Matthew 26:29 But I say unto you, I will not drink henceforth of this fruit of the vine, until that day when I drink it new with you in my Father's kingdom.	**And I give unto you a commandment, that ye shall observe to do the things which ye have seen me do, and bear record of me even unto the end.** But I say unto you, I will not drink henceforth of this fruit of the vine, until that day when I drink it new with you in my Father's kingdom.
	(**NT1** But I say unto you, I will not drink henceforth of this fruit of the vine, until that day when I **shall come and** drink it new with you in my Father's kingdom.)
Matthew 26:31 Then ~~saith~~ Jesus unto them, All ye shall be offended because of me this night: for it is written, I will smite the shepherd, and the sheep of the flock shall be scattered abroad.	Then **said** Jesus unto them, All ye shall be offended because of me this night: for it is written, I will smite the shepherd, and the sheep of the flock shall be scattered abroad.
	(**NT1** Then saith Jesus unto them, All **you** shall be offended because of me this night: for it is written, I will smite the shepherd, and the sheep of the flock shall be scattered abroad.)
Matthew 26:33 Peter answered and said unto him, Though all *men* shall be offended because of thee, ~~yet~~ will ~~I~~ never be offended.	Peter answered and said unto him, Though all men shall be offended because of thee, **I** will never be offended.
	(**NT1 But** Peter answered and said unto him, Though all **my brethren should** be offended because of thee, **I** will never be offended.)
Matthew 26:36 Then cometh Jesus with them unto a place called	Then cometh Jesus with them unto a place called Gethsemane, and **said** unto

Gethsemane, and ~~saith~~ unto the disciples, Sit ye here, while I go and pray yonder.	the disciples, Sit ye here, while I go and pray yonder.

(**NT1** Then cometh Jesus with them unto a place called Gethsemane, and saith unto the disciples, Sit **you** here, while I go **yonder** and pray.) |
| **Matthew 26:38** Then ~~saith~~ he unto them, My soul is exceeding sorrowful, even unto death: tarry ye here, and watch with me. | Then **said** he unto them, My soul is exceeding sorrowful, even unto death: tarry ye here, and watch with me.

(**NT1** Then saith he unto them, My soul is exceeding sorrowful, even unto death: tarry **you** here, and watch with me.) |
| **Matthew 26:40** And he cometh unto the disciples, and findeth them asleep, and ~~saith~~ unto Peter, What, could ye not watch with me one hour? | And he cometh unto the disciples, and findeth them asleep, and **he said** unto Peter, What, could ye not watch with me one hour?

(**NT1** And he cometh unto the disciples, and findeth them asleep, and saith unto Peter, What, could **you** not watch with me one hour?) |
| **Matthew 26:41** Watch and pray, that ye enter not into temptation: the spirit indeed *is* willing, but the flesh *is* weak. | (**NT1** Watch and pray, that **you** enter not into temptation: **he said unto them,** the spirit indeed is willing, but the flesh is weak.) |
| **Matthew 26:45** Then cometh he to his disciples, and ~~saith~~ unto them, Sleep on now, and take ~~your~~ rest: behold, the hour is at hand, and the Son of man is betrayed into the hands of sinners. | Then cometh he to his disciples, and **said** unto them, Sleep on now, and take rest: behold, the hour is at hand, and the Son of man is betrayed into the hands of sinners.

(**NT1** Then cometh he to his disciples, and saith unto them, Sleep on now, and take rest: **and they did so. And when they awoke, Jesus saith unto them,** behold, the hour is at hand, and the Son of man is betrayed into the hands of sinners.) |

Matthew 26:46 ~~Rise~~, let us be going: behold, he is at hand that doth betray me.	**And after they had slept he said unto them, Arise, and** let us be going: behold, he is at hand that doth betray me.
	(**NT1 Arise**, let us be going: behold, he is at hand that doth betray me.)
Matthew 26:47 And while he yet spake, lo, Judas, one of the twelve, came, and with him a great multitude with swords and staves, from the chief priests and elders of the people.	(**NT1** And while he yet spake, **behold**, Judas, one of the twelve, came, and with him a great multitude with swords and staves, **having authority** from the chief priests and elders of the people.)
Matthew 26:50 And Jesus said unto him, ~~Friend~~, wherefore art thou come? Then came they, and laid hands on Jesus, and took him.	And Jesus said unto him, **Judas,** wherefore art thou come **to betray me with a kiss**? Then came they, and laid hands on Jesus, and took him.
	(**NT1** And Jesus said unto him, **Judas, betrayest thou the Son of man with a kiss? And Jesus also said unto the captain,** Friend, wherefore art thou come? **And** then **they** came, and laid hands on Jesus, and took him.)
Matthew 26:51 And, behold, one of them which were with Jesus stretched out *his* hand, and drew his sword, and struck a servant of the high ~~priest's~~, and smote off his ear.	(**NT1** And, behold, one of them **who was** with Jesus **drew his sword, and** stretched out his hand, and struck a servant of the high **priest**, and smote off his ear.)
Matthew 26:52 Then said Jesus unto him, Put up again thy sword into his place: for all they that take the sword shall perish with the sword.	(**NT1** Then said Jesus unto him, Put up thy sword into **its** place: for all they **who** take the sword shall perish with the sword.)
Matthew 26:54 But how then shall the scriptures be fulfilled, that thus it must be?	(**NT1** But how then shall the scriptures be fulfilled, that thus it must be? **And he put forth his hand and touched the servant's ear and it was healed.**)
Matthew 26:55 In that same hour said Jesus ~~to~~ the multitudes, Are ye come out as against a thief with swords and staves for to take me? I sat daily with	In that same hour said Jesus **unto** the multitudes, Are ye come out as against a thief with swords and staves for to take me? I sat daily with you in the

The Testimony of St Matthew

you ~~teaching~~ in the temple, and ye laid no hold on me.

| | temple, **teaching**, and ye laid no hold on me. |

(**NT1** In that same hour Jesus **said** to the **multitude**, Are **you** come out as against a thief with swords and staves to take me? **And yet when** I sat daily with you teaching in the temple, **you** laid no hold on me.)

Matthew 26:59 Now the chief priests, and elders, and all the council, sought false witness against Jesus, to put him to death;

(**NT1** Now the chief priests, and elders, **sought** council against Jesus, to put him to death;)

Matthew 26:60 But found none: yea, though many false witnesses came, ~~yet~~ found ~~they~~ none. At the last came two false witnesses,

But found none: yea, though many false witnesses came, **they** found none **that could accuse him**. At the last came two false witnesses,

(**NT1** But found none: yea, though many false witnesses came, yet they found none **to put him to death**. At the last came two false witnesses,)

Matthew 26:61 And said, This ~~fellow~~ said, I am able to destroy the temple of God, and to build it in three days.

And said, This **man** said, I am able to destroy the temple of God, and to build it in three days.

(**NT1** And said, This **Jesus** said, I am able to destroy the temple of God, and to build it in three days.)

Matthew 26:62 And the high priest arose, and said unto him, Answerest thou nothing? what ~~is it which~~ these witness against thee?

And the high priest arose, and said unto him, Answerest thou nothing? **Knowest thou** what these witness against thee?

(**NT1** And the high priest arose, and said unto him, **Seest** thou what these witness against thee? **What sayest thou for thyself?**)

Matthew 26:63 But Jesus held his peace. And the high priest answered and said unto him, I adjure thee by the

(**NT1** But Jesus held his peace. And the high priest said unto him, **Answerest thou nothing? But he answered**

living God, that thou tell us whether thou be the Christ, the Son of God.

Matthew 26:64 Jesus ~~saith~~ unto him, Thou hast said: nevertheless I say unto you, Hereafter shall ye see the Son of man sitting on the right hand of power, and coming in the clouds of heaven.

Matthew 26:65 Then the high priest rent his clothes, saying, He hath spoken blasphemy; what further need have we of witnesses? behold, now ye have heard his blasphemy.

Matthew 26:66 What think ye? They answered and said, He is guilty of death.

Matthew 26:68 Saying, Prophesy unto us, thou Christ, Who is ~~he~~ that smote thee?

Matthew 26:70 But he denied before *them* all, saying, I know not what thou sayest.

Matthew 26:71 And when he was gone out into the porch, another ~~maid~~ saw him, and said unto them that were there, This ~~fellow~~ was also with Jesus of Nazareth.

Matthew 26:72 And again he denied with an oath, I do not know the man.

Matthew 26:73 And after a while came ~~unto him~~ they that stood by, and said to Peter, Surely thou also art *one* of them; for thy speech ~~bewrayeth~~ thee.

nothing. And the high priest said unto him, I adjure thee by the living God, that thou tell us whether thou be the Christ, the Son of God.)

Jesus **said** unto him, Thou hast said: nevertheless I say unto you, Hereafter shall ye see the Son of man sitting on the right hand of power, and coming in the clouds of heaven.

(**NT1** Jesus saith unto him, Thou hast said: nevertheless I say unto you, Hereafter **you** shall see the Son of man sitting on the right hand of power, and coming in the clouds of heaven.)

(**NT1** Then the high priest rent his clothes, saying, He hath spoken blasphemy; what further need have we of witnesses? behold, now **you** have heard his blasphemy.)

What think ye? They answered and said, He is guilty **and worthy** of death.

Saying, Prophesy unto us, thou Christ, Who is **it** that smote thee?

(**NT1** But he denied before all **the people**, saying, I know what thou sayest.)

And when he was gone out into the porch, another saw him, and said unto them that were there, This **man** was also with Jesus of Nazareth.

And again he denied with an oath, **saying**, I do not know the man.

And after a while came they that stood by, and said to Peter, Surely thou also art one of them; for thy speech **betrayeth** thee.

The Testimony of St Matthew

Matthew 26:75 And Peter remembered the ~~word~~ of Jesus, which said unto him, Before the cock crow, thou shalt deny me thrice. And he went out, and wept bitterly.

Matthew 27:3 Then Judas, ~~which~~ had betrayed him, when he saw that he was condemned, repented himself, and brought again the thirty pieces of silver to the chief priests and elders,

Matthew 27:4 Saying, I have sinned in that I have betrayed the innocent blood. And they said, What *is that* to us? see thou *to* ~~that~~.

Matthew 27:5 And he cast down the pieces of silver in the temple, and departed, and went and hanged himself.

Matthew 27:10 And gave them for the potter's field, as the Lord appointed ~~me~~.

Matthew 27:11 And Jesus stood before the governor: and the governor asked him, saying, Art thou the King of the Jews? And Jesus said unto him, Thou sayest.

Matthew 27:14 And he answered him to never a word; insomuch that the governor marvelled greatly.

Matthew 27:15 Now at ~~that~~ feast the governor was wont to release unto the people a prisoner, whom they would.

Matthew 27:19 When he was set down on the judgment seat, his wife sent unto him, saying, Have thou nothing to do with that just man: for I have suffered

And Peter remembered the **words** of Jesus, which **he** said unto him, Before the cock crow, thou shalt deny me thrice. And he went out, and wept bitterly.

Then Judas, **who** had betrayed him, when he saw that he was condemned, repented himself, and brought again the thirty pieces of silver to the chief priests and elders,

Saying, I have sinned in that I have betrayed the innocent blood. And they said **unto him**, What is that to us? see thou to **it; thy sins be upon thee.**

And he cast down the pieces of silver in the temple, and departed, and went and hanged himself **on a tree. And straightway he fell down, and his bowels gushed out, and he died.**

And therefore they took the pieces of silver, and gave them for the potter's field, as the Lord appointed **by the mouth of Jeremy.**

And Jesus stood before the governor: and the governor asked him, saying, Art thou the King of the Jews? And Jesus said unto him, Thou sayest **truly, for thus it is written of me.**

And he answered him **not to his questions, yea,** never a word; insomuch that the governor marvelled greatly.

Now at **the** feast the governor was wont to release unto the people a prisoner, whom they would.

When he was set down on the judgment seat, his wife sent unto him, saying, Have thou nothing to do with that just man: for I have suffered many

many things this day in a ~~dream~~ because of him.

Matthew 27:21 The governor ~~answered and~~ said unto them, Whether of the twain will ye that I release unto you? They said, Barabbas.

Matthew 27:22 Pilate ~~saith~~ unto them, What shall I do ~~then~~ with Jesus which is called Christ? ~~They~~ all ~~say~~ unto him, Let him be crucified.

Matthew 27:24 When Pilate saw that he could prevail nothing, but ~~that~~ rather a tumult was made, he took water, and washed *his* hands before the multitude, saying, I am innocent of the blood of this just person: see ye ~~to it~~.

Matthew 27:25 Then answered all the people, and said, His blood ~~be~~ on us, and ~~on~~ our children.

Matthew 27:27 Then the soldiers of the governor took Jesus into the common hall, and gathered unto him the whole band ~~of soldiers~~.

Matthew 27:28 And they stripped him, and put on him a ~~scarlet~~ robe.

Matthew 27:29 And when they had platted a crown of thorns, they put *it* upon his head, and a reed in his right hand: and they bowed the knee before him, and mocked him, saying, Hail, King of the Jews!

Matthew 27:33 And when they were come unto a place called Golgotha, that is to say, a place of ~~a skull~~,

Matthew 27:34 They gave him vinegar to drink mingled with gall: and when he had tasted ~~thereof~~, he would not drink.

things this day in a **vision** because of him.

And the governor said unto them, Whether of the twain will ye that I release unto you? They said, Barabbas.

Pilate **said** unto them, What shall I do with Jesus which is called Christ? **And** all **said** unto him, Let him be crucified.

When Pilate saw that he could prevail nothing, but rather a tumult was made, he took water, and washed his hands before the multitude, saying, I am innocent of the blood of this just person: see **that** ye **do nothing unto him**.

Then answered all the people, and said, His blood **come** on us, and our children.

Then the soldiers of the governor took Jesus into the common hall, and gathered unto him the whole band.

And they stripped him, and put on him a **purple** robe.

And when they had platted a crown of thorns, they put it upon his head, and a reed in his right hand: and they bowed the knee before him, and **they** mocked him, saying, Hail, King of the Jews!

And when they were come unto a place called Golgotha, that is to say, a place of **burial**,

They gave him vinegar to drink mingled with gall: and when he had tasted **the vinegar**, he would not drink.

The Testimony of St Matthew

Matthew 27:35 And they crucified him, and parted his garments, casting lots: that it might be fulfilled which was spoken by the prophet, They parted my garments among them, and ~~upon~~ my vesture ~~did~~ they cast lots.	And they crucified him, and parted his garments, casting lots: that it might be fulfilled which was spoken by the prophet, They parted my garments among them, and **for** my vesture they **did** cast lots.
Matthew 27:37 And set up over his head his accusation ~~written~~, THIS IS JESUS THE KING OF THE JEWS.	**And Pilate wrote a title, and put it on the cross, and the writing was, Jesus of Nazareth, the King of the Jews, in letters of Greek, and Latin, and Hebrew. And the chief priest said unto Pilate, It should be written** and set up over his head his accusation, This is **he that said, he was** JESUS THE KING OF THE JEWS. **But Pilate answered and said, What I have written, I have written; let it alone.**
Matthew 27:40 And saying, Thou that destroyest the temple, and buildest *it* in three days, save thyself. If thou be the Son of God, come down from the cross.	And saying, Thou that destroyest the temple, and buildest it **again** in three days, save thyself. If thou be the Son of God, come down from the cross.
Matthew 27:41 Likewise also the chief priests mocking ~~him~~, with the scribes and elders, said,	Likewise also the chief priests mocking, with the scribes and elders, said,
Matthew 27:43 He trusted in God; let him deliver him now, if he will ~~have~~ him: for he said, I am the Son of God.	He trusted in God; let him deliver him now, if he will **save** him, **let him save him**: for he said, I am the Son of God.
Matthew 27:44 The thieves also, which were crucified with him, cast the same in his teeth.	**One of** the thieves also, which were crucified with him, cast the same in his teeth. **But the other rebuked him, saying, Dost thou not fear God, seeing thou art under the same condemnation; and this man is just and hath not sinned; and he cried unto the Lord, that he would save him. And the Lord said unto him, This day thou shalt be with me in Paradise.**
Matthew 27:47 Some of them that stood there, when they heard ~~that~~, said, This *man* calleth for Elias.	Some of them that stood there, when they heard **him**, said, This man calleth for Elias.

Matthew 27:49 The rest said, Let be, let us see whether Elias will come to save him.	The rest said, Let **him** be, let us see whether Elias will come to save him.
Matthew 27:50 Jesus, when he had cried again with a loud voice, yielded up the ghost.	Jesus, when he had cried again with a loud voice, **saying, Father, it is finished, thy will is done,** yielded up the ghost.
Matthew 27:52 And the graves were opened; and ~~many~~ bodies of the saints which slept arose,	And the graves were opened; and **the** bodies of the saints which slept arose, **who were many,**
Matthew 27:53 And came out of the graves after his resurrection, ~~and~~ went into the holy city, and appeared unto many.	And came out of the graves **and** after his resurrection, went into the holy city, and appeared unto many.
Matthew 27:54 Now when the ~~centurion~~, and they that were with him, watching Jesus, ~~saw~~ the earthquake, and those things ~~that~~ were done, they feared greatly, saying, Truly this was the Son of God.	Now when the **centurions**, and they that were with him, watching Jesus, **heard** the earthquake, and **saw** those things **which** were done, they feared greatly, saying, Truly this was the Son of God.
Matthew 27:55 And many women were there beholding afar off, which followed Jesus from Galilee, ministering unto him:	And many women were there beholding afar off, which followed Jesus from Galilee, ministering unto him **for his burial**:
Matthew 27:56 Among ~~which~~ was Mary Magdalene, and Mary the mother of James and Joses, and the mother of Zebedee's children.	Among **whom** was Mary Magdalene, and Mary the mother of James and Joses, and the mother of Zebedee's children.
Matthew 27:57 When the ~~even~~ was come, there came a rich man of Arimathaea, named Joseph, who also himself was Jesus' disciple:	When the **evening** was come, there came a rich man of Arimathaea, named Joseph, who also himself was Jesus' disciple:
Matthew 27:64 Command therefore that the sepulchre be made sure until the third day, lest his disciples come by night, and steal him away, and say unto the people, He is risen from the dead: so ~~the~~ last ~~error shall~~ be worse than the first.	Command therefore that the sepulchre be made sure until the third day, lest his disciples come by night, and steal him away, and say unto the people, He is risen from the dead: so **this** last **imposter will** be worse than the first.

The Testimony of St Matthew

Matthew 27:65 Pilate said unto them, Ye have a watch: go your way, make *it* as sure as ~~ye~~ can.

Matthew 28:1 In the end of the sabbath, as it began to dawn ~~toward~~ the first *day* of the week, came Mary Magdalene and the other Mary to see the sepulchre.

Matthew 28:2 And, behold, there ~~was a~~ great earthquake: for ~~the angel~~ of the Lord descended from heaven, and came and rolled back the stone from the door, and sat upon it.

Matthew 28:3 ~~His~~ countenance was like lightning, and ~~his~~ raiment white as snow:

Matthew 28:4 And for fear of ~~him~~ the keepers did shake, and became as dead ~~men~~.

Matthew 28:5 And the ~~angel~~ answered and said unto the women, Fear not ye: for ~~I~~ know that ye seek Jesus, ~~which~~ was crucified.

Matthew 28:9 And as they went to tell his disciples, behold, Jesus met them, saying, All hail. ~~And~~ they came and held him by the feet, and worshipped him.

Matthew 28:13 Saying, Say ye, His disciples came by night, and stole him ~~away~~ while we slept.

Matthew 28:18 And Jesus came and spake unto them, saying, All power is given unto me in heaven and ~~in~~ earth.

Matthew 28:20 Teaching them to observe all things whatsoever I have commanded you: and, lo, I am with you ~~alway~~, ~~even~~ unto the end of the world. Amen.

Pilate said unto them, Ye have a watch: go your way, make it as sure as **you** can.

In the end of the sabbath **day**, as it began to dawn **towards** the first day of the week, **early in the morning**, came Mary Magdalene and the other Mary to see the sepulchre.

And, behold, there **had been** great earthquake: for **two angels** of the Lord descended from heaven, and came and rolled back the stone from the door, and sat upon it.

And their countenance was like lightning, and **their** raiment white as snow:

And for fear of **them** the keepers did shake, and became as **though they were** dead.

And the **angels** answered and said unto the women, Fear not ye: for **we** know that ye seek Jesus, **who** was crucified.

And as they went to tell his disciples, behold, Jesus met them, saying, All hail. They came and held him by the feet, and worshipped him.

Saying, Say ye, His disciples came by night, and stole him while we slept.

And Jesus came and spake unto them, saying, All power is given unto me in heaven and **on** earth.

Teaching them to observe all things whatsoever I have commanded you: and, lo, I am with you **always**, unto the end of the world. Amen.

The Gospel According to St Mark

King James Version	Joseph Smith Translation
Mark 1:5 And there went out unto him all the land of Judaea, and they of Jerusalem, and were ~~all~~ baptized of him in the river ~~of~~ Jordan, confessing their sins.	And there went out unto him all the land of Judea, and they of Jerusalem, and **many** were baptized of him in the river Jordan, confessing their sins.
Mark 1:7 And preached, saying, There cometh one mightier than I after me, the ~~latchet~~ of whose shoes I am not worthy to stoop down and unloose.	And preached, saying, There cometh one mightier than I after me, the **latchets** of whose shoes I am not worthy to stoop down and unloose.
Mark 1:8 I indeed have baptized you with water: but he shall baptize you with the Holy Ghost.	I indeed have baptized you with water: but he shall **not only** baptize you with **water but with fire and** the Holy Ghost.
Mark 1:11 And there came a voice from heaven, *saying,* Thou art my beloved Son, in whom I am well pleased.	And there came a voice from heaven, saying, Thou art my beloved Son, in whom I am well pleased. **And John bare record of it.**
Mark 1:12 And immediately the Spirit ~~driveth~~ him into the wilderness.	And immediately the Spirit **took** him into the wilderness.
Mark 1:13 And he was there in the wilderness forty days, ~~tempted of~~ Satan; and was with the wild beasts; and the angels ministered unto him.	And he was there in the wilderness forty days, Satan **seeking to tempt him**; and was with the wild beasts; and the angels ministered unto him.
Mark 1:16 Now as he walked by the sea of Galilee, he saw Simon and Andrew his brother casting a net into the sea: for they were fishers.	**And** now as he walked by the sea of Galilee, he saw Simon and Andrew his brother casting a net into the sea: for they were fishers.
Mark 1:20 And ~~straightway~~ he called them: and they left their father Zebedee in the ship with the hired servants, and went after him.	And he called them: and **straightway** they left their father Zebedee in the ship with the hired servants, and went after him.

The Gospel According to St Mark

Mark 1:28 And immediately his fame spread abroad throughout all the ~~region~~ round about Galilee.

Mark 1:30 ~~But~~ Simon's wife's mother lay sick of a fever, and ~~anon~~ they ~~tell~~ him ~~of~~ her.

Mark 1:31 And he came and took her by the hand, and lifted her up; and immediately the fever left her, and she ministered unto them.

Mark 1:32 And at ~~even, when the sun did set~~, they brought unto him all that were diseased, and them that were possessed with devils.

Mark 1:40 And there came a leper to him, beseeching him, and kneeling down to him, and ~~saying unto him~~, If thou wilt, thou canst make me clean.

Mark 1:44 And ~~saith~~ unto him, See thou say nothing to any man: but go thy way, shew thyself to the ~~priest~~, and offer for thy cleansing those things which Moses commanded, for a testimony unto them.

Mark 1:45 But he went out, and began to publish *it* much, and to blaze abroad the matter, insomuch that Jesus could no more openly enter into the city, but was without in ~~desert~~ places: and they came to him from every quarter.

Mark 2:1 And again he entered into Capernaum after ~~some~~ days; and it was noised that he was in the house.

Mark 2:2 And straightway many were gathered together, insomuch that there was no room to receive ~~them~~, no, not so much as about the door: and he preached the word unto them.

And immediately his fame spread abroad throughout all the **regions** round about Galilee.

And Simon's wife's mother lay sick of a fever, and they **besought** him **for** her.

And he came and took her by the hand, and lifted her up; and immediately the fever left her, and she **came and** ministered unto them.

And at **evening, after sunset**, they brought unto him all that were diseased, and them that were possessed with devils.

And there came a leper to him, beseeching him, and kneeling down to him, and **said**, If thou wilt, thou canst make me clean.

And **said** unto him, See thou say nothing to any man: but go thy way, shew thyself to the **priests**, and offer for thy cleansing those things which Moses commanded, for a testimony unto them.

But he went out, and began to publish it much, and to blaze abroad the matter, insomuch that Jesus could no more openly enter into the city, but was without in **solitary** places: and they came to him from every quarter.

And again he entered into Capernaum after **many** days; and it was noised **abroad** that he was in the house.

And straightway many were gathered together, insomuch that there was no room to receive **the multitude**, no, not so much as about the door: and he preached the word unto them.

Mark 2:3 And they ~~come~~ unto him, bringing one sick of the palsy, which was borne of four.	And they **came** unto him, bringing one sick of the palsy, which was borne of four **persons**.
Mark 2:9 ~~Whether~~ is it easier to say to the sick of the palsy, *Thy* sins be forgiven thee; ~~or~~ to say, Arise, and take up thy bed, and walk?	Is it **not** easier to say to the sick of the palsy, Thy sins be forgiven thee; **than** to say, Arise, and take up thy bed, and walk?
Mark 2:10 But that ye may know that the Son of man hath power on earth to forgive sins, (he ~~saith~~ to the sick of the palsy,)	But that ye may know that the Son of man hath power on earth to forgive sins, (he **said** to the sick of the palsy,)
Mark 2:11 I say unto thee, Arise, and take up thy bed, and go thy way into ~~t~~hine house.	I say unto thee, Arise, and take up thy bed, and go thy way into **thy** house.
Mark 2:12 And immediately he arose, took up the bed, and went forth before them all; insomuch that they were all amazed, and glorified God, saying, We never saw ~~it on~~ this ~~fashion~~.	And immediately he arose, took up the bed, and went forth before them all; insomuch that they were all amazed, and **many** glorified God, saying, We never saw **the power of God after** this **manner**.
Mark 2:13 And ~~he~~ went forth again by the sea side; and all the multitude resorted unto him, and he taught them.	And **Jesus** went forth again by the sea side; and all the multitude resorted unto him, and he taught them.
Mark 2:14 And as he passed by, he saw Levi the *son* of Alphaeus sitting at the ~~receipt of custom~~, and said unto him, Follow me. And he arose and followed him.	And as he passed by, he saw Levi the son of Alphaeus sitting at the **place where they receive tribute, as was customary in those days**, and **he** said unto him, Follow me. And he arose and followed him.
Mark 2:15 And it came to pass, that, as Jesus sat at meat in his house, many publicans and sinners sat also together with ~~Jesus~~ and his disciples: for there were many, and they followed him.	And it came to pass, that, as Jesus sat at meat in his house, many publicans and sinners sat also together with **him** and his disciples: for there were many, and they followed him.
Mark 2:17 When Jesus heard ~~it~~, he saith unto them, They that are whole have no need of the physician, but they	When Jesus heard **this**, he saith unto them, They that are whole have no need of the physician, but they that are sick:

that are sick: I came not to call the righteous, but sinners to repentance.	I came not to call the righteous, but sinners to repentance.
Mark 2:18 And the disciples of John and of the Pharisees used to fast: and ~~they come and say unto him~~, Why do the disciples of John and of the Pharisees fast, but thy disciples fast not?	And **they came and said unto him**, the disciples of John and of the Pharisees used to fast: and, Why do the disciples of John and of the Pharisees fast, but thy disciples fast not?
Mark 2:24 And the Pharisees said unto him, Behold, why do ~~they~~ on the sabbath day that which is not lawful?	And the Pharisees said unto him, Behold, why do **thy disciples** on the sabbath day that which is not lawful?
Mark 2:25 And he said unto them, Have ye never read what David did, when he had need, and was an hungred, he, and they ~~that~~ were with him?	And he said unto them, Have ye never read what David did, when he had need, and was a hungred, he, and they **who** were with him?
Mark 2:28 Therefore the Son of man is Lord also of the sabbath.	**Wherefore the sabbath was given unto man for a day of rest; and also that man should glorify God, and not that man should not eat; for the Son of man made the sabbath day,** Therefore the Son of man is Lord also of the sabbath.
Mark 3:1 And he entered again into the synagogue; and there was a man there ~~which~~ had a withered hand.	And he entered again into the synagogue; and there was a man there **that** had a withered hand.
Mark 3:3 And he ~~saith~~ unto the man which had the withered hand, Stand forth.	And he **said** unto the man which had the withered hand, Stand forth.
Mark 3:4 And he ~~saith~~ unto them, Is it lawful to do good on the sabbath days, or to do evil? to save life, or to kill? But they held their peace.	And he **said** unto them, Is it lawful to do good on the sabbath days, or to do evil? to save life, or to kill? But they held their peace.
Mark 3:5 And when he had looked round about on them with anger, being grieved for the hardness of their hearts, he ~~saith~~ unto the man, Stretch forth ~~thine~~ hand. And he stretched ~~it~~ out: and his hand was restored whole as the other.	And when he had looked round about on them with anger, being grieved for the hardness of their hearts, he **said** unto the man, Stretch forth **thy** hand. And he stretched out **his hand**: and his hand was restored whole as the other.

Mark 3:9 And he spake ~~to~~ his disciples, that a small ship should wait on him because of the multitude, lest they should throng him.	And he spake **unto** his disciples, that a small ship should wait on him because of the multitude, lest they should throng him.
Mark 3:12 And he ~~straitly~~ charged them that they should not make him known.	And he **strictly** charged them that they should not make him known.
Mark 3:13 And he goeth up into a mountain, and calleth ~~unto him~~ whom he would: and they came unto him.	And he goeth up into a mountain, and calleth whom he would: and they came unto him.
Mark 3:21 And when his friends heard ~~of it~~, they went out to lay hold on him: for they said, He is beside himself.	And when his friends heard **him speak**, they went out to lay hold on him: for they said, He is beside himself.
Mark 3:22 And the scribes which came down from Jerusalem said, He hath Beelzebub, and by the prince of the devils casteth ~~he~~ out devils.	And the scribes which came down from Jerusalem said, He hath Beelzebub, and by the prince of the devils **he** casteth out devils.
Mark 3:23 And he called them ~~unto him~~, and said unto them in parables, How can Satan cast out Satan?	**Now Jesus knew this,** and he called them, and **he** said unto them in parables, How can Satan cast out Satan?
Mark 3:24 And if a kingdom be divided against itself, that kingdom ~~cannot~~ stand.	And if a kingdom be divided against itself, **how can** that kingdom stand?
Mark 3:26 And if Satan rise up against himself, and be divided, he cannot stand, but hath an end.	And if Satan rise up against himself, and be divided, he cannot stand, but **speedily** hath an end.
Mark 3:28 Verily I say unto you, All sins shall be forgiven unto the sons of men, and blasphemies wherewith soever they shall blaspheme:	**And then came certain men unto him, accusing him, saying, Why do ye receive sinners, seeing thou makest thyself the Son of God? But he answered them, and said,** Verily I say unto you, All sins **which men have committed, when they repent,** shall be forgiven **them; for I came to preach repentance** unto the sons of men, and blasphemies wherewith soever they shall blaspheme, **shall be forgiven them that come unto**

Mark 3:29 But he that shall blaspheme against the Holy Ghost hath never forgiveness, but is in danger of eternal damnation:	me and do the works which they see me do. But **there is a sin which shall not be forgiven,** he that shall blaspheme against the Holy Ghost hath never forgiveness, but is in danger of **being cut down out of the world. And they shall inherit** eternal damnation:
Mark 3:30 Because they said, He hath an unclean spirit.	**And this he said unto them** because they said, He hath an unclean spirit.
Mark 3:31 There came then his brethren and his mother, and, standing without, sent unto him, calling him.	**While he was yet with them, and while he was yet speaking,** there came then **some of** his brethren and his mother, and, standing without, sent unto him, calling **unto** him.
Mark 3:33 And he answered them, saying, Who ~~is~~ my mother, or my brethren?	And he answered them, saying, Who **are** my mother, or **who are** my brethren?
Mark 4:2 And he taught them many things by parables, and said unto them in his doctrine,	And he taught them many things by parables, and **he** said unto them in his doctrine,
Mark 4:8 And other fell on good ground, and did yield fruit that sprang up and increased; and brought forth, some thirty, and some sixty, and some an hundred.	And other **seed** fell on good ground, and did yield fruit that sprang up and increased; and brought forth, some thirty**fold**, and some sixty, and some a hundred.
Mark 4:10 And when he was alone, they that were about him with the twelve asked of him the parable.	And when he was alone **with the twelve and they that believed in him,** they that were about him with the twelve, asked of him the parable.
Mark 4:11 And he said unto them, Unto you it is given to know the mystery of the kingdom of God: but unto them that are without, all ~~these~~ things are done in parables:	And he said unto them, Unto you it is given to know the mystery of the kingdom of God: but unto them that are without, all things are done in parables:
Mark 4:15 And these are they by the way side, where the word is ~~sown~~; but when they have heard, Satan cometh	And these are they by the way side, where the word is **sowed**; but when they have heard, Satan cometh immediately,

immediately, and taketh away the word that was ~~sown~~ in their hearts.

Mark 4:16 And these are they likewise ~~which are sown~~ on stony ground; who, when they have heard the word, immediately receive it with gladness;

Mark 4:17 And have no root in themselves, and so endure but for a time: afterward, when affliction or persecution ariseth for the word's sake, immediately they are offended.

Mark 4:18 And these are they ~~which are sown~~ among thorns; such as hear the word,

Mark 4:20 And these are they ~~which are sown~~ on good ground; such as hear the word, and receive *it,* and bring forth fruit, some thirtyfold, some sixty, and some an hundred.

Mark 4:21 And he said unto them, Is a candle brought to be put under a bushel, or under a bed? and not to be set on a candlestick?

Mark 4:22 For there is nothing hid, which shall not be manifested; neither was any thing kept secret, but that it should come abroad.

Mark 4:24 And he said unto them, Take heed what ~~ye~~ hear: with what measure ~~ye~~ mete, it shall be measured to you: and unto you that ~~hear~~ shall more be given.

Mark 4:25 For he that ~~hath~~, to him shall be given: ~~and~~ he ~~that hath~~ not, from him shall be taken even that which he hath.

and taketh away the word that was **sowed** in their hearts.

And these are they likewise **who receive the word** on stony ground; who, when they have heard the word, immediately receive it with gladness;

And have no root in themselves, and so endure but for a time: **and** afterward, when affliction or persecution ariseth for the word's sake, immediately they are offended.

And these are they **who receive the word** among thorns; such as hear the word,

And these are they **who receive the word** on good ground; such as hear the word, and receive it, and bring forth fruit, some thirtyfold, some sixty, and some a hundred.

And he said unto them, Is a candle brought to be put under a bushel, or under a bed? and not to be set on a candlestick? **I say unto you, Nay;**

For there is nothing hid, which shall not be manifested; neither was any thing kept secret, but that it should **in due time** come abroad.

And he said unto them, Take heed what **you** hear: **for** with what measure **you** mete, it shall be measured to you: and unto you that **continue to receive,** shall more be given.

For he that **receiveth**, to him shall be given: **but** he [that] **continueth** not **to receive,** from him shall be taken even that which he hath.

The Gospel According to St Mark

Mark 4:30 And he said, Whereunto shall ~~we~~ liken the kingdom of God? or with what comparison shall we compare it?

Mark 4:33 And with many such parables spake he the word unto them, as they were able to ~~hear it~~.

Mark 4:34 But without a parable spake he not unto them: and when they were alone, he expounded all things ~~to~~ his disciples.

Mark 4:35 And the same day, when the even was come, he ~~saith~~ unto them, Let us pass over unto the other side.

Mark 4:37 And there arose a great storm of wind, and the waves beat into the ship, ~~so that it was now full~~.

Mark 4:38 And he was in the hinder part of the ship, asleep on a pillow: and they ~~awake~~ him, and ~~say~~ unto him, Master, carest thou not that we perish?

Mark 5:3 Who had ~~his~~ dwelling among the tombs; and no man could bind him, no, not with chains:

Mark 5:8 For he said unto him, Come out of the man, ~~thou~~ unclean spirit.

Mark 5:9 And he ~~asked~~ him, ~~What is~~ thy name? And he answered, saying, My name *is* Legion: for we are many.

Mark 5:13 And forthwith Jesus gave them leave. And the unclean spirits went out, and entered into the swine: and the herd ran violently down a steep place into the sea, (they were about two thousand;) and were choked in the sea.

Mark 5:14 And they that fed the swine fled, and told *it* in the city, and in the

And he said, Whereunto shall **I** liken the kingdom of God? or with what comparison shall we compare it?

And with many such parables spake he the word unto them, as they were able to **bear**.

But without a parable spake he not unto them: and when they were alone, he expounded all things **unto** his disciples.

And the same day, when the even was come, he **said** unto them, Let us pass over unto the other side.

And there arose a great storm of wind, and the waves beat **over** into the ship.

And he was in the hinder part of the ship, asleep on a pillow: and they **awoke** him, and **said** unto him, Master, carest thou not that we perish?

Who had **been** dwelling among the tombs; and no man could bind him, no, not with chains:

For he said unto him, Come out of the man, unclean spirit.

And he **commanded** him, **saying, Declare** thy name. And he answered, saying, My name is Legion: for we are many.

And forthwith Jesus gave them leave. And the unclean spirits went out, and entered into the swine: and the herd ran violently down a steep place into the sea, (**and** they were about two thousand;) and were choked in the sea.

And they that fed the swine fled, and told **the people** in the city, and in the country. And they went out to see what it was that was done.

Mark 5:15 And they ~~come~~ to Jesus, and ~~see~~ him that was possessed with the devil, and had the legion, sitting, and clothed, and in his right mind: and they were afraid.

Mark 5:16 And they that saw ~~it~~ told them how it befell ~~to~~ him that was possessed with the devil, and ~~also~~ concerning the swine.

Mark 5:17 And they began to pray him to depart out of their ~~coasts~~.

Mark 5:18 And when he was come into the ship, he that had been possessed with the devil prayed him that he might be with him.

Mark 5:19 Howbeit Jesus suffered him not, but ~~saith~~ unto him, Go home to thy friends, and tell them how great things the Lord hath done for thee, and hath had compassion on thee.

Mark 5:20 And he departed, and began to publish in Decapolis how great things Jesus had done for him: and all ~~men~~ did marvel.

Mark 5:21 And when Jesus ~~was~~ passed over again by ship unto the other side, much people gathered unto him: and he was nigh unto the sea.

Mark 5:23 And besought him greatly, saying, My little daughter lieth at the point of death: ~~I pray thee,~~ come and lay thy hands on her, that she may be healed; and she shall live.

country, **all that was done unto the swine.** And they went out to see what it was that was done.

And they **came** to Jesus, and **saw** him that was possessed with the devil, and had the legion, sitting, and clothed, and in his right mind: and they were afraid.

And they that saw **the miracle,** told them **that came out,** how it befell him that was possessed with the devil, **and how the devil was cast out,** and concerning the swine.

And they began **immediately** to pray him to depart out of their **coast**.

And when he was come into the ship, he that had been possessed with the devil **spake to Jesus and** prayed him that he might be with him.

Howbeit Jesus suffered him not, but **said** unto him, Go home to thy friends, and tell them how great things the Lord hath done for thee, and hath had compassion on thee.

And he departed, and began to publish in Decapolis how great things Jesus had done for him: and all **that heard him** did marvel.

And when Jesus **had** passed over again by ship unto the other side, much people gathered unto him: and he was nigh unto the sea.

And besought him greatly, saying, My little daughter lieth at the point of death: come and lay thy hands on her, that she may be healed; and she shall live.

The Gospel According to St Mark

Mark 5:24 And ~~Jesus~~ went with him; and much people followed him, and thronged him.

Mark 5:26 And had suffered many things of many physicians, and had spent all that she had, and was nothing ~~bettered~~, but rather grew worse,

Mark 5:27 When she had heard of Jesus, came in the press behind, and touched his garment.

Mark 5:29 And straightway the fountain of her blood was dried up; and she felt in ~~her~~ body that she was healed of that plague.

Mark 5:35 While he yet spake, there came from the ruler of the synagogue's house ~~certain~~ which said, Thy daughter is dead: why troublest thou the Master any further?

Mark 5:36 As soon as Jesus heard the word that was spoken, he ~~saith~~ unto the ruler of the synagogue, Be not afraid, only believe.

Mark 5:39 And when he was come in, he ~~saith~~ unto them, Why make ye this ado, and weep? the damsel is not dead, but sleepeth.

Mark 5:42 And straightway the damsel arose, and walked; for she was ~~of the age of~~ twelve years. And they were astonished with a great astonishment.

Mark 6:1 And he went out from thence, and came into his own country; and his disciples ~~follow~~ him.

Mark 6:2 And when the sabbath day was come, he began to teach in the synagogue: and many hearing ~~him~~ were astonished, saying, From whence hath

And **he** went with him; and much people followed him, and thronged him.

And had suffered many things of many physicians, and had spent all that she had, and was nothing **better**, but rather grew worse,

When she had heard of Jesus, **she** came in the press behind, and touched his garment.

And straightway the fountain of her blood was dried up; and she felt in body that she was healed of that plague.

While he yet spake, there came from the ruler of the synagogue's house, **a man** which said, Thy daughter is dead: why troublest thou the Master any further?

As soon as **he spake,** Jesus heard the word that was spoken, he **said** unto the ruler of the synagogue, Be not afraid, only believe.

And when he was come in, he **said** unto them, Why make ye this ado, and weep? the damsel is not dead, but sleepeth.

And straightway the damsel arose, and walked; for she was twelve years **old.** And they were astonished with a great astonishment.

And he went out from thence, and came into his own country; and his disciples **followed** him.

And when the sabbath day was come, he began to teach in the synagogue: and many hearing were astonished **at his words**, saying, From whence hath this

this *man* these things? and what wisdom *is* this ~~which~~ is given unto him, that even such mighty works are wrought by his hands?

Mark 6:4 But Jesus said unto them, A prophet is not without honour, ~~but~~ in his own country, and among his own kin, and in his own house.

Mark 6:5 And he could ~~there~~ do no mighty ~~work~~, save that he laid his hands upon a few sick ~~folk~~, and healed ~~them~~.

Mark 6:7 And he called ~~unto him~~ the twelve, and began to send them forth by two and two; and gave them power over unclean spirits;

Mark 6:8 And commanded them that they should take nothing for *their* journey, save a staff only; no scrip, ~~no~~ bread, ~~no~~ money in *their* purse:

Mark 6:9 But *be* shod with sandals; and not ~~put on~~ two coats.

Mark 6:10 And he said unto them, In ~~what~~ place ~~soever~~ ye enter into an house, there abide till ye depart from that place.

Mark 6:11 And whosoever shall not receive you, nor hear you, when ye depart thence, shake off the dust ~~under~~ your feet for a testimony against them. Verily I say unto you, It shall be more tolerable for Sodom and Gomorrha in the day of judgment, than for that city.

Mark 6:13 And they cast out many devils, and anointed with oil many that were sick, and healed ~~them~~.

man these things? and what wisdom is this **that** is given unto him, that even such mighty works are wrought by his hands?

But Jesus said unto them, A prophet is not without honour, **save** in his own country, and among his own kin, and in his own house.

And he could do no mighty **works there**, save that he laid his hands upon a few sick **folks**, and **they were** healed.

And he called the twelve, and began to send them forth by two and two; and gave them power over unclean spirits;

And commanded them that they should take nothing for their journey, save a staff only; no scrip, **nor** bread, **nor** money in their purse:

But **should** be shod with sandals; and not **take** two coats.

And he said unto them, In **whatsoever** place ye enter into a house, there abide till ye depart from that place.

And whosoever shall not receive you, nor hear you, when ye depart thence, shake off the dust **of** your feet for a testimony against them. Verily I say unto you, It shall be more tolerable for Sodom and Gomorrha in the day of judgment, than for that city.

And they went out, and preached, that men should repent. And they cast out many devils, and anointed with oil many that were sick, and **they were** healed.

Mark 6:14 And king Herod heard *of him;* (for his name was spread abroad:) and he said, That John the Baptist was risen from the dead, and therefore mighty works do shew forth themselves in him.

Mark 6:16 But when Herod heard ~~thereof~~, he said, It is John, whom I beheaded: he is risen from the dead.

Mark 6:20 For Herod feared John, knowing that he was a just man and an holy, and observed him; and when he heard him, he ~~did~~ many things, and heard him gladly.

Mark 6:21 ~~And~~ when ~~a convenient day~~ was come, ~~that Herod on his birthday~~ made a supper ~~to~~ his lords, high captains, and chief ~~estates~~ of Galilee;

Mark 6:22 And when the daughter of ~~the said~~ Herodias came in, and danced, and pleased Herod and them that sat with him, the king said unto the damsel, Ask of me whatsoever thou wilt, and I will give ~~it~~ thee.

Mark 6:23 And he sware unto her, Whatsoever thou shalt ask of me, I will give ~~it~~ thee, unto the half of my kingdom.

Mark 6:26 And the king was exceeding sorry; ~~yet~~ for his oath's sake, and for their sakes which sat with him, he would not reject her.

Mark 6:29 And when ~~his~~ disciples heard *of it,* they came and took up his corpse, and laid it in a tomb.

Mark 6:30 ~~And~~ the apostles gathered themselves together unto Jesus, and

And king Herod heard of **Jesus**; for his name was spread abroad: and he said, That John the Baptist was risen from the dead, and therefore mighty works do shew forth themselves in him.

But when Herod heard **of him**, he said, It is John, whom I beheaded: he is risen from the dead.

For Herod feared John, knowing that he was a just man and a holy **man, and one who feared God**, and observed **to worship** him; and when he heard him, he [did] many things **for him**, and heard him gladly.

But when **Herod's birthday** was come, **he** made a supper **for** his lords, high captains, and **the** chief **priests** of Galilee;

And when the daughter of Herodias came in, and danced, and pleased Herod and them that sat with him, the king said unto the damsel, Ask of me whatsoever thou wilt, and I will give thee.

And he sware unto her, Whatsoever thou shalt ask of me, I will give thee, unto the half of my kingdom.

And the king was exceeding sorry; **but** for his oath's sake, and for their sakes which sat with him, he would not reject her.

And when **John's** disciples heard of it, they came and took up his corpse, and laid it in a tomb.

Now the apostles gathered themselves together unto Jesus, and told him all told him all things, both what they had done, and what they had taught.

Mark 6:31 And he said unto them, Come ye yourselves apart into a ~~desert~~ place, and rest a while: for there were many coming and going, and they had no leisure so much as to eat.

Mark 6:32 And they departed into a ~~desert~~ place by ship privately.

Mark 6:33 And the people saw them departing, and many knew ~~him~~, and ran afoot thither out of all cities, and ~~outwent~~ them, and came together unto him.

Mark 6:34 And Jesus, when he came out, saw much people, and was moved with compassion ~~toward~~ them, because they were as sheep not having a shepherd: and he began to teach them many things.

Mark 6:35 And when the day was now far spent, his disciples came unto him, and said, This is a ~~desert~~ place, and now the time *is* ~~far passed~~:

Mark 6:37 He answered and said unto them, Give ye them to eat. And they say unto him, Shall we go and buy two hundred pennyworth of bread, and give them to eat?

Mark 6:38 He ~~saith~~ unto them, How many loaves have ye? go and see. And when they knew, they say, Five, and two fishes.

Mark 6:41 And when he had taken the five loaves and ~~the~~ two fishes, he looked up to heaven, and blessed, and brake the loaves, and gave ~~them~~ to his disciples

things, both what they had done, and what they had taught.

And he said unto them, Come ye yourselves apart into a **solitary** place, and rest a while: for there were many coming and going, and they had no leisure, **not** so much as to eat.

And they departed into a **solitary** place by ship privately.

And the people saw them departing, and many knew **Jesus**, and ran afoot thither out of all cities, and **outran** them, and came together unto him.

And Jesus, when he came out, saw much people, and was moved with compassion **towards** them, because they were as sheep not having a shepherd: and he began to teach them many things.

And when the day was now far spent, his disciples came unto him, and said, This is a **solitary** place, and now the time **for departure** is **come**:

And he answered and said unto them, Give ye them to eat. And they say unto him, Shall we go and buy two hundred pennyworth of bread, and give them to eat?

He **said** unto them, How many loaves have ye? go and see. And when they knew, they say, Five, and two fishes.

And when he had taken the five loaves and two fishes, he looked up to heaven, and blessed, and brake the loaves, and gave to his disciples to set before **the**

to set before ~~them~~; and the two fishes divided he among them all.

Mark 6:45 And straightway he constrained his disciples to get into the ship, and to go to the other side before unto Bethsaida, while he sent away the people.

Mark 6:48 And he saw them toiling in rowing; for the wind was contrary unto them: and about the fourth watch of the night he cometh unto them, walking upon the sea, ~~and~~ would have passed by them.

Mark 6:49 ~~But~~ when they saw him walking upon the sea, they supposed it had been a spirit, and cried out:

Mark 6:50 For they all saw him, and were troubled. And immediately he talked with them, and ~~saith~~ unto them, Be of good cheer: it is I; be not afraid.

Mark 6:52 For they considered not ~~the miracle~~ of the loaves: for their ~~heart was~~ hardened.

Mark 6:54 And when they were come out of the ship, straightway ~~they~~ knew him,

Mark 6:56 And whithersoever he entered, into villages, or cities, or country, they laid the sick in the streets, and besought him that they might touch if it were but the border of his ~~garment~~: and as many as touched him were made whole.

Mark 7:2 And when they saw some of his disciples eat bread with defiled, that is to say, with unwashen, hands, they found fault.

multitude; and the two fishes divided he among them all.

And straightway he constrained his disciples to get into the ship, and to go to the other side before **him** unto Bethsaida, while he sent away the people.

And he saw them toiling in rowing; for the wind was contrary unto them: and about the fourth watch of the night he cometh unto them, walking upon the sea, **as if he** would have passed by them.

And when they saw him walking upon the sea, they supposed it had been a spirit, and cried out:

For they all saw him, and were troubled. And immediately he talked with them, and **said** unto them, Be of good cheer: it is I; be not afraid.

For they considered not of the loaves: for their **hearts were** hardened.

And when they were come out of the ship, straightway **the people** knew him,

And whithersoever he entered, into villages, or cities, or country, they laid the sick in the streets, and besought him that they might touch if it were but the border of his **garments**: and as many as touched him were made whole.

And when they saw some of his disciples eat bread with defiled (that is to say, with unwashen) hands, they found fault.

Mark 7:3 For the Pharisees, and all the Jews, except they wash ~~their~~ hands oft, eat not, holding the tradition of the elders.	For the Pharisees, and all the Jews, except they wash hands oft, eat not, holding the tradition of the elders.
Mark 7:4 And *when they* ~~come~~ from the market, except they wash, they eat not. And many other things there be, which they have received to hold, *as* the washing of cups, and pots, brasen vessels, and of tables.	And when they **came** from the market, except they wash **their bodies**, they eat not. And many other things there be, which they have received to hold, as the washing of cups, and pots, brasen vessels, and of tables.
Mark 7:5 ~~Then~~ the Pharisees and scribes asked him, Why walk not thy disciples according to the ~~tradition~~ of the elders, but eat bread with unwashen hands?	**And** the Pharisees and scribes asked him, Why walk not thy disciples according to the **traditions** of the elders, but eat bread with unwashen hands?
Mark 7:6 He answered and said unto them, Well hath Esaias prophesied of you hypocrites, as it is written, This people honoureth me with *their* lips, but their heart is far from me.	He answered and said unto them, Well hath Isaiah prophesied of you hypocrites, as it is written, This people honoureth me with their lips, but their heart is far from me.
Mark 7:7 Howbeit in vain do they worship me, teaching ~~for~~ doctrines ~~the~~ commandments of men.	Howbeit in vain do they worship me, teaching **the** doctrines **and** commandments of men.
Mark 7:8 For laying aside the commandment of God, ye hold the tradition of men, ~~as~~ the washing of pots and cups: and many other such like things ye do.	For laying aside the commandment of God, ye hold the tradition of men, the washing of pots and **of** cups: and many other such like things ye do.
Mark 7:9 And he said unto them, ~~Full well~~ ye reject the commandment of God, that ye may keep your own ~~tradition~~.	And he said unto them, **Yea, altogether** ye reject the commandment of God, that ye may keep your own **traditions**. **Full well is it written of you, by the prophets whom ye have rejected.**
Mark 7:10 For Moses said, Honour thy father and thy mother; and, Whoso curseth father or mother, let him die the death:	**They testified these things of a truth, and their blood shall be upon you. Ye have kept not the ordinances of God,** for Moses said, Honour thy father and thy mother; and, Whoso curseth father or mother, let him die the death **of the**

	transgressor, as it is written in your law; but ye keep not the law.
Mark 7:11 ~~But~~ ye say, If a man shall say to his father or mother, ~~It is~~ Corban, that is to say, a gift, by whatsoever thou mightest be profited by me; ~~he shall be free~~.	Ye say, If a man shall say to his father or mother, Corban, that is to say, a gift, by whatsoever thou mightest be profited by me, **he is of age**;
Mark 7:14 And when he had called all the people ~~unto him~~, he said unto them, Hearken unto me every one ~~of you~~, and understand:	And when he had called all the people, he said unto them, Hearken unto me every one, and understand:
Mark 7:15 There is nothing from without a man, that entering into him can defile him: but the things which come out of him, those are they that defile the man.	There is nothing from without **that entering into** a man can defile him, **which is food**: but the things which come out of him, those are they that defile the man, **that proceedeth forth out of the heart**.
Mark 7:17 And when he was entered into the house from the people, his disciples asked him concerning the parable.	And when he was entered into the house from **among** the people, his disciples asked him concerning the parable.
Mark 7:18 And he ~~saith~~ unto them, Are ye ~~so~~ without understanding also? Do ye not perceive, that whatsoever thing from without entereth into the man, ~~it~~ cannot defile him;	And he **said** unto them, Are ye without understanding also? Do ye not perceive, that whatsoever thing from without entereth into the man, cannot defile him;
Mark 7:20 And he said, That which cometh out of ~~the~~ man, ~~that~~ defileth the man.	And he said, That which cometh out of **a** man, defileth the man.
Mark 7:21 For from within, out of the ~~heart~~ of men, proceed evil thoughts, adulteries, fornications, murders,	For from within, out of the **hearts** of men, proceed evil thoughts, adulteries, fornications, murders,
Mark 7:24 And from thence he arose, and went into the borders of Tyre and Sidon, and entered into an house, and would ~~have~~ no man ~~know it~~: but he could not ~~be hid~~.	And from thence he arose, and went into the borders of Tyre and Sidon, and entered into a house, and would **that** no man **should come unto him**. But he could not **deny them, for he had compassion upon all men**.

Mark 7:25 For a ~~certain~~ woman, whose young daughter had an unclean spirit, heard of him, and came and fell at his feet:	For a woman, whose young daughter had an unclean spirit, heard of him, and came and fell at his feet:
Mark 7:27 But Jesus said unto her, Let the children first be filled: for it is not meet to take the children's bread, and ~~to~~ cast *it* unto the dogs.	But Jesus said unto her, Let the children **of the kingdom** first be filled: for it is not meet to take the children's bread, and cast it unto the dogs.
Mark 7:28 And she answered and said unto him, Yes, Lord: yet the dogs under the table eat of the children's crumbs.	And she answered and said unto him, Yes, Lord: **thou sayest truly,** yet the dogs under the table eat of the children's crumbs.
Mark 7:30 And when she was come to her house, she found the devil gone out, and her daughter laid upon the bed.	And when she was come to her house, she found **that** the devil **had** gone out, and her daughter **was** laid upon the bed.
Mark 7:31 And again, departing from the ~~coasts~~ of Tyre and Sidon, he came unto the sea of Galilee, through the midst of the coasts of Decapolis.	And again, departing from the **coast** of Tyre and Sidon, he came unto the sea of Galilee, through the midst of the coasts of Decapolis.
Mark 7:34 And looking up to heaven, he sighed, and ~~saith~~ unto him, Ephphatha, that is, Be opened.	And looking up to heaven, he sighed, and **said** unto him, Ephphatha, that is, Be opened.
Mark 7:36 And he charged them that they should tell no man: but the more he charged them, so much the more a great deal they published ~~it~~;	And he charged them that they should tell no man: but the more he charged them, so much the more a great deal they published **him**;
Mark 8:1 In those days the multitude being very great, and having nothing to eat, Jesus called his disciples ~~unto him~~, and ~~saith~~ unto them,	In those days the multitude being very great, and having nothing to eat, Jesus called his disciples, and **said** unto them,
Mark 8:3 And if I send them away fasting to their own houses, they will faint by the way: for divers of them came from ~~far~~.	And if I send them away fasting to their own houses, they will faint by the way: for divers of them came from **afar**.
Mark 8:4 And his disciples answered him, From whence can a man satisfy	And his disciples answered him, From whence can a man satisfy these **so great**

these ~~men~~ with bread here in the wilderness?

Mark 8:6 And he commanded the people to sit down on the ground: and he took the seven loaves, and gave thanks, and brake, and gave to his disciples to set before ~~them~~; and they did set *them* before the people.

Mark 8:7 And they had a few small fishes: and he blessed, and commanded to set them also before ~~them~~.

Mark 8:8 So they did eat, and were filled: and they took up of the broken ~~meat~~ that was left seven baskets.

Mark 8:10 And straightway he entered into a ship with his disciples, and came into the ~~parts~~ of Dalmanutha.

Mark 8:12 And he sighed deeply in his spirit, and ~~saith~~, Why doth this generation seek after a sign? verily I say unto you, There shall no sign be given unto this generation.

Mark 8:13 And he left them, and entering into the ship again departed to the other side.

Mark 8:14 Now *the* ~~disciples~~ had forgotten to take bread, neither had they in the ship with them more than one loaf.

Mark 8:15 And he charged them, saying, Take heed, beware of the leaven of the Pharisees, and ~~of~~ the leaven of Herod.

a multitude with bread here in the wilderness?

And he commanded the people to sit down on the ground: and he took the seven loaves, and gave thanks, and brake, and gave to his disciples to set before **the people**; and they did set them before the people.

And they had a few small fishes: and he blessed **them**, and commanded to set them also before **the people, that they should eat.**

So they did eat, and were filled: and they took up of the broken **bread** that was left seven baskets.

And straightway he entered into a ship with his disciples, and came into the **ports** of Dalmanutha.

And he sighed deeply in his spirit, and **said**, Why doth this generation seek after a sign? verily I say unto you, There shall no sign be given unto this generation, **save the sign of the prophet Jonah; for as Jonah was three days and three nights in the whale's belly, so likewise shall the Son of man be buried in the bowels of the earth**.

And he left them, and entering into the ship again, **he** departed to the other side.

Now the **multitude** had forgotten to take bread, neither had they in the ship with them more than one loaf.

And he charged them, saying, Take heed, **and** beware of the leaven of the Pharisees, and the leaven of Herod.

Mark 8:16 And they reasoned among themselves, saying, ~~It is~~ because we have no bread.

Mark 8:17 And when Jesus knew *it,* he ~~saith~~ unto them, Why reason ye, because ye have no bread? perceive ye not yet, neither understand? ~~have ye~~ your ~~heart~~ yet hardened?

Mark 8:19 When I brake the five loaves among five thousand, how many baskets full of fragments took ye up? They say unto him, Twelve.

Mark 8:20 And when the seven among four thousand, how many baskets full of fragments took ye up? And they said, Seven.

Mark 8:23 And he took the blind man by the hand, and led him out of the town; and when he had spit ~~on~~ his eyes, and put his hands upon him, he asked him if he saw ought.

Mark 8:24 And he looked up, and said, I see men as trees, walking.

Mark 8:26 And he sent him away to his house, saying, Neither go into the town, nor tell ~~it~~ to any in the town.

Mark 8:29 And he ~~saith~~ unto them, But whom say ye that I am? And Peter ~~answereth~~ and saith unto him, Thou art the Christ.

Mark 8:31 And he began to teach them, that the Son of man must suffer many things, and be rejected of the elders, and ~~of~~ the chief priests, and scribes, and be killed, and after three days rise again.

And they reasoned among themselves, saying, **He hath said this** because we have no bread.

And when **they said this among themselves,** Jesus knew it, **and** he **said** unto them, Why reason ye, because ye have no bread? perceive ye not yet, neither understand **ye**? **Are** your **hearts** yet hardened?

When I brake the five loaves among **the** five thousand, how many baskets full of fragments took ye up? They say unto him, Twelve.

And when the seven among **the** four thousand, how many baskets full of fragments took ye up? And they said, Seven.

And he took the blind man by the hand, and led him out of the town; and when he had spit **upon** his eyes, and put his hands upon him, he asked him if he saw aught.

And he looked up, and **he** said, I see men as trees, walking.

And he sent him away to his house, saying, Neither go into the town, nor tell **what is done,** to any in the town.

And he **said** unto them, But whom say ye that I am? And Peter **answered** and saith unto him, Thou art the Christ, **the son of the living God.**

And he began to teach them, that the Son of man must suffer many things, and be rejected of the elders, and the chief priests, and scribes, and be killed, and after three days rise again.

The Gospel According to St Mark

Mark 8:32 And he ~~spake~~ that saying openly. And Peter took him, and began to rebuke him.	And he **spoke** that saying openly. And Peter took him, and began to rebuke him.
Mark 8:33 But when he had turned about and looked ~~on~~ his disciples, he rebuked Peter, saying, Get thee behind me, Satan: for thou savourest not the things that be of God, but the things that be of men.	But when he had turned about and looked **upon** his disciples, he rebuked Peter, saying, Get thee behind me, Satan: for thou savourest not the things that be of God, but the things that be of men.
Mark 8:34 And when he had called the people ~~unto him~~ with his disciples also, he said unto them, Whosoever will come after me, let him deny himself, and take up his cross, and follow me.	And when he had called the people with his disciples also, he said unto them, Whosoever will come after me, let him deny himself, and take up his cross, and follow me.
Mark 8:35 For whosoever will save his life shall lose it; but whosoever shall lose his life for my sake and the gospel's, the same shall save it.	For whosoever will save his life shall lose it; **or whosoever will save his life, shall be willing to lay it down for my sake; and if he is not willing to lay it down for my sake, he shall lose it; but whosoever shall be willing** to lose his life for my sake and the gospel's, the same shall save it.
Mark 8:38 Whosoever ~~therefore~~ shall be ashamed of me and of my words in this adulterous and sinful generation; of him also shall the Son of man be ashamed, when he cometh in the glory of his Father with the holy angels.	**Therefore deny yourselves of these, and be not ashamed of me.** Whosoever shall be ashamed of me and of my words in this adulterous and sinful generation; of him also shall the Son of man be ashamed, when he cometh in the glory of his Father with the holy angels. **And they shall not have part in that resurrection when he cometh. For verily I say unto you, that he shall come; and he that layeth down his life for my sake and the gospel's, shall come with him, and shall be clothed with his glory, in the cloud, on the right hand of the Son of man.**
Mark 9:1 And he said unto them, Verily I say unto you, That there be some of them that stand here, which shall not	And he said unto them **again**, Verily I say unto you, That there be some of them that stand here, which shall not

taste of death, till they have seen the kingdom of God come with power.

Mark 9:2 And after six days Jesus taketh ~~with him~~ Peter, and James, and John, and leadeth them up into an high mountain apart by themselves: and he was transfigured before them.

Mark 9:3 And his raiment became shining, exceeding white as snow; so as no fuller on earth ~~can~~ white them.

Mark 9:4 And there appeared unto them Elias with Moses: and they were talking with Jesus.

Mark 9:6 For he ~~wist~~ not what to say; for they were sore afraid.

Mark 9:8 And suddenly, when they had looked round about, they saw no man any more, save Jesus only with themselves.

Mark 9:9 And as they came down from the mountain, he charged them that they should tell no man what things they had seen, till the Son of man ~~were~~ risen from the dead.

Mark 9:12 And he answered and told them, Elias verily cometh first, and ~~restoreth~~ all things; and how it is written of the Son of man, that he must suffer many things, and be set at nought.

Mark 9:13 ~~But~~ I say unto you, That Elias is indeed come, ~~and~~ they have done unto him whatsoever they listed, as it is written of him.

taste of death, till they have seen the kingdom of God come with power.

And after six days Jesus taketh Peter, and James, and John, **who asked him many questions concerning his saying;** and **Jesus** leadeth them up into a high mountain apart by themselves: and he was transfigured before them.

And his raiment became shining, exceeding white as snow; so **white** as no fuller on earth **could** white them.

And there appeared unto them Elias with Moses, **or in other words, John the Baptist and Moses**: and they were talking with Jesus.

For he **knew** not what to say; for they were sore afraid.

And suddenly, when they had looked round about **with great astonishment**, they saw no man any more, save Jesus only with themselves. **And immediately they departed.**

And as they came down from the mountain, he charged them that they should tell no man what things they had seen, till the Son of man **was** risen from the dead.

And he answered and told them, **saying,** Elias verily cometh first, and **prepareth** all things; and **teacheth you of the prophets;** how it is written of the Son of man, that he must suffer many things, and be set at nought.

Again I say unto you, That Elias is indeed come, **but** they have done unto him whatsoever they listed, **and even** as it is written of him; **and he bore record**

| | of me, and they received him not. Verily this was Elias. |

Mark 9:14 And when he came to ~~his~~ disciples, he saw a great multitude about them, and the scribes questioning with them.

And when he came to **the** disciples, he saw a great multitude about them, and the scribes questioning with them.

Mark 9:16 And ~~he~~ asked the scribes, What ~~question~~ ye with them?

And **Jesus** asked the scribes, What **questioned** ye with them?

Mark 9:17 And one of the multitude answered and said, Master, I have brought unto thee my son, ~~which~~ hath a dumb spirit;

And one of the multitude answered and said, Master, I have brought unto thee my son, **who** hath a dumb spirit **that is a devil**;

Mark 9:18 And ~~wheresoever~~ he ~~taketh~~ him, he teareth him: and he foameth, and gnasheth with his teeth, and pineth away: and I spake to thy disciples that they ~~should~~ cast him out; and they could not.

And **when he seizeth** him, he teareth him: and he foameth, and gnasheth with his teeth, and pineth away: and I spake to thy disciples that they **might** cast him out; and they could not.

Mark 9:19 ~~He answereth~~ him, and ~~saith~~, O faithless generation, how long shall I be with you? how long shall I suffer you? bring him unto me.

Jesus spake unto him, and **said**, O faithless generation, how long shall I be with you? how long shall I suffer you? bring him unto me.

Mark 9:20 And they brought him unto ~~him~~: and when ~~he~~ saw him, ~~straightway~~ the spirit ~~tare him~~; and he fell on the ground, and wallowed foaming.

And they brought him unto **Jesus**: and when **the man** saw him, **immediately he was torn by** the spirit; and he fell on the ground, and wallowed foaming.

Mark 9:21 And ~~he~~ asked his father, How long is it ~~ago~~ since this came unto him? And ~~he~~ said, ~~Of~~ a child.

And **Jesus** asked his father, How long **a time** is it since this came unto him? And **his father** said, **When** a child.

Mark 9:22 And ofttimes it hath cast him into the fire, and into the waters, to destroy him: but if thou canst ~~do any thing~~, have compassion on us, and help us.

And ofttimes it hath cast him into the fire, and into the waters, to destroy him: but if thou canst, **I ask thee to** have compassion on us, and help us.

Mark 9:23 Jesus said unto him, If thou ~~canst~~ believe, all things ~~are~~ possible to him that believeth.

Jesus said unto him, If thou **wilt** believe, all things **I shall say unto you, this is** possible to him that believeth.

Mark 9:24 And ~~straightway~~ the father of the child cried out, and said with tears, Lord, I believe; help thou mine unbelief.

Mark 9:25 When Jesus saw that the people came running together, he rebuked the foul spirit, saying unto him, ~~Thou dumb and deaf spirit~~, I charge thee, come out of him, and enter no more into him.

Mark 9:26 ~~And~~ the spirit cried, and rent him sore, and came out of him: and he was as one dead; insomuch that many said, He is dead.

Mark 9:28 ~~And~~ when he was come into the house, his disciples asked him privately, Why could not we cast him out?

Mark 9:30 And they departed thence, and passed through Galilee; ~~and~~ he would not that any man should know it.

Mark 9:31 ~~For~~ he taught his disciples, and said unto them, The Son of man is delivered into the hands of men, and they shall kill him; and after that he is killed, he shall rise the third day.

Mark 9:33 And he came to Capernaum: and being in the house he asked them, ~~What~~ was it that ye disputed among yourselves by the way?

Mark 9:34 But they held their peace: for by the way they had disputed among themselves, who ~~should be~~ the greatest.

Mark 9:35 ~~And he~~ sat down, and called the twelve, and ~~saith~~ unto them, If any man desire to be first, ~~the same~~ shall be last of all, and servant of all.

And **immediately** the father of the child cried out, and said with tears, Lord, I believe; help thou mine unbelief.

When Jesus saw that the people came running together, he rebuked the foul spirit, saying unto him, I charge thee **to** come out of him, and enter no more into him.

Now the **dumb and deaf** spirit cried, and rent him sore, and came out of him: and he was as one dead; insomuch that many said, He is dead.

When **Jesus** was come into the house, his disciples asked him privately, Why could not we cast him out?

And they departed thence, and passed through Galilee **privately; for** he would not that any man should know it.

And he taught his disciples, and said unto them, The Son of man is delivered into the hands of men, and they shall kill him; and after that he is killed, he shall rise the third day.

And he came to Capernaum: and being in the house he asked them, **Why** was it that ye disputed among yourselves by the way?

But they held their peace, **being afraid**: for by the way they had disputed among themselves, who **was** the greatest **among them**.

Now Jesus sat down, and called the twelve, and **said** unto them, If any man desire to be first, **he** shall be last of all, and servant of all.

Mark 9:36 And he took a child, and ~~set him~~ in the midst of them: and when he had taken ~~him~~ in his arms, he said unto them,	And he took a child, and **sat** in the midst of them: and when he had taken **the child** in his arms, he said unto them,
Mark 9:37 Whosoever shall ~~receive one~~ of ~~such~~ children ~~in my name~~, receiveth me: and whosoever shall receive me, receiveth not me, but him that sent me.	Whosoever shall **humble himself like one** of **these** children **and** receiveth me, **ye shall receive in my name**. And whosoever shall receive me, receiveth not me **only**, but him that sent me, **even the Father**.
Mark 9:38 And John **spake unto** him, saying, Master, we saw one casting out devils in thy name, and he ~~followeth~~ not us: and we forbad him, because he followeth not us.	And John **spake unto** him, saying, Master, we saw one casting out devils in thy name, and he **followed** not us: and we forbade him, because he followeth not us.
Mark 9:39 But Jesus said, Forbid him not: for there is no man which shall do a miracle in my name, that can ~~lightly~~ speak evil of me.	But Jesus said, Forbid him not: for there is no man which shall do a miracle in my name, that can speak evil of me.
Mark 9:41 ~~For~~ whosoever shall give you a cup of water to drink in my name, because ye belong to Christ, verily I say unto you, he shall not lose his reward.	**And** whosoever shall give you a cup of water to drink in my name, because ye belong to Christ, verily I say unto you, he shall not lose his reward.
Mark 9:43 ~~And~~ if thy hand offend thee, cut it off: it is better for thee to enter into life maimed, than having two hands to go into hell, into the fire that never shall be quenched:	**Therefore** if thy hand offend thee, cut it off: **or if thy brother offend thee, and confess not, and forsake not, he shall be cut off**. It is better for thee to enter into life maimed, than having two hands to go into hell; **for it is better for thee to enter into life without thy brother, than for thee and thy brother to be cast into hell**; into the fire that never shall be quenched:
Mark 9:45 And if thy foot offend thee, cut it off: it is better for thee to enter halt into life, than having two feet to be cast into hell, into the fire that never shall be quenched:	And **again**, if thy foot offend thee, cut it off: **for he that is thy standard, by whom thou walkest, if he become a transgressor, he shall be cut off**. It is better for thee to enter halt into life, than having two feet to be cast into hell,

Mark 9:46 ~~Where their worm dieth not, and the fire is not quenched~~.	into the fire that never shall be quenched:
	Therefore, let every man stand, or fall by himself, and not for another; or not trusting another. Seek unto my Father, and it shall be done in that very moment what ye shall ask, if ye ask in faith, believing that ye shall receive,
Mark 9:47 And if thine eye offend thee, pluck ~~it~~ out: it is better for thee to enter into the kingdom of God with one eye, than having two eyes to be cast into hell fire~~:~~	And if thine eye, **which seeth for thee, him that is appointed to watch over thee to shew thee light, become a transgressor and** offend thee, pluck **him** out: it is better for thee to enter into the kingdom of God with one eye, than having two eyes to be cast into hell fire.
Mark 9:48 Where their worm dieth not, and the fire is not quenched.	**For it is better that thyself should be saved, than to be cast into hell with thy brother,** where their worm dieth not, and **where** the fire is not quenched.
Mark 9:50 Salt ~~is~~ good: ~~but~~ if the salt have lost his saltness, wherewith will ye season it? Have salt in yourselves, and have peace one with another.	**For everyone shall be salted with fire, and every sacrifice shall be salted with salt; but the** salt **must be good. For if** the salt have lost his saltness, wherewith will ye season it **(the sacrifice)**? **Therefore it must needs be, that ye** have salt in yourselves, and have peace one with another.
Mark 10:1 And he arose from thence, and cometh into the coasts of Judaea by the farther side of Jordan: and the people resort unto him again; and, as he was ~~wont~~, he taught them again.	And he arose from thence, and cometh into the coasts of Judea by the farther side of Jordan: and the people resort unto him again; and, as he was **accustomed to teach**, he **also** taught them again.
Mark 10:2 And the Pharisees came to him, and asked him, Is it lawful for a man to put away *his* wife? ~~tempting~~ him.	And the Pharisees came to him, and asked him, Is it lawful for a man to put away his wife? **This they said, thinking to tempt** him.

The Gospel According to St Mark

Mark 10:5 ~~And~~ Jesus answered and said unto them, For the hardness of your ~~heart~~ he wrote you this precept.

Mark 10:8 And they ~~twain~~ shall be one flesh: so then they are no more ~~twain~~, but one flesh.

Mark 10:11 And he ~~saith~~ unto them, Whosoever shall put away his wife, and marry another, committeth adultery against her.

Mark 10:13 And they brought young children to him, that he should touch them: and *his* disciples rebuked those that brought *them*.

Mark 10:14 But when Jesus saw ~~it~~, he was much displeased, and said unto them, Suffer the little children to come unto me, and forbid them not: for of such is the kingdom of God.

Mark 10:16 And he took them up in his arms, put *his* hands upon them, and blessed them.

Mark 10:18 And Jesus said unto him, Why callest thou me good? ~~there is~~ none good but one, *that is,* God.

Mark 10:20 And ~~he~~ answered and said unto him, Master, all these have I observed from my youth.

Mark 10:22 And ~~he~~ was sad at that saying, and went away grieved: for he had great possessions.

Mark 10:23 And Jesus looked round about, and ~~saith~~ unto his disciples, How hardly shall they that have riches enter into the kingdom of ~~God~~!

Mark 10:24 And the disciples were astonished at his words. But Jesus

Jesus answered and said unto them, For the hardness of your **hearts** he wrote you this precept.

And they **two** shall be one flesh: so then they are no more **two**, but one flesh.

And he **said** unto them, Whosoever shall put away his wife, and marry another, committeth adultery against her.

And they brought young children to him, that he should touch them: and **the** disciples rebuked those that brought them.

But when Jesus saw **and heard them**, he was much displeased, and said unto them, Suffer the little children to come unto me, and forbid them not: for of such is the kingdom of God.

And he took them up in his arms, **and** put his hands upon them, and blessed them.

And Jesus said unto him, Why callest thou me good? None **is** good but one, that is, God.

And **the man** answered and said unto him, Master, all these have I observed from my youth.

And **the man** was sad at that saying, and went away grieved: for he had great possessions.

And Jesus looked round about, and **said** unto his disciples, How hardly shall they that have riches enter into the kingdom of **my Father.**

And the disciples were astonished at his words. But Jesus **spake** again, and **said**

answereth again, and saith unto them, Children, how hard is it for them that trust in riches to enter into the kingdom of God!

Mark 10:27 And Jesus looking upon them saith, With men it is impossible, but not with God: for with God all things are possible.

Mark 10:31 But many that are first shall be last; and the last first.

Mark 10:32 And they were in the way going up to Jerusalem; and Jesus went before them: and they were amazed; and as they followed, they were afraid. And he took again the twelve, and began to tell them what things should happen unto him,

Mark 10:33 Saying, Behold, we go up to Jerusalem; and the Son of man shall be delivered unto the chief priests, and unto the scribes; and they shall condemn him to death, and shall deliver him to the Gentiles:

Mark 10:35 And James and John, the sons of Zebedee, come unto him, saying, Master, we would that thou shouldest do for us whatsoever we shall desire.

Mark 10:36 And he said unto them, What would ye that I should do for you?

Mark 10:39 And they said unto him, We can. And Jesus said unto them, Ye shall indeed drink of the cup that I drink of; and with the baptism that I am baptized withal shall ye be baptized:

unto them, Children, how hard is it for them **who** trust in riches to enter into the kingdom of God!

And Jesus looking upon them **said**, With men **that trust in riches**, it is impossible, but not **impossible** with **men who trust in** God, **and leave all for my sake;** for with **such**, all **these** things are possible.

But **there are** many **who make themselves** first **that** shall be last; and the last first.

This he said, rebuking Peter; and they were in the way going up to Jerusalem; and Jesus went before: and they were amazed; and as they followed, they were afraid. And he took again the twelve, and began to tell them what things should happen unto him,

And Jesus said, Behold, we go up to Jerusalem; and the Son of man shall be delivered unto the chief priests, and unto the scribes; and they shall condemn him to death, and shall deliver him to the Gentiles:

And James and John, the sons of Zebedee, **came** unto him, saying, Master, we would that thou shouldest do for us whatsoever we shall desire.

And he said unto them, What **will** ye that I should do **unto** you?

And they said unto him, We can. And Jesus said unto them, Ye shall indeed drink of the cup that I drink of; and **be baptized** with the baptism that I am baptized **with:**

The Gospel According to St Mark

Mark 10:40 But to sit on my right hand and on my left hand is not mine to give; but ~~it~~ *shall* ~~be given to them~~ for whom it is prepared.

But to sit on my right hand and on my left hand is not mine to give; but **they** shall **receive it** for whom it is prepared.

Mark 10:41 And when the ten heard ~~it~~, they began to be much displeased with James and John.

And when the ten heard, they began to be much displeased with James and John.

Mark 10:42 But Jesus called them ~~to him~~, and ~~saith~~ unto them, Ye know that they ~~which~~ are ~~accounted~~ to rule over the Gentiles exercise lordship over them; and their great ones exercise authority upon them.

But Jesus called them, and **said** unto them, Ye know that they **who** are **appointed** to rule over the Gentiles exercise lordship over them; and their great ones exercise authority upon them.

Mark 10:43 But ~~so shall~~ it not be among you: but whosoever will be great among you, shall be your minister:

But it **shall** not be **so** among you: but whosoever will be great among you, shall be your minister:

Mark 10:47 And when he heard that it was Jesus of Nazareth, he began to cry out, and say, Jesus, ~~thou~~ Son of David, have mercy on me.

And when he heard that it was Jesus of Nazareth, he began to cry out, and say, Jesus, Son of David, have mercy on me.

Mark 10:48 And many charged him that he should hold his peace: but he cried the more ~~a great deal, Thou~~ Son of David, have mercy on me.

And many charged him that he should hold his peace: but he cried the more **exceedingly**, **saying**, Son of David, have mercy on me.

Mark 10:49 And Jesus stood still, and commanded him to be called. And they ~~call~~ the blind man, saying unto him, Be of good comfort, ~~rise~~; he calleth thee.

And Jesus stood still, and commanded him to be called. And they **called** the blind man, saying unto him, Be of good comfort, **arise**; he calleth thee.

Mark 10:50 And he, casting away his garment, ~~rose~~, and came to Jesus.

And he, casting away his garment, **arose**, and came to Jesus.

Mark 10:51 And Jesus ~~answered and~~ said unto him, What wilt thou that I should do unto thee? The blind man said unto him, Lord, that I might receive my sight.

And Jesus said unto him, What wilt thou that I should do unto thee? **And** the blind man said unto him, Lord, that I might receive my sight.

Mark 10:52 And Jesus said unto him, Go thy way; thy faith ~~hath~~ made thee

And Jesus said unto him, Go thy way; thy faith **has** made thee whole. And whole. And immediately he received his sight, and followed Jesus in the way.

Mark 11:2 And ~~saith~~ unto them, Go your way into the village over against you: and as soon as ye ~~be~~ entered into it, ye shall find a colt tied, whereon ~~never~~ man sat; loose him, and bring *him*.

Mark 11:4 And they went their way, and found the colt tied by the door without in a place where two ways met; and they ~~loose~~ him.

Mark 11:5 And certain of them ~~that~~ stood ~~there~~ said unto ~~them~~, ~~What do~~ ye, ~~loosing~~ the colt?

Mark 11:7 And they brought the colt to Jesus, and cast their garments on ~~him~~; and ~~he~~ sat upon ~~him~~.

Mark 11:8 And many spread their garments in the way: and others cut down branches off the trees, and ~~strawed~~ *them* in the way.

Mark 11:9 And they that went before, and they that followed, cried, saying, Hosanna; Blessed *is* he that cometh in the name of the Lord:

Mark 11:10 ~~Blessed be~~ the kingdom of our father David, that cometh in the name of the Lord: Hosanna in the highest.

Mark 11:11 And Jesus entered into Jerusalem, and into the temple: and when he had looked round about upon all things, and ~~now~~ the eventide was come, he went out unto Bethany with the twelve.

immediately he received his sight, and followed Jesus in the way.

And **said** unto them, Go your way into the village over against you: and as soon as ye **have** entered into it, ye shall find a colt tied, whereon **no** man **ever** sat; loose him, and bring him **to me**.

And they went their way, and found the colt tied by the door without in a place where two ways met; and they **loosed** him.

And certain of them **who** stood **by** said unto **the disciples, Why loose** ye the colt?

And they brought the colt to Jesus, and cast their garments on **it**; and **Jesus** sat upon **it**.

And many spread their garments in the way: and others cut down branches off **of** the trees, and **strewed** them in the way.

And they that went before **him**, and they that followed **after**, cried, saying, Hosanna; Blessed is he that cometh in the name of the Lord:

That bringeth the kingdom of our father **David; blessed is he** that cometh in the name of the Lord: Hosanna in the highest.

And Jesus entered into Jerusalem, and into the temple: and when he had looked round about upon all things, and **blessed the disciples,** the eventide was come, **and** he went out unto Bethany with the twelve.

Mark 11:12 And on the morrow, when they ~~were come~~ from Bethany, he was hungry:	And on the morrow, when they **came** from Bethany, he was hungry:
Mark 11:13 And seeing a fig tree afar off having leaves, he came, ~~if haply~~ he might find any thing thereon: and when he came to it, ~~he found~~ nothing but leaves; for the ~~time of~~ figs ~~was~~ not ~~yet~~.	And seeing a fig tree afar off having leaves, he came **to it with his disciples; and as they supposed**, he **came to it to see if he** might find any thing thereon: and when he came to it, **there was** nothing but leaves; for **as yet** the figs **were** not **ripe**.
Mark 11:14 And Jesus ~~answered~~ and said unto it, No man eat fruit of thee hereafter for ever. And his disciples heard ~~it~~.	And Jesus **spake** and said unto it, No man eat fruit of thee hereafter for ever. And his disciples heard **him**.
Mark 11:15 And they ~~come~~ to Jerusalem: and Jesus went into the temple, and began to cast out them that sold and bought in the temple, and overthrew the tables of the moneychangers, and the seats of them ~~that~~ sold doves;	And they **came** to Jerusalem: and Jesus went into the temple, and began to cast out them that sold and bought in the temple, and overthrew the tables of the moneychangers, and the seats of them **who** sold doves;
Mark 11:16 And would not suffer that any man should carry ~~any~~ vessel through the temple.	And would not suffer that any man should carry **a** vessel through the temple.
Mark 11:18 And the scribes and chief ~~priests~~ heard ~~it~~, and sought how they might destroy him: for they feared him, because all the people ~~was~~ astonished at his doctrine.	And the scribes and chief **priest** heard **him**, and sought how they might destroy him: for they feared him, because all the people **were** astonished at his doctrine.
Mark 11:21 And Peter calling to remembrance ~~saith~~ unto him, Master, behold, the fig tree which thou cursedst is withered away.	And Peter calling to remembrance **said** unto him, Master, behold, the fig tree which thou cursedst is withered away.
Mark 11: 22 And Jesus ~~answering saith~~ unto ~~them~~, Have faith in God.	And Jesus **spake and said** unto **him**, Have faith in God.
Mark 11:23 For verily I say unto you, That whosoever shall say unto this mountain, Be thou removed, and be	For verily I say unto you, That whosoever shall say unto this mountain, Be thou removed, and be thou cast into the

thou cast into the sea; and shall not doubt in his heart, but shall believe that those things which he saith shall come to pass; he shall have whatsoever he saith.

Mark 11:24 Therefore I say unto you, ~~What~~ things ~~soever~~ ye desire, when ye pray, believe that ye receive ~~them~~, and ye shall have ~~them~~.

Mark 11:25 And when ye stand praying, forgive, if ye have ought against any: that your Father also ~~which~~ is in heaven may forgive you your trespasses.

Mark 11:26 But if ~~ye~~ do not forgive, neither will your Father ~~which~~ is in heaven forgive your trespasses.

Mark 11:27 And they ~~come~~ again to Jerusalem: and as he was walking in the temple, there ~~come~~ to him the chief ~~priests~~, and the scribes, and the elders,

Mark 11:28 And ~~say~~ unto him, By what authority doest thou these things? and who gave thee this authority to do these things?

Mark 11:29 And Jesus answered and said unto them, I will also ask of you one question, ~~and~~ answer me, and I will tell you by what authority I do these things.

Mark 11:30 ~~The~~ baptism of John, ~~was it~~ from heaven, or of men? answer me.

Mark 11:32 But if we shall say, Of men; ~~they feared~~ the people: for all ~~men counted~~ John, that he was a prophet indeed.

Mark 11:33 And they answered and said unto Jesus, We cannot tell. And

sea; and shall not doubt in his heart, but shall believe that those things which he saith shall come to pass; he shall have whatsoever he saith **fulfilled**.

Therefore I say unto you, **Whatsoever** things ye desire, when ye pray, believe that ye receive, and ye shall have **whatsoever ye ask**.

And when ye stand praying, forgive, if ye have aught against any: that your Father also **who** is in heaven may forgive you your trespasses.

But if **you** do not forgive, neither will your Father **who** is in heaven forgive your trespasses.

And they **came** again to Jerusalem: and as he was walking in the temple, there **came** to him the chief **priest**, and the scribes, and the elders,

And **said** unto him, By what authority doest thou these things? and who gave thee this authority to do these things?

And Jesus answered and said unto them, I will also ask of you one question, answer me, and **then** I will tell you by what authority I do these things.

Was the baptism of John from heaven, or of men? answer me.

But if we shall say, Of men; **we shall offend** the people. **Therefore they feared the people**: for all **people believed** John, that he was a prophet indeed.

And they answered and said unto Jesus, We cannot tell. And Jesus answering

Jesus answering ~~saith~~ unto them, Neither do I tell you by what authority I do these things.

Mark 12:1 And ~~he~~ began to speak unto them by parables. A ~~certain~~ man planted a vineyard, and set ~~an~~ hedge about *it*, and digged ~~a place for~~ the ~~winefat~~, and built a tower, and let it out to husbandmen, and went into a far country.

Mark 12:3 And they caught *him*, and beat him, and sent *him* away empty.

Mark 12:8 And they took him, ~~and killed *him*~~, and cast *him* out of the vineyard.

Mark 12:9 What shall therefore the lord of the vineyard do? he will come and destroy the husbandmen, and will give the vineyard unto others.

Mark 12:10 ~~And~~ have ye not read this scripture; The stone which the builders rejected is become the head of the corner:

Mark 12:12 And they sought to lay hold on him, but feared the people: for they knew that he had spoken the parable against them: and they left him, and went their way.

Mark 12:13 And they ~~send~~ unto him certain of the Pharisees and of the Herodians, to catch him in ~~his~~ words.

Mark 12:14 And when they were come, they ~~say~~ unto him, Master, we know that thou art true, and carest for no man: for thou regardest not the person of men, but teachest the way of God in truth: Is it lawful to give tribute to Caesar or not?

said unto them, Neither do I tell you by what authority I do these things.

And **Jesus** began to speak unto them by parables, **saying**, A man planted a vineyard, and set **a** hedge about it, and digged the **winevat**, and built a tower, and let it out to husbandmen, and went into a far country.

And they caught **the servant**, and beat him, and sent him away empty.

And they took him, and cast him out of the vineyard **and killed him**.

What shall therefore the lord of the vineyard do? **Lo**; he will come and destroy the husbandmen, and will give the vineyard unto others.

Again have ye not read this scripture; The stone which the builders rejected is become the head of the corner:

And now they were angry when they heard these words; and they sought to lay hold on him, but feared the people: for they knew that he had spoken the parable against them: and they left him, and went their way.

And they **sent** unto him certain of the Pharisees and of the Herodians, to catch him in [his] words.

And when they were come, they **said** unto him, Master, we know that thou art true, and carest for no man: for thou regardest not the person of men, but teachest the way of God in truth: Is it lawful to give tribute to Caesar or not?

Mark 12:16 And they brought ~~it~~. And he ~~saith~~ unto them, Whose ~~is this~~ image and superscription? And they said unto him, Caesar's.

Mark 12:17 And Jesus answering said unto them, Render to Caesar the things ~~that~~ are Caesar's, and to God the things that are God's. And they marvelled at ~~him~~.

Mark 12:18 Then ~~come~~ unto him the Sadducees, ~~which~~ say there is no resurrection; and they asked him, saying,

Mark 12:19 Master, Moses wrote unto us, If a man's brother die, and leave ~~his~~ wife ~~behind him~~, and leave no children, that his brother should take his wife, and raise up seed unto his brother.

Mark 12:20 Now there were seven brethren: ~~and~~ the first took a wife, and dying left no seed.

Mark 12:24 And Jesus answering said unto them, ~~Do~~ ye ~~not therefore~~ err, because ye know not the scriptures, neither the power of God?

Mark 12:25 For when they shall rise from the dead, they neither marry, nor are given in marriage; but are as the angels ~~which~~ are in heaven.

Mark 12:27 He is not the God of the dead, but the God of the living: ye therefore do greatly err.

Mark 12:29 And Jesus answered him, The first of all the commandments *is*, Hear, O Israel; The Lord our God is one Lord:

Mark 12:31 And the second *is* like, ~~namely~~ this, Thou shalt love thy

And they brought **the penny;** and he **said** unto them, Whose image and superscription **is this**? And they said unto him, Caesar's.

And Jesus answering said unto them, Render to Caesar the things **which** are Caesar's, and to God the things that are God's. And they marvelled at **it**.

Then **came** unto him the Sadducees, **who** say there is no resurrection; and they asked him, saying,

Master, Moses wrote unto us **in his law**, If a man's brother die, and leave **a** wife, and leave no children, that his brother should take his wife, and raise up seed unto his brother.

Now there were seven brethren: the first took a wife, and dying left no seed.

And Jesus answering said unto them, Ye **do** err **therefore**, because ye know not **and understand not** the scriptures, neither the power of God;

For when they shall rise from the dead, they neither marry, nor are given in marriage; but are as the angels **of God who** are in heaven.

He is not **therefore** the God of the dead, but the God of the living; **for he raiseth them up out of their graves.** Ye therefore do greatly err.

And Jesus answered him, The first of all the commandments is, **Hearken and** hear, O Israel; The Lord our God is one Lord:

And the second is like this, Thou shalt love thy neighbour as thyself. There is

neighbour as thyself. There is none other commandment greater than these.

Mark 12:32 And the scribe said unto him, Well, Master, thou hast said the truth: for there is one God; and there is none other but ~~he~~:

Mark 12:34 And when Jesus saw that he answered discreetly, he said unto him, Thou art not far from the kingdom of God. And no man after that durst ask him ~~any question~~.

Mark 12:35 And Jesus ~~answered~~ and said, while he taught in the temple, How say the scribes that Christ is the Son of David?

Mark 12:36 For David himself said by the Holy Ghost, The Lord said ~~to~~ my Lord, Sit thou on my right hand, ~~till~~ I make thine enemies thy footstool.

Mark 12:37 David therefore himself calleth him Lord; and whence is he ~~then~~ his son? And the common people heard him gladly.

Mark 12:38 And he said unto them in his doctrine, Beware of the scribes, which love to go in long clothing, and ~~love~~ salutations in the marketplaces,

Mark 12:40 ~~Which~~ devour widows' houses, and for a pretence make long prayers: these shall receive greater damnation.

Mark 12:41 And Jesus sat over against the treasury, and beheld how the people cast money into the treasury: and many that were rich cast in much.

none other commandment greater than these.

And the scribe said unto him, Well, Master, thou hast said the truth: for there is one God; and there is none other but **him**:

And when Jesus saw that he answered discreetly, he said unto him, Thou art not far from the kingdom of God. And no man after that durst ask him **saying, Who art thou?**

And Jesus **spake** and said, while he taught in the temple, How say the scribes that Christ is the Son of David?

For David himself said by the Holy Ghost, The Lord said **unto** my Lord, Sit thou on my right hand, **until** I make thine enemies thy footstool.

David therefore himself calleth him Lord; and whence is he his son? And the common people heard him gladly; **but the high priest and the elders were offended at him.**

And he said unto them in his doctrine, Beware of the scribes, which love to go in long clothing, and **have** salutations in the marketplaces,

Who devour widows' houses, and for a pretence make long prayers: these shall receive greater damnation.

And **after this,** Jesus sat over against the treasury, and beheld how the people cast money into the treasury: and many that were rich cast in much.

Mark 12:42 And there came a certain poor widow, and she ~~threw~~ in two mites, which make a farthing.

Mark 12:43 And ~~he~~ called ~~unto him~~ his disciples, and ~~saith~~ unto them, Verily I say unto you, That this poor widow hath cast more in, than all they ~~which~~ have cast into the treasury:

Mark 12:44 For all ~~they~~ did cast in of their abundance; but she ~~of~~ her want did cast in all that she had, *even* all her living.

Mark 13:1 And as ~~he~~ went out of the temple, ~~one of~~ his disciples ~~saith unto him~~, Master, ~~see what manner~~ of ~~stones and what buildings are here~~!

Mark 13:2 And Jesus ~~answering~~ said unto ~~him, Seest thou~~ these ~~great buildings~~? there shall not be left one stone upon another, that shall not be thrown down.

Mark 13:3 And as he sat upon the mount of Olives ~~over against the temple, Peter and James and John and Andrew asked~~ him privately,

Mark 13:4 Tell us, when shall these things be? and what ~~shall be~~ the sign ~~when all these things shall be fulfilled~~?

And there came a certain poor widow, and she **cast** in two mites, which make a farthing.

And **Jesus** called his disciples, and **said** unto them, Verily I say unto you, That this poor widow hath cast more in, than all they **who** have cast into the treasury:

For all **the rich** did cast in of their abundance; but she **notwithstanding** her want did cast in all that she had, **yea**, even all her living.

And as **Jesus** went out of the temple, his disciples **came to him for to hear him,** saying, Master, **shew us concerning the** buildings of the temple.

And he said unto them, Behold ye these stones of the temple, and all this great work, and buildings of the temple? Verily I say unto you, they shall be thrown down and left unto the Jews desolate. And Jesus said unto **them**, See you not all these **things and do you not understand them? Verily I say unto you**, there shall not be left **here upon this temple** one stone upon another, that shall not be thrown down.

And Jesus left them and went upon the mount of Olives. And as he sat upon the mount of Olives, **the disciples came unto** him privately, **saying,**

Tell us, when shall these things be **which thou hast said, concerning the destruction of the temple, and the Jews?** and what **is** the sign **of thy coming, and of the end of the world, (or the destruction of the wicked, which is the end of the world?)**

Mark 13:5 And Jesus ~~answering~~ them ~~began to say~~, Take heed ~~lest any~~ *man* deceive you:	And Jesus **answered and said unto** them, Take heed **that no** man deceive you:
Mark 13:7 ~~And when ye shall hear of wars and rumours of wars, be ye not troubled: for~~ *such things* ~~must needs be; but the end~~ *shall* ~~not~~ *be* ~~yet.~~	
Mark 13:8 ~~For nation shall rise against nation, and kingdom against kingdom: and there shall be earthquakes in divers places, and there shall be famines and troubles: these~~ *are* ~~the beginnings of sorrows.~~	
Mark 13:9 ~~But take heed to yourselves: for they shall deliver you up to councils; and in the synagogues ye shall be beaten: and ye shall be brought before rulers and kings for my sake, for a testimony against them.~~	
Mark 13:10 ~~And the gospel must first be published among all nations.~~	
Mark 13:11 ~~But when they~~ shall ~~lead you, and~~ deliver you up, ~~take no thought beforehand what ye shall speak, neither do ye premeditate: but whatsoever shall be given you in that hour, that speak ye: for it is not ye that speak, but the Holy Ghost.~~	Then shall **they** deliver you up **to be** afflicted, and shall kill you, and ye shall be hated of all nations for my name's sake.
Mark 13:12 ~~Now the brother~~ shall betray ~~the brother to death, and the father the son; and children shall rise up against~~ *their* parents, ~~and shall cause them to be put to death.~~	And then shall many be offended, and shall betray **one another; and many false prophets shall rise, and shall deceive many; and because iniquity shall abound, the love of many shall wax cold;**
Mark 13:13 ~~And ye shall be hated of all~~ *men* ~~for my name's sake:~~ but he that shall endure unto the end, the same shall be saved.	But he that shall endure unto the end, the same shall be saved.

Mark 13:14 ~~But~~ when ~~ye~~ shall see the ~~abomination~~ of desolation, spoken of by Daniel the prophet, ~~standing where it ought not, (let him that~~ readeth understand~~,)~~ then let them ~~that~~ be in Judaea flee ~~to~~ the mountains:

Mark 13:15 ~~And~~ let him ~~that~~ is on the housetop ~~not go down into the house, neither enter therein~~, to take any thing out of his house:

Mark 13:16 ~~And~~ let him ~~that~~ is in the field ~~not turn~~ back ~~again for~~ to take ~~up~~ his ~~garment~~.

Mark 13:17 ~~But~~ woe ~~to~~ them that are with child, and ~~to~~ them ~~that~~ give suck in those days!

Mark 13:18 ~~And~~ pray ye that your flight be not in the winter.

Mark 13:19 For *in* those days shall be ~~affliction~~, such as was not ~~from~~ the beginning of ~~the creation which God created unto~~ this time, ~~neither~~ shall be.

Mark 13:20 And except ~~that the Lord had shortened~~ those days, no flesh ~~should~~ be saved: but for the elect's sake, ~~whom he hath chosen, he hath~~ shortened ~~the days~~.

Mark 13:21 And then if any man shall say ~~to~~ you, Lo, here *is* Christ; or, ~~lo, he is~~ there; believe *him* not:

When **you therefore** shall see the **abominations** of desolation, spoken of by Daniel the prophet **concerning the destruction of Jerusalem, then you shall stand in the holy place. Whoso** readeth, **let him** understand. Then let them **who** be in Judea flee **into** the mountains:

Let him **who** is on the housetop **flee, and not return** to take any thing out of his house:

Neither let him **who** is in the field, **return** back to take his **clothes**.

And woe **unto** them that are with child, and **unto** them **who** give suck in those days!

Therefore pray ye **the Lord** that your flight be not in the winter, **neither on the Sabbath day.**

For **then**, in those days shall be **great tribulations on the Jews, and upon the inhabitants of Jerusalem;** such as was not **before sent upon Israel, of God,** since the beginning of **their kingdom (for it is written, their enemies shall scatter them) until** this time; **no, nor ever** shall be **sent again upon Israel.**

All these things are the beginnings of sorrows. And except those days **should be shortened, there should** no flesh be saved: but for the elect's sake, **according to the covenants, those days shall be shortened. Behold, these things I have spoken unto you concerning the Jews.**

And then **immediately after the tribulation of those days, which shall come upon Jerusalem,** if any man shall say

The Gospel According to St Mark

Mark 13:22 For false Christs and false prophets ~~shall rise~~, and shall shew signs and wonders, ~~to seduce,~~ if ~~it were~~ possible, ~~even~~ the elect.

Mark 13:23 ~~But take ye heed: behold, I have foretold you all things~~.

unto you, Lo, here is Christ; or there; believe him not:

For **in those days there shall also arise** false Christs and false prophets, and shall shew **great** signs and wonders; insomuch, **that** if possible, **they shall deceive the very elect, who are the elect according to the covenant. Behold, I speak these things unto you for the elect's sake. And you also shall hear of wars, and rumour of wars; see that ye be not troubled;**

For all I have told you must come to pass, but the end is not yet. Behold, I have told you before, wherefore if they shall say unto you, Behold, he is in the desert; go not forth; Behold, he is in the secret chambers; believe it not. For as the light of the morning cometh out of the east, and shineth even unto the west, and covereth the whole earth, so shall also the coming of the Son of man be. And now I shew unto you a parable, Behold, wheresoever the carcass is, there will the eagles be gathered together; so likewise shall mine elect be gathered from the four quarters of the earth. And they shall hear of wars and rumours of wars. Behold, I speak unto you for mine elect's sake. For nation shall rise against nation, and kingdom against kingdom; there shall be famines, and pestilences, and earthquakes in divers places. And again, because iniquity shall abound, the love of men shall wax cold; but he who shall not be overcome, the same shall be saved. And again this gospel of the kingdom shall be preached in all the world, for a witness unto all nations, and then shall the end come, or the destruction of the wicked. And

Mark 13:24 ~~But in those days,~~ after ~~that~~ tribulation, the sun shall be darkened, and the moon shall not give her light,	again shall the abomination of desolation, spoken of by Daniel the prophet, be fulfilled.
	And immediately after the tribulation of those days, the sun shall be darkened, and the moon shall not give her light,
Mark 13:25 And the stars ~~of heaven~~ shall fall, and the powers ~~that are in~~ heaven shall be shaken.	And the stars shall fall from heaven, and the powers of heaven shall be shaken. Verily I say unto you, this generation in the which these things shall be shewn forth, shall not pass away, till all I have told you shall be fulfilled. Although the days will come that heaven and earth shall pass away, yet my words shall not pass away, but all shall be fulfilled. And as I said before, After the tribulations of those days, and the powers of the heavens shall be shaken, then shall appear the sign of the Son of man in heaven; and then shall all the tribes of the earth mourn,
Mark 13:26 And ~~then~~ shall ~~they~~ see the Son of man coming in the clouds with ~~great~~ power and glory.	And they shall see the Son of man coming in the clouds of heaven, with power and great glory, and whoso treasureth up my word shall not be deceived; for the Son of man shall come;
Mark 13:27 And ~~then~~ shall ~~he~~ send his angels, and shall gather together his elect from the four winds, from ~~the uttermost part of the earth to the uttermost part~~ of heaven.	And he shall send his angels before him with the great sound of a trumpet, and they shall gather together his elect from the four winds, from one end of heaven to the other.
Mark 13:28 Now learn a parable of the fig tree; When ~~her branch is~~ yet tender, and putteth forth leaves, ~~ye~~ know that summer is ~~near:~~	Now learn a parable of the fig tree. When his branches are yet tender, and putteth forth leaves, you know that summer is nigh at hand.
Mark 13:29 So ~~ye in like manner~~, when ~~ye~~ shall see these things ~~come to pass~~, know that ~~it~~ is ~~nigh~~, *even* at the doors.	So likewise, mine elect, when they shall see all these things, they shall know that he is near, even at the doors.

The Gospel According to St Mark

Mark 13:30 ~~Verily I say unto you, that this generation shall not pass, till all these things be done~~.

Mark 13:31 ~~Heaven and earth shall pass away: but my words shall not pass away~~.

Mark 13:32 But of that day and ~~that~~ hour knoweth ~~no man~~, no, not the angels ~~which are~~ in heaven, ~~neither the Son,~~ but ~~the~~ Father.

But of that day and hour, **no one** knoweth, no, not the angels **of God** in heaven, but **my** Father **only**.

Mark 13:33 ~~Take ye heed, watch and pray: for ye know not when the time is~~.

But as it was in the days of Noah, so it shall be also at the coming of the Son of man; for it shall be with them as it was in the days which were before the flood. Until the day that Noah entered into the ark, they were eating and drinking, marrying and giving in marriage, and knew not until the flood came and took them all away; so shall also the coming of the Son of man be.

Mark 13:34 ~~For the Son of man is~~ as a ~~man taking a far journey, who left his house, and gave authority to his servants, and to every man his work, and commanded the porter to watch~~.

Then shall be fulfilled that which is written, that in the last days, two shall be in the field; one shall be taken, and the other left. Two shall be grinding at the mill; the one taken, and the other left. And what I say unto one, I say unto all men.

Mark 13:35 Watch ~~ye~~ therefore: for ye know not ~~when~~ the ~~master~~ of the house ~~cometh, at even, or at midnight, or at the cockcrowing, or in the morning~~:

Watch therefore: for ye know not **at what hour your Lord doth come**. But know this, if the **goodman** of the house had known in what watch the thief would come, he would have watched, and would not have suffered his house to have been broken up; but would have been ready.

Mark 13:36 ~~Lest coming suddenly he find you sleeping~~.

Therefore, be ye also ready, for in such an hour as you think not, the Son of man cometh. Who then is a faithful and wise servant, whom [his] Lord hath made ruler over his household, to give them meat in due season? Blessed is that servant whom his Lord, when he cometh, shall find so doing. And verily I say unto you, he shall make him ruler over all his goods. But if that evil servant shall say in his heart, My Lord delayeth his coming; and shall begin to smite his fellow servants, and to eat and drink with the drunken; the Lord of that servant shall come in a day when he looketh not for him, and in an hour that he is not aware of, and shall cut him asunder, and shall appoint him his portion with the hypocrites. There shall be weeping and gnashing of teeth; and thus cometh the end.

Mark 13:37 ~~And what I say unto you I say unto all, Watch~~.

Mark 14:1 After two days was ~~*the feast of*~~ the passover, and of unleavened bread: and the chief priests and the scribes sought how they might take ~~him~~ by craft, and put *him* to death.

After two days was the passover, and **the feast** of unleavened bread: and the chief priests and the scribes sought how they might take **Jesus** by craft, and put him to death.

Mark 14:2 But they said, Not on the feast *day,* lest there be an uproar ~~of~~ the people.

But they said **among themselves, Let us** not **take him** on the feast day, lest there be an uproar **among** the people.

Mark 14:3 And being in Bethany in the house of Simon the leper, as he sat at meat, there came a woman having an alabaster box of ointment of spikenard very precious; and she brake the box, and poured ~~it~~ on his head.

And **Jesus** being in Bethany in the house of Simon the leper, as he sat at meat, there came a woman having an alabaster box of ointment of spikenard very precious; and she brake the box, and poured **the ointment** on his head.

Mark 14:4 ~~And~~ there were some ~~that~~ had indignation within themselves, and said, Why was this waste of the ointment made?

There were some **among the disciples who** had indignation within themselves, and said, Why was this waste of the ointment made?

Mark 14:6 And Jesus said, Let her alone; why trouble ye her? she hath wrought a good work on me.

And Jesus said **unto them**, Let her alone; why trouble ye her? **for** she hath wrought a good work on me.

The Gospel According to St Mark

Mark 14:7 ~~For~~ ye have the poor with you always, and whensoever ~~ye~~ will ~~ye~~ may do them good: but me ye have not always.

Mark 14:8 She ~~hath~~ done what she could: she ~~is~~ come ~~aforehand~~ to anoint my body to the burying.

Mark 14:9 Verily I say unto you, Wheresoever this gospel shall be preached throughout the whole world, ~~this also that~~ she hath done shall be spoken of for a memorial of her.

Mark 14:10 ~~And Judas Iscariot, one of the twelve, went unto the chief priests, to betray him unto them.~~

Mark 14:11 ~~And when they heard it, they were glad, and promised to give him money. And he sought how he might conveniently betray him.~~

Mark 14:12 And the first day of unleavened bread, when they killed the passover, his disciples said unto him, Where wilt thou that we go and prepare that thou mayest eat the passover?

Mark 14:18 And as they sat and did eat, Jesus said, Verily I say unto you, One of you ~~which~~ eateth with me shall betray me.

Mark 14:19 And they began to be sorrowful, and to say unto him one by one, *Is* it I? and another *said, Is* it I?

Mark 14:20 And he answered and said unto them, *It is* one of the twelve, ~~that~~ dippeth with me in the dish.

Ye have the poor with you always, and whensoever **you** will **you** may do them good: but me ye have not always.

She **has** done what she could, **and this which she has done unto me shall be had in remembrance in generations to come, wheresoever my gospel shall be preached; for verily** she **has** come **beforehand** to anoint my body to the burying.

Verily I say unto you, Wheresoever this gospel shall be preached throughout the whole world, **what** she hath done shall be spoken of **also** for a memorial of her.

And **now** the first day of unleavened bread, when they killed the passover, his disciples said unto him, Where wilt thou that we go and prepare that thou mayest eat the passover?

And as they sat and did eat, Jesus said, Verily I say unto you, One of you **who** eateth with me shall betray me.

And they **all** began to be **very** sorrowful, and **began** to say unto him one by one, Is it I? and another said, Is it I?

And he answered and said unto them, It is one of the twelve, **who** dippeth with me in the dish.

Mark 14:22 And as they did eat, Jesus took bread, and blessed, and brake ~~it~~, and gave to them, and said, Take, eat: this is my body.	And as they did eat, Jesus took bread, and blessed **it**, and brake, and gave to them, and said, Take **it, and** eat: **Behold,** this is **for you to do in remembrance of** my body; **for as oft as ye do this you will remember this hour that I was with you.**
Mark 14:24 And he said unto them, This is my blood ~~of~~ the new testament, which ~~is shed for many~~.	And he said unto them, This is **in remembrance of** my blood, **which is** shed for many, **and** the new testament, which **I give unto you; for of me, ye shall bear record unto all the world. And as oft as ye do this ordinance, you will remember me in this hour that I was with you, and drank with you of this cup, even the last time in my ministry.**
Mark 14:25 Verily I say unto you, I will ~~drink~~ no more of the fruit of the vine, until that day that I drink it new in the kingdom of God.	Verily I say unto you, **Of this ye shall bear record; for** I will no more **drink** of the fruit of the vine **with you**, until that day that I drink it new in the kingdom of God. **And now they were grieved, and wept over him.**
Mark 14:27 And Jesus ~~saith~~ unto them, All ye shall be offended because of me this night: for it is written, I will smite the shepherd, and the sheep shall be scattered.	And Jesus **said** unto them, All ye shall be offended because of me this night: for it is written, I will smite the shepherd, and the sheep shall be scattered.
Mark 14:28 But after that I am risen, I will go before you into Galilee.	But after that I am risen, I will go before you into Galilee. **And he said unto Judas Iscariot, what thou doest, do quickly; but beware of innocent blood. Nevertheless, Judas Iscariot, even one of the twelve, went unto the chief priests to betray Jesus unto them; for he turned away from him, and was offended because of his words. And when the chief priests heard of him, they were glad, and promised to give him money; and he sought how he might conveniently betray Jesus.**

The Gospel According to St Mark

Mark 14:29 But Peter said unto ~~him~~, Although all shall be offended, yet *will* ~~not I~~.	But Peter said unto **Jesus**, Although all **men** shall be offended **with thee**, yet **I** will **never be offended**.
Mark 14:30 And Jesus ~~saith~~ unto him, Verily I say unto thee, That this day, *even* in this night, before the cock crow twice, thou shalt deny me thrice.	And Jesus **said** unto him, Verily I say unto thee, That **at** this day, even in this night, before the cock crow twice, thou shalt deny me thrice.
Mark 14:31 But he spake the more vehemently, If I should die with thee, I ~~will~~ not deny thee in any wise. Likewise also said they all.	But he spake the more vehemently, If I should die with thee, **yet will** I not deny thee in any wise. Likewise also said they all.
Mark 14:32 And they came to a place which was named Gethsemane: and he ~~saith~~ to his disciples, Sit ~~ye~~ here, while I shall pray.	And they came to a place which was named Gethsemane, **which was a garden; and the disciples began to be sore amazed, and to be very heavy, and to complain in their hearts, wondering if this be the Messiah. And Jesus, knowing their hearts,** he **said** to his disciples, Sit **you** here, while I shall pray.
Mark 14:33 And he taketh with him Peter and James and John, and ~~began to be sore amazed, and to be very heavy~~;	And he taketh with him Peter and James and John, and **rebuked them,**
Mark 14:34 And saith unto them, My soul is exceeding sorrowful unto death: tarry ye here, and watch.	And saith unto them, My soul is exceeding sorrowful, **even** unto death: tarry ye here, and watch.
Mark 14:36 And he said, Abba, Father, all things *are* possible unto thee; take away this cup from me: nevertheless not ~~what I~~ will, but ~~what thou wilt~~.	And he said, Abba, Father, all things are possible unto thee; take away this cup from me: nevertheless not **my** will, but **thine be done.**
Mark 14:37 And he cometh, and findeth them sleeping, and saith unto Peter, Simon, sleepest thou? couldest not ~~thou~~ watch one hour?	And he cometh, and findeth them sleeping, and saith unto Peter, Simon, sleepest thou? couldest **thou** not watch one hour?
Mark 14:38 Watch ye and pray, lest ye enter into temptation. The spirit truly *is* ready, but the flesh *is* weak.	Watch ye and pray, lest ye enter into temptation. **And they said unto him,** The spirit truly is ready, but the flesh is weak.

Mark 14:40 And when he returned, he found them asleep again, (for their eyes were heavy,) neither ~~wist~~ they what to answer him.

Mark 14:41 And he ~~cometh~~ the third time, and saith unto them, Sleep on now, and take ~~your~~ rest: it is enough, the hour is come; behold, the Son of man is betrayed into the ~~hands~~ of sinners.

Mark 14:42 Rise up, let us go; lo, he ~~that~~ betrayeth me is at hand.

Mark 14:44 And he ~~that~~ betrayed him had given them a token, saying, Whomsoever I shall kiss, that same is he; take him, and lead *him* away safely.

Mark 14:45 And as soon as he was come, he goeth straightway to him, and ~~saith~~, Master, master; and kissed him.

Mark 14:47 And one of them ~~that~~ stood by drew ~~a~~ sword, and smote a servant of the high priest, and cut off his ear.

Mark 14:48 And Jesus answered and said unto them, Are ye come out, as against a thief, with swords and ~~with~~ staves to take me?

Mark 14:49 I was daily with you in the temple teaching, and ye took me not: but the ~~scriptures~~ must be fulfilled.

Mark 14:50 And they all forsook him, and fled.

Mark 14:51 And there followed him a certain young man, having a linen

And when he returned, he found them asleep again, (for their eyes were heavy,) neither **knew** they what to answer him.

And he **came to them** the third time, and **he** saith unto them, Sleep on now, and take rest: it is enough, the hour is come; behold, the Son of man is betrayed into the **hand** of sinners.

And after they had finished their sleep, he said, Rise up, let us go; lo, he **who** betrayeth me is at hand.

And he **who** betrayed him had given them a token, saying, Whomsoever I shall kiss, that same is he; take him, and lead him away safely.

And as soon as he was come, he goeth straightway to him, and **said**, Master, master; and kissed him.

And one of them **who** stood by drew **his** sword, and smote a servant of the high priest, and cut off his ear. **But Jesus commanded him to return his sword, saying, He who taketh the sword shall perish with the sword. And he put forth his finger, and healed the servant of the high priest.**

And Jesus answered and said unto them, Are ye come out, as against a thief, with swords and staves to take me?

I was daily with you in the temple teaching, and ye took me not: but the **scripture** must be fulfilled.

And **the disciples, when** they **heard this saying,** all forsook him, and fled.

And there followed him a certain young man, **a disciple,** having a linen cloth

cloth cast about *his* naked *body;* and the young men laid hold on him:

Mark 14:52 And he left the linen cloth, and fled from them naked.

Mark 14:55 And the chief ~~priests~~ and all the council sought for witness against Jesus to put him to death; ~~and~~ found none.

Mark 14:56 ~~For~~ many bare false witness against him, ~~but~~ their witness agreed not together.

Mark 14:57 And there arose certain, and bare false witness against him, saying,

Mark 14:59 But neither ~~so~~ did their witness agree together.

Mark 14:60 And the high priest stood up in the midst, and asked Jesus, saying, Answerest thou nothing? what ~~is it which~~ these witness against thee?

Mark 14:63 Then the high priest rent his clothes, and ~~saith~~, What need we any further witnesses?

Mark 14:66 And as Peter was beneath in the palace, there ~~cometh~~ one of the maids of the high priest:

Mark 14:67 And when she saw Peter warming himself, she looked upon him, and said, ~~And~~ thou also wast with Jesus of Nazareth.

Mark 14:68 But he denied, saying, I know not, neither understand I what thou ~~sayest~~. And he went out into the porch; and the cock crew.

cast about his naked body; and the young men laid hold on him:

And he left the linen cloth, and fled from them naked, **and saved himself out of their hands**.

And the chief **priest** and all the council sought for witness against Jesus to put him to death; **but** found none.

Though many bare false witness against him, **yet** their witness agreed not together.

And there arose certain **men**, and bare false witness against him, saying,

But neither did their witness agree together.

And the high priest stood up in the midst, and asked Jesus, saying, Answerest thou nothing? **Knowest thou not** what these witness against thee?

Then the high priest rent his clothes, and **said**, What need we any further witnesses?

And as Peter was beneath in the palace, there **came** one of the maids of the high priest:

And when she saw Peter warming himself, she looked upon him, and said, Thou also wast with Jesus of Nazareth.

But he denied, saying, I know not, neither understand I what thou **saith**. And he went out into the porch; and the cock crew.

Mark 14:69 And a maid saw him again, and began to say to them ~~that~~ stood by, This is *one* of them.

Mark 14:70 And he denied it again. And a little after, they ~~that~~ stood by said again to Peter, Surely thou art *one* of them: for thou art a Galilaean, ~~and~~ thy speech agreeth *thereto.*

Mark 14:72 And the second time the cock crew. And Peter called to mind the ~~word that~~ Jesus said unto him, Before the cock crow twice, thou shalt deny me thrice. And ~~when~~ he ~~thought thereon,~~ ~~he~~ wept.

Mark 15:1 And straightway in the morning the chief priests held a consultation with the elders and scribes and the whole council, and bound ~~Jesus~~, and carried *him* away, and delivered *him* to Pilate.

Mark 15:2 And Pilate asked him, Art thou the King of the Jews? And ~~he~~ answering said unto him, Thou sayest ~~it~~.

Mark 15:6 Now at ~~that~~ feast ~~he released~~ unto them one prisoner, whomsoever they desired.

Mark 15:7 And there was ~~one~~ named Barabbas, ~~which lay~~ bound with them ~~that~~ had made insurrection with him, who had committed murder in the insurrection.

Mark 15:8 And the multitude crying aloud began to desire *him to* ~~do as he had ever done~~ unto them.

Mark 15:9 But Pilate answered them, saying, Will ye that I release unto you the King of the Jews?

And a maid saw him again, and began to say to them **who** stood by, This is one of them.

And he denied it again. And a little after, they **who** stood by said again to Peter, Surely thou art one of them: for thou art a Galilaean, thy speech agreeth thereto.

And the second time the cock crew. And Peter called to mind the **words which** Jesus said unto him, Before the cock crow twice, thou shalt deny me thrice. And he **went out, and fell upon his face, and** wept **bitterly**.

And straightway in the morning the chief priests held a consultation with the elders and scribes; and the whole council **condemned him**, and bound **him**, and carried him away, and delivered him to Pilate.

And Pilate asked him, Art thou the King of the Jews? And **Jesus** answering said unto him, **I am even as** thou sayest.

Now **it was common** at the feast **for Pilate to release** unto them one prisoner, whomsoever they desired.

And there was **a man** named Barabbas, bound with them **who** had made insurrection with him, who had committed murder in the insurrection.

And the multitude crying aloud began to desire him to **deliver Jesus** unto them.

But Pilate answered **unto** them, saying, Will ye that I release unto you the King of the Jews?

The Gospel According to St Mark

Mark 15:10 For he knew that the chief ~~priests~~ had delivered him for envy.

Mark 15:11 But the chief priests moved the people, that he should rather release Barabbas unto them.

Mark 15:12 And Pilate ~~answered~~ and said ~~again~~ unto them, What will ye then that I shall do ~~unto~~ *him* whom ye call the King of the Jews?

Mark 15:13 And they cried out again, Crucify him.

Mark 15:14 Then Pilate said unto them, Why, what evil hath he done? ~~And~~ they cried out the more exceedingly, Crucify him.

Mark 15:15 And ~~so~~ Pilate, willing to content the people, released Barabbas unto them, and delivered Jesus, when he had scourged *him*, to be crucified.

Mark 15:16 And the soldiers led him away into the hall, called Praetorium; and they ~~call~~ together the whole band.

Mark 15:17 And they clothed him with purple, and platted a crown of thorns, and put it ~~about~~ his *head,*

Mark 15:18 And began to salute him, Hail, King of the Jews!

Mark 15:21 And they ~~compel~~ one Simon a Cyrenian, who passed by, coming out of the country, the father of ~~Alexander~~ and Rufus, to bear his cross.

Mark 15:22 And they bring him unto the place Golgotha, which is, being interpreted, The place of a ~~skull~~.

For he knew that the chief **priest** had delivered him for envy.

But the chief priests moved the people, that he should rather release Barabbas unto them, **as he had before done unto them.**

And Pilate **spake again** and said unto them, What will ye then that I shall do **with** him whom ye call the King of the Jews?

And they cried out again, **Deliver him unto us to be crucified. Away with him.** Crucify him.

Then Pilate said unto them, Why, what evil hath he done? **But** they cried out the more exceedingly, Crucify him.

And **now** Pilate, willing to content the people, released Barabbas unto them, and delivered Jesus, when he had scourged him, to be crucified.

And the soldiers led him away into the hall, called Praetorium; and they **called** together the whole band.

And they clothed him with purple, and platted a crown of thorns, and put it **upon** his head,

And began to salute him, **saying**, Hail, King of the Jews!

And they **compelled** one Simon a Cyrenian, who passed by, coming out of the country, the father of **Alexandria** and Rufus, to bear his cross.

And they bring him unto the place **called** Golgotha, which is, (being interpreted) the place of a **burial**.

Mark 15:23 And they gave him to drink ~~wine~~ mingled with ~~myrrh: but~~ he ~~received it~~ not.

Mark 15:25 And it was the third hour, ~~and~~ they crucified him.

Mark 15:26 And ~~the superscription of~~ his accusation ~~was written over~~, THE KING OF THE JEWS.

Mark 15:27 And with him they ~~crucify~~ two thieves; the one on his right hand, and the other on his left.

Mark 15:28 And the scripture was fulfilled, which ~~saith~~, And he was numbered with the transgressors.

Mark 15:29 And they ~~that~~ passed by railed on him, wagging their heads, and saying, Ah, thou ~~that~~ destroyest the temple, and buildest ~~it~~ in three days,

Mark 15:32 Let Christ the King of Israel descend now from the cross, that we may see and believe. And ~~they that were~~ crucified with him reviled him.

Mark 15:34 And at the ninth hour Jesus cried with a loud voice, saying, Eloi, Eloi, lama sabachthani? which is, being interpreted, My God, my God, why hast thou forsaken me?

Mark 15:35 And some of them ~~that~~ stood by, when they heard ~~it~~, said, Behold, he calleth Elias.

And they gave him to drink **vinegar** mingled with **gall: and when** he **had tasted the vinegar, he would** not **drink**.

And it was the third hour, **when** they crucified him.

And **Pilate wrote** his accusation, **and put it upon the cross**, THE KING OF THE JEWS. **There were certain of the high priests who stood by, that said unto Pilate, Write that he said, I am king of the Jews. But Pilate said unto them, What I have written, I have written.**

And with him they **crucified** two thieves; the one on his right hand, and the other on his left.

And the scripture was fulfilled, which **said**, And he was numbered with the transgressors.

And they **who** passed by railed on him, wagging their heads, and saying, Ah, thou **who** destroyest the temple, and buildest it in three days,

Let Christ the King of Israel descend now from the cross, that we may see and believe. And **one of them who was** crucified with him reviled him **also, saying, If thou art the Christ, save thyself and us.**

And at the ninth hour Jesus cried with a loud voice, saying, Eloi, Eloi, lama sabachthani? which is, (being interpreted) My God, my God, why hast thou forsaken me?

And some of them **who** stood by, when they heard **him**, said, Behold, he calleth Elias.

The Gospel According to St Mark

Mark 15:36 And one ran and filled a spunge full of vinegar, and put ~~it~~ on a reed, and gave him to drink, saying, Let alone; let us see whether Elias will come to take him down.

Mark 15:39 And when the centurion, ~~which~~ stood over against him, saw that he so cried out, and gave up the ghost, he said, Truly this man ~~was~~ the Son of God.

Mark 15:40 There were also women looking on afar off: among whom was Mary Magdalene, and Mary the mother of James the ~~less~~ and of Joses, and Salome;

Mark 15:41 ~~(~~Who also, when he was in Galilee, followed him, and ministered unto him;~~)~~ and many other women ~~which~~ came ~~up~~ with him unto Jerusalem.

Mark 15:42 And now when the even was come, because it was the preparation, that is, the day before the sabbath,

Mark 15:43 Joseph of Arimathaea, an honourable counsellor, ~~which~~ also waited for the kingdom of God, came, and went in boldly unto Pilate, and craved the body of Jesus.

Mark 15:44 And Pilate marvelled if he were already dead: and calling ~~unto him~~ the centurion, he asked him ~~whether~~ he had been any while dead.

Mark 15:46 And ~~he~~ bought fine linen, and took him down, and wrapped him in the linen, and laid him in a sepulchre which was hewn out of a rock, and rolled a stone unto the door of the sepulchre.

And one ran and filled a spunge full of vinegar, and put on a reed, and gave him to drink; **others spake**, saying, Let **him** alone; let us see whether Elias will come to take him down.

And when the centurion, **who** stood over against him, saw that he so cried out, and gave up the ghost, he said, Truly this man **is** the Son of God.

There were also women looking on afar off: among whom was Mary Magdalene, and Mary the mother of James the **younger** and of Joses, and Salome;

Who also, when he was in Galilee, followed him, and ministered unto him; and many other women **who** came with him unto Jerusalem.

And now when the even was come, because it was the preparation **day**, that is, the day before the sabbath,

Joseph of Arimathaea, an honourable counsellor, **who** also waited for the kingdom of God, came, and went in boldly unto Pilate, and craved the body of Jesus.

And Pilate marvelled **and asked him** if he were already dead: and calling the centurion, he asked him **if** he had been any while dead.

And **Joseph** bought fine linen, and took him down, and wrapped him in the linen, and laid him in a sepulchre which was hewn out of a rock, and rolled a stone unto the door of the sepulchre.

Mark 16:1 And when the sabbath was past, Mary Magdalene, and Mary the *mother* of James, and Salome, ~~had~~ bought sweet spices, that they might come and anoint him.

Mark 16:4 ~~And~~ when they looked, they saw that the stone was rolled away: for it was very great.

Mark 16:5 And ~~entering into the sepulchre, they saw a young man~~ sitting ~~on the right side~~, clothed in ~~a~~ long white ~~garment~~; and they were affrighted.

Mark 16:6 ~~And he saith~~ unto them, Be not affrighted: Ye seek Jesus of Nazareth, ~~which~~ was crucified: he is risen; he is not here: behold the place where they laid him.

Mark 16:7 ~~But~~ go your way, tell his disciples and Peter that he goeth before you into Galilee: there shall ~~ye~~ see him, as he said unto you.

Mark 16:8 And they went out quickly, and fled from the sepulchre; for they trembled and were amazed: neither said they any thing to any *man;* for they were afraid.

Mark 16:9 Now when *Jesus* was risen early the first *day* of the week, he appeared first to Mary Magdalene, out of whom he had cast seven devils.

Mark 16:10 *And* she went and told them ~~that~~ had been with him, as they mourned and wept.

Mark 16:14 Afterward he appeared unto the eleven as they sat at meat, and upbraided them with their unbelief and

And when the sabbath was past, Mary Magdalene, and Mary the mother of James, and Salome, bought sweet spices, that they might come and anoint him.

But when they looked, they saw that the stone was rolled away: (for it was very great.)**;**

And **two angels** sitting **thereon**, clothed in long white **garments**; and they were affrighted.

But the angels said unto them, Be not affrighted: Ye seek Jesus of Nazareth, **who** was crucified: he is risen; he is not here: behold the place where they laid him.

And go your way, tell his disciples and Peter that he goeth before you into Galilee: there shall **you** see him, as he said unto you.

And they, entering into the sepulchre, saw the place where they laid Jesus. And they went out quickly, and fled from the sepulchre; for they trembled and were amazed: neither said they any thing to any man; for they were afraid.

Now when Jesus was risen early **on** the first day of the week, he appeared first to Mary Magdalene, out of whom he had cast seven devils.

And she went and told them **who** had been with him, as they mourned and wept.

Afterward he appeared unto the eleven as they sat at meat, and upbraided them with their unbelief and hardness of

hardness of heart, because they believed not them ~~which~~ had seen him after he was risen.	heart, because they believed not them **who** had seen him after he was risen.

The Gospel According to St Luke

King James Version

Luke 1:1 ~~Forasmuch as~~ many have taken in hand to set forth in order a declaration of those things which are most surely believed among us,

Luke 1:2 Even as they delivered them unto us, ~~which~~ from the beginning were eyewitnesses, and ministers of the word;

Luke 1:5 There was in the days of Herod, the king of Judaea, a certain priest named Zacharias, of the course of Abia: and his wife ~~was~~ of the daughters of Aaron, and her name ~~was~~ Elisabeth.

Luke 1:6 ~~And they~~ were both righteous before God, walking in all the commandments and ordinances of the Lord blameless.

Luke 1:7 And they had no child, ~~because that~~ Elisabeth was barren, and they both ~~were now~~ well stricken in years.

Luke 1:8 And ~~it came to pass, that~~ while he executed the priest's office before God in the order of his ~~course~~,

Luke 1:9 According to the ~~custom of the priest's office~~, his lot was to burn incense when he went into the temple of the Lord.

Luke 1:10 ~~And~~ the whole multitude of the people were praying without at the time of incense.

Joseph Smith Translation

As I am a messenger of Jesus Christ, and knowing that many have taken in hand to set forth in order a declaration of those things which are most surely believed among us,

Even as they delivered them unto us, **who** from the beginning were eyewitnesses, and ministers of the word;

There was in the days of Herod, the king of Judea, a certain priest named Zacharias, of the course of Abia: and his wife **being** of the daughters of Aaron, and her name Elisabeth,

Were both righteous before God, walking in all the commandments and ordinances of the Lord blameless.

And they had no child. Elisabeth was barren, and they **were** both well stricken in years.

And while he executed the priest's office before God in the order of his **priesthood**,

According to the **law** (his lot was to burn incense when he went into the temple of the Lord),

The whole multitude of the people were praying without at the time of incense.

Luke 1:12 And when Zacharias saw ~~him~~, he was troubled, and fear fell upon him.

Luke 1:14 ~~And~~ thou shalt have joy and gladness; and many shall rejoice at his birth.

Luke 1:17 And he shall go before ~~him~~ in the spirit and power of Elias, to turn the hearts of the fathers to the children, and the disobedient to the wisdom of the just; to make ready a people prepared for the Lord.

Luke 1:18 And Zacharias said unto the angel, Whereby shall I know this? for I am an old man, and my wife well stricken in years.

Luke 1:19 And the angel answering said unto him, I am Gabriel, ~~that~~ stand in the presence of God; and am sent to speak unto thee, and to shew thee these glad tidings.

Luke 1:23 And ~~it came to pass, that~~, as soon as the days of his ministration were accomplished, he departed to his own house.

Luke 1:25 Thus hath the Lord dealt with me in the days wherein he looked on *me,* to take away my reproach among men.

Luke 1:28 And the angel came in unto her, and said, Hail, *thou ~~that~~ art* highly favoured, the Lord *is* with thee: blessed ~~art thou~~ among women.

Luke 1:29 And when she saw ~~him~~, she was troubled at his saying, and ~~cast~~ in her mind what manner of salutation this should be.

And when Zacharias saw **the angel**, he was troubled, and fear fell upon him.

Thou shalt have joy and gladness; and many shall rejoice at his birth.

And he shall go before **the Lord** in the spirit and power of Elias, to turn the hearts of the fathers to the children, and the disobedient to the wisdom of the just; to make ready a people prepared for the Lord.

And Zacharias said unto the angel, Whereby shall I know this? for I am an old man, and my wife **is** well stricken in years.

And the angel answering said unto him, I am Gabriel, **who** stand[s] in the presence of God; and am sent to speak unto thee, and to shew thee these glad tidings.

And as soon as the days of his ministration were accomplished, he departed to his own house.

Thus hath the Lord dealt with me in the days wherein he looked on me, to take away my reproach **from** among men.

And the angel came in unto her, and said, Hail, thou **virgin who** art highly favoured **of the Lord**. The Lord is with thee, **for thou art chosen and** blessed among women.

And when she saw **the angel**, she was troubled at his saying, and **pondered** in her mind what manner of salutation this should be.

Luke 1:31 And, behold, thou shalt conceive ~~in thy womb~~, and bring forth a son, and ~~shalt~~ call his name JESUS.	And, behold, thou shalt conceive, and bring forth a son, and **shall** call his name JESUS.
Luke 1:34 Then said Mary unto the angel, How ~~shall~~ this be, ~~seeing I know not a man~~?	Then said Mary unto the angel, How **can** this be?
Luke 1:35 And the angel answered and said unto her, The Holy Ghost ~~shall come upon thee~~, and the power of the Highest ~~shall overshadow thee~~: therefore also that holy ~~thing which~~ shall be born of thee shall be called the Son of God.	And the angel answered and said unto her, **Of** the Holy Ghost, and the power of the Highest. Therefore also that holy **child that** shall be born of thee shall be called the Son of God.
Luke 1:36 And, behold, thy cousin Elisabeth, she hath also conceived a son in her old age: and this is the sixth month with her, who ~~was~~ called barren.	And, behold, thy cousin Elisabeth, she hath also conceived a son in her old age: and this is the sixth month with her, who **is** called barren.
Luke 1:37 For with God nothing ~~shall~~ be impossible.	For with God nothing **can** be impossible.
Luke 1:39 And Mary ~~arose in those days, and~~ went into the hill country with haste, into a city of Juda;	And **in those days,** Mary went into the hill country with haste, into a city of Juda;
Luke 1:43 And ~~whence~~ is this ~~to~~ me, that the mother of my Lord should come to me?	And **why** is **it that** this **blessing is upon** me, that the mother of my Lord should come to me?
Luke 1:45 And blessed ~~is she that~~ believed: for ~~there shall be a performance of~~ those things which were told ~~her from~~ the Lord.	And blessed **art thou who** believed: for those things which were told **of the angel of** the Lord **shall be fulfilled**.
Luke 1:47 And my spirit ~~hath rejoiced~~ in God my Saviour.	And my spirit **rejoiceth** in God my Saviour.
Luke 1:49 For he ~~that~~ is mighty hath done to me great things; and holy ~~is his~~ name.	For he **who** is mighty hath done to me great things; and **I will magnify his** holy name,
Luke 1:50 ~~And~~ his mercy ~~is~~ on ~~them that~~ fear him from generation to generation.	**For** his mercy on **those who** fear him from generation to generation.

The Gospel According to St Luke

Luke 1:52 He hath put down the mighty from *their* seats, and exalted them of low degree.

Luke 1:53 He hath filled the hungry with good things; ~~and~~ the rich he hath sent empty away.

Luke 1:54 He hath ~~holpen~~ his servant Israel, in remembrance of ~~his~~ mercy;

Luke 1:56 And Mary abode with ~~her~~ about three months, and returned to her own house.

Luke 1:57 Now Elisabeth's full time came that she should be delivered; and she brought forth a son.

Luke 1:58 And her neighbours and her cousins heard how the Lord had shewed great mercy ~~upon~~ her; and they rejoiced with her.

Luke 1:62 And they made signs to his father, how he would have him called.

Luke 1:63 And he asked for a writing table, and wrote, saying, His name is John. And they marvelled ~~all~~.

Luke 1:64 And his mouth was opened immediately, and his tongue ~~loosed, and he spake~~, and praised God.

Luke 1:65 And fear came on all ~~that~~ dwelt round about them: and all these sayings were noised abroad throughout all the hill country of Judaea.

Luke 1:66 And all they that heard *them* laid *them* up in their hearts, saying, What manner of child shall this be! And the hand of the Lord was with ~~him~~.

He hath put down the mighty from their **high** seats, and exalted them of low degree.

He hath filled the hungry with good things; **but** the rich he hath sent empty away.

He hath **helped** his servant Israel, in remembrance of mercy;

And Mary abode with **Elisabeth** about three months, and returned to her own house.

And now Elisabeth's full time came that she should be delivered; and she brought forth a son.

And her neighbours and her cousins heard how the Lord had shewed great mercy **unto** her; and they rejoiced with her.

And they made signs to his father, **and asked him** how he would have him called.

And he asked for a writing table, and wrote, saying, His name is John. And they **all** marvelled.

And his mouth was opened immediately, and **he spake with** his tongue, and praised God.

And fear came on all **who** dwelt round about them: and all these sayings were noised abroad throughout all the hill country of Judea.

And all they that heard them laid them up in their hearts, saying, What manner of child shall this be? And the hand of the Lord was with **it**.

Luke 1:67 And ~~his~~ father Zacharias was filled with the Holy Ghost, and prophesied, saying,	And **its** father Zacharias was filled with the Holy Ghost, and prophesied, saying,
Luke 1:70 As he spake by the mouth of his holy prophets, ~~which have been~~ since the world began:	As he spake by the mouth of his holy prophets, **ever** since the world began:
Luke 1:71 That we should be saved from our enemies, and from the hand of all ~~that~~ hate us;	That we should be saved from our enemies, and from the hand of all **those who** hate us;
Luke 1:75 In holiness and righteousness before him, all the days of our ~~life~~.	In holiness and righteousness before him, all the days of our **lives**.
Luke 1:77 To give knowledge of salvation unto his people by the remission of their sins,	To give knowledge of salvation unto his people by **baptism for** the remission of their sins,
Luke 1:79 To give light to them ~~that~~ sit in darkness and ~~in~~ the shadow of death, to guide our feet into the way of peace.	To give light to them **who** sit in darkness and the shadow of death, to guide our feet into the way of peace.
Luke 1:80 And the child grew, and waxed strong in spirit, and was in the deserts ~~till~~ the day of his shewing unto Israel.	And the child grew, and waxed strong in spirit, and was in the deserts **until** the day of his shewing unto Israel.
Luke 2:1 And it came to pass in those days, that there went out a decree from Caesar Augustus, that all ~~the world~~ should be taxed.	And it came to pass in those days, that there went out a decree from Caesar Augustus, that all **his empire** should be taxed.
Luke 2:2 ~~(And~~ this taxing was ~~first made~~ when Cyrenius was governor of Syria.~~)~~	This **same** taxing was when Cyrenius was governor of Syria.
Luke 2:3 And all went to be taxed, every one ~~into~~ his own city.	And all went to be taxed, every one **in** his own city.
Luke 2:5 To be taxed with Mary his espoused wife, being great with child.	To be taxed with Mary his espoused wife, **she** being great with child.
Luke 2:7 And she brought forth her firstborn son, and wrapped him in swaddling clothes, and laid him in a manger; because there was ~~no~~ room for them in the ~~inn~~.	And she brought forth her firstborn son, and wrapped him in swaddling clothes, and laid him in a manger; because there was **none to give** room for them in the **inns**.

The Gospel According to St Luke

Luke 2:8 And there were in the same country shepherds abiding in the field, keeping watch over their ~~flock~~ by night.

Luke 2:9 And, lo, ~~the~~ angel of the Lord ~~came upon~~ them, and the glory of the Lord shone round about them: and they were sore afraid.

Luke 2:10 ~~And~~ the angel said unto them, Fear not: for, behold, I bring you good tidings of great joy, which shall be to all people.

Luke 2:11 For unto you is born this day in the city of David a Saviour, ~~which~~ is Christ the Lord.

Luke 2:12 And this ~~shall be a sign unto~~ you; ~~Ye~~ shall find the babe wrapped in swaddling clothes, lying in a manger.

Luke 2:14 Glory to God in the highest, and on earth peace, good will ~~toward~~ men.

Luke 2:15 And it came to pass, ~~as~~ the angels were gone away from them into heaven, the shepherds said one to another, Let us now go even unto Bethlehem, and see this thing which is come to pass, which the Lord ~~hath~~ made known unto us.

Luke 2:17 And when they had seen *it*, they made known abroad the saying which was told them concerning this child.

Luke 2:18 ~~And~~ all they ~~that~~ heard *it* wondered at those things which were told them by the shepherds.

Luke 2:19 But Mary kept all ~~these~~ things, and pondered *them* in her heart.

And there were in the same country shepherds abiding in the field, keeping watch over their **flocks** by night.

And, lo, **an** angel of the Lord **appeared unto** them, and the glory of the Lord shone round about them: and they were sore afraid.

But the angel said unto them, Fear not: for, behold, I bring you good tidings of great joy, which shall be to all people.

For unto you is born this day in the city of David a Saviour, **who** is Christ the Lord.

And this **is the way** you shall find the babe, **he is** wrapped in swaddling clothes, **and is lying** in a manger.

Glory to God in the highest, and on earth peace, good will **to** men.

And it came to pass, **when** the angels were gone away from them into heaven, the shepherds said one to another, Let us now go even unto Bethlehem, and see this thing which is come to pass, which the Lord **has** made known unto us.

And when they had seen, they made known abroad the saying which was told them concerning this child.

All they **who** heard it wondered at those things which were told them by the shepherds.

But Mary kept all **those** things, and pondered them in her heart.

Luke 2:20 And the shepherds returned, glorifying and praising God for all the things ~~that~~ they had heard and seen, as ~~it was told~~ unto them.	And the shepherds returned, glorifying and praising God for all the things **which** they had heard and seen, as **they were manifested** unto them.
Luke 2:21 And when eight days were accomplished for the circumcising of the child, his name was called JESUS, which was so named of the angel before he was conceived ~~in the womb~~.	And when eight days were accomplished for the circumcising of the child, his name was called JESUS, which was so named of the angel before he was conceived.
Luke 2:23 ~~(~~As it is written in the law of the Lord, Every male ~~that~~ openeth the womb shall be called holy to the Lord;~~)~~	As it is written in the law of the Lord, Every male **which** openeth the womb shall be called holy to the Lord;
Luke 2:24 And to offer a sacrifice according to that which is ~~said~~ in the law of the Lord, A pair of turtledoves, or two young pigeons.	And to offer a sacrifice according to that which is **written** in the law of the Lord, A pair of turtledoves, or two young pigeons.
Luke 2:25 And, behold, there was a man ~~in~~ Jerusalem, whose name *was* Simeon; and the same man *was* just and devout, waiting for the consolation of Israel: and the Holy Ghost was upon him.	And, behold, there was a man **at** Jerusalem, whose name was Simeon; and the same man was just and devout, waiting for the consolation of Israel: and the Holy Ghost was upon him.
Luke 2:27 And he came by the Spirit into the temple: and when the parents brought in the child Jesus, to do for him after the custom of the law,	And he came by the Spirit into the temple: and when the parents brought in the child, **even** Jesus, to do for him after the custom of the law,
Luke 2:29 Lord, now lettest ~~thou~~ thy servant depart in peace, according to thy word:	Lord, now lettest thy servant depart in peace, according to thy word:
Luke 2:33 And Joseph and ~~his mother~~ marvelled at those things which were spoken of ~~him~~.	And Joseph and **Mary** marvelled at those things which were spoken of **the child**.
Luke 2:34 And Simeon blessed them, and said unto Mary ~~his mother~~, Behold, this *child* is set for the fall and rising again of many in Israel; and for a sign which shall be spoken against;	And Simeon blessed them, and said unto Mary, Behold, this child is set for the fall and rising again of many in Israel; and for a sign which shall be spoken against;

The Gospel According to St Luke

Luke 2:35 (Yea, a ~~sword~~ shall pierce through ~~thy~~ own soul also,) that the thoughts of many hearts may be revealed.

Luke 2:36 And there was one Anna, a prophetess, the daughter of Phanuel, of the tribe of Aser: she was of ~~a~~ great age, and had lived with an husband seven ~~years from her virginity~~;

Luke 2:37 And she ~~was~~ a widow ~~of~~ about fourscore and four years, ~~which~~ departed not from the temple, but served *God* with fastings and prayers night and day.

Luke 2:38 And she coming in that instant gave thanks likewise unto the Lord, and spake of him to all them ~~that~~ looked for redemption in Jerusalem.

Luke 2:39 And when they had performed all things according to the law of the Lord, they returned into Galilee, ~~to~~ their own city Nazareth.

Luke 2:40 And the child grew, and waxed strong in spirit, filled with wisdom: and the grace of God was upon him.

Luke 2:42 And when he was twelve years old, they went up to Jerusalem after the custom ~~of~~ the feast.

Luke 2:43 And when they had fulfilled the days, as they returned, the child Jesus tarried behind in Jerusalem; and Joseph and his mother knew not ~~of it~~.

Luke 2:44 But they, supposing him to have been in the company, went a day's journey; and they sought him among ~~their~~ ~~kinsfolk~~ and acquaintance.

Yea, **a spear** shall pierce through **him to the wounding of thine** own soul also, that the thoughts of many hearts may be revealed.

And there was one Anna, a prophetess, the daughter of Phanuel, of the tribe of Aser: she was of great age, and had lived with a husband **only** seven years, **whom she married in her youth,**

And she **lived** a widow about fourscore and four years, **who** departed not from the temple, but served God with fastings and prayers night and day.

And she coming in that instant gave thanks likewise unto the Lord, and spake of him to all them **who** looked for redemption in Jerusalem.

And when they had performed all things according to the law of the Lord, they returned into Galilee, **unto** their own city Nazareth.

And the child grew, and waxed strong in spirit, **being** filled with wisdom: and the grace of God was upon him.

And when he was twelve years old, they went up to Jerusalem after the custom, **to** the feast.

And when they had fulfilled the days, as they returned, the child Jesus tarried behind in Jerusalem; and Joseph and his mother knew not **that he tarried;**

But they, supposing him to have been in the company, went a day's journey; and they sought him among **his kindred** and acquaintance.

Luke 2:46 And it came to pass, ~~that~~ after three days they found him in the temple, sitting in the midst of the doctors, ~~both~~ hearing ~~them~~, and asking ~~them~~ questions.	And it came to pass, after three days they found him in the temple, sitting in the midst of the doctors, **and they were** hearing **him**, and asking **him** questions.
Luke 2:47 And all ~~that~~ heard him were astonished at his understanding and answers.	And all **who** heard him were astonished at his understanding and answers.
Luke 2:48 And when ~~they~~ saw him, they were amazed: and his mother said unto him, Son, why hast thou thus dealt with us? behold, thy father and I have sought thee sorrowing.	And when **his parents** saw him, they were amazed: and his mother said unto him, Son, why hast thou thus dealt with us? behold, thy father and I have sought thee sorrowing.
Luke 2:49 And he said unto them, ~~How~~ is it that ye sought me? ~~wist~~ ye not that I must be about my Father's business?	And he said unto them, **Why** is it that ye sought me? **knew** ye not that I must be about my Father's business?
Luke 2:51 And he went down with them, and came to Nazareth, and was subject unto them: ~~but~~ his mother kept all these sayings in her heart.	And he went down with them, and came to Nazareth, and was subject unto them: **and** his mother kept all these sayings in her heart.
Luke 3:2 Annas and Caiaphas being the high priests, the word of God came unto John the son of Zacharias in the wilderness.	Annas and Caiaphas being the high priests. **Now, in this same year,** the word of God came unto John the son of Zacharias in the wilderness.
Luke 3:4 As it is written in the book of the ~~words of Esaias the~~ prophet, saying, The voice of one crying in the wilderness, Prepare ye the way of the Lord, make his paths straight.	As it is written in the book of the prophet **Esaias, and these are the words**, saying, The voice of one crying in the wilderness, Prepare ye the way of the Lord, **and** make his paths straight. **For behold, and lo, he shall come as it is written in the book of the prophets, to take away the sins of the world, and to bring salvation unto the heathen nations; to gather together those who are lost, which are of the sheepfold of Israel; yea, even her dispersed and afflicted; and also to prepare the way, and make possible the preaching of the gospel unto the Gentiles. And to be a light unto all who sit in darkness,**

	unto the uttermost parts of the earth; to bring to pass the resurrection from the dead, and to ascend up on high, to dwell on the right hand of the Father, until the fulness of time, and the law and the testimony shall be sealed, and the keys of the kingdom shall be delivered up again unto the Father; to administer justice unto all; to come down in judgment upon all, and to convince all the ungodly of their ungodly deeds, which they have committed; and all this in the day that he shall come, for it is a day of power.
Luke 3:5 Every valley shall be filled, and every mountain and hill shall be brought low; ~~and~~ the crooked shall be made straight, and the rough ways ~~shall be~~ made smooth;	**Yea,** every valley shall be filled, and every mountain and hill shall be brought low; the crooked shall be made straight, and the rough ways made smooth;
Luke 3:7 Then said ~~he~~ to the multitude that came forth to be baptized of him, O generation of vipers, who hath warned you to flee from the wrath to come?	Then said **John** to the multitude that came forth to be baptized of him, **crying against them with a loud voice, saying,** O generation of vipers, who hath warned you to flee from the wrath to come?
Luke 3:8 Bring forth therefore fruits worthy of repentance, and begin not to say within yourselves, ~~We have~~ Abraham ~~to~~ *our* father: for I say unto you, That God is able of these stones to raise up children unto Abraham.	Bring forth therefore fruits worthy of repentance, and begin not to say within yourselves, Abraham **is** our father; **we have kept the commandments of God, and none can inherit the promises but the children of Abraham**: for I say unto you, That God is able of these stones to raise up children unto Abraham.
Luke 3:9 And now also the axe is laid unto the root of the trees: every tree therefore which bringeth not forth good fruit ~~is~~ hewn down, and cast into the fire.	And now also the axe is laid unto the root of the trees: every tree therefore which bringeth not forth good fruit **shall be** hewn down, and cast into the fire.
Luke 3:11 He answereth and saith unto them, He that hath two coats, let him	He answereth and saith unto them, He that hath two coats, let him impart to

impart to him ~~that~~ hath none; and he that hath meat, let him do likewise.

Luke 3:13 And he said unto them, Exact no more than that which is appointed you.

Luke 3:16 John answered, saying unto ~~them~~ all, I indeed baptize you with water; but one mightier than I ~~cometh~~, the latchet of whose shoes I am not worthy to unloose: he shall baptize you with the Holy Ghost and with fire:

Luke 3:19 But Herod the tetrarch, being reproved ~~by~~ him for Herodias his brother Philip's wife, and for all the evils which Herod had done,

Luke 3:21 Now when all the people were baptized, it came to pass, that Jesus also being baptized, and praying, the heaven was opened,

Luke 3:22 And the Holy Ghost descended in ~~a~~ bodily shape like a dove upon him, and a voice came from heaven, which said, Thou art my beloved Son; in thee I am well pleased.

Luke 3:23 And Jesus himself began to be about thirty years of age, being {as was supposed} the son of Joseph, ~~which~~ was ~~the son~~ of Heli,

him **who** hath none; and he that hath meat, let him do likewise.

And he said unto them, Exact no more than that which is appointed **unto** you. **For it is well known unto you, Theophilus, that after the manner of the Jews, and according to the custom of their law, in receiving money in the treasury, that out of the abundance which was received was appointed unto the poor, every man his portion; and after this manner did the publicans also, wherefore John said unto them, Exact no more than that which is appointed you.**

John answered, **and** saying unto all, I indeed baptize you with water; but **there cometh** one mightier than I, the latchet of whose shoes I am not worthy to unloose: he shall baptize you with the Holy Ghost and with fire:

But Herod the tetrarch, being reproved **of** him for Herodias his brother Philip's wife, and for all the evils which Herod had done,

Now when all the people were baptized, it came to pass, that Jesus also **came unto John, and** being baptized **of him**, and praying, the heaven was opened,

And the Holy Ghost descended in bodily shape like a dove upon him, and a voice came from heaven, which said, Thou art my beloved Son; in thee I am well pleased.

And Jesus himself began to be about thirty years of age, **having lived with his father**, being as was supposed **of the world**, the son of Joseph, **who** was **from the loins** of Heli,

The Gospel According to St Luke

Luke 3:24 ~~Which~~ was *the son* of Matthat, ~~which~~ was *the son* of Levi, ~~which~~ was ~~*the son*~~ of Melchi, ~~which was the son~~ of Janna, ~~which was the son~~ of Joseph,

Luke 3:25 ~~Which was the son~~ of Mattathias, ~~which was the son~~ of Amos, ~~which was the son~~ of Naum, ~~which was the son~~ of Esli, ~~which was the son~~ of Nagge,

Luke 3:26 ~~Which was the son~~ of Maath, ~~which was the son~~ of Mattathias, ~~which was the son~~ of Semei, ~~which was the son~~ of Joseph, ~~which was the son~~ of Juda,

Luke 3:27 ~~Which was the son~~ of Joanna, ~~which was the son~~ of Rhesa, ~~which was the son~~ of Zorobabel, ~~which was the son~~ of Salathiel, ~~which~~ was *the son* of Neri,

Luke 3:28 ~~Which~~ was ~~*the son*~~ of Melchi, ~~which was the son~~ of Addi, ~~which was the son~~ of Cosam, ~~which was the son~~ of Elmodam, ~~which was the son~~ of Er,

Luke 3:29 ~~Which was the son~~ of Jose, ~~which was the son~~ of Eliezer, ~~which was the son~~ of Jorim, ~~which was the son~~ of Matthat, ~~which was the son~~ of Levi,

Luke 3:30 ~~Which was the son~~ of Simeon, ~~which was the son~~ of Juda, ~~which was the son~~ of Joseph, ~~which was the son~~ of Jonan, ~~which was the son~~ of Eliakim,

Luke 3:31 ~~Which was the son~~ of Melea, ~~which was the son~~ of Menan, ~~which was the son~~ of Mattatha, ~~which was the son~~ of Nathan, ~~which was the son~~ of David,

Luke 3:32 ~~Which was the son~~ of Jesse, ~~which was the son~~ of Obed, ~~which was~~

Who was from the loins of Matthat, who was the son of Levi, who was a descendant of Melchi, and of Janna, and of Joseph,

And of Mattathias, and of Amos, and of Naum, and of Esli, and of Nagge,

And of Maath, and of Mattathias, and of Semei, and of Joseph, and of Juda,

And of Joanna, and of Rhesa, and of Zorobabel, and of Salathiel, who was the son of Neri,

Who was a descendant of Melchi, and of Addi, and of Cosam, and of Elmodam, and of Er,

And of Jose, and of Eliezer, and of Jorim, and of Matthat, and of Levi,

And of Simeon, and of Juda, and of Joseph, and of Jonan, and of Eliakim,

And of Melea, and of Menan, and of Mattatha, and of Nathan, and of David,

And of Jesse, and of Obed, and of Booz, and of Salmon, and of Naasson,

~~the son~~ of Booz, ~~which was the son~~ of Salmon, ~~which was the son~~ of Naasson,

Luke 3:33 ~~Which was the son~~ of Aminadab, ~~which was the son~~ of Aram, ~~which was the son~~ of Esrom, ~~which was the son~~ of Phares, ~~which was the son~~ of Juda,

Luke 3:34 ~~Which was the son~~ of Jacob, ~~which was the son~~ of Isaac, ~~which was the son~~ of Abraham, ~~which was the son~~ of Thara, ~~which was the son~~ of Nachor,

Luke 3:35 ~~Which was the son~~ of Saruch, ~~which was the son~~ of Ragau, ~~which was the son~~ of Phalec, ~~which was the son~~ of Heber, ~~which was the son~~ of Sala,

Luke 3:36 ~~Which was the son~~ of Cainan, ~~which was the son~~ of Arphaxad, ~~which was the son~~ of Sem, ~~which was the son~~ of Noe, ~~which was the son~~ of Lamech,

Luke 3:37 ~~Which was the son~~ of Mathusala, ~~which was the son~~ of Enoch, ~~which was the son~~ of Jared, ~~which was the son~~ of Maleleel, ~~which was the son~~ of Cainan,

Luke 3:38 ~~Which was the son~~ of Enos, ~~which was the son~~ of Seth, ~~which was the son~~ of Adam, ~~which~~ was ~~the son~~ of God.

Luke 4:2 ~~Being~~ forty days ~~tempted of~~ the devil. And in those days he did eat nothing: and when they were ended, he ~~afterward~~ hungered.

Luke 4:5 And the ~~devil, taking~~ him up into an high mountain, ~~shewed unto him~~ all the kingdoms of the world in a moment of time.

And of Aminadab, **and** of Aram, **and** of Esrom, **and** of Phares, **and** of Juda,

And of Jacob, **and** of Isaac, **and** of Abraham, **and** of Thara, **and** of Nachor,

And of Saruch, **and** of Ragau, **and** of Phalec, **and** of Heber, **and** of Sala,

And of Cainan, **and** of Arphaxad, **and** of Shem, **and** of Noah, **and** of Lamech,

And of Mathusala, **and** of Enoch, **and** of Jared, **and** of Maleleel, **and** of Cainan,

And of Enos, **and** of Seth, **and** of Adam, **who** was **formed** of God; **and the first man upon the earth.**

And after forty days, the devil **came unto him, to tempt him.** And in those days he did eat nothing: and when they were ended, he **afterwards** hungered.

And the **spirit taketh** him up into an high mountain, **and he beheld** all the kingdoms of the world in a moment of time.

The Gospel According to St Luke

Luke 4:6 And the devil said unto him, All this power will I give thee, and the glory of them: for ~~that is~~ delivered unto me; and to whomsoever I will I give ~~it~~.

Luke 4:8 ~~And~~ Jesus answered and said unto him, Get thee behind me, Satan: for it is written, Thou shalt worship the Lord thy God, and him only shalt thou serve.

Luke 4:9 And ~~he~~ brought him to Jerusalem, and set him on a pinnacle of the temple, and said unto him, If thou be the Son of God, cast thyself down from hence:

Luke 4:11 And in ~~their~~ hands they shall bear thee up, lest at any time thou dash thy foot against a stone.

Luke 4:12 And Jesus answering said unto him, It is ~~said~~, Thou shalt not tempt the Lord thy God.

Luke 4:15 And he taught in their synagogues, being glorified of all.

Luke 4:18 The Spirit of the Lord *is* upon me, because he hath anointed me to preach the gospel to the poor; he hath sent me to heal the brokenhearted, to preach deliverance to the captives, and recovering of sight to the blind, to set at liberty them ~~that~~ are bruised,

Luke 4:20 And he closed the book, and he gave *it* again to the minister, and sat down. And the eyes of all ~~them that~~ were in the synagogue were fastened on him.

And the devil **came unto him, and** said unto him, All this power will I give **unto** thee, and the glory of them: for **they are** delivered unto me; and to whomsoever I will, I give **them**.

Jesus answered and said unto him, Get thee behind me, Satan: for it is written, Thou shalt worship the Lord thy God, and him only shalt thou serve.

And **the spirit** brought him to Jerusalem, and set him on a pinnacle of the temple, and **the devil came unto him and** said unto him, If thou be the Son of God, cast thyself down from hence:

And in **his** hands they shall bear thee up, lest at any time thou dash thy foot against a stone.

And Jesus answering said unto him, It is **written**, Thou shalt not tempt the Lord thy God.

And he taught in their synagogues, being glorified of all **who believed on his name**.

The Spirit of the Lord is upon me, because he hath anointed me to preach the gospel to the poor; he hath sent me to heal the brokenhearted, to preach deliverance to the captives, and **the** recovering of sight to the blind, to set at liberty them **who** are bruised,

And he closed the book, and he gave it again to the minister, and **he** sat down. And the eyes of all **those who** were in the synagogue were fastened on him.

Luke 4:23 And he said unto them, Ye will surely say unto me this proverb, Physician, heal thyself: whatsoever we have heard done in Capernaum, do also here in thy country.

Luke 4:25 But I tell you ~~of a~~ truth, many widows were in Israel in the days of Elias, when the heaven was shut up three years and six months, ~~when~~ great famine was throughout all the land;

Luke 4:26 But unto none of them was Elias sent, save unto Sarepta, ~~a city~~ of Sidon, unto a woman ~~that~~ *was* a widow.

Luke 4:27 And many lepers were in Israel in the time of Eliseus the prophet; and none of them ~~was~~ cleansed, ~~saving~~ Naaman the Syrian.

Luke 4:32 And they were astonished at his doctrine: for his ~~word was~~ with power.

Luke 4:33 And in the synagogue there was a man, ~~which~~ had a spirit of an unclean devil, and cried out with a loud voice,

Luke 4:34 Saying, Let *us* alone; what have we to do with thee, ~~thou~~ Jesus of Nazareth? art thou come to destroy us? I know thee who thou art; the Holy One of God.

Luke 4:35 ~~And~~ Jesus rebuked him, saying, Hold thy peace, and come out of him. And when the devil had thrown him in the midst, he came out of him, and hurt him not.

Luke 4:36 And they were all amazed, and spake ~~among~~ themselves, saying, What a word *is* this! for with authority

And he said unto them, Ye will surely say unto me this proverb, Physician, heal thyself: whatsoever we have heard **was** done in Capernaum, do also here in thy country.

But I tell you **the** truth, many widows were in Israel in the days of Elias, when the heaven was shut up three years and six months, **and** great famine was throughout all the land;

But unto none of them was Elias sent, save unto Sarepta, of Sidon, unto a woman **who** was a widow.

And many lepers were in Israel in the time of Eliseus the prophet; and none of them **were** cleansed, **save** Naaman the Syrian.

And they were astonished at his doctrine: for his **words were** with power.

And in the synagogue there was a man, **who** had a spirit of an unclean devil, and **he** cried out with a loud voice,

Saying, Let us alone; what have we to do with thee, Jesus of Nazareth? art thou come to destroy us? I know thee who thou art; the Holy One of God.

Jesus rebuked him, saying, Hold thy peace, and come out of him. And when the devil had thrown him in the midst, he came out of him, and hurt him not.

And they were all amazed, and spake **amongst** themselves, saying, What a word is this! for with authority and

The Gospel According to St Luke

and power he commandeth the unclean spirits, and they come out.

Luke 4:37 And the fame of him went out ~~into~~ every place ~~of the country~~ round about.

Luke 4:38 And he arose out of the synagogue, and entered into Simon's house. And Simon's wife's mother was taken with a great fever; and they besought him for her.

Luke 4:39 And he stood over her, and rebuked the fever; and it left her: and immediately she arose and ~~ministered~~ unto them.

Luke 4:40 Now when the sun was setting, all they ~~that~~ had any sick with divers diseases brought them unto him; and he laid his hands on every one of them, and healed them.

Luke 4:42 And when it was day, he departed and went into a ~~desert~~ place: and the people sought him, and came unto him, and ~~stayed~~ him, that he should not depart from them.

Luke 4:43 ~~And~~ he said unto them, I must preach the kingdom of God to other cities also: for therefore am I sent.

Luke 5:1 And it came to pass, ~~that~~, as the people pressed upon him to hear the word of God, he stood by the lake of Gennesaret,

Luke 5:2 And saw two ships standing ~~by~~ the lake: but the fishermen were gone out of them, and were ~~washing~~ *their* nets.

Luke 5:4 Now when he had ~~left~~ speaking, he said unto Simon, Launch out

power he commandeth the unclean spirits, and they come out.

And the fame of him went out **in** every place round about.

And he arose **and went** out of the synagogue, and entered into Simon's house. And Simon's wife's mother was taken with a great fever; and they besought him for **to heal** her.

And he stood over her, and rebuked the fever; and it left her: and immediately she arose and **administered** unto them.

Now when the sun was setting, all they **who** had any sick with divers diseases brought them unto him; and he laid his hands on every one of them, and healed them.

And when it was day, he departed and went into a **solitary** place: and the people sought him, and came unto him, and **desired** him that he should not depart from them.

But he said unto them, I must preach the kingdom of God to other cities also: for therefore am I sent.

And it came to pass, as the people pressed upon him to hear the word of God, he stood by the lake of Gennesaret,

And saw two ships standing **on** the lake: but the fishermen were gone out of them, and were **wetting** their nets.

Now when he had **done** speaking, he said unto Simon, Launch out into the into the deep, and let down your nets for a draught.

Luke 5:6 And when they had ~~this~~ done, they inclosed a great multitude of fishes: and their net brake.

Luke 5:7 And they beckoned unto ~~their~~ partners, ~~which~~ were in the other ship, that they should come and help them. And they came, and filled both the ships, so that they began to sink.

Luke 5:8 When Simon Peter saw ~~it~~, he fell down at Jesus' knees, saying, Depart from me; for I am a sinful man, O Lord.

Luke 5:9 For he was astonished, and all ~~that~~ were with him, at the draught of the fishes which they had taken:

Luke 5:10 And so ~~was~~ also James, and John, the sons of Zebedee, ~~which~~ were partners with Simon. And Jesus said unto Simon, Fear not; from henceforth thou shalt catch men.

Luke 5:14 And he charged him to tell no man: but go, and shew thyself to the ~~priest~~, and offer for thy cleansing, according as Moses commanded, for a testimony unto them.

Luke 5:17 And it came to pass on a certain day, as he was teaching, that there were Pharisees and doctors of the law sitting by, ~~which~~ were come out of every town of Galilee, and Judaea, and Jerusalem: and the power of the Lord was *present* to heal them.

Luke 5:18 And, behold, men brought in a bed a man ~~which~~ was taken with a palsy: and they sought ~~means~~ to bring him in, and to lay *him* before ~~him~~.

deep, and let down your nets for a draught.

And when they had done **this**, they inclosed a great multitude of fishes: and their net brake.

And they beckoned unto partners, **who** were in the other ship, that they should come and help them. And they came, and filled both the ships, so that they began to sink.

When Simon Peter saw **the multitude of fishes**, he fell down at Jesus' knees, saying, Depart from me; for I am a sinful man, O Lord.

For he was astonished, and all **who** were with him, at the draught of the fishes which they had taken:

And so **were** also James, and John, the sons of Zebedee, **who** were partners with Simon. And Jesus said unto Simon, Fear not; from henceforth, **for** thou shalt catch men.

And he charged him to tell no man: but **said unto him**, go, and shew thyself to the **priests**, and offer for thy cleansing, according as Moses commanded, for a testimony unto them.

And it came to pass on a certain day, as he was teaching, that there were Pharisees and doctors of the law sitting by, **who** were come out of every town of Galilee, and Judea, and Jerusalem: and the power of the Lord was present to heal them.

And, behold, men brought in a bed a man **who** was taken with a palsy: and they sought to bring him in, and to lay him before **Jesus**.

Luke 5:19 And when they could not ~~find by what~~ *way* ~~they might~~ bring him in ~~because of~~ the multitude, they went upon the housetop, and let him down through the tiling with *his* couch into the midst before Jesus.

Luke 5:20 ~~And when~~ he saw their faith, ~~he~~ said unto ~~him~~, Man, thy sins are forgiven thee.

Luke 5:21 And the scribes and the Pharisees began to reason, saying, Who is this ~~which~~ speaketh blasphemies? Who can forgive sins, but God alone?

Luke 5:22 But ~~when~~ Jesus perceived their thoughts, he ~~answering~~ said unto them, What reason ye in your hearts?

Luke 5:23 ~~Whether is easier~~, to ~~say, Thy~~ sins ~~be forgiven thee; or~~ to ~~say~~, Rise up and walk?

Luke 5:24 But that ye may know that the Son of man hath power upon earth to forgive sins, ~~(~~he said unto the sick of the palsy,~~)~~ I say unto thee, Arise, and take up thy couch, and go into ~~thine~~ house.

Luke 5:27 And after these things he went forth, and saw a publican, named Levi, sitting at the ~~receipt of~~ custom: and he said unto him, Follow me.

Luke 5:31 ~~And~~ Jesus answering said unto them, They that are whole need not a physician; but they ~~that~~ are sick.

Luke 5:33 And they said unto him, Why do the disciples of John fast often, and make ~~prayers~~, and likewise *the disciples* of the Pharisees; but thine eat and drink?

And when **found that they** could not bring him in **for** the multitude, they went upon the housetop, and let him down through the tiling with his couch into the midst before Jesus.

Now he saw their faith, **and** said unto **the** man, Thy sins are forgiven thee.

And the scribes and Pharisees began to reason, saying, Who is this **that** speaketh blasphemies? Who can forgive sins, but God alone?

But Jesus perceived their thoughts, **and** he said unto them, What reason ye in your hearts?

Does it require more power to **forgive** sins **than to make the sick** rise up and walk?

But that ye may know that the Son of man hath power upon earth to forgive sins, **I said it. And** he said unto the sick of the palsy, I say unto thee, Arise, and take up thy couch, and go into **thy** house.

And after these things he went forth, and saw a publican, named Levi, sitting at the **place where they received** custom: and he said unto him, Follow me.

Jesus answering said unto them, They that are whole need not a physician; but they **who** are sick.

And they said unto him, Why do the disciples of John fast often, and make **prayer**, and likewise the disciples of the Pharisees; but thine eat and drink?

Luke 5:36 And he spake also a parable unto them; No man putteth a piece of ~~a~~ new ~~garment~~ upon an old; if ~~otherwise~~, then ~~both~~ the new maketh a rent, and ~~the piece that was taken out of the new~~ agreeth not with the old.

Luke 5:39 No man also having drunk old *wine* ~~straightway~~ desireth new: for he saith, The old is better.

Luke 6:1 And it came to pass on the second sabbath after ~~the first~~, that he went through the corn fields; and his disciples plucked the ears of corn, and did eat, rubbing *them* in *their* hands.

Luke 6:3 ~~And~~ Jesus answering them said, Have ye not read so much as this, what David did, when himself was an hungred, and they ~~which~~ were with him;

Luke 6:4 How he went into the house of God, and did take and eat the shewbread, and gave also to them ~~that~~ were with him; which it is not lawful to eat but for the priests alone?

Luke 6:8 But he knew their thoughts, and said to the man ~~which~~ had the withered hand, Rise up, and stand forth in the midst. And he arose and stood forth.

Luke 6:9 Then said Jesus unto them, I will ask you one thing; Is it lawful on the sabbath days to do good, or to do evil? to save life, or to destroy ~~it~~?

Luke 6:13 And when it was day, he called ~~unto him~~ his disciples: and of them he chose twelve, whom also he named apostles;

And he spake also a parable unto them, **saying**, No man putteth a piece of new **cloth** upon an old **garment**; if **so**, then the new maketh a rent, and agreeth not with the old.

No man also having drunk old wine desireth new: for he saith, The old is better.

And it came to pass on the second sabbath after **this**, that he went through the corn fields; and his disciples plucked the ears of **the** corn, and did eat, rubbing them in their hands.

Jesus answering them said, Have ye not read so much as this, what David did, when **he** himself was a hungred, and they **who** were with him;

How he went into the house of God, and did take and eat the shewbread, and gave also to them **who** were with him; which it is not lawful to eat but for the priests alone?

But he knew their thoughts, and said to the man **who** had the withered hand, Rise up, and stand forth in the midst. And he arose and stood forth.

Then said Jesus unto them, I will ask you one thing; Is it lawful on the sabbath days to do good, or to do evil? to save life, or to destroy?

And when it was day, he called his disciples: and of them he chose twelve, whom also he named apostles;

The Gospel According to St Luke

Luke 6:16 And Judas *the brother* of James, and Judas Iscariot, ~~which~~ also was the traitor.

And Judas the brother of James, and Judas Iscariot, **who** also was the traitor.

Luke 6:17 And he came down with them, and stood in the plain, and the company of his disciples, and a great multitude of people out of all Judaea and Jerusalem, and from the sea ~~coast~~ of Tyre and Sidon, ~~which~~ came to hear him, and to be healed of their diseases;

And he came down with them, and stood in the plain, and the company of his disciples, and a great multitude of people out of all Judea and Jerusalem, and from the sea **coasts** of Tyre and Sidon, **who** came to hear him, and to be healed of their diseases;

Luke 6:18 And they ~~that~~ were vexed with unclean spirits: and they were healed.

And they **who** were vexed with unclean spirits: and they were healed.

Luke 6:20 And he lifted up his eyes on his disciples, and said, Blessed ~~be ye~~ poor: for ~~yours~~ is the kingdom of God.

And he lifted up his eyes on his disciples, and said, Blessed **are the** poor: for **theirs** is the kingdom of God.

Luke 6:21 Blessed *are* ~~ye that~~ hunger now: for ~~ye~~ shall be filled. Blessed *are* ~~ye that~~ weep now: for ~~ye~~ shall laugh.

Blessed are **they who** hunger now: for **they** shall be filled. Blessed are **they who** weep now: for **they** shall laugh.

Luke 6:22 Blessed are ~~ye~~, when men shall hate you, and when they shall separate you *from* ~~their company~~, and shall reproach *you,* and cast out your name as evil, for the Son of man's sake.

Blessed are **you**, when men shall hate you, and when they shall separate you from **among them**, and shall reproach you, and cast out your name as evil, for the Son of man's sake.

Luke 6:23 Rejoice ye in that day, and leap for joy: for, behold, your reward *is* great in heaven: for in the like manner did their fathers unto the prophets.

Rejoice ye in that day, and leap for joy: for, behold, your reward **shall be** great in heaven: for in the like manner did their fathers unto the prophets.

Luke 6:25 Woe unto you ~~that~~ are full! for ye shall hunger. Woe unto you ~~that~~ laugh now! for ye shall mourn and weep.

Woe unto you **who** are full! for ye shall hunger. Woe unto you **who** laugh now! for ye shall mourn and weep.

Luke 6:26 Woe unto you, when all men shall speak ~~well~~ of you! for so did their fathers to the false prophets.

Woe unto you, when all men shall speak **evil** of you! for so did their fathers to the false prophets.

Luke 6:27 But I say unto you ~~which~~ hear, Love your enemies, do good to them ~~which~~ hate you,

But I say unto you **who** hear **my words**, Love your enemies, do good to them **who** hate you,

Luke 6:28 Bless them ~~that~~ curse you, and pray for them ~~which~~ despitefully use you.	Bless them **who** curse you, and pray for them **who** despitefully use you **and persecute you**.
Luke 6:29 And unto him ~~that~~ smiteth thee on the ~~one~~ cheek offer also the other; ar.d him ~~that~~ taketh away thy cloke forbid not *to take thy* coat also.	And unto him **who** smiteth thee on the cheek offer also the other; **or in other words, it is better to offer the other, than to revile again.** And him **who** taketh away thy cloke forbid not to take thy coat also. **For it is better that thou suffer thine enemy to take these things than to contend with him. Verily I say unto you, Your heavenly Father, who seeth in secret, shall bring that wicked one into judgment.**
Luke 6:30 Give to every man ~~that~~ asketh of thee; and of him ~~that~~ taketh away thy goods ask *them* not again.	**Therefore** give to every man **who** asketh of thee; and of him **who** taketh away thy goods ask them not again.
Luke 6:32 For if ~~ye~~ love them ~~which~~ love you, what ~~thank~~ have ~~ye~~? for sinners also ~~love those that love them~~.	For if **you** love them **only who** love you, what **reward** have **you**? for sinners also **do even the same**.
Luke 6:33 ~~And if ye do good to them which do good to you, what thank have ye? for sinners also do even the same~~.	
Luke 6:34 And if ye lend *to them* of whom ye hope to receive, what ~~thank~~ have ~~ye~~? for sinners also lend to sinners, to receive as much again.	And if ye lend to them of whom ye hope to receive, what **reward** have **you**? for sinners also lend to sinners, to receive as much again.
Luke 6:35 But love ye your enemies, and do good, and lend, hoping for nothing again; and your reward shall be great. and ye shall be the children of the Highest: for he is kind unto the unthankful and ~~to~~ the evil.	But love ye your enemies, and do good, and lend, hoping for nothing again; and your reward shall be great, and ye shall be the children of the Highest: for he is kind unto the unthankful and the evil.
Luke 6:40 ~~The~~ disciple is not above his master: but every one that is perfect shall be as his master.	**A** disciple is not above his master: but every one that is perfect shall be as his master.
Luke 6:41 And why beholdest thou the mote ~~that~~ is in thy brother's eye, but	And why beholdest thou the mote **which** is in thy brother's eye, but

perceivest not the beam ~~that~~ is in thine own eye?

Luke 6:42 ~~Either~~ how canst thou say to thy brother, ~~Brother,~~ let me pull out the mote that is in thine eye, when thou thyself beholdest not the beam ~~that~~ is in thine own eye? Thou hypocrite, cast out first the beam out of thine own eye, and then shalt thou see clearly to pull out the mote ~~that~~ is in thy brother's eye.

Luke 6:48 He is like a man ~~which~~ built an house, and digged deep, and laid the foundation on a rock: and when the flood arose, the stream beat vehemently upon that house, and could not shake it: for it was founded upon a rock.

Luke 6:49 But he ~~that~~ heareth, and doeth not, is like a man that without a foundation built an house upon the earth; against which the stream did beat vehemently, and immediately it fell; and the ruin of that house was great.

Luke 7:1 Now when he had ended all ~~his~~ sayings in the audience of the people, he entered into Capernaum.

Luke 7:7 Wherefore neither thought I myself worthy to come unto thee: but say ~~in a~~ word, and my servant shall be healed.

Luke 7:9 When Jesus heard these things, he marvelled at him, and turned him about, and said unto the people ~~that~~ followed him, I say unto you, I have not found so great faith, no, not in Israel.

Luke 7:10 And they ~~that~~ were sent, returning to the house, found the servant whole ~~that~~ had been sick.

perceivest not the beam **which** is in thine own eye?

Again, how canst thou say to thy brother, Let me pull out the mote that is in thine eye, when thou thyself beholdest not the beam **which** is in thine own eye? Thou hypocrite, cast out first the beam out of thine own eye, and then shalt thou see clearly to pull out the mote **which** is in thy brother's eye.

He is like a man **who** built a house, and digged deep, and laid the foundation on a rock: and when the flood arose, the stream beat vehemently upon that house, and could not shake it: for it was founded upon a rock.

But he **who** heareth, and doeth not, is like a man that without a foundation built a house upon the earth; against which the stream did beat vehemently, and immediately it fell; and the ruin of that house was great.

Now when he had ended all **these** sayings in the audience of the people, he entered into Capernaum.

Wherefore neither thought I myself worthy to come unto thee: but say **the** word, and my servant shall be healed.

When Jesus heard these things, he marvelled at him, and turned him about, and said unto the people **who** followed him, I say unto you, I have not found so great faith, no, not in Israel.

And they **who** were sent, returning to the house, found the servant whole **who** had been sick.

Luke 7:12 Now when he came nigh to the gate of the city, behold, there was a dead man carried out, the only son of his mother, and she was a widow: and ~~much~~ people of the city ~~was~~ with her.

Luke 7:13 And ~~when~~ the Lord saw her, he had compassion on her, and said unto her, Weep not.

Luke 7:14 And he came and touched the bier: and they ~~that~~ bare ~~him~~ stood still. And he said, Young man, I say unto thee, Arise.

Luke 7:15 And he ~~that~~ was dead sat up, and began to speak. And he delivered him to his mother.

Luke 7:19 And John calling ~~unto him~~ two of his disciples sent *them* to Jesus, saying, Art thou he that should come? or look we for another?

Luke 7:20 When the men were come unto him, they said, John Baptist hath sent us unto thee, saying, Art thou he ~~that~~ should come? or look we for another?

Luke 7:21 And in ~~that~~ same hour he cured many of ~~their~~ infirmities and plagues, and of evil spirits; and unto many ~~that were~~ blind he gave sight.

Luke 7:22 Then Jesus answering said unto them, Go your way, and tell John what things ye have seen and heard; how that the blind see, the lame walk, the lepers are cleansed, the deaf hear, the dead are raised, to the poor the gospel is preached.

Luke 7:23 And blessed ~~is he, whosoever~~ shall not be offended in me.

Now when he came nigh to the gate of the city, behold, there was a dead man carried out, the only son of his mother, and she was a widow: and **many** people of the city **were** with her.

And **now** the Lord saw her, **and** he had compassion on her, and **he** said unto her, Weep not.

And he came and touched the bier: and they **who** bare **it** stood still. And he said, Young man, I say unto thee, Arise.

And he **who** was dead sat up, and began to speak. And he delivered him to his mother.

And John calling two of his disciples sent them to Jesus, saying, Art thou he that should come? or look we for another?

When the men were come unto him, they said, John Baptist hath sent us unto thee, saying, Art thou he **who** should come? or look we for another?

And in **the** same hour he cured many of infirmities and plagues, and of evil spirits; and unto many blind he gave sight.

Then Jesus answering said unto them, Go your way, and tell John what things ye have seen and heard; how that the blind see, the lame walk, the lepers are cleansed, the deaf hear, the dead are raised, **and** to the poor the gospel is preached.

And blessed **are they who** shall not be offended in me.

Luke 7:24 And when the messengers of John were departed, he began to speak unto the people concerning John, What went ye out into the wilderness ~~for~~ to see? A reed shaken with the wind?	And when the messengers of John were departed, he began to speak unto the people concerning John, What went ye out into the wilderness to see? A reed shaken with the wind?
Luke 7:25 ~~But what went ye out for to see?~~ A man clothed in soft raiment? Behold, they ~~which~~ are gorgeously apparelled, and live delicately, are in kings' courts.	**Or** a man clothed in soft raiment? Behold, they **who** are gorgeously apparelled, and live delicately, are in kings' courts.
Luke 7:26 But what went ~~ye~~ out for to see? A prophet? Yea, I say unto you, and much more than a prophet.	But what went **you** out for to see? A prophet? Yea, I say unto you, and much more than a prophet.
Luke 7:27 This is ~~he,~~ of whom it is written, Behold, I send my messenger before thy face, ~~which~~ shall prepare thy way before thee.	This is **the one** of whom it is written, Behold, I send my messenger before thy face, **who** shall prepare thy way before thee.
Luke 7:28 For I say unto you, Among those ~~that~~ are born of women there is not a greater prophet than John the Baptist: but he ~~that~~ is least in the kingdom of God is greater than he.	For I say unto you, Among those **who** are born of women there is not a greater prophet than John the Baptist: but he **who** is least in the kingdom of God is greater than he.
Luke 7:29 And all the people ~~that~~ heard *him,* and the publicans, justified God, being baptized with the baptism of John.	And all the people **who** heard him, and the publicans, justified God, being baptized with the baptism of John.
Luke 7:32 They are like unto children sitting in the marketplace, and calling one to another, and saying, We have piped ~~unto~~ you, and ye have not danced; we have mourned ~~to~~ you, and ye have not wept.	They are like unto children sitting in the marketplace, and calling one to another, and saying, We have piped **for** you, and ye have not danced; we have mourned **for** you, and ye have not wept.
Luke 7:37 And, behold, a woman in the city, ~~which~~ was a sinner, when she knew that *Jesus* sat at meat in the Pharisee's house, brought an alabaster box of ointment,	And, behold, a woman in the city, **who** was a sinner, when she knew that Jesus sat at meat in the Pharisee's house, brought an alabaster box of ointment,

Luke 7:38 And stood at his feet ~~behind him~~ weeping, and began to wash his feet with tears, and did wipe *them* with the hairs of her head, and kissed his feet, and anointed *them* with the ointment.	And stood at his feet weeping, and began to wash his feet with tears, and did wipe them with the hairs of her head, and kissed his feet, and anointed them with the ointment.
Luke 7:39 Now when the Pharisee ~~which~~ had bidden him saw ~~it~~, he spake within himself, saying, This man, if he were a prophet, would have known who ~~and~~ what manner of woman *this is* ~~that~~ toucheth him: for she is a sinner.	Now when the Pharisee **who** had bidden him saw **this**, he spake within himself, saying, This man, if he were a prophet, would have known who **or** what manner of woman this is **who** toucheth him: for she is a sinner.
Luke 7:41 There was a certain creditor ~~which~~ had two debtors: the one owed five hundred pence, and the other fifty.	**And Jesus said**, There was a certain creditor **who** had two debtors: the one owed five hundred pence, and the other fifty.
Luke 7:42 And when they had nothing to pay, he frankly forgave them both. Tell me therefore, which of them will love him most?	And when **he found** they had nothing to pay, he frankly forgave them both. Tell me therefore, which of them will love him most?
Luke 7:43 Simon answered and said, I suppose ~~that he~~, to whom he forgave most. And he said unto him, Thou hast rightly judged.	Simon answered and said, I suppose **the man** to whom he forgave most. And he said unto him, Thou hast rightly judged.
Luke 7:44 And he turned to the woman, and said unto Simon, Seest thou this woman? I entered into ~~thine~~ house, thou gavest me no water for my feet: but she hath washed my feet with tears, and wiped *them* with the hairs of her head.	And he turned to the woman, and said unto Simon, Seest thou this woman? I entered into **thy** house, thou gavest me no water for my feet: but she hath washed my feet with tears, and wiped them with the hairs of her head.
Luke 7:49 And they ~~that~~ sat at meat with him began to say within themselves, Who is this that forgiveth sins also?	And they **who** sat at meat with him began to say within themselves, Who is this that forgiveth sins also?
Luke 8:1 And it came to pass afterward, that he went throughout every city and village, preaching and shewing the glad tidings of the kingdom of God: and the twelve *were* with him,	And it came to pass afterward, that he went throughout every city and village, preaching and shewing the glad tidings of the kingdom of God: and the twelve **who were ordained of him**, were with him,

Luke 8:2 And certain women, ~~which~~ had been healed of evil spirits and infirmities, Mary called Magdalene, out of whom went seven devils,	And certain women, **who** had been healed of evil spirits and infirmities, Mary called Magdalene, out of whom went seven devils,
Luke 8:3 And Joanna the wife of Chuza Herod's steward, and Susanna, and many others, ~~which~~ ministered unto him ~~of~~ their substance.	And Joanna the wife of Chuza Herod's steward, and Susanna, and many others, **who** ministered unto him **with** their substance.
Luke 8:4 And when much people were gathered together, and were come to him out of every city, he spake by a parable:	And when much people were gathered together, and were come to him out of every city, he spake by a parable **saying,**
Luke 8:8 And ~~other~~ fell on good ground, and sprang up, and bare fruit an hundredfold. And when he had said these things, he cried, He **who** hath ears to hear, let him hear.	And **others** fell on good ground, and sprang up, and bare fruit a hundredfold. And when he had said these things, he cried, He **who** hath ears to hear, let him hear.
Luke 8:12 ~~Those~~ by the way side are they ~~that~~ hear; ~~then cometh~~ the devil, and taketh away the word out of their hearts, lest they should believe and be saved.	**That which fell** by the way side are they **who** hear; **and** the devil **cometh,** and taketh away the word out of their hearts, lest they should believe and be saved.
Luke 8:13 ~~They~~ on the rock *are they,* ~~which~~, when they hear, receive the word with joy; and ~~these~~ have no root, ~~which~~ for a while believe, and in time of temptation fall away.	**That which fell** on the rock are they, **who,** when they hear, receive the word with joy; and **they** have no root, **but** for a while believe, and in **a** time of temptation fall away.
Luke 8:14 And that which fell among thorns are they, ~~which~~, when they have heard, go forth, and are choked with cares and riches and pleasures of ~~this~~ life, and bring no fruit to perfection.	And that which fell among thorns are they, **who,** when they have heard, go forth, and are choked with cares and riches and pleasures of life, and bring no fruit to perfection.
Luke 8:15 But that on the good ground are they, ~~which~~ in an honest and good heart, having heard the word, ~~keep it~~, and ~~bring~~ forth fruit with patience.	But that **which fell** on the good ground are they, **who receive the word** in an honest and good heart, having heard the word, **keepeth what they hear,** and **bringeth** forth fruit with patience.

Luke 8:16 No man, when he hath lighted a candle, covereth it with a vessel, or putteth *it* under a bed; but ~~setteth~~ *it* on a candlestick, that they ~~which~~ enter in may see the light.	**For** no man, when he hath lighted a candle, covereth it with a vessel, or putteth it under a bed; but **sitteth** it on a candlestick, that they **who** enter in may see the light.
Luke 8:17 For nothing is secret, ~~that~~ shall not be made manifest; neither ~~any thing~~ hid, ~~that~~ shall not be known and ~~come~~ abroad.	For nothing is secret, **which** shall not be made manifest; neither hid, **which** shall not be **made** known and **go** abroad.
Luke 8:18 Take heed therefore how ye hear: for whosoever ~~hath,~~ to him shall be given; and whosoever ~~hath~~ not, from him shall be taken even that which he seemeth to have.	Take heed therefore how ye hear: for whosoever **receiveth**, to him shall be given; and whosoever **receiveth** not, from him shall be taken even that which he seemeth to have.
Luke 8:19 Then came to him *his* mother and his brethren, and could not ~~come at~~ him for the ~~press~~.	Then came to him his mother and his brethren, and could not **speak to** him for the **multitude**.
Luke 8:20 And ~~it was told him~~ *by* ~~certain which~~ said, Thy mother and thy brethren stand without, desiring to see thee.	And **some who stood** by said **unto him**, Thy mother and thy brethren stand without, desiring to see thee.
Luke 8:21 And he answered and said unto them, My mother and my brethren are ~~these which~~ hear the word of God, and do it.	And he answered and said unto them, My mother and my brethren are **those who** hear the word of God, and do it.
Luke 8:23 But as they sailed he fell asleep: and there came down a storm of wind on the lake; and they were filled *with* ~~water,~~ and were in ~~jeopardy~~.	But as they sailed he fell asleep: and there came down a storm of wind on the lake; and they were filled with **fear**, and were in **danger**.
Luke 8:27 And when he went forth to land, there met him out of the city a certain man, ~~which~~ had devils long time, and ware no clothes, neither abode in ~~any~~ house, but in the tombs.	And when he went forth to land, there met him out of the city a certain man, **who** had devils **for a** long time, and **he would** ware no clothes, neither abode in a house, but in the tombs.
Luke 8:29 (For he had commanded the unclean spirit to come out of the man. For ~~oftentimes~~ it had caught him: and he was kept bound with chains and in	(For he had commanded the unclean spirit to come out of the man. For **oft times** it had caught him: and he was kept bound with chains and in fetters;

fetters; and he brake the bands, and was driven of the devil into the wilderness.)

Luke 8:30 ~~And~~ Jesus asked him, saying, What is thy name? And he said, Legion: because many devils were entered into him.

Luke 8:31 ~~And they besought him that he would not command them to go out into the deep~~.

Luke 8:32 And there was there an herd of many swine feeding on the mountain: and they besought him that he would suffer them to enter into ~~them~~. And he suffered them.

Luke 8:34 When they ~~that~~ fed ~~them~~ saw what was done, they fled, and went and told ~~it~~ in the city and in the country.

Luke 8:36 They also ~~which~~ saw ~~it~~ told them by what means he ~~that~~ was possessed of the devils was healed.

Luke 8:37 Then the whole multitude of the country of the Gadarenes round about besought ~~him~~ to depart from them; for they were taken with great fear: and ~~he~~ went up into the ship, and returned back again.

Luke 8:40 And it came to pass, that, when Jesus was returned, the people ~~gladly~~ received him: for they were all waiting for him.

Luke 8:43 And a woman having an issue of blood twelve years, ~~which~~ had spent all her living upon physicians, neither could be healed of any,

and he brake the bands, and was driven of the devil into the wilderness.)

Jesus asked him, saying, What is thy name? And he said, Legion: because many devils were entered into him.

And there was there a herd of many swine feeding on the mountain: and they besought him that he would suffer them to enter into **the swine**. And he suffered them. **And they besought him also, that he would not command them to go out into the deep. And he said unto them, Come out of the man.**

When they **who** fed **the swine** saw what was done, they fled, and went and told **the people** in the city and in the country.

They also, **who** saw **the miracle**, told them by what means he **who** was possessed of the devils was healed.

Then the whole multitude of the country of the Gadarenes round about besought **Jesus** to depart from them; for they were taken with great fear: and **Jesus** went up into the ship, and returned back again.

And it came to pass, that, when Jesus was returned, **that** the people received him: for they were all waiting for him.

And a woman having an issue of blood twelve years, **who** had spent all her living upon physicians, neither could be healed of any,

Luke 8:44 Came behind ~~him~~, and touched the border of his garment: and immediately her issue of blood stanched.

Luke 8:45 And Jesus said, Who touched me? When all denied, Peter and they ~~that~~ were with him said, Master, the multitude throng thee and press *thee*, and sayest thou, Who touched me?

Luke 8:46 And Jesus said, ~~Somebody~~ hath touched me: for I perceive that virtue is gone out of me.

Luke 8:47 And when the woman ~~saw~~ that she was not hid, she came trembling, and falling down before him, she declared unto him before all the people for what cause she had touched him, and how she was healed immediately.

Luke 8:50 But ~~when~~ Jesus heard ~~it~~, he ~~answered him, saying~~, Fear not: believe only, and she shall be made whole.

Luke 8:52 And all wept, and bewailed her: but he said, Weep not; she is not dead, but sleepeth.

Luke 8:54 And he put them all out, and took her by the hand, and called, saying, Maid, arise.

Luke 9:1 Then he called his twelve disciples together, and gave them power and authority over all devils, and to cure diseases.

Luke 9:4 And whatsoever house ye enter ~~into~~, there abide, ~~and~~ thence ~~depart~~.

Luke 9:7 Now Herod the tetrarch heard of all that was done by ~~him~~: and he was perplexed, because that it was said

Came behind **Jesus**, and touched the border of his garment: and immediately her issue of blood stanched.

And Jesus said, Who touched me? When all denied, Peter and they **who** were with him said, Master, the multitude throng thee and press **upon** thee, and sayest thou, Who touched me?

And Jesus said, **Someone** hath touched me: for I perceive that virtue is gone out of me.

And when the woman **found** that she was not hid, she came trembling, and falling down before him, she declared unto him before all the people for what cause she had touched him, and how she was healed immediately.

But Jesus heard **him, and** he **said unto the ruler of the synagogue**, Fear not: believe only, and she shall be made whole.

And all wept, and bewailed her: but he said, Weep not; **for** she is not dead, but sleepeth.

And he put them all out, and took her by the hand, and **he** called, saying, Maid, arise.

Then he called his twelve disciples together, and **he** gave them power and authority over all devils, and to cure diseases.

And **into** whatsoever house ye enter, there abide **until ye depart** thence.

Now Herod the tetrarch heard of all that was done by **Jesus**: and he was perplexed, because that it was said of some,

The Gospel According to St Luke

of some, that John was risen from the dead;

Luke 9:10 And the apostles, when they ~~were~~ returned, told ~~him~~ all that they had done. And he took them, and went aside privately into a ~~desert~~ place belonging to the city called Bethsaida.

Luke 9:11 And the people, when they knew *it,* followed him: and he received them, and spake unto them of the kingdom of God, and healed them ~~that~~ had need of healing.

Luke 9:12 And when the day began to wear away, then came the twelve, and said unto him, Send the multitude away, that they may go into the towns and country round about, and lodge, and get victuals: for we are here in a ~~desert~~ place.

Luke 9:13 But he said unto them, Give ye them to eat. And they said, We have ~~no more~~ but five loaves and two fishes; except we should go and buy meat for all this ~~people~~.

Luke 9:14 For they were about five thousand men. And ~~he~~ said to his disciples, Make them sit down by fifties in a company.

Luke 9:17 And they did eat, and were all filled: and there ~~was~~ taken up of fragments ~~that~~ remained ~~to them~~ twelve baskets.

Luke 9:18 And it came to pass, as he ~~was~~ alone ~~praying~~, his disciples ~~were with him: and~~ he asked them, saying, ~~Whom~~ say the people that I am?

that John was risen from the dead;

And the apostles, when they returned, told **Jesus** all that they had done. And he took them, and went aside privately into a **solitary** place belonging to the city called Bethsaida.

And the people, when they knew it, followed him: and he received them, and spake unto them of the kingdom of God, and healed them **who** had need of healing.

And when the day began to wear away, then came the twelve, and said unto him, Send the multitude away, that they may go into the towns and country round about, and lodge, and get victuals: for we are here in a **solitary** place.

But he said unto them, Give ye them to eat. And they said, We have but five loaves and two fishes; **and** except we should go and buy meat, **we can provide no more food** for all this **multitude**.

For they were **in number** about five thousand men. And **Jesus** said to his disciples, Make them sit down by fifties in a company.

And they did eat, and were all filled: and there **were** taken up of fragments **which** remained twelve baskets.

And it came to pass, as he **went** alone **with** his disciples **to pray** he asked them, saying, **Who** say the people that I am?

Luke 9:19 They answering said, John the Baptist; but ~~some~~ say, Elias; and others ~~say~~, that one of the old prophets is risen again.

Luke 9:20 He said unto them, But ~~whom~~ say ye that I am? Peter answering said, The Christ of God.

Luke 9:21 And he straitly charged them, and commanded *them* to tell no man ~~that thing~~;

Luke 9:23 And he said ~~to~~ *them* all, If any ~~man~~ will come after me, let him deny himself, and take up his cross daily, and follow me.

Luke 9:24 For whosoever will save his life ~~shall~~ lose it: ~~but~~ whosoever will lose his life for my sake, the same shall save it.

Luke 9:25 For what ~~is~~ a man ~~advantaged~~, if he gain the whole world, and lose himself, ~~or~~ be cast away?

Luke 9:26 For whosoever shall be ashamed of me and of my words, of him shall the Son of man be ashamed, when he shall come in his own ~~glory, and~~ *in his* ~~Father's~~, ~~and of~~ the holy angels.

Luke 9:27 ~~But~~ I tell you of a truth, there ~~be~~ some standing here, ~~which~~ shall not taste of death, ~~till~~ they see the kingdom of God.

Luke 9:28 And it came to pass ~~about an~~ eight days after these sayings, he took Peter and John and James, and went up into a mountain to pray.

They answering said, **Some say**, John the Baptist; but **others** say, Elias; and others, that one of the old prophets is risen again.

He said unto them, But **who** say ye that I am? Peter answering said, The Christ, **the Son** of God.

And he straitly charged them, and commanded them to tell no man **of him**;

And he said **unto** them, If any man will come after me, let him deny himself, and take up his cross daily, and follow me.

For whosoever will save his life **must be willing to** lose it **for my sake: and** whosoever will **be willing to** lose his life for my sake, the same shall save it.

For what **doth it profit** a man, if he gain the whole world, and **yet he receive him not whom God hath ordained, and he** lose **his own soul, and he himself** be a cast away?

For whosoever shall be ashamed of me and of my words, of him shall the Son of man be ashamed, when he shall come in his own **kingdom, clothed** in **the glory of** his **Father, with** the holy angels.

Verily I tell you of a truth, there **are** some standing here, **who** shall not taste of death, **until** they see the kingdom of God **coming in power.**

And it came to pass eight days after these sayings, **that** he took Peter and John and James, and went up into a mountain to pray.

The Gospel According to St Luke

Luke 9:29 And as he prayed, the fashion of his countenance was ~~altered~~, and his raiment ~~was~~ white *and* ~~glistering~~.	And as he prayed, the fashion of his countenance was **changed**, and his raiment **became** white and **glittering**.
Luke 9:30 And, behold, there talked with him two men, ~~which were~~ Moses and Elias:	And, behold, there **came and** talked with him two men, **even** Moses and Elias:
Luke 9:31 Who appeared in glory, and spake of his ~~decease~~ which he should accomplish at Jerusalem.	Who appeared in glory, and spake of his **death, and also his resurrection**, which he should accomplish at Jerusalem.
Luke 9:32 But Peter and they ~~that~~ were with him were heavy with sleep: and when they were awake, they saw his glory, and the two men ~~that~~ stood with him.	But Peter and they **who** were with him were heavy with sleep: and when they were awake, they saw his glory, and the two men **who** stood with him.
Luke 9:33 And ~~it came to pass, as they~~ departed from him, Peter said unto Jesus, Master, it is good for us to be here: ~~and~~ let us make three tabernacles; one for thee, and one for Moses, and one for Elias: not knowing what he said.	And **after the two men** departed from him, Peter said unto Jesus, Master, it is good for us to be here: let us make three tabernacles; one for thee, and one for Moses, and one for Elias: not knowing what he said.
Luke 9:34 While he thus spake, there came a cloud, and overshadowed them: and they feared as they entered into the cloud.	While he thus spake, there came a cloud, and overshadowed them **all**: and they feared as they entered into the cloud.
Luke 9:36 And when the voice was past, Jesus was found alone. And they kept ~~it~~ close, and told no man in those days any of ~~those~~ things which they had seen.	And when the voice was past, Jesus was found alone. And **these things** they kept close, and **they** told no man in those days any of **the** things which they had seen.
Luke 9:39 And, lo, a spirit taketh him, and he suddenly crieth out; and it teareth him that he foameth ~~again~~, and bruising him hardly departeth from him.	And, lo, a spirit taketh him, and he suddenly crieth out; and it teareth him that he foameth, and bruising him hardly, departeth from him.
Luke 9:42 And as he was ~~yet a~~ coming, the devil threw him down, and tare *him*. And Jesus rebuked the unclean spirit,	And as he was coming, the devil threw him down, and tare him **again**. And Jesus rebuked the unclean spirit, and

and healed the child, and delivered him again to his father.

Luke 9:44 Let these sayings sink down into your ~~ears~~: for the Son of man shall be delivered into the hands of ~~men~~.

Luke 9:46 Then there arose a reasoning among them, ~~which~~ of them should be greatest.

Luke 9:47 And Jesus, perceiving the ~~thought~~ of their ~~heart~~, took a child, and set him ~~by him~~,

Luke 9:48 And said unto them, Whosoever shall receive this child in my name receiveth me: and whosoever shall receive me receiveth him that sent me: for he ~~that~~ is least among you all, the same shall be great.

Luke 9:49 And John ~~answered~~ and said, Master, we saw one casting out devils in thy name; and we forbad him, because he followeth not with us.

Luke 9:50 And Jesus said unto him, Forbid ~~him~~ not: for he that is not against us is for us.

Luke 9:53 And ~~they did~~ not receive him, because his face was as though he would go to Jerusalem.

Luke 9:54 And when his disciples James and John saw ~~this~~, they said, Lord, wilt thou that we command fire to come down from heaven, and consume them, even as Elias did?

Luke 9:57 And it came to pass, ~~that~~, as they went in the way, a certain *man* said unto him, Lord, I will follow thee whithersoever thou goest.

healed the child, and delivered him again to his father.

Let these sayings sink down into your **hearts**: for the Son of man shall be delivered into the hands of **man**.

Then there arose a reasoning among them, **who** of them should be greatest.

And Jesus, perceiving the **thoughts** of their **hearts**, took a child, and set him **in the midst**,

And said unto them, Whosoever shall receive this child in my name receiveth me: and whosoever shall receive me receiveth him that sent me: for he **who** is least among you all, the same shall be great.

And John **spake** and said, Master, we saw one casting out devils in thy name; and we forbad him, because he followeth not with us.

And Jesus said unto him, Forbid not **any**: for he that is not against us is for us.

And **the Samaritans would** not receive him, because his face was **turned** as though he would go to Jerusalem.

And when his disciples James and John saw **that they would not receive him**, they said, Lord, wilt thou that we command fire to come down from heaven, and consume them, even as Elias did?

And it came to pass, as they went in the way, a certain man said unto him, Lord, I will follow thee whithersoever thou goest.

Luke 9:58 And Jesus said unto him, Foxes have holes, and birds of the air ~~have~~ nests; but the Son of man hath not where to lay *his* head.

Luke 9:61 And another also said, Lord, I will follow thee; but let me first go bid them farewell, ~~which~~ are ~~at home~~ at my house.

Luke 10:1 After these things the Lord appointed other seventy also, and sent them two and two before his face into every city and place, ~~whither~~ he himself would come.

Luke 10:2 ~~Therefore~~ said ~~he~~ unto them, The harvest truly *is* great, but the labourers ~~are~~ few: pray ye therefore the Lord of the harvest, that he would send forth labourers into his harvest.

Luke 10:4 Carry neither purse, nor scrip, nor shoes: ~~and~~ salute ~~no~~ man by the way.

Luke 10:5 And into whatsoever house ~~ye~~ enter, first say, Peace ~~be~~ to this house.

Luke 10:7 And in ~~the same~~ house remain, eating and drinking such things as they give: for the labourer is worthy of his hire. Go not from house to house.

Luke 10:8 And into whatsoever city ~~ye~~ enter, and they receive you, eat such things as are set before you:

Luke 10:9 And heal the sick that are therein, and say ~~unto them~~, The kingdom of God is come nigh unto you.

Luke 10:10 But into whatsoever city ~~ye~~ enter, and they receive you not, go your ways out into the streets of the same, and say,

And Jesus said unto him, Foxes have holes, and birds of the air nests; but the Son of man hath not where to lay his head.

And another also said, Lord, I will follow thee; but let me first go bid them farewell, **who** are at my house.

After these things the Lord appointed other seventy also, and sent them two and two before his face into every city and place, **where** he himself would come.

And he said unto them, The harvest truly is great, but the labourers few: pray ye therefore the Lord of the harvest, that he would send forth labourers into his harvest.

Carry neither purse, nor scrip, nor shoes: **nor** salute **any** man by the way.

And into whatsoever house **you** enter, first say, Peace to this house.

And in **whatsoever** house **they receive you**, remain, eating and drinking such things as they give: for the labourer is worthy of his hire. Go not from house to house.

And into whatsoever city **you** enter, and they receive you, eat such things as are set before you.

And heal the sick that are therein, and say, The kingdom of God is come nigh unto you.

But into whatsoever city **you** enter, and they receive you not, go your ways out into the streets of the same, and say,

Luke 10:11 Even the very dust of your city, which cleaveth on us, we do wipe off against you: notwithstanding be ~~ye~~ sure of this, that the kingdom of God is come nigh unto you.

Luke 10:12 But I say unto you, that it shall be more tolerable in ~~that~~ day for Sodom, than for that city.

Luke 10:13 Woe unto thee, Chorazin! woe unto thee, Bethsaida! for if the mighty works had been done in Tyre and Sidon, which have been done in you, they ~~had a great while ago~~ repented, sitting in sackcloth and ashes.

Luke 10:14 But it shall be more tolerable for Tyre and Sidon ~~at~~ the judgment, than for you.

Luke 10:15 And thou, Capernaum, which art exalted to heaven, ~~shalt~~ be ~~thrust~~ down to hell.

Luke 10:16 He that heareth you heareth me; and he that despiseth you despiseth me; and he that despiseth me despiseth him ~~that~~ sent me.

Luke 10:18 And he said unto them, I beheld Satan ~~as lightning fall from heaven~~.

Luke 10:19 Behold, I give unto you ~~power to tread on~~ serpents and scorpions, and over all the power of the enemy: and nothing shall by any means hurt you.

Luke 10:21 In that hour Jesus rejoiced in spirit, and said, I thank thee, O

Even the very dust of your city, which cleaveth on us, we do wipe off against you: notwithstanding be sure of this, that the kingdom of God is come nigh unto you.

But I say unto you, that it shall be more tolerable in **the** day **of judgment,** for Sodom, than for that city.

Then began he to upbraid the people in every city wherein his mighty works were done, who received him not, saying, Woe unto thee, Chorazin! woe unto thee, Bethsaida! for if the mighty works had been done in Tyre and Sidon, which have been done in you, they **would have** repented, sitting in sackcloth and ashes.

But it shall be more tolerable for Tyre and Sidon **in** the **day of** judgment, than for you.

And thou, Capernaum, which art exalted to heaven, **shall** be **cast** down to hell.

And he said unto his disciples, He that heareth you heareth me; and he that despiseth you despiseth me; and he that despiseth me despiseth him **who** sent me.

And he said unto them, **As lightning falleth from heaven,** I beheld Satan **also falling**.

Behold, I **will** give unto you power **over** serpents and scorpions, and over all the power of the enemy: and nothing shall by any means hurt you.

In that hour Jesus rejoiced in spirit, and said, I thank thee, O Father, Lord

Father, Lord of heaven and earth, that thou hast hid these things from ~~the~~ wise and prudent, and hast revealed them unto babes: even so, Father; for so it seemed good in thy sight.

Luke 10:22 All things are delivered to me of my Father: and no man knoweth ~~who~~ the Son is~~, but~~ the Father; and ~~who~~ the Father is, ~~but~~ the Son, ~~and he~~ to whom the Son will reveal ~~him~~.

Luke 10:23 And he turned him unto ~~his~~ disciples, and said privately, Blessed *are* the eyes which see the things that ye see:

Luke 10:30 And Jesus answering said, A certain *man* went down from Jerusalem to Jericho, and fell among thieves, ~~which~~ stripped him of his raiment, and wounded *him,* and departed, leaving *him* half dead.

Luke 10:31 And by chance there came down a certain priest that way: and when he saw him, he passed by on the other side.

Luke 10:32 And likewise a Levite, when he was at the place, came and looked ~~on~~ *him,* and passed by on the other side.

Luke 10:35 And on the morrow when he departed, he took ~~out two pence~~, and gave ~~them~~ to the host, and said unto him, Take care of him; and whatsoever thou spendest more, when I come again, I will repay thee.

Luke 10:36 ~~Which~~ now of these three, thinkest thou, was neighbour unto him ~~that~~ fell among the thieves?

of heaven and earth, that thou hast hid these things from **them who think they are** wise and prudent, and hast revealed them unto babes: even so, Father; for so it seemed good in thy sight.

All things are delivered to me of my Father: and no man knoweth **that** the Son is the Father; and **that** the Father is the Son, **but him** to whom the Son will reveal **it**.

And he turned him unto **the** disciples, and said privately, Blessed are the eyes which see the things that ye see:

And Jesus answering said, A certain man went down from Jerusalem to Jericho, and fell among thieves, **who** stripped him of his raiment, and wounded him, and departed, leaving him half dead.

And by chance there came down a certain priest that way: and when he saw him, he passed by on the other side **of the way.**

And likewise a Levite, when he was at the place, came and looked **upon** him, and passed by on the other side **of the way; for they desired in their hearts that it might not be known that they had seen him.**

And on the morrow when he departed, he took **money**, and gave to the host, and said unto him, Take care of him; and whatsoever thou spendest more, when I come again, I will repay thee.

Who now of these three, thinkest thou, was neighbour unto him **who** fell among the thieves?

Luke 10:37 And he said, He ~~that~~ shewed mercy on him. Then said Jesus unto him, Go, and do ~~thou~~ likewise.

Luke 10:38 Now it came to pass, as they went, that ~~he~~ entered into a certain village: and a certain woman named Martha received him into her house.

Luke 10:39 And she had a sister called Mary, ~~which~~ also sat at Jesus' feet, and heard his word.

Luke 11:1 And it came to pass, ~~that~~, as ~~he~~ was praying in a certain place, when he ceased, one of his disciples said unto him, Lord, teach us to pray, as John also taught his disciples.

Luke 11:2 And he said unto them, When ye pray, say, Our Father ~~which~~ art in heaven, Hallowed be thy name. Thy kingdom come. Thy will be done, as in heaven, so in earth.

Luke 11:4 And forgive us our sins; for we also forgive every one ~~that~~ is indebted to us. And ~~lead~~ us not ~~into~~ temptation; but deliver us from evil.

Luke 11:5 And he ~~said unto them~~, Which of you shall have a friend, and shall go unto him at midnight, and say unto him, Friend, lend me three loaves;

Luke 11:6 For a friend of mine in his journey ~~is come to me~~, and I have nothing to set before him?

Luke 11:10 For every one ~~that~~ asketh receiveth; and he that seeketh findeth; and to him that knocketh it shall be opened.

And he said, He **who** shewed mercy on him. Then said Jesus unto him, Go, and do likewise.

Now it came to pass, as they went, that **they** entered into a certain village: and a certain woman named Martha received him into her house.

And she had a sister called Mary, **who** also sat at Jesus' feet, and heard his word.

And it came to pass, as **Jesus** was praying in a certain place, when he ceased, one of his disciples said unto him, Lord, teach us to pray, as John also taught his disciples.

And he said unto them, When ye pray, say, Our Father **who** art in heaven, Hallowed be thy name. Thy kingdom come. Thy will be done, as in heaven, so in earth.

And forgive us our sins; for we also forgive every one **who** is indebted to us. And **let** us not **be led unto** temptation; but deliver us from evil; **for thine is the kingdom, and power. Amen. And he said unto them, Your heavenly Father will not fail to give unto you whatsoever ye ask of him.**

And he **spake a parable, saying**, Which of you shall have a friend, and shall go unto him at midnight, and say unto him, Friend, lend me three loaves;

For a friend of mine **has come to me** in his journey, and I have nothing to set before him?

For every one **who** asketh receiveth; and he that seeketh findeth; and to him that knocketh it shall be opened.

The Gospel According to St Luke

Luke 11:11 If a son shall ask bread of any of you ~~that~~ is a father, will he give him a stone? or if ~~he ask~~ a fish, will he for a fish give him a serpent?

Luke 11:13 If ye then, being evil, know how to give good gifts unto your children: how much more shall *your* heavenly Father give the Holy Spirit to them ~~that~~ ask him?

Luke 11:14 And he was casting ~~out~~ a devil, and ~~it~~ was dumb. And it came to pass, when the devil was gone out, the dumb spake; and the people wondered.

Luke 11:16 And others, tempting ~~him~~, sought of him a sign from heaven.

Luke 11:17 But he, knowing their thoughts, said unto them, Every kingdom divided against itself is brought to desolation; and a house *divided* ~~against a house~~ falleth.

Luke 11:18 If Satan also be divided against himself, how ~~shall~~ his kingdom stand? because ~~ye~~ say ~~that~~ I cast out devils through Beelzebub.

Luke 11:19 And if I by Beelzebub cast out devils, by whom do your sons cast ~~them~~ out? therefore shall they be your judges.

Luke 11:20 But if I with the finger of God cast out devils, no doubt the kingdom of God ~~is~~ come upon you.

Luke 11:22 But when a stronger than he shall come upon him, and overcome him, he taketh from him all his armour wherein he trusted, and divideth his ~~spoils~~.

If a son shall ask bread of any of you **who** is a father, will he give him a stone? or if a fish, will he for a fish give him a serpent?

If ye then, being evil, know how to give good gifts unto your children: how much more shall your heavenly Father give **good gifts, through** the Holy Spirit, to them **who** ask him?

And he was casting a devil **out of a man**, and **he** was dumb. And it came to pass, when the devil was gone out, the dumb spake; and the people wondered.

And others, tempting, sought of him a sign from heaven.

But he, knowing their thoughts, said unto them, Every kingdom divided against itself is brought to desolation; and a house divided **cannot stand, but** falleth.

If Satan also be divided against himself, how **can** his kingdom stand? **I say this** because **you** say I cast out devils through Beelzebub.

And if I by Beelzebub cast out devils, by whom do your sons cast out **devils**? therefore shall they be your judges.

But if I with the finger of God cast out devils, no doubt the kingdom of God **has** come upon you.

But when a stronger than he shall come upon him, and overcome him, he taketh from him all his armour wherein he trusted, and divideth his **goods**.

Luke 11:23 He that is not with me is against me: and he ~~that~~ gathereth not with me scattereth.	He that is not with me is against me: and he **who** gathereth not with me scattereth.
Luke 11:24 When the unclean spirit is gone out of a man, ~~he~~ walketh through dry places, seeking rest; and finding none, ~~he~~ saith, I will return ~~unto my~~ house whence I came out.	When the unclean spirit is gone out of a man, **it** walketh through dry places, seeking rest; and finding none, **it** saith, I will return **into mine** house whence I came out.
Luke 11:25 And when ~~he~~ cometh, ~~he~~ findeth ~~it~~ swept and garnished.	And when **it** cometh, **it** findeth **the house** swept and garnished.
Luke 11:26 Then goeth ~~he~~, and taketh ~~to him~~ seven other spirits more wicked than himself; and they enter in, and dwell there: and the last ~~state~~ of that man is worse than the first.	Then goeth **the evil spirit**, and taketh seven other spirits more wicked than himself; and they enter in, and dwell there: and the last **end** of that man is worse than the first.
Luke 11:27 And it came to pass, as he spake these things, a certain woman of the company lifted up her voice, and said unto him, Blessed *is* the womb ~~that~~ bare thee, and the paps which thou hast sucked.	And it came to pass, as he spake these things, a certain woman of the company lifted up her voice, and said unto him, Blessed is the womb **which** bare thee, and the paps which thou hast sucked.
Luke 11:28 ~~But~~ he said, Yea ~~rather~~, blessed *are* they ~~that~~ hear the word of God, and keep it.	**And** he said, Yea, **and** blessed are **all** they **who** hear the word of God, and keep it.
Luke 11:29 ~~And~~ when the people were gathered thick together, he began to say, This is an evil generation: they seek a sign; and there shall no sign be given ~~it~~, but the sign of Jonas the prophet.	When the people were gathered thick together, he began to say, This is an evil generation: they seek a sign; and there shall no sign be given **them**, but the sign of Jonas the prophet.
Luke 11:31 The queen of the south shall rise up in the judgment with the men of this generation, and condemn them: for she came from the utmost parts of the earth to hear the wisdom of Solomon; and, behold, a greater than Solomon *is* here.	The queen of the south shall rise up in the **day of** judgment with the men of this generation, and condemn them: for she came from the utmost parts of the earth to hear the wisdom of Solomon; and, behold, a greater than Solomon is here.
Luke 11:32 The men of Nineve shall rise up in the judgment with this	The men of Nineveh shall rise up in the **day of** judgment with this generation,

generation, and shall condemn it: for they repented at the preaching of Jonas; and, behold, a greater than Jonas *is* here.

Luke 11:33 No man, when he hath lighted a candle, putteth *it* in a secret place, neither under a bushel, but on a candlestick, that they ~~which~~ come in may see the light.

Luke 11:36 If thy whole body therefore ~~be~~ full of light, having no part dark, the whole shall be full of light, as when the bright shining of a candle doth give thee light.

Luke 11:38 And when the Pharisee saw ~~it~~, he marvelled that he had not first washed before dinner.

Luke 11:39 And the Lord said unto him, Now do ~~ye~~ Pharisees make clean the outside of the cup and the platter; but your inward part is full of ravening and wickedness.

Luke 11:40 ~~Ye~~ fools, did not he ~~that~~ made that which is without make that which is within also?

Luke 11:41 But rather give alms of such things as ye have; and, ~~behold,~~ all things ~~are~~ clean ~~unto you~~.

Luke 11:42 But woe unto you, Pharisees! for ye tithe mint and rue and all manner of herbs, and pass over judgment and the love of God: these ought ye to have done, and not to leave the other undone.

Luke 11:43 Woe unto you, Pharisees! for ~~ye~~ love the uppermost seats in the synagogues, and greetings in the markets.

and shall condemn it: for they repented at the preaching of Jonas; and, behold, a greater than Jonas is here.

No man, when he hath lighted a candle, putteth it in a secret place, neither under a bushel, but on a candlestick, that they **who** come in may see the light.

If thy whole body therefore **is** full of light, having no part dark, the whole shall be full of light, as when the bright shining of a candle **lighteneth a room, and** doth give thee light **in all the room**.

And when the Pharisee saw **him**, he marvelled that he had not first washed before dinner.

And the Lord said unto him, Now do **you** Pharisees make clean the outside of the cup and the platter; but your inward part is full of ravening and wickedness.

O, fools, did not he **who** made that which is without make that which is within also?

But **if ye would** rather give alms of such things as ye have; and, **observe to do** all things **which I have commanded you, then would your inward parts be** clean **also**.

But **I say unto you,** Woe **be** unto you, Pharisees! for ye tithe mint and rue and all manner of herbs, and pass over judgment and the love of God: these ought ye to have done, and not to leave the other undone.

Woe unto you, Pharisees! for **you** love the uppermost seats in the synagogues, and greetings in the markets.

Luke 11:44 Woe unto you, scribes and Pharisees, hypocrites! for ye are ~~as~~ graves which appear not, and the men ~~that~~ walk over ~~them~~ are not aware *of them*.

Luke 11:46 And he said, Woe unto you ~~also, ye~~ lawyers! for ye lade men with burdens grievous to be borne, and ye yourselves touch not the burdens with one of your fingers.

Luke 11:47 Woe unto you! for ~~ye~~ build the sepulchres of the prophets, and your fathers killed them.

Luke 11:51 From the blood of Abel unto the blood of Zacharias, ~~which~~ perished between the altar and the temple: verily I say unto you, It shall be required of this generation.

Luke 11:52 Woe unto you, lawyers! for ye have taken away the key of knowledge: ye ~~entered~~ not in yourselves, and them ~~that~~ were entering in ye hindered.

Luke 11:53 And as he said these things unto them, the scribes and ~~the~~ Pharisees began to urge ~~him~~ vehemently, ~~and~~ to provoke him to speak of many things:

Luke 12:2 For there is nothing covered, ~~that~~ shall not be revealed; neither hid, ~~that~~ shall not be known.

Luke 12:4 And I say unto you my friends, Be not afraid of them ~~that~~ kill the body, and after that have no more that they can do.

Luke 12:5 But I will forewarn you whom ye shall fear: Fear him, ~~which~~ after he hath killed hath power to cast into hell; yea, I say unto you, Fear him.

Woe unto you, scribes and Pharisees, hypocrites! for ye are graves which appear not, and the men **who** walk over are not aware of them.

And he said, Woe unto you, lawyers, **also**! for ye lade men with burdens grievous to be borne, and ye yourselves touch not the burdens with one of your fingers.

Woe unto you! for **you** build the sepulchres of the prophets, and your fathers killed them.

From the blood of Abel unto the blood of Zacharias, **who** perished between the altar and the temple: verily I say unto you, It shall be required of this generation.

Woe unto you, lawyers! for ye have taken away the key of knowledge, **the fulness of the scriptures. Ye enter** not in yourselves **into the kingdom**, and them **who** were entering in ye hindered.

And as he said these things unto them, the scribes and Pharisees began to **be angry, and to** urge vehemently, **endeavouring** to provoke him to speak of many things:

For there is nothing covered, **which** shall not be revealed; neither hid, **which** shall not be known.

And I say unto you my friends, Be not afraid of them **who** kill the body, and after that have no more that they can do.

But I will forewarn you whom ye shall fear: Fear him, **who** after he hath killed hath power to cast into hell; yea, I say unto you, Fear him.

Luke 12:9 But he ~~that~~ denieth me before men shall be denied before the angels of God.	But he **who** denieth me before men shall be denied before the angels of God. **Now his disciples knew that he said this, because they had spoken evil against him before the people; for they were afraid to confess him before men. And they reasoned among themselves, saying, He knoweth our hearts, and he speaketh to our condemnation, and we shall not be forgiven.**
Luke 12:10 And whosoever shall speak a word against the Son of man, it shall be forgiven him: but unto him ~~that~~ blasphemeth against the Holy Ghost it shall not be forgiven.	**But he answered them, and said unto them,** Whosoever shall speak a word against the Son of man, **and repenteth,** it shall be forgiven him: but unto him **who** blasphemeth against the Holy Ghost it shall not be forgiven **him**.
Luke 12:11 And ~~when~~ they bring you unto the synagogues, and ~~unto~~ magistrates, and powers, take ye no thought how or what thing ye shall answer, or what ye shall say:	And **again I say unto you,** They **shall** bring you unto the synagogues, and **before** magistrates, and powers, **when they do this,** take ye no thought how or what thing ye shall answer, or what ye shall say:
Luke 12:21 So ~~is he that~~ layeth up treasure for himself, and is not rich toward God.	So **shall it be with him who** layeth up treasure for himself, and is not rich toward God.
Luke 12:23 The life is more than meat, and the body ~~is more~~ than raiment.	**For** the life is more than meat, and the body than raiment.
Luke 12:24 Consider the ravens: for they neither sow nor reap; which neither have storehouse nor barn; ~~and~~ God feedeth them: ~~how much more~~ are ye better than the fowls?	Consider the ravens: for they neither sow nor reap; which neither have storehouse nor barn; **nevertheless** God feedeth them: are ye **not** better than the fowls?
Luke 12:25 And ~~which~~ of you ~~with~~ taking thought can add to his stature one cubit?	And **who** of you **by** taking thought can add to his stature one cubit?
Luke 12:26 If ye then be not able to do that ~~thing~~ which is least, why take ye thought for the rest?	If ye then be not able to do that which is least, why take ye thought for the rest?

Luke 12:28 If then God so clothe the grass, which is to day in the field, and to morrow is cast into the oven; how much more *will he clothe* you, O ye of little faith?

Luke 12:29 And seek not ye what ye shall eat, or what ye shall drink, neither be ye of doubtful mind.

Luke 12:30 For all these things do the nations of the world seek after: and your Father knoweth that ye have need of these things.

Luke 12:31 But rather seek ye the kingdom of God; and all these things shall be added unto you.

Luke 12:33 Sell that ye have, and give alms; provide yourselves bags which wax old, a treasure in the heavens that faileth not, where no thief approacheth, neither moth corrupteth.

Luke 12:35 Let your loins be girded about, and *your* lights burning;

Luke 12:36 And ye yourselves like unto men that wait for their lord, when he will return from the wedding; that when he cometh and knocketh, they may open unto him immediately.

Luke 12:37 Blessed *are* those servants, whom the lord when he cometh shall find watching: he shall gird himself, and make them to sit down to meat, and will come forth and serve them.

If then God so clothe the grass, which is to day in the field, and to morrow is cast into the oven; how much more will he **provide for** you, **if** ye **are not** of little faith?

Therefore seek not what ye shall eat, or what ye shall drink, neither be ye of doubtful mind.

For all these things do the nations of the world seek after: and your Father **who is in heaven** knoweth that ye have need of these things. **And ye are sent unto them to be their ministers, and the labourer is worthy of his hire; for the law saith, that a man shall not muzzle the ox that treadeth out the corn.**

Therefore, seek ye **to bring forth** the kingdom of God; and all these things shall be added unto you.

This he spake unto his disciples, saying, Sell that **you** have, and give alms; provide **not for** yourselves bags which wax old, **but rather provide** a treasure in the heavens that faileth not, where no thief approacheth, neither moth corrupteth.

Let your loins be girded about, and **have** your lights burning;

That ye yourselves **may be** like unto men **who** wait for their lord, when he will return from the wedding; that when he cometh and knocketh, they may open unto him immediately.

Verily I say unto you, Blessed are those servants, whom the lord when he cometh shall find watching: **for** he shall gird himself, and make them sit down to meat, and will come forth and serve them. **For behold, he cometh in the**

The Gospel According to St Luke

Luke 12:38 ~~And if~~ he shall come in the second watch, or come in the third watch, ~~and find them so~~, blessed are those servants.	first watch of the night, and he shall also come in the second watch, and again he shall come in the third watch.
	And verily I say unto you; he hath already come as it is written of him; and again, when he shall come in the second watch, or come in the third watch, blessed are those servants **when he cometh, that he shall find so doing; for the Lord of those servants shall gird himself, and make them to sit down to meat, and will come forth and serve them. And now, verily I say these things unto you, that ye may know this, that the coming of the Lord is as a thief in the night; and it is like unto a man who is an householder, who, if he watcheth not his goods, the thief cometh in an hour of which he is not aware, and taketh his goods, and divideth them among his fellows.**
Luke 12:39 And ~~this know, that~~ if the goodman of the house had known what hour the thief would come, he would have watched, and not have suffered his house to be broken through.	And **they said among themselves, If** the goodman of the house had known what hour the thief would come, he would have watched, and not have suffered his house to be broken through, **and the loss of his goods.**
Luke 12:40 Be ye therefore ready also: for the Son of man cometh at an hour when ye think not.	**And he saith unto them, Verily I say unto you,** Be ye therefore ready also: for the Son of man cometh at an hour when ye think not.
Luke 12:41 Then Peter said unto him, Lord, speakest thou this parable unto us, or ~~even to~~ all?	Then Peter said unto him, Lord, speakest thou this parable unto us, or **unto** all?
Luke 12:42 And the Lord said, ~~Who then is that faithful and wise steward~~, whom ~~his~~ lord shall make ~~ruler~~ over his household, to give ~~them~~ *their* portion of meat in due season?	And the Lord said, **I speak unto those** whom **the Lord** shall make **rulers** over his household, to give **his children** their portion of meat in due season?

Luke 12:43 Blessed ~~is~~ that servant, whom his lord when he cometh ~~shall find~~ so doing.	And they said, Who then is that faithful and wise servant? And the Lord said unto them, it is that servant who watcheth, to impart his portion of meat in due season. Blessed **be** that servant, whom his lord **shall find** when he cometh so doing.
Luke 12:45 But and if that servant say in his heart, My lord delayeth his coming; and shall begin to beat the ~~menservants~~ and maidens, and to eat and drink, and to be drunken;	But **the evil servant is he who is not found watching.** And if that servant **is not found watching, he will** say in his heart, My lord delayeth his coming; and shall begin to beat the **manservants** and **the** maidens, and to eat and drink, and to be drunken;
Luke 12:46 The lord of that servant will come in a day ~~when~~ he looketh not for ~~him~~, and at an hour when he is not aware, and will cut him ~~in sunder~~, and will appoint him his portion with the unbelievers.	The lord of that servant will come in a day he looketh not for, and at an hour when he is not aware, and will cut him **down**, and will appoint him his portion with the unbelievers.
Luke 12:47 And that servant, ~~which~~ knew his lord's will, and prepared not ~~himself~~, neither did according to his will, shall be beaten with many *stripes*.	And that servant, **who** knew his lord's will, and prepared not **for his Lord's coming**, neither did according to his will, shall be beaten with many stripes.
Luke 12:48 But he that knew not, and did commit things worthy of stripes, shall be beaten with few ~~stripes~~. For unto whomsoever much is given, of him shall be much required: and to whom ~~men have~~ committed much, of him ~~they~~ will ask the more.	But he that knew not **his Lord's will,** and did commit things worthy of stripes, shall be beaten with few. For unto whomsoever much is given, of him shall be much required: and to whom **the Lord has** committed much, of him **men** will ask the more; **for they are not well pleased with the Lord's doings**.
Luke 12:49 I am come to send fire on the earth; and what ~~will I~~, if it be already kindled?	**Therefore** I am come to send fire on the earth; and what **is it to you** if **I will that** it be already kindled?
Luke 12:50 But I have a baptism to be baptized with; and how am I straitened ~~till~~ it be accomplished!	But I have a baptism to be baptized with; and how am I straitened **until** it be accomplished!

Luke 12:53 The father shall be divided against the son, and the son against the father; ~~the~~ mother against the daughter, and ~~the~~ daughter against the mother; the mother in law against her daughter in law, and the daughter in law against her mother in law.

Luke 12:54 And he said also ~~to~~ the people, When ye see a cloud rise out of the west, straightway ~~ye say~~, There cometh a shower; and so it is.

Luke 12:55 And when ~~ye see~~ the south wind ~~blow~~, ye say, There will be heat; and it cometh to pass.

Luke 12:56 ~~Ye~~ hypocrites, ye can discern the face of the sky and of the earth; but how is it that ~~ye~~ do not discern this time?

Luke 12:58 ~~When~~ thou ~~goest with~~ thine adversary ~~to the~~ magistrate, ~~as~~ *thou art* in the way, give diligence that thou mayest be delivered from him; lest he hale thee to the judge, and the judge deliver thee to the officer, and the officer cast thee into prison.

Luke 13:1 There were present at that ~~season~~ some ~~that told~~ him of the Galilaeans, whose blood Pilate had mingled with their sacrifices.

Luke 13:2 And Jesus ~~answering~~ said unto them, Suppose ye that these Galilaeans were sinners above all the Galilaeans, because they suffered such things?

Luke 13:3 I tell you, Nay: but, except ~~ye~~ repent, ~~ye~~ shall all likewise perish.

Luke 13:4 Or those eighteen, ~~upon~~ whom the tower in Siloam fell, and slew

The father shall be divided against the son, and the son against the father; mother against the daughter, and daughter against the mother; the mother in law against her daughter in law, and the daughter in law against her mother in law.

And he said also **unto** the people, When ye see a cloud rise out of the west, **ye say**, straightway, There cometh a shower; and so it is.

And when the south wind **blows**, ye say, There will be heat; and it cometh to pass.

O hypocrites, ye can discern the face of the sky and of the earth; but how is it that **you** do not discern this time?

Why goest thou **to** thine adversary **for** a magistrate, **when** thou art in the way **with thine enemy? Why not** give diligence that thou mayest be delivered from him; lest he hale thee to the judge, and the judge deliver thee to the officer, and the officer cast thee into prison.

And there were present at that **time**, some **who spake unto** him of the Galilaeans, whose blood Pilate had mingled with their sacrifices.

And Jesus said unto them, Suppose ye that these Galilaeans were sinners above all the Galilaeans, because they suffered such things?

I tell you, Nay: but, except **you** repent, **you** shall all likewise perish.

Or those eighteen, **on** whom the tower in Siloam fell, and slew them, think ye them, think ye that they were sinners above all men ~~that~~ dwelt in Jerusalem?

Luke 13:6 He spake also this parable; A certain ~~man~~ had a fig tree planted in his vineyard; ~~and~~ he came and sought fruit thereon, and found none.

Luke 13:7 Then said he unto the dresser of his vineyard, Behold, these three years I ~~come~~ seeking fruit on this fig tree, and find none: cut it down; why cumbereth it the ground?

Luke 13:8 And he answering said unto him, Lord, let it alone this year also, till I shall dig about ~~it~~, and dung *it:*

Luke 13:9 And if it bear fruit, ~~well~~: and if not, ~~then~~ after that thou shalt cut it down.

Luke 13:10 And he was teaching in one of the synagogues on the sabbath.

Luke 13:11 ~~And~~, behold, there was a woman ~~which~~ had a spirit of infirmity eighteen years, and was bowed together, and could in no wise ~~lift~~ up ~~herself~~.

Luke 13:12 And when Jesus saw her, he called ~~her to him~~, and said unto her, Woman, thou art loosed from thine ~~infirmity~~.

Luke 13:13 And he laid ~~his~~ hands on her: and immediately she was made straight, and glorified God.

Luke 13:14 And the ruler of the synagogue ~~answered~~ with indignation, because that Jesus had healed on the sabbath day, and said unto the people, There are six days in which men ought to work: in them therefore come and be healed, and not on the sabbath day.

that they were sinners above all men **who** dwelt in Jerusalem?

He spake also this parable; A certain **husbandman** had a fig tree planted in his vineyard. He came and sought fruit thereon, and found none.

Then said he unto the dresser of his vineyard, Behold, these three years I **came** seeking fruit on this fig tree, and find none: cut it down; why cumbereth it the ground?

And he answering said unto him, Lord, let it alone this year also, till I shall dig about, and dung it:

And if it bear fruit, **the tree is saved**: and if not, after that thou shalt cut it down. **And many other parables spake he unto the people.**

And **after this, as** he was teaching in one of the synagogues on the sabbath.

Behold, there was a woman **who** had a spirit of infirmity eighteen years, and was bowed together, and could in no wise **straighten** up.

And when Jesus saw her, he called and said unto her, Woman, thou art loosed from thine **infirmities**.

And he laid hands on her: and immediately she was made straight, and glorified God.

And the ruler of the synagogue **was filled** with indignation, because that Jesus had healed on the sabbath day, and said unto the people, There are six days in which men ought to work: in them therefore come and be healed, and not on the sabbath day.

The Gospel According to St Luke

Luke 13:15 The Lord then ~~answered him, and~~ said, ~~Thou~~ hypocrite, doth not each one of you on the sabbath loose his ox or ~~his~~ ass from the stall, and lead *him* away to watering?

Luke 13:17 And when he had said these things, all his adversaries were ashamed: and all ~~the people~~ rejoiced for all the glorious things ~~that~~ were done by him.

Luke 13:19 It is like a grain of mustard ~~seed~~, which a man took, and cast into his garden; and it grew, and waxed a great tree; and the fowls of the air lodged in the branches of it.

Luke 13:23 ~~Then~~ said one unto him, Lord, are there few that be saved? And he ~~said unto them~~,

Luke 13:24 Strive to enter in at the strait gate: for ~~many~~, I say unto you, ~~will~~ seek to enter in, and shall not be able.

Luke 13:25 When once the ~~master~~ of the ~~house~~ is risen up, and hath shut ~~to~~ the door, ~~and~~ ye ~~begin to~~ stand without, and ~~to~~ knock at the door, saying, Lord, Lord, open unto us; ~~and he~~ shall answer and say unto you, I know ~~you~~ not whence ye are:

Luke 13:27 But he shall say, I tell you, I know ~~you~~ not whence ye are; depart from me, all ~~ye~~ workers of iniquity.

Luke 13:28 There shall be weeping and gnashing of teeth, when ye shall see Abraham, and Isaac, and Jacob, and all the prophets, in the kingdom of God, and you ~~yourselves~~ thrust out.

The Lord then said **unto him**, O hypocrite, doth not each one of you on the sabbath loose his ox or **an** ass from the stall, and lead him away to watering?

And when he had said these things, all his adversaries were ashamed: and all **his disciples** rejoiced for all the glorious things **which** were done by him.

It is like a grain of mustard, which a man took, and cast into his garden; and it grew, and waxed a great tree; and the fowls of the air lodged in the branches of it.

And there said one unto him, Lord, are there few **only** that be saved? And he **answered him and said**,

Strive to enter in at the strait gate: for I say unto you, **many shall** seek to enter in, and shall not be able; **for the Lord shall not always strive with man.**

Therefore, When once the **Lord** of the **kingdom** is risen up, and hath shut the door **of the kingdom, then** ye **shall** stand without, and knock at the door, saying, Lord, Lord, open unto us; **but the Lord** shall answer and say unto you, I **will not receive you, for ye** know not **from** whence ye are:

But he shall say, I tell you, **ye** know not **from** whence ye are; depart from me, all workers of iniquity.

There shall be weeping and gnashing of teeth **among you**, when ye shall see Abraham, and Isaac, and Jacob, and all the prophets, in the kingdom of God, and you **are** thrust out.

Luke 13:29 And they shall come from the east, and ~~from~~ the west, and from the north, and ~~from~~ the south, and shall sit down in the kingdom of God.

Luke 13:30 And, behold, there are last which shall be first, and there are first which shall be last.

Luke 13:31 ~~The same day~~ there came certain of the Pharisees, saying unto him, Get thee out, and depart hence: for Herod will kill thee.

Luke 13:32 And he said unto them, Go ye, and tell ~~that fox~~, Behold, I cast out devils, and ~~I~~ do cures to day and to morrow, and the third *day* I shall be perfected.

Luke 13:33 Nevertheless I must walk to day, and to morrow, and the *day* ~~following~~: for it cannot be that a prophet perish out of Jerusalem.

Luke 13:34 O Jerusalem, Jerusalem, ~~which~~ killest the prophets, and stonest them ~~that~~ are sent unto thee; how often would I have gathered thy children together, as a hen ~~doth gather~~ her brood under *her* wings, and ye would not!

Luke 13:35 Behold, your house is left unto you desolate: and verily I say unto you, Ye shall not ~~see~~ me, until *the time* come when ye shall say, Blessed *is* he ~~that~~ cometh in the name of the Lord.

And **verily I say unto you,** They shall come from the east, and the west, and from the north, and the south, and shall sit down in the kingdom of God.

And, behold, there are last which shall be first, and there are first which shall be last, **and shall be saved therein.**

And as he was thus teaching there came **to him** certain of the Pharisees, saying unto him, Get thee out, and depart hence: for Herod will kill thee.

And he said unto them, Go ye, and tell **Herod**, Behold, I cast out devils, and do cures to day and to morrow, and the third day I shall be perfected.

Nevertheless I must walk to day, and to morrow, and the **third** day: for it cannot be that a prophet perish out of Jerusalem. **This he spake signifying of his death.**

And in this very hour, he began **to weep over Jerusalem, saying,** O Jerusalem, Jerusalem, **thou who** killest the prophets, and stonest them **who** are sent unto thee; how often would I have gathered thy children together, as a hen her brood under her wings, and ye would not!

Behold, your house is left unto you desolate: and verily I say unto you, Ye shall not **know** me, **until ye have received from the hand of the Lord a just recompense for all your sins;** until the time come when ye shall say, Blessed is he **who** cometh in the name of the Lord.

The Gospel According to St Luke

Luke 14:2 And, behold, there was a certain man before him ~~which~~ had the dropsy.

Luke 14:3 And Jesus ~~answering~~ spake unto the lawyers and Pharisees, saying, Is it lawful to heal on the sabbath day?

Luke 14:4 And they held their peace. And he took ~~him~~, and healed him, and let him go;

Luke 14:5 And ~~answered~~ them, saying, Which of you shall have an ass or an ox fallen into a pit, and will not straightway pull him out on the sabbath day?

Luke 14:6 And they could not answer him ~~again~~ to these things.

Luke 14:7 And he put forth a parable ~~to~~ those ~~which~~ were bidden, ~~when he marked~~ how they chose out the chief rooms; ~~saying~~ unto them,

Luke 14:8 When thou art bidden of any *man* to a wedding, sit not down in ~~the~~ highest room; lest a more honourable man than thou be bidden of him;

Luke 14:9 And he ~~that~~ bade thee ~~and~~ him come and say to thee, Give this man place; and thou begin with shame to take the lowest room.

Luke 14:10 But when thou art bidden, go and sit down in the lowest room; that when he ~~that~~ bade thee cometh, he may say unto thee, Friend, go up higher: then shalt thou have ~~worship~~ in the presence of them ~~that~~ sit at meat with thee.

And, behold, there was a certain man before him **who** had the dropsy.

And Jesus spake unto the lawyers and Pharisees, saying, Is it lawful to heal on the sabbath day?

And they held their peace. And he took **the man**, and healed him, and let him go;

And **spake unto** them **again**, saying, Which of you shall have an ass or an ox fallen into a pit, and will not straightway pull him out on the sabbath day?

And they could not answer him to these things.

And he put forth a parable **unto them, concerning** those **who** were bidden **to a wedding, for he knew** how they chose out the chief rooms **and exalted themselves one above another. Wherefore he spake** unto them, **saying,**

When thou art bidden of any man to a wedding, sit not down in **a** highest room; lest a more honourable man than thou be bidden of him;

And he **who** bade thee **with** him **who is more honourable,** come and say to thee, Give this man place; and thou begin with shame to take the lowest room.

But when thou art bidden, go and sit down in the lowest room; that when he **who** bade thee cometh, he may say unto thee, Friend, go up higher: then shalt thou have **honour of God** in the presence of them **who** sit at meat with thee.

Luke 14:11 For whosoever exalteth himself shall be abased; and he ~~that~~ humbleth himself shall be exalted.	For whosoever exalteth himself shall be abased; and he **who** humbleth himself shall be exalted.
Luke 14:12 Then said he also ~~to~~ him ~~that~~ bade him, When thou makest a dinner or a supper, call not thy friends, nor thy brethren, neither thy kinsmen, nor ~~thy~~ rich neighbours; lest they also bid thee again, and a recompence be made thee.	Then said he also **concerning** him **who** bade him **to the wedding**, When thou makest a dinner or a supper, call not thy friends, nor thy brethren, neither thy kinsmen, nor rich neighbours; lest they also bid thee again, and a recompence be made thee.
Luke 14:15 And when one of them ~~that~~ sat at meat with him heard these things, he said unto him, Blessed *is* he ~~that~~ shall eat bread in the kingdom of God.	And when one of them **who** sat at meat with him heard these things, he said unto him, Blessed is he **who** shall eat bread in the kingdom of God.
Luke 14:17 And sent his ~~servant~~ at supper time to say to them ~~that~~ were bidden, Come; for all things are now ready.	And sent his **servants** at supper time to say to them **who** were bidden, Come; for all things are now ready.
Luke 14:20 And another said, I have married a wife, ~~and~~ therefore I cannot come.	And another said, I have married a wife, therefore I cannot come.
Luke 14:21 So that servant came, and shewed his lord these things. Then the master of the house being angry said to his ~~servant~~, Go out quickly into the streets and lanes of the city, and bring ~~in~~ hither the poor, and the maimed, and the halt, and the blind.	So that servant came, and shewed his lord these things. Then the master of the house being angry said to his **servants**, Go out quickly into the streets and lanes of the city, and bring hither the poor, and the maimed, and the halt, and the blind.
Luke 14:23 ~~And~~ the lord said unto ~~the~~ servant, Go out into the highways and hedges, and compel ~~them~~ to come in, that my house may be filled.	The lord said unto **his** servant, Go out into the highways and hedges, and compel **men** to come in, that my house may be filled.
Luke 14:24 For I say unto you, That none of those men ~~which~~ were bidden shall taste of my supper.	For I say unto you, That none of those men **who** were bidden shall taste of my supper.
Luke 14:25 And there went great multitudes with him: and he turned, and said unto them,	And **when he had finished these sayings, he departed thence, and** there went great multitudes with him: and he turned, and said unto them,

Luke 14:26 If any ~~man~~ come to me, and hate not his father, and mother, and wife, and children, and brethren, and sisters, yea, and ~~his~~ own life also, ~~he~~ cannot be my disciple.	If any **one** come to me, and hate not his father, and mother, and wife, and children, and brethren, and sisters **or husband**, yea, and **their** own life also, **or in other words, is afraid to lay down their life for my sake,** cannot be my disciple.
	Wherefore, settle this in your hearts, that ye will do the things which I shall teach and command you. For which of you, intending to build a tower, sitteth not down first, and counteth the cost, whether he **has money** to finish **his work**?
Luke 14:28 For which of you, intending to build a tower, sitteth not down first, and counteth the cost, whether he ~~have sufficient~~ to finish ~~it~~?	
Luke 14:29 Lest ~~haply~~, after he ~~hath~~ laid the foundation, and is not able to finish ~~it~~, all ~~that~~ behold ~~it~~ begin to mock him,	Lest **unhappily**, after he **has** laid the foundation, and is not able to finish **his work**, all **who** behold begin to mock him,
Luke 14:30 Saying, This man began to build, and was not able to finish.	Saying, This man began to build, and was not able to finish. **And this he said, signifying there should not any man follow him, unless he was able to continue, saying,**
Luke 14:31 Or what king, going to make war against another king, sitteth not down first, and consulteth whether he be able with ten thousand to meet him ~~that~~ cometh against him with twenty thousand?	Or what king, going to make war against another king, sitteth not down first, and consulteth whether he be able with ten thousand to meet him **who** cometh against him with twenty thousand?
Luke 14:33 So likewise, whosoever ~~he be~~ of you ~~that~~ forsaketh not all that he hath, he cannot be my disciple.	So likewise, whosoever of you forsaketh not all that he hath, he cannot be my disciple. **Then certain of them came to him, saying, Good master, we have Moses and the prophets, and whosoever shall live by them, shall he not have life? And Jesus answered, saying, Ye know not Moses, neither the prophets, for if ye had known them ye would have believed on me; for to this intent they were written. For I am sent that ye might have life.**

Luke 14:34 Salt *is* good: but if the salt ~~have~~ lost ~~his~~ savour, wherewith shall it be seasoned?	**Therefore I will liken it unto** salt **which** is good: but if the salt **has** lost **its** savour, wherewith shall it be seasoned?
Luke 14:35 It is neither fit for the land, nor yet for the dunghill; ~~but~~ men cast it out. He ~~that~~ hath ears to hear, let him hear.	It is neither fit for the land, nor yet for the dunghill; men cast it out. He **who** hath ears to hear, let him hear. **These things he said, signifying; That which was written verily must all be fulfilled.**
Luke 15:1 Then drew near unto him ~~all~~ the publicans and sinners for to hear him.	Then drew near unto him **many of** the publicans and sinners for to hear him.
Luke 15:4 What man of you, having an hundred sheep, if he lose one of them, doth not leave the ninety and nine ~~in~~ the wilderness, ~~and go~~ after that which is lost, until he find it?	What man of you, having an hundred sheep, if he lose one of them, doth not leave the ninety and nine **and go into** the wilderness after that which is lost, until he find it?
Luke 15:6 And when he cometh home, he calleth together *his* friends and neighbours, ~~saying~~ unto them, Rejoice with me; for I have found my sheep which was lost.	And when he cometh home, he calleth together his friends and neighbours, **and saith** unto them, Rejoice with me; for I have found my sheep which was lost.
Luke 15:7 I say unto you, that likewise joy shall be in heaven over one sinner that repenteth, more than over ninety and nine just persons, ~~which need~~ no repentance.	I say unto you, that likewise joy shall be in heaven over one sinner that repenteth, more than over ninety and nine just persons, **who needeth** no repentance.
Luke 15:9 And when she hath found *it,* she calleth ~~her~~ friends and ~~her~~ neighbours together, saying, Rejoice with me; for I have found the piece which I had lost.	And when she hath found it, she calleth friends and neighbours together, saying, Rejoice with me; for I have found the piece which I had lost.
Luke 15:10 Likewise, I say unto you, there is joy in the presence of the angels of God over one sinner ~~that~~ repenteth.	Likewise, I say unto you, there is joy in the presence of the angels of God over one sinner **who** repenteth.
Luke 15:12 And the younger of them said unto *his* father, Father, give me the portion of goods ~~that~~ falleth *to me*. And he divided unto ~~them~~ *his* living.	And the younger of them said to his father, Father, give me the portion of goods **which** falleth to me. And he divided unto **him** his living.

Luke 15:16 And he would fain have filled his belly with the husks ~~that~~ the swine did eat: and no man gave unto him.

Luke 15:20 And he arose, and came to his father. ~~But~~ when he was yet a great way off, his father saw him, and had compassion, and ran, and fell on his neck, and kissed him.

Luke 15:22 But the father said ~~to~~ his servants, Bring forth the best robe, and put ~~it~~ on him; and put a ring on his ~~hand~~, and shoes on *his* feet:

Luke 15:29 And he answering said to *his* father, Lo, these many years do I serve thee, neither transgressed I at any time thy commandment: and ~~yet~~ thou never gavest me a kid, that I might make merry with my friends:

Luke 15:30 But as soon as this thy son was come, ~~which~~ hath devoured thy living with harlots, thou hast killed for him the fatted calf.

Luke 15:31 And he said unto him, Son, thou art ever with me, and all ~~that~~ I have is thine.

Luke 16:1 And he said also unto his disciples, There was a certain rich man, ~~which~~ had a steward; and the same was accused unto him that he had wasted his goods.

Luke 16:5 So he called every one of his lord's debtors ~~unto him~~, and said unto the first, How much owest thou unto my lord?

Luke 16:8 And the lord commended the unjust steward, because he had done wisely: for the children of this world are

And he would fain have filled his belly with the husks **which** the swine did eat: and no man gave unto him.

And he arose, and came to his father. **And** when he was yet a great way off, his father saw him, and had compassion, and ran, and fell on his neck, and kissed him.

But the father said **unto** his servants, Bring forth the best robe, and put [it] on him; and put a ring on his **finger**, and shoes on his feet:

And he answering said to his father, Lo, these many years do I serve thee, neither transgressed I at any time thy commandment: and thou never gavest me a kid, that I might make merry with my friends:

But as soon as this thy son was come, **who** hath devoured thy living with harlots, thou hast killed for him the fatted calf.

And he said unto him, Son, thou art ever with me, and all I have is thine.

And he said also unto his disciples, There was a certain rich man, **who** had a steward; and the same was accused unto him that he had wasted his goods.

So he called every one of his lord's debtors, and said unto the first, How much owest thou unto my lord?

And the lord commended the unjust steward, because he had done wisely: for the children of this world are **wiser** in their generation ~~wiser~~ than the children of light.

Luke 16:10 He ~~that~~ is faithful in that which is least is faithful also in much: and he ~~that~~ is unjust in the least is ~~unjust~~ also in much.

Luke 16:12 And if ye have not been faithful in that which is another man's, who shall give you that which is your own?

Luke 16:15 And he said unto them, Ye are they ~~which~~ justify yourselves before men; but God knoweth your hearts: for that which is highly esteemed among men is abomination in the sight of God.

Luke 16:16 The law and the prophets ~~were~~ until John: since that time the kingdom of God is preached, and every man presseth into it.

Luke 16:17 And it is easier for heaven and earth to pass, than one tittle of the law to fail.

in their generation than the children of light.

He **who** is faithful in that which is least is faithful also in much: and he **who** is unjust in the least is also **unjust** in much.

And if ye have not been faithful in that which is another man's, who shall give **unto** you that which is your own?

And he said unto them, Ye are they **who** justify yourselves before men; but God knoweth your hearts: for that which is highly esteemed among men is **an** abomination in the sight of God.

And they said unto him, We have the law and the prophets, but as for this man we will not receive him to be our ruler; for he maketh himself to be a judge over us. Then said Jesus unto them, The law and the prophets **testify of me; yea, and all the prophets who have written, even** until John, **have foretold of these days.** Since that time the kingdom of God is preached, and every man **who seeketh truth,** presseth into it.

And it is easier for heaven and earth to pass, than **for** one tittle of the law to fail. **And why teach ye the law, and deny that which is written; and condemn him who the Father hath sent to fulfill the law, that you might all be redeemed? O fools! For you have said in your hearts, There is no God. And you pervert the right way; and the kingdom of heaven suffereth violence of you; and you persecute the meek; and in your violence you seek to**

	destroy the kingdom; and ye take the children of the kingdom by force.
Luke 16:18 Whosoever putteth away his wife, and marrieth another, committeth adultery: and whosoever marrieth her ~~that~~ is put away from *her* husband committeth adultery.	Wo unto you, ye adulterers! And they reviled him again, being angry for the saying, that they were adulterers. But he continued, saying, Whosoever putteth away his wife, and marrieth another, committeth adultery: and whosoever marrieth her **who** is put away from her husband committeth adultery.
Luke 16:19 There was a certain rich man, ~~which~~ was clothed in purple and fine linen, and fared sumptuously every day:	Verily I say unto you, I will liken you unto the rich man. For there was a certain rich man, **who** was clothed in purple and fine linen, and fared sumptuously every day:
Luke 16:20 And there was a certain beggar named Lazarus, ~~which~~ was laid at his gate, full of sores,	And there was a certain beggar named Lazarus, **who** was laid at his gate, full of sores,
Luke 16:22 And it came to pass, that the beggar died, and was carried ~~by~~ the angels into Abraham's bosom: the rich man also died, and was buried;	And it came to pass, that the beggar died, and was carried **of** the angels into Abraham's bosom: the rich man also died, and was buried;
Luke 16:23 And in hell he ~~lift~~ up his eyes, being in torments, and ~~seeth~~ Abraham afar off, and Lazarus in his bosom.	And in hell he **lifted** up his eyes, being in torments, and **saw** Abraham afar off, and Lazarus in his bosom.
Luke 16:26 And ~~beside~~ all this, between us and you there is a great gulf fixed: so that they ~~which~~ would pass from hence to you cannot; neither can they pass to us, that *would come* from thence.	And **besides** all this, between us and you there is a great gulf fixed: so that they **who** would pass from hence to you cannot; neither can they pass to us, that would come from thence.
Luke 16:31 And he said unto him, If they hear not Moses and the prophets, neither will they be persuaded, though one ~~rose~~ from the dead.	And he said unto him, If they hear not Moses and the prophets, neither will they be persuaded, though one **should rise** from the dead.
Luke 17:1 Then said he unto the disciples, It is impossible but that offences	Then said he unto the disciples, It is impossible but that offences will come:

will come: but woe ~~unto~~ *him,* through whom they come!

Luke 17:3 Take heed to yourselves: If ~~thy~~ brother trespass against ~~thee~~, rebuke him; and if he repent, forgive him.

Luke 17:4 And if he trespass against ~~thee~~ seven times in a day, and seven times in a day turn ~~again~~ to ~~thee~~, saying, I repent; ~~thou shalt~~ forgive him.

Luke 17:5 And the apostles said unto ~~the~~ Lord, Increase our faith.

Luke 17:6 And the Lord said, If ~~ye~~ had faith as a grain of mustard seed, ~~ye~~ might say unto this sycamine tree, Be thou plucked up by the ~~root~~, and be thou planted in the sea; and it should obey you.

Luke 17:7 But ~~which~~ of you, having a servant plowing or feeding cattle, will say unto him ~~by and by~~, when he is come from the field, Go and sit down to meat?

Luke 17:8 ~~And~~ will not rather say unto him, Make ready wherewith I may sup, and gird ~~thyself~~, and serve me, till I have eaten and drunken; and afterward ~~thou shalt~~ eat and drink?

Luke 17:9 Doth he thank that servant because he ~~did~~ the things ~~that~~ were commanded him? I ~~trow not~~.

Luke 17:10 So likewise ye, when ye shall have done all those things which are commanded you, say, We are unprofitable servants: we have done that which was our duty to do.

Luke 17:11 ~~And~~ it came to pass, as he went to Jerusalem, that he passed through the midst of ~~Samaria~~ and ~~Galilee~~.

but woe **to** him, through whom they come!

Take heed to yourselves: If **your** brother trespass against **you**, rebuke him; and if he repent, forgive him.

And if he trespass against **you** seven times in a day, and seven times in a day turn to **you again**, saying, I repent; **you shall** forgive him.

And the apostles said unto **him**, Lord, Increase our faith.

And the Lord said, If **you** had faith as a grain of mustard seed, **you** might say unto this sycamore tree, Be thou plucked up by the **roots**, and be thou planted in the sea; and it should obey you.

But **who** of you, having a servant plowing or feeding cattle, will say unto him when he is come from the field, Go and sit down to meat?

Will **he** not rather say unto him, Make ready wherewith I may sup, and gird **yourself**, and serve me, till I have eaten and drunken; and afterward, **by and by, you shall** eat and drink?

Doth he thank that servant because he **doeth** the things **which** were commanded him? I **say unto you, Nay**.

So likewise ye, when ye shall have done all those things which are commanded you, say, We are unprofitable servants: we have done that which was **no more than** our duty to do.

It came to pass, as he went to Jerusalem, that he passed through the midst of **Galilee** and **Samaria**.

The Gospel According to St Luke

Luke 17:12 And as he entered into a certain village, there met him ten men ~~that~~ were lepers, ~~which~~ stood afar off:

Luke 17:14 And ~~when he saw them~~, he said unto them, Go shew yourselves unto the priests. And it came to pass, ~~that,~~ as they went, they were cleansed.

Luke 17:15 ~~And~~ one of them, when he saw ~~that~~ he was healed, turned back, and with a loud voice glorified God,

Luke 17:16 And fell down on *his* face at ~~his~~ feet, giving him thanks: and he was a Samaritan.

Luke 17:18 There are not found that ~~returned~~ to give glory to God, save this stranger.

Luke 17:21 Neither shall they say, Lo here! or, lo there! for, behold, the kingdom of God ~~is within~~ you.

Luke 17:22 And he said unto ~~the~~ disciples, The days will come, when ~~ye shall~~ desire to see one of the days of the Son of man, and ~~ye~~ shall not see *it*.

Luke 17:23 And they shall say to you, See here; or, see there: go not after *them*, nor follow *them*.

Luke 17:24 For as the ~~lightning~~, that ~~lighteneth~~ out of the one *part* under heaven, ~~shineth unto~~ the other *part* under heaven; so shall also the Son of man be in his day.

Luke 17:25 But first must ~~he~~ suffer many things, and be rejected of this generation.

Luke 17:31 In that day, ~~he which~~ shall be ~~upon~~ the housetop, and his stuff in the house, let him not come down to

And as he entered into a certain village, there met him ten men **who** were lepers, **who** stood afar off:

And he said unto them, Go shew yourselves unto the priests. And it came to pass, as they went, they were cleansed.

One of them, when he saw he was healed, turned back, and with a loud voice glorified God,

And fell down on his face at **Jesus'** feet, giving him thanks: and he was a Samaritan.

There are not found that **return** to give glory to God, save this stranger.

Neither shall they say, Lo here! or, lo there! for, behold, the kingdom of God **has already come unto** you.

And he said unto **his** disciples, The days will come, when **they will** desire to see one of the days of the Son of man, and **they** shall not see it.

And **if** they shall say to you, See here; or, see there: go not after them, nor follow them.

For as the **light of the morning** that shineth out of the one part under heaven, **and lighteneth to** the other part under heaven; so shall also the Son of man be in his day.

But first **he** must suffer many things, and be rejected of this generation.

In that day, **the disciple who** shall be **on** the housetop, and his stuff in the house, let him not come down to take it away:

take it away: and he ~~that~~ is in the field, let him likewise not return back.

Luke 17:34 I tell you, in that night there shall be two ~~men~~ in one bed; the one shall be taken, and the other shall be left.

Luke 17:35 Two ~~women~~ shall be grinding together; the one shall be taken, and the other left.

Luke 17:36 Two ~~men~~ shall be in the field; the one shall be taken, and the other left.

Luke 17:37 And they answered and said unto him, Where, Lord? And he said unto them, Wheresoever the body *is,* thither will the eagles be gathered together.

and he **who** is in the field, let him likewise not return back.

I tell you, in that night there shall be two in one bed; the one shall be taken, and the other shall be left.

Two shall be grinding together; the one shall be taken, and the other left.

Two shall be in the field; the one shall be taken, and the other left.

And they answered and said unto him, Where, Lord, **shall they be taken?** And he said unto them, Wheresoever the body is **gathered; or, in other words, whithersoever the saints are gathered**, thither will the eagles be gathered together, **or thither will the remainder be gathered together. This he spake signifying the gathering of his saints; and of angels descending and gathering the remainder unto them; the one from the bed, the other from the grinding, and the other from the field, whithersoever he listeth. For verily there shall be new heavens and a new earth, wherein dwelleth righteousness. And there shall be no unclean thing; for the earth becoming old, even as a garment, having waxed in corruption, wherefore it vanisheth away, and the footstool remaineth sanctified, cleansed from all sin.**

Luke 18:1 And he spake a parable unto them ~~to this end~~, ~~that~~ men ought always to pray, and not ~~to~~ faint;

And he spake a parable unto them, **saying**, Men ought always to pray, and not faint;

Luke 18:2 Saying, There was in a city a judge, which feared not God, ~~neither~~ regarded man:

Saying, There was in a city a judge, which feared not God, **nor** regarded man:

The Gospel According to St Luke

Luke 18:7 And shall not God avenge his own elect, ~~which~~ cry day and night unto him, though he bear long with ~~them~~?

Luke 18:8 I tell you that he will avenge ~~them~~ speedily. Nevertheless when the Son of man cometh, shall he find faith on the earth?

Luke 18:9 ~~And~~ he spake this parable unto certain ~~which~~ trusted in themselves that they were righteous, and despised others:

Luke 18:10 Two men went up into the temple to pray; the one a Pharisee, ~~and~~ the other a publican.

Luke 18:11 The Pharisee stood and prayed thus with himself, God, I thank thee, that I am not as other men ~~are,~~ extortioners, unjust, adulterers, or even as this publican.

Luke 18:13 ~~And~~ the publican, standing afar off, would not lift up so much as *his* eyes unto heaven, but smote upon his breast, saying, God be merciful to me a sinner.

Luke 18:14 I tell you, this man went down to his house justified *rather* than the other: for every one ~~that~~ exalteth himself shall be abased; and he ~~that~~ humbleth himself shall be exalted.

Luke 18:15 And they brought unto him also infants, that he ~~would~~ touch them: but when *his* disciples saw *it,* they rebuked them.

Luke 18:16 But Jesus called them ~~unto him~~, and said, Suffer little children to come unto me, and forbid them not: for of such is the kingdom of God.

And shall not God avenge his own elect, **who** cry day and night unto him, though he bear long with **men**?

I tell you that he will **come; and when** [he] **does come, he will** avenge **his saints** speedily. Nevertheless when the Son of man cometh, shall he find faith on the earth?

He spake this parable unto certain **men who** trusted in themselves that they were righteous, and despised others:

Two men went up into the temple to pray; the one a Pharisee, the other a publican.

The Pharisee stood and prayed thus with himself, God, I thank thee, that I am not as other men, extortioners, unjust, adulterers, or even as this publican.

But the publican, standing afar off, would not lift up so much as his eyes unto heaven, but smote upon his breast, saying, God be merciful to me a sinner.

I tell you, this man went down to his house justified rather than the other: for every one **who** exalteth himself shall be abased; and he **who** humbleth himself shall be exalted.

And they brought unto him also infants, that he **might** touch them: but when his disciples saw it, they rebuked them.

But Jesus called them, and said, Suffer little children to come unto me, and forbid them not: for of such is the kingdom of God.

Luke 18:17 Verily I say unto you, Whosoever ~~shall~~ not receive the kingdom of God as a little child shall in no wise enter therein.

Luke 18:22 Now when Jesus heard these things, he said unto him, Yet lackest ~~thou~~ one thing: sell all that thou hast, and distribute unto the poor, and thou shalt have treasure in heaven: and come, follow me.

Luke 18:24 And when Jesus saw that he was very sorrowful, he said, How hardly shall they ~~that~~ have riches enter into the kingdom of God!

Luke 18:26 And they ~~that~~ heard ~~it~~ said, Who then can be saved?

Luke 18:27 And he said, ~~The things which are~~ impossible ~~with men are~~ possible with God.

Luke 18:29 And he said unto them, Verily I say unto you, There is no man ~~that hath~~ left house, or parents, or brethren, or wife, or children, for the kingdom of God's sake,

Luke 18:30 Who shall not receive ~~manifold~~ more in this present time, and in the world to come life everlasting.

Luke 18:31 Then he took ~~unto him~~ the twelve, and said unto them, Behold, we go up to Jerusalem, and all things ~~that~~ are written by the prophets concerning the Son of man shall be accomplished.

Luke 18:33 And they shall scourge ~~him~~, and put him to death: and the third day he shall rise again.

Verily I say unto you, Whosoever **will** not receive the kingdom of God as a little child shall in no wise enter therein.

Now when Jesus heard these things, he said unto him, Yet **thou** lackest one thing: sell all that thou hast, and distribute unto the poor, and thou shalt have treasure in heaven: and come, follow me.

And when Jesus saw that he was very sorrowful, he said, How hardly shall they **who** have riches enter into the kingdom of God!

And they **who** heard said **unto him**, Who then can be saved?

And he said **unto them, It is** impossible **for them who trust in riches to enter into the kingdom of God; but he who forsaketh the things which are of this world, it is** possible with God, **that he should enter in**.

And he said unto them, Verily I say unto you, There is no man **who has** left house, or parents, or brethren, or wife, or children, for the kingdom of God's sake,

Who shall not receive **many fold** more in this present time, and in the world to come life everlasting.

Then he took the twelve, and said unto them, Behold, we go up to Jerusalem, and all things **which** are written by the prophets concerning the Son of man shall be accomplished.

And they shall scourge and put him to death: and the third day he shall rise again.

The Gospel According to St Luke

Luke 18:34 And they understood none of these things: and this saying was hid from them, neither ~~knew~~ they the things which were spoken.

Luke 18:35 And it came to pass, ~~that~~ as he was come nigh unto Jericho, a certain blind man sat by the way side begging:

Luke 18:37 And they told him, that Jesus of Nazareth ~~passeth~~ by.

Luke 18:38 And he cried, saying, Jesus, ~~thou~~ Son of David, have mercy on me.

Luke 18:39 And they ~~which~~ went before rebuked him, that he should hold his peace: but he cried so much the more, ~~Thou~~ Son of David, have mercy on me.

Luke 18:42 And Jesus said unto him, Receive thy sight: thy faith ~~hath~~ saved thee.

Luke 18:43 And immediately he received his sight, and followed him, glorifying God: and all the ~~people~~, when they saw ~~it~~, gave praise unto God.

Luke 19:2 And, behold, *there was* a man named Zacchaeus, ~~which~~ was ~~the~~ chief among the publicans, and he was rich.

Luke 19:7 And when ~~they~~ saw *it,* they all murmured, saying, That he was gone to be guest with a man ~~that~~ is a sinner.

Luke 19:8 And Zacchaeus stood, and said unto the Lord; Behold, Lord, the half of my goods I give to the poor; and if I have taken any thing from any man by ~~false accusation~~, I restore ~~him~~ fourfold.

And they understood none of these things: and this saying was hid from them, neither **remembered** they the things which were spoken.

And it came to pass, as he was come nigh unto Jericho, a certain blind man sat by the way side begging:

And they told him, that Jesus of Nazareth **passed** by.

And he cried, saying, Jesus, Son of David, have mercy on me.

And they **who** went before rebuked him, **telling him** that he should hold his peace: but he cried so much the more, **saying,** Son of David, have mercy on me.

And Jesus said unto him, Receive thy sight: thy faith **has** saved thee.

And immediately he received his sight, and **he** followed him, glorifying God: and all the **disciples**, when they saw **this**, gave praise unto God.

And, behold, there was a man named Zacchaeus, **who** was chief among the publicans, and he was rich.

And when **the disciples** saw it, they all murmured, saying, That he was gone to be **a** guest with a man **who** is a sinner.

And Zacchaeus stood, and said unto the Lord; Behold, Lord, the half of my goods I give to the poor; and if I have taken any thing from any man by **unjust means**, I restore fourfold.

Luke 19:9 And Jesus said unto him, This day is salvation come to this house, ~~forsomuch~~ as he also is a son of Abraham.

Luke 19:11 And as they heard these things, he added and spake a parable, because he was nigh to Jerusalem, and because ~~they thought~~ that the kingdom of God should immediately appear.

Luke 19:13 And he called his ten servants, and delivered them ten pounds, and said unto them, Occupy till I come.

Luke 19:14 But his citizens hated him, and sent a ~~message~~ after him, saying, We will not have this *man* to reign over us.

Luke 19:17 And he said unto him, Well, thou good servant: because thou hast been faithful in a very little, have thou authority over ten cities.

Luke 19:20 And another came, saying, Lord, behold, ~~here is~~ thy pound, which I have kept laid up in a napkin:

Luke 19:21 For I feared thee, because thou art an austere man: thou takest up that thou layedst not down, and reapest that thou didst not sow.

Luke 19:22 And he ~~saith~~ unto him, Out of thine own mouth will I judge thee, ~~thou~~ wicked servant. Thou knewest that I was an austere man, taking up that I laid not down, and reaping that I did not sow:

Luke 19:23 Wherefore then gavest not thou my money into the bank, that at my coming I might have ~~required mine~~ own with usury?

And Jesus said unto him, This day is salvation come to this house, **forasmuch** as he also is a son of Abraham.

And as they heard these things, he added and spake a parable, because he was nigh to Jerusalem, and because **the Jews taught** that the kingdom of God should immediately appear.

And he called his ten servants, and **he** delivered them ten pounds, and said unto them, Occupy till I come.

But his citizens hated him, and sent a **messenger** after him, saying, We will not have this man to reign over us.

And he said unto him, Well **done**, thou good servant: because thou hast been faithful in a very little, have thou authority over ten cities.

And another came, saying, Lord, behold, thy pound, which I have kept laid up in a napkin:

For I feared thee, because thou art an austere man: thou takest up that thou layedst not down, and reapest that **which** thou didst not sow.

And he **said** unto him, Out of thine own mouth will I judge thee, **O** wicked servant. Thou knewest that I was an austere man, taking up that I laid not down, and reaping that I did not sow:

Wherefore then gavest not thou my money into the bank, that at my coming I might have **received my** own with usury?

Luke 19:24 And he said unto them ~~that~~ stood by, Take from him the pound, and give ~~it~~ to him ~~that~~ hath ten pounds.

Luke 19:25 ~~(And they said unto him, Lord, he hath ten pounds.)~~

Luke 19:26 For I say unto you, That unto every one ~~which hath~~ shall be given; and from him ~~that hath~~ not, even that he hath shall be taken away from him.

Luke 19:27 But those mine enemies, ~~which~~ would not that I should reign over them, bring hither, and slay *them* before me.

Luke 19:30 Saying, Go ye into the village over against *you;* in the which at your entering ye shall find a colt tied, whereon yet never man sat: loose him, and bring *him* ~~hither~~.

Luke 19:31 And if any man ask you, Why do ~~ye~~ loose ~~him~~? thus shall ye say unto him, Because the Lord hath need of him.

Luke 19:32 And they ~~that~~ were sent went their way, and found even as he had said unto them.

Luke 19:37 And when he was come nigh, even now at the descent of the mount of Olives, the whole multitude of the disciples began to rejoice and praise God with a loud voice for all the mighty works ~~that~~ they had seen;

Luke 19:38 Saying, Blessed ~~be~~ the King ~~that~~ cometh in the name of the Lord: peace in heaven, and glory in the highest.

And he said unto them **who** stood by, Take from him the pound, and give to him **who** hath ten pounds.

For I say unto you, That unto every one **who occupieth**, shall be given; and from him **who occupieth** not, even that he hath **received** shall be taken away from him.

But those mine enemies, **who** would not that I should reign over them, bring **them** hither, and slay them before me.

Saying, Go ye into the village over against you; in the which at your entering ye shall find a colt tied, whereon yet never man sat: loose him, and bring **him to me**.

And if any man ask you, Why do **you** loose **the colt**? thus shall ye say unto him, Because the Lord hath need of him.

And they **who** were sent went their way, and found even as he had said unto them.

And when he was come nigh, even now at the descent of the mount of Olives, the whole multitude of the disciples began to rejoice and praise God with a loud voice for all the mighty works **which** they had seen;

Saying, Blessed **is** the King **who** cometh in the name of the Lord: peace in heaven, and glory in the highest.

Luke 19:40 And he answered and said unto them, ~~I tell you that~~, if these should hold their peace, the stones would immediately cry out.

Luke 19:45 And he went into the temple, and began to cast out them ~~that~~ sold therein, and them ~~that~~ bought;

Luke 19:46 Saying unto them, It is written, My house is ~~the~~ house of prayer: but ~~ye~~ have made it a den of thieves.

Luke 20:2 And spake unto him, saying, Tell us, by what authority doest thou these things? or who is he ~~that~~ gave thee this authority?

Luke 20:3 And he answered and said unto them, I will also ask you one thing; ~~and~~ answer me:

Luke 20:6 ~~But~~ and if we say, Of men; all the people will stone us: for they ~~be~~ persuaded that John was a prophet.

Luke 20:8 ~~And~~ Jesus said unto them, Neither tell I you by what authority I do ~~these~~ things.

Luke 20:9 Then began he to speak to the people this parable; A certain man planted a vineyard, and let it ~~forth~~ to husbandmen, and went into a far country for a long time.

Luke 20:10 And at the season he sent ~~a~~ servant to the husbandmen, that they should give him of the fruit of the vineyard: but the husbandmen beat him, and sent *him* away empty.

Luke 20:16 He shall come and destroy these husbandmen, and shall give the vineyard to others. And when they heard ~~it~~, they said, God forbid.

And he answered and said unto them, If these should hold their peace, the stones would immediately cry out.

And he went into the temple, and began to cast out them **who** sold therein, and them **who** bought;

Saying unto them, It is written, My house is **a** house of prayer: but **you** have made it a den of thieves.

And spake unto him, saying, Tell us, by what authority doest thou these things? or who is he **who** gave thee this authority?

And he answered and said unto them, I will also ask you one thing; answer me:

And if we say, Of men; all the people will stone us: for they **are** persuaded that John was a prophet.

Jesus said unto them, Neither tell I you by what authority I do **those** things.

Then began he to speak to the people this parable; A certain man planted a vineyard, and let it **out** to husbandmen, and went into a far country for a long time.

And at the season **of the harvest**, he sent **his** servant to the husbandmen, that they should give him of the fruit of the vineyard: but the husbandmen beat him, and sent him away empty.

He shall come and destroy these husbandmen, and shall give the vineyard to others. And when they heard **this**, they said, God forbid.

Luke 20:17 And he beheld them, and said, What is this then ~~that~~ is written, The stone which the builders rejected, the same is become the head of the corner?

Luke 20:18 Whosoever shall fall upon that stone shall be broken; but on whomsoever it shall fall, it ~~will~~ grind him to powder.

Luke 20:19 And the chief priests and the scribes the same hour sought to lay hands on him; ~~and~~ they feared the people: for they perceived that he had spoken this parable against them.

Luke 20:20 And they watched *him,* and sent forth spies, ~~which~~ should feign themselves just men, that they might take hold of his words, that so they might deliver him unto the power and authority of the governor.

Luke 20:21 And they asked him, saying, Master, we know that thou sayest and teachest rightly, neither ~~acceptest~~ thou the person *of any,* but teachest the way of God truly:

Luke 20:27 Then came ~~to~~ *him* certain of the Sadducees, ~~which~~ deny that there is any resurrection; and they asked him,

Luke 20:28 Saying, Master, Moses wrote unto us, If any man's brother die, having a wife, and he die without children, that his brother should take his wife, and raise up seed unto his brother.

Luke 20:29 There were therefore seven brethren: ~~and~~ the first took a wife, and died without children.

And he beheld them, and said, What is this then **which** is written, The stone which the builders rejected, the same is become the head of the corner?

Whosoever shall fall upon that stone shall be broken; but on whomsoever it shall fall, it **shall** grind him to powder.

And the chief priests and the scribes the same hour sought to lay hands on him; **but** they feared the people: for they perceived that he had spoken this parable against them.

And they watched him, and sent forth spies, **who** should feign themselves just men, that they might take hold of his words, that so **doing,** they might deliver him unto the power and authority of the governor.

And they asked him, saying, Master, we know that thou sayest and teachest rightly, neither **regardest** thou the person of any, but teachest the way of God truly:

Then came **unto** him certain of the Sadducees, **who** deny that there is any resurrection; and they asked him,

Saying, Master, Moses wrote unto us, **saying,** If any man's brother die, having a wife, and he die without children, that his brother should take his wife, and raise up seed unto his brother.

There were therefore seven brethren. The first took a wife, and died without children.

Luke 20:31 And the third took her; ~~and~~ in like manner the seven also: and they left no children, and died.	And the third took her in like manner **and** the seven also: and they left no children, and died.
Luke 20:32 Last of all the woman died also.	**And** last of all the woman died also.
Luke 20:35 But they ~~which~~ shall be accounted worthy to obtain that world, ~~and the~~ resurrection from the dead, neither marry, nor are given in marriage:	But they **who** shall be accounted worthy to obtain that world, **through** resurrection from the dead, neither marry, nor are given in marriage:
Luke 20:37 Now that the dead are raised, even Moses shewed at the bush, when he calleth the Lord the God of Abraham, ~~and~~ the God of Isaac, and the God of Jacob.	Now that the dead are raised, even Moses shewed at the bush, when he calleth the Lord the God of Abraham, the God of Isaac, and the God of Jacob.
Luke 20:42 And David himself ~~saith~~ in the book of Psalms, The L<small>ORD</small> said unto my Lord, Sit thou on my right hand,	And David himself **said** in the book of Psalms, The L<small>ORD</small> said unto my Lord, Sit thou on my right hand,
Luke 20:46 Beware of the scribes, ~~which~~ desire to walk in long robes, and love greetings in the markets, and the highest seats in the synagogues, and the chief rooms at feasts;	Beware of the scribes, **who** desire to walk in long robes, and love greetings in the markets, and the highest seats in the synagogues, and the chief rooms at feasts;
Luke 20:47 ~~Which~~ devour widows' houses, and for a shew make long prayers: the same shall receive greater damnation.	**Who** devour widows' houses, and for a shew make long prayers: the same shall receive greater damnation.
Luke 21:1 And he looked up, and saw the rich men casting their gifts into the treasury.	And he looked up, and saw the rich men casting **in** their gifts into the treasury.
Luke 21:4 For all these have of their abundance cast in unto the offerings of God: but she of her penury ~~hath~~ cast in all the living that she had.	For all these have of their abundance cast in unto the offerings of God: but she of her penury **has** cast in all the living that she had.
Luke 21:6 ~~As for~~ these things which ye behold, the days will come, in the	These things which ye behold, the days will come, in the which there shall not

which there shall not be left one stone upon another, ~~that~~ shall not be thrown down.

Luke 21:7 And ~~they~~ asked him, saying, Master, ~~but~~ when shall these things be? and what sign ~~will there be~~ when these things shall come to pass?

Luke 21:8 And he said, Take heed that ye be not deceived: for many shall come in my name, saying, I am *Christ;* ~~and the time draweth near:~~ go ye not therefore after them.

Luke 21:9 ~~But~~ when ye shall hear of wars and commotions, be not terrified: for these things must first come to pass; but the end ~~is not by and by~~.

Luke 21:12 But before all these, they shall lay their hands on you, and persecute *you,* delivering *you* up to the synagogues, and into prisons, being brought before kings and rulers for my name's sake.

Luke 21:13 ~~And it shall turn to you for a testimony~~.

Luke 21:14 Settle ~~it~~ therefore in your hearts, not to meditate before what ye shall answer:

Luke 21:15 For I will give you a mouth and wisdom, which all your adversaries shall not be able to gainsay nor resist.

Luke 21:17 And ye shall be hated of all ~~men~~ for my name's sake.

Luke 21:21 Then let them ~~which~~ are in Judaea flee to the mountains; and let them ~~which~~ are in the midst of it depart out; and let not them ~~that~~ are in the countries enter ~~thereinto~~.

be left one stone upon another, **which** shall not be thrown down.

And **the disciples** asked him, saying, Master, when shall these things be? and what sign **wilt thou shew** when these things shall come to pass?

And he said, **The time draweth near, and therefore** take heed that ye be not deceived: for many shall come in my name, saying, I am Christ; go ye not therefore after them.

And when ye shall hear of wars and commotions, be not terrified: for these things must first come to pass; but **this is not** the end.

But before all these **things shall come**, they shall lay their hands on you, and persecute you, delivering you up to the synagogues, and into prisons, being brought before kings and rulers for my name's sake.

Settle **this** therefore in your hearts, not to meditate before what ye shall answer:

For I will give you a mouth and wisdom, which all your adversaries shall not be able to gainsay nor resist. **And it shall turn to you for a testimony.**

And ye shall be hated of all **the world** for my name's sake.

Then let them **who** are in Judea flee to the mountains; and let them **who** are in the midst of it depart out; and let not them **who** are in the countries **return to** enter **into the city**.

Luke 21:23 But woe unto them ~~that~~ are with child, and to them ~~that~~ give suck, in those days! for there shall be great distress in the land, and wrath upon this people.	But woe unto them **who** are with child, and to them **who** give suck, in those days! for there shall be great distress in the land, and wrath upon this people.
Luke 21:25 ~~And~~ there shall be signs in the sun, and in the moon, and in the stars; and upon the earth distress of nations, with perplexity; the sea and the waves roaring;	**Now these things he spake unto them concerning the destruction of Jerusalem. And then his disciples asked him, saying, Master, tell us concerning thy coming. And he answered them, and said, In the generation in which the times of the Gentiles shall be fulfilled,** there shall be signs in the sun, and in the moon, and in the stars; and upon the earth distress of nations, with perplexity; **like** the sea and the waves roaring;
Luke 21:26 Men's hearts failing them for fear, and for looking after those things which are coming on the earth: for the powers of heaven shall be shaken.	**The earth also shall be troubled, and the waters of the great deep;** men's hearts failing them for fear, and for looking after those things which are coming on the earth: for the powers of heaven shall be shaken.
Luke 21:27 ~~And then shall they see the Son of man coming in a cloud with power and great glory~~.	
Luke 21:28 And when these things begin to come to pass, then look up, and lift up your heads; for your redemption draweth nigh.	And when these things begin to come to pass, then look up, and lift up your heads; for **the day of** your redemption draweth nigh. **And then shall they see the Son of man coming in a cloud, with power and great glory.**
Luke 21:29 And he spake to them a parable; Behold the fig tree, and all the trees;	And he spake to them a parable, **saying,** Behold the fig tree, and all the trees;
Luke 21:32 Verily I say unto you, This generation shall not pass away, till all be fulfilled.	Verily I say unto you, This generation, **the generation when the times of the Gentiles be fulfilled,** shall not pass away, till all be fulfilled.

The Gospel According to St Luke

Luke 21:34 ~~And~~ take heed to ~~yourselves~~, lest at any time ~~your~~ hearts be overcharged with surfeiting, and drunkenness, and cares of this life, and ~~so~~ that day come upon ~~you~~ unawares.

Luke 21:35 For as a snare shall ~~it~~ come on all them ~~that~~ dwell on the face of the whole earth.

Luke 21:36 Watch ye therefore, and pray always, that ye may be ~~accounted~~ worthy to escape all these things ~~that~~ shall come to pass, and to stand before the Son of man.

Luke 21:37 And in the day time he was teaching in the temple; and at night he went out, and abode in the mount that is called ~~the mount of~~ Olives.

Luke 21:38 And ~~all~~ the people came early in the morning to him in the temple, for to hear him.

Luke 22:2 And the chief priests and scribes sought how they might kill him; ~~for~~ they feared the people.

Luke 22:6 And he promised, and sought opportunity to betray him unto them in the absence of the multitude.

Luke 22:10 And he said unto them, Behold, when ye ~~are~~ entered into the city, there shall a man meet you, bearing a pitcher of water; follow him into the house where he entereth in.

Luke 22:11 And ye shall say unto the goodman of the house, The Master saith unto ~~thee~~, Where is the guestchamber, where I shall eat the passover with my disciples?

Let my disciples therefore take heed to **themselves**, lest at any time **their** hearts be overcharged with surfeiting, and drunkenness, and cares of this life, and that day come upon **them** unawares.

For as a snare **it** shall come on all them **who** dwell on the face of the whole earth.

And what I say unto one, I say unto all, Watch ye therefore, and pray always, **and keep my commandments,** that ye may be **counted** worthy to escape all these things **which** shall come to pass, and to stand before the Son of man **when he shall come clothed in the glory of his Father.**

And in the day time he was teaching in the temple; and at night he went out, and abode in the mount that is called Olives.

And the people came early in the morning to him in the temple, for to hear him.

And the chief priests and **the** scribes sought how they might kill him; **but** they feared the people.

And he promised **them**, and sought opportunity to betray him unto them in the absence of the multitude.

And he said unto them, Behold, when ye **have** entered into the city, there shall a man meet you, bearing a pitcher of water; follow him into the house where he entereth in.

And ye shall say unto the goodman of the house, The Master saith unto **you**, Where is the guestchamber, where I shall eat the passover with my disciples?

Luke 22:16 For I say unto you, I will not any more eat thereof, until it be fulfilled in the kingdom of God.	For I say unto you, I will not any more eat thereof, until it be fulfilled, **which is written in the prophets concerning me. Then I will partake with you,** in the kingdom of God.
Luke 22:17 And he took the cup, and gave thanks, and said, Take this, and divide ~~it~~ among yourselves:	And he took the cup, and gave thanks, and said, Take this, and divide among yourselves:
Luke 22:18 For I say unto you, I will not drink of the fruit of the vine, until the kingdom of God shall come.	For I say unto you, **that** I will not drink of the fruit of the vine, until the kingdom of God shall come.
Luke 22:19 And he took bread, and gave thanks, and brake ~~it~~, and gave unto them, saying, This is my body which is given for you: this do in remembrance of me.	And he took bread, and gave thanks, and brake, and gave unto them, saying, This is my body which is given for you: this do in remembrance of me.
Luke 22:21 But, behold, the hand of him ~~that~~ betrayeth me *is* with me on the table.	But, behold, the hand of him **who** betrayeth me is with me on the table.
Luke 22:23 And they began to enquire among themselves, ~~which~~ of them it was ~~that~~ should do this thing.	And they began to enquire among themselves, **who** of them it was **who** should do this thing.
Luke 22:24 ~~And~~ there was also a strife among them, ~~which~~ of them should be accounted the greatest.	There was also a strife among them, **who** of them should be accounted the greatest.
Luke 22:25 And he said unto them, The kings of the Gentiles exercise lordship over them; and they ~~that~~ exercise authority upon them are called benefactors.	And he said unto them, The kings of the Gentiles exercise lordship over them; and they **who** exercise authority upon them are called benefactors.
Luke 22:26 But ~~ye shall~~ not *be* so: but he ~~that~~ is greatest among you, let him be as the younger; and he ~~that~~ is chief, as he ~~that~~ doth serve.	But **it ought** not to be so **with you**: but he **who** is greatest among you, let him be as the younger; and he **who** is chief, as he **who** doth serve.
Luke 22:27 For whether *is* greater, ~~he that~~ sitteth at meat, or he ~~that~~ serveth? *is* not he ~~that~~ sitteth at meat? but I am among you as he ~~that~~ serveth.	For whether is **he** greater, **who** sitteth at meat, or he **who** serveth? **I am** not **as** he **who** sitteth at meat, but I am among you as he **who** serveth.

The Gospel According to St Luke

Luke 22:28 Ye are they ~~which~~ have continued with me in my temptations.

Luke 22:30 That ~~ye~~ may eat and drink at my table in my kingdom, and sit on thrones judging the twelve tribes of Israel.

Luke 22:31 And the Lord said, Simon, Simon, behold, Satan hath desired ~~to have~~ you, that he may sift ~~you~~ as wheat:

Luke 22:32 But I have prayed for ~~thee~~, that ~~thy~~ faith fail not: and when ~~thou art~~ converted, strengthen ~~thy~~ brethren.

Luke 22:33 And he said unto him, Lord, I am ready to go with ~~thee~~, both into prison, and ~~to~~ death.

Luke 22:34 And ~~he~~ said, I tell ~~thee~~, Peter, the cock shall not crow this day, before that ~~thou shalt~~ thrice deny that ~~thou knowest~~ me.

Luke 22:35 And he said unto them, When I sent you without purse, and scrip, ~~and~~ shoes, lacked ye any thing? And they said, Nothing.

Luke 22:36 Then said he unto them, ~~But now~~, he ~~that~~ hath a purse, let him take *it,* and likewise ~~his~~ scrip: and he ~~that~~ hath no sword, let him sell his garment, and buy one.

Luke 22:37 For I say unto you, ~~that~~ this that is written must yet be accomplished in me, And he was reckoned among the transgressors: for the things concerning me have an end.

Luke 22:39 And he came out, and went, as he was ~~wont~~, to the mount of Olives; and his disciples ~~also~~ followed him.

Ye are they **who** have continued with me in my temptations.

That **you** may eat and drink at my table in my kingdom, and sit on **twelve** thrones judging the twelve tribes of Israel.

And the Lord said, Simon, Simon, behold, Satan hath desired you, that he may sift **the children of the kingdom** as wheat:

But I have prayed for **you**, that **your** faith fail not: and when **you are** converted, strengthen **your** brethren.

And he said unto him, **being aggrieved,** Lord, I am ready to go with **you**, both into prison, and **unto** death.

And **the Lord** said, I tell **you**, Peter, **that** the cock shall not crow this day, before that **you will** thrice deny that **you know** me.

And he said unto them, When I sent you without purse, and scrip, **or** shoes, lacked ye any thing? And they said, Nothing.

Then said he unto them, **I say unto you again**, he **who** hath a purse, let him take it, and likewise **a** scrip: and he **who** hath no sword, let him sell his garment, and buy one.

For I say unto you, this that is written must yet be accomplished in me, And he was reckoned among the transgressors: for the things concerning me have an end.

And he came out, and went, as he was **accustomed**, to the mount of Olives; and his disciples followed him.

Luke 22:42 Saying, Father, if thou be willing, remove this cup from me: nevertheless not my will, but thine, be done.

Luke 22:44 And being in an agony he prayed more earnestly: and ~~his~~ sweat ~~was~~ as it were great drops of blood falling down to the ground.

Luke 22:45 And when he rose up from prayer, and was come to his disciples, he found them sleeping for sorrow,

Luke 22:46 And said unto them, Why sleep ye? rise and pray, lest ~~ye~~ enter into temptation.

Luke 22:47 And while he yet spake, behold a multitude, and he ~~that~~ was called Judas, one of the twelve, went before them, and drew near unto Jesus to kiss him.

Luke 22:49 When they ~~which~~ were about him saw what would follow, they said unto him, Lord, shall we smite with ~~the~~ sword?

Luke 22:52 Then Jesus said unto the chief priests, and captains of the temple, and ~~the~~ elders, ~~which~~ were come to him, ~~Be~~ ye come out, as against a thief, with swords and staves?

Luke 22:55 And when they had kindled a fire in the midst of the hall, and were ~~set~~ down together, Peter sat down among them.

Luke 22:59 And about the space of one hour ~~after~~ another confidently affirmed, saying, Of a truth this ~~fellow~~ also ~~was~~ with him: for he is a Galilaean.

Saying, Father, if thou be willing **to** remove this cup from me: nevertheless not my will, but thine, be done.

And being in an agony he prayed more earnestly: and **he** sweat as it were great drops of blood falling down to the ground.

And when he rose up from prayer, and was come to his disciples, he found them sleeping; for **they were filled with** sorrow,

And said unto them, Why sleep ye? rise and pray, lest **you** enter into temptation.

And while he yet spake, behold a multitude, and he **who** was called Judas, one of the twelve, went before them, and drew near unto Jesus to kiss him.

When they **who** were about him saw what would follow, they said unto him, Lord, shall we smite with **a** sword?

Then Jesus said unto the chief priests, and captains of the temple, and elders, **who** were come to him, **Are** ye come out, as against a thief, with swords and staves?

And when they had kindled a fire in the midst of the hall, and were **sat** down together, Peter sat down among them.

And about the space of one hour another confidently affirmed, saying, Of a truth this **man was** also with him: for he is a Galilaean.

The Gospel According to St Luke

Luke 22:63 And the men ~~that~~ held Jesus mocked him, and smote *him*.	And the men **who** held Jesus mocked him, and smote him.
Luke 22:64 And when they had blindfolded him, they struck him on the face, and asked him, saying, Prophesy, who is it ~~that~~ smote thee?	And when they had blindfolded him, they struck him on the face, and asked him, saying, Prophesy, who is it **who** smote thee?
Luke 22:68 And if I also ask *you*, ~~ye~~ will not answer me, nor let *me* go.	And if I also ask you, **you** will not answer me, nor let me go.
Luke 22:71 And they said, What need we any further witness? for we ourselves have heard of his own mouth.	And they said, What need we **of** any further witness? for we ourselves have heard of his own mouth.
Luke 23:2 And they began to accuse him, saying, We found this ~~fellow~~ perverting the nation, and forbidding to give tribute to Caesar, saying that he himself is Christ a King.	And they began to accuse him, saying, We found this **man** perverting the nation, and forbidding to give tribute to Caesar, saying that he himself is Christ a King.
Luke 23:3 And Pilate asked him, saying, Art thou the King of the Jews? And he answered him and said, Thou sayest *it*.	And Pilate asked him, saying, Art thou the King of the Jews? And he answered him and said, **Yea**, thou sayest it.
Luke 23:4 Then said Pilate to the chief priests and ~~to the~~ people, I find no fault in this man.	Then said Pilate to the chief priests and people, I find no fault in this man.
Luke 23:8 And when Herod saw Jesus, he was exceeding glad: for he was desirous to see him of a long ~~season~~, because he had heard many things of him; and he hoped to have seen some miracle done by him.	And when Herod saw Jesus, he was exceeding glad: for he was desirous to see him of a long **time**, because he had heard many things of him; and he hoped to have seen some miracle done by him.
Luke 23:10 And the chief ~~priests~~ and scribes stood and vehemently accused him.	And the chief **priest** and scribes stood and vehemently accused him.
Luke 23:12 And the same day Pilate and Herod were made friends together: for before they were at enmity between themselves.	And the same day Pilate and Herod were made friends together: for before **this**, they were at enmity between themselves.

Luke 23:13 And Pilate, when he had called together the chief ~~priests~~ and the rulers and the people,

Luke 23:14 Said unto them, ~~Ye~~ have brought this man unto me, as one that perverteth the people: and, behold, I, having examined *him* before you, have found no fault in this man touching those things whereof ye accuse him:

Luke 23:18 ~~And~~ they cried out all at once, saying, Away with this *man,* and release unto us Barabbas:

Luke 23:23 And they were instant ~~with~~ loud voices, requiring that he might be crucified. And the voices of them and ~~of~~ the chief priests prevailed.

Luke 23:25 And he released unto them him ~~that~~ for sedition and murder was cast into prison, whom they had desired; ~~but he~~ delivered Jesus to their will.

Luke 23:27 And there followed him a great company of people, and of women, ~~which~~ also bewailed and lamented him.

Luke 23:28 But Jesus ~~turning~~ unto them said, Daughters of Jerusalem, weep not for me, but weep for yourselves, and for your children.

Luke 23:29 For, behold, the days are coming, in the which they shall say, Blessed *are* the barren, and the wombs ~~that~~ never bare, and the paps which never gave suck.

Luke 23:31 ~~For~~ if ~~they do~~ these things in ~~a~~ green tree, what shall be done in the dry?

And Pilate, when he had called together the chief **priest** and the rulers and the people,

Said unto them, **You** have brought this man unto me, as one **who** perverteth the people: and, behold, I, having examined him before you, have found no fault in this man touching those things whereof ye accuse him:

But they cried out all at once, saying, Away with this man, and release unto us Barabbas:

And they were instant **in** loud voices, requiring that he might be crucified. And the voices of them and the chief priests prevailed.

And he released unto them him **who** for sedition and murder was cast into prison, whom they had desired; **and** delivered Jesus to their will.

And there followed him a great company of people, and of women, **who** also bewailed and lamented him.

But Jesus **turned** unto them **and** said, Daughters of Jerusalem, weep not for me, but weep for yourselves, and for your children.

For, behold, the days are coming, in the which they shall say, Blessed are the barren, and the wombs **which** never bare, and the paps which never gave suck.

And if these things **are done** in the green tree, what shall be done in the dry **tree? This he spake, signifying the scattering of Israel, and the desolation**

	of the heathen, or in other words, the Gentiles.
Luke 23:32 And there were also two ~~other~~, malefactors, led with him to be put to death.	And there were also two **others**, malefactors, led with him to be put to death.
Luke 23:34 Then said Jesus, Father, forgive them; for they know not what they do. And they parted his raiment, and cast lots.	Then said Jesus, Father, forgive them; for they know not what they do **(meaning the soldiers who crucified him)**. And they parted his raiment, and cast lots.
Luke 23:35 And the people stood beholding. And the rulers also with them derided ~~him~~, saying, He saved others; let him save himself, if he be Christ, the chosen of God.	And the people stood beholding. And the rulers also with them derided, saying, He saved others; let him save himself, if he be Christ, the chosen of God.
Luke 23:36 And ~~the~~ soldiers also mocked him, coming to him, and offering him vinegar,	And soldiers also mocked him, coming to him, and offering him vinegar,
Luke 23:39 And one of the malefactors ~~which were hanged~~ railed on him, saying, If thou be Christ, save thyself and us.	And one of the malefactors **who was crucified with him** railed on him, saying, If thou be **the** Christ, save thyself and us.
Luke 23:40 But the other answering rebuked him, saying, Dost not ~~thou~~ fear God, seeing thou art in the same condemnation?	But the other answering rebuked him, saying, Dost **thou** not fear God, seeing thou art in the same condemnation?
Luke 23:48 And all the people ~~that~~ came together to that sight, beholding the things which were done, smote their breasts, and returned.	And all the people **who** came together to that sight, beholding the things which were done, smote their breasts, and returned.
Luke 23:49 And all his acquaintance, and ~~the~~ women ~~that~~ followed him from Galilee, stood afar off, beholding these things.	And all his acquaintance, and women **who** followed him from Galilee, stood afar off, beholding these things.
Luke 23:50 And, behold, ~~there was~~ a man named Joseph, a counsellor; ~~and he was~~ a good man, and a just:	And, behold, a man named Joseph, a counsellor, a good man, and a just **one**:

Luke 23:51 {The same had not consented to the counsel and deed of them;} ~~he was~~ of Arimathaea, a city of the Jews: who also himself waited for the kingdom of God.	The same **day** had not consented to the counsel and deed of them; **a man** of Arimathaea, a city of the Jews: who also himself waited for the kingdom of God.
Luke 23:52 ~~This man~~ went unto Pilate, and begged the body of Jesus.	**He** went unto Pilate, and begged the body of Jesus.
Luke 23:53 And he took it down, and wrapped it in linen, and laid it in a sepulchre ~~that~~ was ~~hewn~~ in stone, wherein never man before was laid.	And he took it down, and wrapped it in linen, and laid it in a sepulchre **which** was **hewed** in **a** stone, wherein never man before was laid.
Luke 23:55 And the women also, ~~which~~ came with him from Galilee, followed after, and beheld the sepulchre, and how his body was laid.	And the women also, **who** came with him from Galilee, followed after, and beheld the sepulchre, and how his body was laid.
Luke 24:1 Now upon the first *day* of the week, very early in the morning, ~~they~~ came unto the sepulchre, bringing the spices which they had prepared, and certain *others* with them.	Now upon the first day of the week, very early in the morning, **the women** came unto the sepulchre, bringing the spices which they had prepared, and certain others with them.
Luke 24:2 And they found the stone rolled away from the sepulchre.	And they found the stone rolled away from the sepulchre, **and two angels standing by it in shining garments.**
Luke 24:3 And they entered ~~in~~, and ~~found~~ not the body of the Lord Jesus.	And they entered **into the sepulchre**, and not **finding** the body of the Lord Jesus,
Luke 24:4 ~~And it came to pass, as~~ they were much perplexed thereabout, ~~behold, two men stood by them in shining garments~~:	They were much perplexed thereabout:
Luke 24:5 And ~~as they~~ were ~~afraid~~, and bowed down *their* faces to the earth, ~~they~~ said unto them, Why seek ye the living among the dead?	And were **affrighted**, and bowed down their faces to the earth, **but behold, the angels** said unto them, Why seek ye the living among the dead?
Luke 24:10 It was Mary Magdalene, and Joanna, and Mary *the mother* of James, and other *women* ~~that~~ were with	It was Mary Magdalene, and Joanna, and Mary the mother of James, and other women **who** were with them, **who**

them, ~~which~~ told these things unto the apostles.

Luke 24:12 Then arose Peter, and ran unto the sepulchre; and ~~stooping down~~, he beheld the linen clothes laid by themselves, and departed, wondering in himself at that which was come to pass.

Luke 24:13 And, behold, two of them went that same day to a village called Emmaus, which was from Jerusalem ~~about~~ threescore furlongs.

Luke 24:16 But their eyes were holden that they ~~should~~ not know him.

Luke 24:17 And he said unto them, What manner of communications *are* these ~~that ye~~ have one ~~to~~ another, as ye walk, and are sad?

Luke 24:18 And ~~the~~ one of them, whose name was Cleopas, answering said unto him, Art thou ~~only~~ a stranger in Jerusalem, and hast not known the things which are come to pass there in these days?

Luke 24:19 And he said unto them, What things? And they said unto him, Concerning Jesus of Nazareth, ~~which~~ was a prophet mighty in deed and word before God and all the people:

Luke 24:21 But we trusted that it had been he ~~which~~ should have redeemed Israel: and ~~beside~~ all this, to day is the third day since these things were done.

Luke 24:22 Yea, and certain women also of our company made us astonished, ~~which~~ were early at the sepulchre;

Luke 24:23 And when they found not his body, they came, saying, that they

told these things unto the apostles.

Then arose Peter, and ran unto the sepulchre; and **went in, and** he beheld the linen clothes laid by themselves, and **he** departed, wondering in himself at that which was come to pass.

And, behold, two of them went that same day to a village called Emmaus, which was from Jerusalem threescore furlongs.

But their eyes were holden, **or covered**, that they **could** not know him.

And he said unto them, What manner of communications are these **which you** have one **with** another, as ye walk, and are sad?

And one of them, whose name was Cleopas, answering said unto him, Art thou a stranger in Jerusalem, and hast not known the things which are come to pass there in these days?

And he said unto them, What things? And they said unto him, Concerning Jesus of Nazareth, **who** was a prophet mighty in deed and word before God and all the people:

But we trusted that it had been he **who** should have redeemed Israel: and **besides** all this, to day is the third day since these things were done.

Yea, and certain women also of our company made us astonished, **who** were early at the sepulchre;

And when they found not his body, they came, saying, that they had also had also seen a vision of angels, ~~which~~ said that he was alive.

Luke 24:24 And certain of them ~~which~~ were with us went to the sepulchre, and found ~~it~~ even so as the women had said: but him they saw not.

Luke 24:28 And they drew nigh unto the village, whither they went: and he made as though he would have gone ~~further~~.

Luke 24:30 And it came to pass, as he sat at meat with them, he took bread, and blessed ~~it,~~ and brake, and gave to them.

Luke 24:31 And their eyes were opened, and they knew him; and he ~~vanished~~ out of their sight.

Luke 24:32 And they said one to another, Did not our ~~heart~~ burn within us, while he talked with us by the way, and while he opened to us the scriptures?

Luke 24:33 And they rose up the same hour, and returned to Jerusalem, and found the eleven gathered together, and ~~them that~~ were with them,

Luke 24:35 And they told what things ~~were done~~ in the way, and how he was known ~~of~~ them in breaking of bread.

Luke 24:36 And as they thus spake, Jesus himself stood in the midst of them, and ~~saith~~ unto them, Peace ~~be~~ unto you.

Luke 24:38 And he said unto them, Why are ~~ye~~ troubled? and why do thoughts arise in your hearts?

seen a vision of angels, **who** said that he was alive.

And certain of them **who** were with us went to the sepulchre, and found even so as the women had said: but him they saw not.

And they drew nigh unto the village, whither they went: and he made as though he would have gone **farther**.

And it came to pass, as he sat at meat with them, he took bread, and blessed, and brake, and gave to them.

And their eyes were opened, and they knew him; and he **was taken up** out of their sight.

And they said one to another, Did not our **hearts** burn within us, while he talked with us by the way, and while he opened to us the scriptures?

And they rose up the same hour, and returned to Jerusalem, and found the eleven gathered together, and **those who** were with them,

And they told what things **they saw and heard** in the way, and how he was known **to** them in breaking of bread.

And as they thus spake, Jesus himself stood in the midst of them, and **said** unto them, Peace be unto you.

And he said unto them, Why are **you** troubled? and why do thoughts arise in your hearts?

The Gospel According to St Luke

Luke 24:39 Behold my hands and my feet, that it is I myself: handle me, and see; for a spirit hath not flesh and bones, as ~~ye~~ see me have.	Behold my hands and my feet, that it is I myself: handle me, and see; for a spirit hath not flesh and bones, as **you** see me have.
Luke 24:40 And when he had thus spoken, he shewed them *his* hands and ~~*his*~~ feet.	And when he had thus spoken, he shewed them his hands and feet.
Luke 24:41 And while they yet believed not for joy, ~~and wondered~~, he said unto them, Have ye here any meat?	And while they yet **wondered, and** believed not for joy, he said unto them, Have ye here any meat?
Luke 24:42 And they gave him a piece of a broiled fish, and ~~of~~ an honeycomb.	And they gave him a piece of a broiled fish, and a honeycomb.
Luke 24:51 And it came to pass, while he blessed them, he was ~~parted~~ from them, and carried up into heaven.	And it came to pass, while he blessed them, he was **taken** from them, and carried up into heaven.

The Testimony of John

King James Version	Joseph Smith Translation
John 1:1 In the beginning was the Word, and the Word was with God, and the ~~Word~~ was God.	In the beginning was the **gospel preached through the Son. And the gospel was the** Word, and the Word was with **the Son, and the Son was with** God, and the **Son** was **of** God.
John 1:3 All things were made by him; and without him was not any thing made ~~that~~ was made.	All things were made by him; and without him was not any thing made **which** was made.
John 1:4 In him was ~~life~~; and the life was the light of men.	In him was **the gospel**; and **the gospel was** the life, **and the life** was the light of men;
John 1:5 And the light shineth in ~~darkness~~; and the ~~darkness comprehended~~ it not.	And the light shineth in **the world**; and the **world perceiveth** it not.
John 1:7 The same came for a witness, to bear witness of the Light, ~~that~~ all ~~men~~ through him might believe.	The same came **into the world** for a witness, to bear witness of the Light, **to bear record of the gospel through the Son, unto** all, **that** through him **men** might believe.
John 1:8 He was not that Light, but ~~was sent~~ to bear witness of that Light.	He was not that Light, but **came** to bear witness of that Light
John 1:9 ~~That~~ was the true Light, which lighteth every man ~~that~~ cometh into the world.	**Which** was the true Light, which lighteth every man **who** cometh into the world.
John 1:10 He was in the world, and the world was made by him, and the world knew him not.	**Even the Son of God. He who** was in the world, and the world was made by him, and the world knew him not.
John 1:12 But as many as received him, to them gave he power to become the sons of God, ~~even~~ to them ~~that~~ believe on his name:	But as many as received him, to them gave he power to become the sons of God, **only** to them **who** believe on his name:

224

The Testimony of John

John 1:13 ~~Which were~~ born, not of blood, nor of the will of the flesh, nor of the will of man, but of God.

John 1:14 And the Word was made flesh, and dwelt among us, {and we beheld his glory, the glory as of the only begotten of the Father,} full of grace and truth.

John 1:15 John bare witness of him, and cried, saying, This ~~was~~ he of whom I spake, He ~~that~~ cometh after me is preferred before me: for he was before me.

John 1:16 And of his fulness have all we received, and grace ~~for grace~~.

John 1:17 For the law was given ~~by~~ Moses, *but* ~~grace~~ and truth came ~~by~~ Jesus Christ.

John 1:18 No man hath seen God at any time; ~~the only begotten~~ Son, ~~which is in the bosom of the Father, he hath declared~~ *him*.

John 1:20 And he confessed, and denied not; but confessed, I am not the Christ.

John 1:21 And they asked him, ~~What~~ then? Art thou Elias? And he ~~saith~~, I am not. Art thou that prophet? And he answered, No.

He **was** born, not of blood, nor of the will of the flesh, nor of the will of man, but of God.

And the **same** Word was made flesh, and dwelt among us, and we beheld his glory, the glory as of the only begotten of the Father, full of grace and truth.

John bare witness of him, and cried, saying, This **is** he of whom I spake, He **who** cometh after me is preferred before me: for he was before me. **For in the beginning was the Word, even the Son, who is made flesh, and sent unto us by the will of the Father.**

And **as many as believe on his name shall receive** of his fullness. **And of his fullness** have all we received, **even immortality** and eternal life through his grace.

For the law was given **through** Moses, but **life** and truth came **through** Jesus Christ. **For the law was after a carnal commandment, to the administration of death; but the gospel was after the power of an endless life, through Jesus Christ, the only begotten Son, who is in the bosom of the Father.**

And no man hath seen God at any time; **except he hath born record of the Son, for except it is through him no man can be saved.**

And he confessed, and denied not **that he was Elias**; but confessed, **saying,** I am not the Christ.

And they asked him, **saying, How** then art thou Elias? And he **said**, I am not **that Elias who was to restore all things.**

	And they asked him, saying, Art thou that prophet? And he answered, No.
John 1:22 Then said they unto him, Who art thou? that we may give an answer to them ~~that~~ sent us. What sayest thou of thyself?	Then said they unto him, Who art thou? that we may give an answer to them **who** sent us. What sayest thou of thyself?
John 1:24 And they ~~which~~ were sent were of the Pharisees.	And they **who** were sent were of the Pharisees.
John 1:25 And they asked him, and said unto him, Why baptizest thou then, if thou be not ~~that~~ Christ, nor Elias, neither that prophet?	And they asked him, and said unto him, Why baptizest thou then, if thou be not **the** Christ, nor Elias **who was to restore all things**, neither that prophet?
John 1:27 He it is, who coming after me is preferred before me, whose shoe's latchet I am not worthy to unloose.	He it is **of whom I bear record. He is that prophet, even Elias,** who coming after me is preferred before me, whose shoe's latchet I am not worthy to unloose, **or whose place I am not able to fill: for he shall baptize, not only with water, but with fire, and with the Holy Ghost.**
John 1:28 ~~These things were done in Bethabara beyond Jordan, where John was baptizing.~~	
John 1:29 The next day John seeth Jesus coming unto him, and ~~saith~~, Behold the Lamb of God, ~~which~~ taketh away the sin of the world.	The next day John seeth Jesus coming unto him, and **said**, Behold the Lamb of God, **who** taketh away the sin of the world!
John 1:30 This is he of whom I said, After me cometh a man ~~which~~ is preferred before me: for he was before me.	**And John bear record of him unto the people, saying,** This is he of whom I said, After me cometh a man **who** is preferred before me: for he was before me.
John 1:31 And I knew him ~~not: but~~ that he should be made manifest to Israel, therefore am I come baptizing with water.	And I knew him **and** that he should be made manifest to Israel, therefore am I come baptizing with water.
John 1:32 And John bare record, saying, I saw the Spirit descending from	And John bare record, saying, **When he was baptized of me,** I saw the Spirit

The Testimony of John

heaven like a dove, and it abode upon him.

John 1:33 And I knew him ~~not: but~~ he ~~that~~ sent me to baptize with water, the same said unto me, Upon whom thou shalt see the Spirit descending, and remaining on him, the same is he ~~which~~ baptizeth with the Holy Ghost.

John 1:34 And I saw, and bare record that this is the Son of God.

John 1:36 And looking upon Jesus as he walked, he ~~saith~~, Behold the Lamb of God!

John 1:38 Then Jesus turned, and saw them following, and ~~saith~~ unto them, What seek ye? They ~~said~~ unto him, Rabbi, (which is to say, being interpreted, Master,) where dwellest thou?

John 1:39 He saith unto them, Come and see. They came and saw where he dwelt, and abode with him that day: for it was about the tenth hour.

John 1:40 One of the two ~~which~~ heard John ~~speak~~, and followed ~~him~~, was Andrew, Simon Peter's brother.

John 1:41 He first findeth his own brother Simon, and ~~saith~~ unto him, We have found the Messias, which is, being interpreted, the Christ.

John 1:42 And he brought him to Jesus. And when Jesus beheld him, he said, Thou art Simon the son of Jona: thou shalt be called Cephas, which is by interpretation, A stone.

---

descending from heaven like a dove, and it abode upon him.

And I knew him: **for** he **who** sent me to baptize with water, the same said unto me, Upon whom thou shalt see the Spirit descending, and remaining on him, the same is he **who** baptizeth with the Holy Ghost.

And I saw, and bare record that this is the Son of God. **These things were done in Bethabara, beyond Jordan where John was baptizing.**

And looking upon Jesus as he walked, he **said**, Behold the Lamb of God!

Then Jesus turned, and saw them following **him**, and **said** unto them, What seek ye? They **say** unto him, Rabbi, (which is to say, being interpreted, Master,) where dwellest thou?

He saith unto them, Come and see. **And** they came and saw where he dwelt, and abode with him that day: for it was about the tenth hour.

One of the two **who** heard John, and followed **Jesus**, was Andrew, Simon Peter's brother.

He first findeth his own brother Simon, and **said** unto him, We have found the Messias, which is, being interpreted, the Christ.

And he brought him to Jesus. And when Jesus beheld him, he said, Thou art Simon the son of Jona: thou shalt be called Cephas, which is by interpretation, **A seer, or** a stone. **And they were fishermen. And they straightway left all, and followed Jesus.**

John 1:43 The day following Jesus would go forth into Galilee, and findeth Philip, and ~~saith~~ unto him, Follow me.

John 1:44 Now Philip was ~~of~~ Bethsaida, the city of Andrew and Peter.

John 1:45 Philip findeth Nathanael, and ~~saith~~ unto him, We have found him, of whom Moses in the law, and the prophets, did write, Jesus of Nazareth, the son of Joseph.

John 1:46 And Nathanael said unto him, Can there any good thing come out of Nazareth? Philip ~~saith~~ unto him, Come and see.

John 1:47 Jesus saw Nathanael coming ~~to~~ him, and ~~saith~~ of him, Behold an Israelite indeed, in whom is no guile!

John 1:48 Nathanael ~~saith~~ unto him, Whence knowest thou me? Jesus ~~answered and~~ said unto him, Before ~~that~~ Philip called thee, when thou wast under the fig tree, I saw thee.

John 1:49 Nathanael answered and ~~saith~~ unto him, Rabbi, thou art the Son of God; thou art the King of Israel.

John 1:51 And he ~~saith~~ unto him, Verily, verily, I say unto you, Hereafter ye shall see heaven open, and the angels of God ascending and descending upon the Son of man.

John 2:1 And the third day there was a marriage in Cana of Galilee; and the mother of Jesus was there:

John 2:2 And ~~both~~ Jesus was called, and his disciples, to the marriage.

The day following Jesus would go forth into Galilee, and findeth Philip, and **said** unto him, Follow me.

Now Philip was **at** Bethsaida, the city of Andrew and Peter.

Philip findeth Nathanael, and **said** unto him, We have found him, of whom Moses in the law, and the prophets, did write, Jesus of Nazareth, the son of Joseph.

And Nathanael said unto him, Can there any good thing come out of Nazareth? Philip **said** unto him, Come and see.

Jesus saw Nathanael coming **unto** him, and **said** of him, Behold an Israelite indeed, in whom is no guile!

Nathanael **said** unto him, Whence knowest thou me? Jesus **answering** said unto him, Before Philip called thee, when thou wast under the fig tree, I saw thee.

Nathanael answered and **said** unto him, Rabbi, thou art the Son of God; thou art the King of Israel.

And he **said** unto him, Verily, verily, I say unto you, Hereafter ye shall see heaven open, and the angels of God ascending and descending upon the Son of man.

And **on** the third day **of the week** there was a marriage in Cana of Galilee; and the mother of Jesus was there:

And Jesus was called, and his disciples, to the marriage.

The Testimony of John

John 2:3 And when they wanted wine, the mother of Jesus saith unto him, They have no wine.

John 2:4 Jesus saith unto her, Woman, what have I to do with thee? mine hour is not yet come.

John 2:5 His mother saith unto the servants, Whatsoever he saith unto you, do it.

John 2:6 And there were set there six waterpots of stone, after the manner of the purifying of the Jews, containing two or three firkins apiece.

John 2:7 Jesus saith unto them, Fill the waterpots with water. And they filled them up to the brim.

John 2:8 And he saith unto them, Draw out now, and bear unto the governor of the feast. And they bare it.

John 2:9 When the ruler of the feast had tasted the water that was made wine, and knew not whence it was: (but the servants which drew the water knew;) the governor of the feast called the bridegroom,

John 2:10 And saith unto him, Every man at the beginning doth set forth good wine; and when men have well drunk, then that which is worse: but thou hast kept the good wine until now.

John 2:11 This beginning of miracles did Jesus in Cana of Galilee, and manifested forth his glory; and his disciples believed on him.

John 2:14 And found in the temple those that sold oxen and sheep and doves, and the changers of money sitting:

And when they wanted wine, **his** mother **said** unto him, They have no wine.

Jesus **said** unto her, Woman, what **wilt thou** have **me** to do **for** thee? **that will I do, for** mine hour is not yet come.

His mother **said** unto the servants, Whatsoever he saith unto you, **see that ye** do it.

There were set there six waterpots of stone, after the manner of the purifying of the Jews, containing two or three firkins apiece.

Jesus **said** unto them, Fill the waterpots with water. And they filled them up to the brim.

And he **said**, Draw out now, and bear unto the governor of the feast. And they bare **unto him**.

When the **governor** of the feast had tasted the water **which** was made wine, (he knew not whence it was: but the servants **who** drew the water knew;) the governor of the feast called the bridegroom,

And **said** unto him, Every man at the beginning doth set forth good wine; and when men have well drunk, then that which is worse: but thou hast kept the good wine until now.

This beginning of miracles did Jesus in Cana of Galilee, and manifested forth his glory; and **the faith of** his disciples **was strengthened in** him.

And found in the temple **those who** sold oxen and sheep and doves, and changers of money sitting:

John 2:16 And said unto them ~~that~~ sold doves, Take these things hence; make not my Father's house an house of merchandise.

John 2:17 And his disciples remembered that it was written, The zeal of ~~thine~~ house hath eaten me up.

John 2:18 Then ~~answered~~ the Jews and said unto him, What sign shewest thou unto us, seeing ~~that~~ thou doest these things?

John 2:22 When therefore he was risen from the dead, his disciples remembered that he had said this unto them; and they ~~believed~~ the scripture, and the word which Jesus had said.

John 2:23 Now when he was in Jerusalem at the passover, ~~in~~ the feast day, many believed in his name, when they saw the miracles which he did.

John 2:24 But Jesus did not commit himself unto them, because he knew all ~~men~~,

John 3:2 The same came to Jesus by night, and said unto him, Rabbi, we know that thou art a teacher come from God: for no man can do these miracles ~~that~~ thou doest, except God be with him.

John 3:4 Nicodemus ~~saith~~ unto him, How can a man be born when he is old? ~~can~~ he enter the second time into his mother's womb, and be born?

John 3:5 Jesus answered, Verily, verily, I say unto thee, Except a man be born of water and ~~of~~ the Spirit, he cannot enter into the kingdom of God.

And said unto them **who** sold doves, Take these things hence; make not my Father's house a house of merchandise.

And his disciples remembered that it was written, The zeal of **thy** house hath eaten me up.

Then **spake** the Jews and said unto him, What sign shewest thou unto us, seeing thou doest these things?

When therefore he was risen from the dead, his disciples remembered that he had said this unto them; and they **remembered** the scripture, and the word which Jesus had said **unto them**.

Now when he was in Jerusalem at the passover, **on** the feast day, many believed **on** his name, when they saw the miracles which he did.

But Jesus did not commit himself unto them, because he knew all **things**,

The same came to Jesus by night, and said unto him, Rabbi, we know that thou art a teacher come from God: for no man can do these miracles **which** thou doest, except God be with him.

Nicodemus **said** unto him, How can a man be born when he is old? **Can** he enter the second time into his mother's womb, and be born?

Jesus answered, Verily, verily, I say unto thee, Except a man be born of water and the Spirit, he cannot enter into the kingdom of God.

The Testimony of John

John 3:8 The wind bloweth where it listeth, and thou hearest the sound thereof, but canst not tell whence it cometh, and whither it goeth: so is every one ~~that~~ is born of the Spirit.	The wind bloweth where it listeth, and thou hearest the sound thereof, but canst not tell whence it cometh, and whither it goeth: so is every one **who** is born of the Spirit.
John 3:10 Jesus answered and said ~~unto him~~, Art thou a master of Israel, and knowest not these things?	Jesus answered and said, Art thou a master of Israel, and knowest not these things?
John 3:12 If I have told you earthly things, and ye believe not, how shall ye believe, if I tell you ~~of~~ heavenly things?	If I have told you earthly things, and ye believe not, how shall ye believe, if I tell you heavenly things?
John 3:13 ~~And~~ no man hath ascended up to heaven, but he ~~that~~ came down from heaven, ~~even~~ the Son of man ~~which~~ is in heaven.	**I tell you**, no man hath ascended up to heaven, but he **who** came down from heaven, the Son of man **who** is in heaven.
John 3:15 That whosoever believeth ~~in~~ him should not perish, but have eternal life.	That whosoever believeth **on** him should not perish, but have eternal life.
John 3:16 For God so loved the world, that he gave his only begotten Son, that whosoever believeth ~~in~~ him should not perish, but have everlasting life.	For God so loved the world, that he gave his only begotten Son, that whosoever believeth **on** him should not perish, but have everlasting life.
John 3:18 He ~~that~~ believeth on him is not condemned: but he ~~that~~ believeth not is condemned already, because he hath not believed ~~in~~ the name of the only begotten Son of God.	He **who** believeth on him is not condemned: but he **who** believeth not is condemned already, because he hath not believed **on** the name of the only begotten Son of God, **which before was preached by the mouth of the holy prophets; for they testified of me.**
John 3:19 And this is the condemnation, that light is come into the world, and men ~~loved~~ darkness rather than light, because their deeds ~~were~~ evil.	And this is the condemnation, that light is come into the world, and men **love** darkness rather than light, because their deeds **are** evil.
John 3:20 For every one ~~that~~ doeth evil hateth the light, neither cometh to the light, lest his deeds should be reproved.	For every one **who** doeth evil hateth the light, neither cometh to the light, lest his deeds should be reproved.
John 3:21 But he ~~that doeth~~ truth cometh to the light, that his deeds may	But he **who loveth** truth cometh to the light, that his deeds may be made

be made manifest, ~~that~~ they are ~~wrought in~~ God.

John 3:23 And John also was baptizing in Aenon near to Salim, because there was much water there: and they came, and were baptized.

John 3:26 And they came unto John, and said unto him, Rabbi, he ~~that~~ was with thee beyond Jordan, to whom thou barest witness, behold, the same baptizeth, and all ~~men~~ come ~~to~~ him.

John 3:29 He ~~that~~ hath the bride is the bridegroom: but the friend of the bridegroom, ~~which~~ standeth and heareth him, rejoiceth greatly because of the bridegroom's voice: this my joy ~~therefore~~ is fulfilled.

John 3:31 He ~~that~~ cometh from above is above all: he ~~that~~ is of the earth is earthly, and speaketh of the earth: he ~~that~~ cometh from heaven is above all.

John 3:32 And what he hath seen and heard, that he testifieth; and ~~no man~~ receiveth his testimony.

John 3:33 He ~~that~~ hath received his testimony hath set to his seal that God is true.

John 3:34 For he whom God hath sent speaketh the words of God: for God giveth not the Spirit by measure ~~unto~~ him.

John 3:35 The Father loveth the Son, and hath given all things into his ~~hand~~.

John 3:36 He ~~that~~ believeth on the Son hath everlasting life: ~~and~~ he ~~that~~

manifest. **And he who obeyeth the truth, the works which he doeth,** they are **of** God.

And John also was baptizing in Aenon near to Salim, because there was much water there: and they came, and were baptized; **for John was not yet cast into prison.**

And they came unto John, and said unto him, Rabbi, he **who** was with thee beyond Jordan, to whom thou barest witness, behold, the same baptizeth, and **he receiveth of** all **people who** come **unto** him.

He **who** hath the bride is the bridegroom: but the friend of the bridegroom, **who** standeth and heareth him, rejoiceth greatly because of the bridegroom's voice: this my joy **is** therefore fulfilled.

He **who** cometh from above is above all: he **who** is of the earth is earthly, and speaketh of the earth: he **who** cometh from heaven is above all.

And what he hath seen and heard, that he testifieth; and **but few men** receiveth his testimony.

He **who** hath received his testimony hath set to his seal that God is true.

For he whom God hath sent speaketh the words of God: for God giveth **him** not the Spirit by measure, **for he dwelleth in him, even the fullness.**

The Father loveth the Son, and hath given all things into his **hands,**

And he **who** believeth on the Son hath everlasting life: **and shall receive of his**

The Testimony of John

believeth not the Son shall not ~~see life; but~~ the wrath of God ~~abideth on~~ him.

John 4:1 When therefore ~~the Lord knew how~~ the Pharisees had heard that Jesus made and baptized more disciples than John,

John 4:2 (Though ~~Jesus~~ himself baptized not, ~~but~~ his disciples,)

John 4:3 He left Judaea, and departed again into Galilee.

John 4:4 And ~~he~~ must needs go through Samaria.

John 4:5 Then ~~cometh~~ he to ~~a~~ city of Samaria, which is called Sychar, near to the parcel of ground ~~that~~ Jacob gave to his son Joseph.

John 4:6 ~~Now~~ Jacob's well was ~~there~~. Jesus ~~therefore,~~ being ~~wearied~~ with *his* journey, sat ~~thus~~ on the well: ~~and it was about the sixth hour.~~

John 4:7 There ~~cometh~~ a woman of Samaria to draw water: Jesus ~~saith~~ unto her, Give me to drink.

John 4:8 (~~For~~ his disciples were gone away ~~unto~~ the city to buy meat.)

John 4:9 ~~Then saith~~ the woman of Samaria unto him, How is it that thou, being a Jew, askest drink of me, ~~which~~ am a woman of Samaria? ~~for~~ the Jews have no dealings with the Samaritans.

fullness, **but** he **who** believeth not the Son shall not **receive of his fullness, for** the wrath of God **is upon** him.

When therefore the Pharisees had heard that Jesus made and baptized more disciples than John, **they sought more diligently some means that they might put him to death; for many received John as a prophet, but they believed not on Jesus. Now the Lord knew this,**

Though **he** himself baptized not **so many as** his disciples, **for he suffered them for an example, preferring one another.**

And he left Judea, and departed again into Galilee,

And **saith unto his disciples, I** must needs go through Samaria.

Then **he** cometh to **the** city of Samaria, which is called Sychar, near to the parcel of ground **which** Jacob gave to his son Joseph,

The place where Jacob's well was. **Now** Jesus being **weary** with his journey, **it being about the sixth hour,** sat **down** on the well.

And there **came** a woman of Samaria to draw water: Jesus **said** unto her, Give me to drink.

(**Now** his disciples were gone away **into** the city to buy meat.)

Wherefore, he being alone, the woman of Samaria **said** unto him, How is it that thou, being a Jew, askest drink of me, **who** am a woman of Samaria? the Jews have no dealings with the Samaritans.

John 4:10 Jesus answered and said unto her, If thou knewest the gift of God, and who it is ~~that~~ saith to thee, Give me to drink; thou wouldest have asked of him, and he would have given thee living water.

John 4:11 The woman ~~saith~~ unto him, Sir, thou hast nothing to draw with, and the well is deep: from whence then hast thou that living water?

John 4:12 Art thou greater than our father Jacob, ~~which~~ gave us the well, and drank thereof himself, and his children, and his cattle?

John 4:13 Jesus answered and said unto her, Whosoever ~~drinketh~~ of this ~~water~~ shall thirst again:

John 4:14 But whosoever drinketh of the water ~~that~~ I shall give him shall never thirst; but the water that I shall give him shall be in him a well of water springing up into everlasting life.

John 4:15 The woman ~~saith~~ unto him, Sir, give me this water, that I thirst not, neither come hither to draw.

John 4:16 Jesus ~~saith~~ unto her, Go, call thy husband, and come hither.

John 4:19 The woman ~~saith~~ unto him, Sir, I perceive that thou art a prophet.

John 4:21 Jesus ~~saith~~ unto her, Woman, believe me, the hour cometh, when ye shall neither in this mountain, nor yet at Jerusalem, worship the Father.

John 4:22 Ye worship ye know not what: we know what we worship: ~~for~~ salvation is of the Jews.

Jesus answered and said unto her, If thou knewest the gift of God, and who it is **who** saith to thee, Give me to drink; thou wouldest have asked of him, and he would have given thee living water.

The woman **said** unto him, Sir, thou hast nothing to draw with, and the well is deep: from whence then hast thou that living water?

Art thou greater than our father Jacob, **who** gave us the well, and drank thereof himself, and his children, and his cattle?

Jesus answered and said unto her, Whosoever **shall drink** of this **well** shall thirst again:

But whosoever drinketh of the water **which** I shall give him shall never thirst; but the water that I shall give him shall be in him a well of water springing up into everlasting life.

The woman **said** unto him, Sir, give me **of** this water, that I thirst not, neither come hither to draw.

Jesus **said** unto her, Go, call thy husband, and come hither.

The woman **said** unto him, Sir, I perceive that thou art a prophet.

Jesus **said** unto her, Woman, believe me, the hour cometh, when ye shall neither in this mountain, nor yet at Jerusalem, worship the Father.

Ye worship ye know not what: we know what we worship: **and** salvation is of the Jews.

The Testimony of John

John 4:23 ~~But~~ the hour cometh, and now is, when the true worshippers shall worship the Father in spirit and in truth: for the Father seeketh such to worship him.

John 4:24 God ~~is a~~ Spirit: and they ~~that~~ worship him must worship ~~him~~ in spirit and in truth.

John 4:25 The woman ~~saith~~ unto him, I know that Messias cometh, ~~which~~ is called Christ: when he is come, he will tell us all things.

John 4:26 Jesus ~~saith~~ unto her, I ~~that~~ speak unto thee am ~~he~~.

John 4:29 Come, see a man, ~~which~~ told me all things that ~~ever~~ I ~~did~~: is not this the Christ?

John 4:31 In the mean ~~while~~ his disciples prayed him, saying, Master, eat.

John 4:33 Therefore said the disciples one to another, Hath any man brought him ~~ought~~ to eat?

John 4:34 Jesus ~~saith~~ unto them, My meat is to do the will of him ~~that~~ sent me, and to finish his work.

John 4:35 Say not ye, There are yet four months, ~~and~~ *then* cometh harvest? behold, I say unto you, Lift up your eyes, and look on the fields; for they are white already to harvest.

John 4:36 And he ~~that~~ reapeth receiveth wages, and gathereth fruit unto life eternal: that both he ~~that~~ soweth and he ~~that~~ reapeth may rejoice together.

John 4:38 I sent you to reap that whereon ye bestowed no labour: ~~other~~

And the hour cometh, and now is, when the true worshippers shall worship the Father in spirit and in truth: for the Father seeketh such to worship him.

For unto such hath God **promised his** Spirit: and they **who** worship him must worship in spirit and in truth.

The woman **said** unto him, I know that Messias cometh, **who** is called Christ: when he is come, he will tell us all things.

Jesus **said** unto her, I **who** speak unto thee am **the Messias**.

Come, see a man, **who** told me all things that I **have ever done**: is not this the Christ?

In the mean **time** his disciples prayed him, saying, Master, eat.

Therefore said the disciples one to another, Hath any man brought him **meat** to eat?

Jesus **said** unto them, My meat is to do the will of him **who** sent me, and to finish his work.

Say not ye, There are yet four months, then cometh harvest? behold, I say unto you, Lift up your eyes, and look on the fields; for they are white already to harvest.

And he **who** reapeth receiveth wages, and gathereth fruit unto life eternal: that both he **who** soweth and he **who** reapeth may rejoice together.

I **have** sent you to reap that whereon ye **have** bestowed no labour: **the prophets** men laboured, and ye ~~are~~ entered into their labours.

John 4:39 And many of the Samaritans of that city believed on him for the saying of the woman, ~~which~~ testified, He told me all that ~~ever~~ I ~~did~~.

John 4:42 And said unto the woman, Now we believe, not because of thy saying: ~~for~~ we have heard ourselves, and know that this is indeed the Christ ~~him~~, the Saviour of the world.

John 4:45 Then when he ~~was~~ come into Galilee, the Galilaeans received him, having seen all the things ~~that~~ he ~~did~~ at Jerusalem at the feast: for they also went unto the feast.

John 4:47 When he heard ~~that~~ Jesus was come out of Judaea into Galilee, he went unto him, and besought him that he would come down, and heal his son: for he was at the point of death.

John 4:49 The nobleman ~~saith~~ unto him, Sir, come down ~~ere~~ my child die.

John 4:50 Jesus ~~saith~~ unto him, Go thy way; thy son liveth. And the man believed the word ~~that~~ Jesus had spoken unto him, and he went his way.

John 4:51 And as he was now going down, his servants met him, and ~~told him~~, saying, Thy son liveth.

John 4:53 So the father knew that ~~it was at~~ the same hour, in the which Jesus said unto him, Thy son liveth: and himself believed, and his whole house.

John 4:54 This ~~is again~~ the second miracle ~~that~~ Jesus ~~did~~, when he ~~was~~ come out of Judaea into Galilee.

have laboured, and ye **have** entered into their labours.

And many of the Samaritans of that city believed on him for the saying of the woman, **who** testified, He told me all that I **have ever done**.

And said unto the woman, Now we believe, not because of thy saying: we have heard **for** ourselves, and know that this is indeed the Christ, the Saviour of the world.

Then when he **had** come into Galilee, the Galilaeans received him, having seen all the things **which** he **had done** at Jerusalem at the feast: for they also went unto the feast.

When he heard Jesus was come out of Judea into Galilee, he went unto him, and besought him that he would come down, and heal his son: for he was at the point of death.

The nobleman **said** unto him, Sir, come down **before** my child die.

Jesus **said** unto him, Go thy way; thy son liveth. And the man believed the word **which** Jesus had spoken unto him, and he went his way.

And as he was now going down **to his house**, his servants met him, and **spake**, saying, Thy son liveth.

So the father knew that **his son was healed in** the same hour, in the which Jesus said unto him, Thy son liveth: and himself believed, and his whole house.

This **being** the second miracle **which** Jesus **had done**, when he **had** come out of Judea into Galilee.

The Testimony of John

John 5:3 In these lay a great ~~multitude of~~ impotent folk, of blind, halt, withered, waiting for the moving of the water.	In these **porches** lay a great **many** impotent folk, of blind, halt, withered, waiting for the moving of the water.
John 5:5 And a certain man was there, ~~which~~ had an infirmity thirty and eight years.	And a certain man was there, **who** had an infirmity thirty and eight years.
John 5:6 ~~When~~ Jesus saw him lie, and knew that he had been now a long time ~~in that case~~, he ~~saith~~ unto him, Wilt thou be made whole?	**And** Jesus saw him lie, and knew that he had been now a long time **afflicted, and** he **said** unto him, Wilt thou be made whole?
John 5:8 Jesus ~~saith~~ unto him, Rise, take up thy bed, and walk.	Jesus **said** unto him, Rise, take up thy bed, and walk.
John 5:9 And immediately the man was made whole, and took up his bed, and walked: and ~~on the same day~~ was the sabbath.	And immediately the man was made whole, and took up his bed, and walked: and **it** was **on** the Sabbath **day**.
John 5:10 The Jews therefore said unto him ~~that~~ was cured, It is the sabbath day: it is not lawful for thee to carry *thy* bed.	The Jews therefore said unto him **who** was cured, It is the sabbath day: it is not lawful for thee to carry thy bed.
John 5:11 He answered them, He ~~that~~ made me whole, ~~the same~~ said unto me, Take up thy bed, and walk.	He answered them, He **who** made me whole, said unto me, Take up thy bed, and walk.
John 5:12 Then ~~asked~~ they him, What man is ~~that which~~ said unto thee, Take up thy bed, and walk?	Then **answered** they him **saying**, What man is **he who** said unto thee, Take up thy bed, and walk?
John 5:13 And he that was healed ~~wist~~ not who it was: for Jesus had conveyed himself away, a multitude being in ~~that~~ place.	And he that was healed **knew** not who it was: for Jesus had conveyed himself away, a multitude being in **the** place.
John 5:15 The man departed, and told the Jews that it was Jesus~~, which~~ had made him whole.	The man departed, and told the Jews that it was Jesus **who** had made him whole.
John 5:18 Therefore the Jews sought the more to kill him, because he not only ~~had~~ broken the sabbath, but said	Therefore the Jews sought the more to kill him, because he **had** not only broken the sabbath, but said also that God

also that God was his Father, making himself equal with God.

John 5:23 That all ~~men~~ should honour the Son, even as they honour the Father. He ~~that~~ honoureth not the Son honoureth not the Father ~~which~~ hath sent him.

John 5:24 Verily, verily, I say unto you, He ~~that~~ heareth my word, and believeth on him ~~that~~ sent me, hath everlasting life, and shall not come into condemnation; but is passed from death ~~unto~~ life.

John 5:25 Verily, verily, I say unto you, The hour is coming, and now is, when the dead shall hear the voice of the Son of God: and they ~~that~~ hear shall live.

John 5:28 Marvel not at this: for the hour is coming, in the which all ~~that~~ are in ~~the~~ graves shall hear his voice,

John 5:29 And shall come forth; they ~~that~~ have done good, ~~unto~~ the resurrection of ~~life~~; and they ~~that~~ have done evil, ~~unto~~ the resurrection of ~~damnation~~.

John 5:30 ~~I can of mine own self do nothing~~: as I hear, I judge: and my judgment is just; because I seek not mine own will, but the will of the Father ~~which~~ hath sent me.

John 5:31 If I bear witness of myself, my witness is ~~not~~ true.

John 5:32 There is another ~~that~~ beareth witness of me; and I know that the ~~witness~~ which he ~~witnesseth~~ of me is true.

John 5:33 Ye sent unto John, and he bare witness unto the truth.

was his Father, making himself equal with God.

That all should honour the Son, even as they honour the Father. He **who** honoureth not the Son honoureth not the Father **who** hath sent him.

Verily, verily, I say unto you, He **who** heareth my word, and believeth on him **who** sent me, hath everlasting life, and shall not come into condemnation; but is passed from death **into** life.

Verily, verily, I say unto you, The hour is coming, and now is, when the dead shall hear the voice of the Son of God: and they **who** hear shall live.

Marvel not at this: for the hour is coming, in the which all **who** are in **their** graves shall hear his voice,

And shall come forth; they **who** have done good, **in** the resurrection of **the just**; and they **who** have done evil, **in** the resurrection of **the unjust; and shall all be judged of the Son of man.**

For as I hear, I judge: and my judgment is just; **for I can of mine own self do nothing**; because I seek not mine own will, but the will of the Father **who** hath sent me.

Therefore if I bear witness of myself, **yet** my witness is true.

For I am not alone, there is another **who** beareth witness of me; and I know that the **testimony** which he **giveth** of me is true.

Ye sent unto John, and he bare witness **also** unto the truth.

The Testimony of John

John 5:34 ~~But I receive~~ not testimony ~~from~~ man: but ~~these things I say, that ye might be saved~~.	And he received not his testimony of man, but of God. And ye yourselves say that he is a prophet, therefore ye ought to receive his testimony. These things I say that ye might be saved.
John 5:35 He was a burning and ~~a~~ shining light: and ye were willing for a season to rejoice in his light.	He was a burning and shining light: and ye were willing for a season to rejoice in his light.
John 5:36 But I have greater witness than ~~that~~ of John: for the works which the Father hath given me to finish, the same works that I do, bear witness of me, that the Father hath sent me.	But I have **a** greater witness than **the testimony** of John: for the works which the Father hath given me to finish, the same works that I do, bear witness of me, that the Father hath sent me.
John 5:37 And the Father himself, ~~which hath~~ sent me, hath borne witness of me. Ye have ~~neither~~ heard his voice at any time, nor seen his shape.	And the Father himself, **who** sent me, hath borne witness of me. **And verily I testify unto you, that** ye have **never** heard his voice at any time, nor seen his shape.
John 5:38 ~~And ye~~ have not his word abiding in you: ~~for~~ whom he hath sent, ~~him~~ ye believe not.	**For you** have not his word abiding in you: **and him** whom he hath sent, ye believe not.
John 5:40 And ye will not come to me, that ye might have life.	And ye will not come to me, that ye might have life, **lest ye should honor me.**
John 5:44 How can ye believe, ~~which receive honour one of another, and~~ seek ~~not the~~ honour ~~that~~ cometh from God only?	How can ye believe, **who** seek honour **one of another and seek not the honour which** cometh from God only?
John 5:45 Do not think that I will accuse you to the Father: there is ~~one that~~ accuseth you, ~~even Moses~~, in whom ye trust.	Do not think that I will accuse you to the Father: there is **Moses who** accuseth you, in whom ye trust.
John 5:46 For had ye believed Moses, ~~ye~~ would have believed me: for he wrote of me.	For had ye believed Moses, **you** would have believed me: for he wrote of me.
John 6:12 When they ~~were filled~~, he said unto his disciples, Gather up the	When they **had eaten and were satisfied**, he said unto his disciples, Gather

John 6:17 And entered into a ship, and went over the sea toward Capernaum. And it was now dark, and Jesus ~~was~~ not come to them.

John 6:19 So when they had rowed about five and twenty or thirty furlongs, they ~~see~~ Jesus walking on the sea, and drawing nigh unto the ship: and they were afraid.

John 6:25 And when they had found him on the other side of the sea, they said unto him, Rabbi, ~~when~~ camest thou hither?

John 6:26 Jesus answered them and said, Verily, verily, I say unto you, Ye seek me, not because ye saw the miracles, but because ye ~~did~~ eat of the loaves, and were filled.

John 6:27 Labour not for the meat which perisheth, but for that meat which endureth unto everlasting life, which the Son of man ~~shall~~ give unto you: for him hath God the Father sealed.

John 6:40 And this is the will of him that sent me, that every one which seeth the Son, and believeth on him, may have everlasting life: and I will raise him up at the last day.

John 6:44 No man can come to me, except ~~the~~ Father ~~which~~ hath sent me ~~draw him: and~~ I will raise ~~him~~ up ~~at the last day~~.

up the fragments that remain, that nothing be lost.

And entered into a ship, and went over the sea toward Capernaum. And it was now dark, and Jesus **had** not come to them.

So when they had rowed about five and twenty or thirty furlongs, they **saw** Jesus walking on the sea, and drawing nigh unto the ship: and they were afraid.

And when they had found him on the other side of the sea, they said unto him, Rabbi, **how** camest thou hither?

Jesus answered them and said, Verily, verily, I say unto you, Ye seek me, not because ye **desire to keep my sayings, neither because ye** saw the miracles, but because ye eat of the loaves, and were filled.

Labour not for the meat which perisheth, but for that meat which endureth unto everlasting life, which the Son of man **hath power to** give unto you: for him hath God the Father sealed.

And this is the will of him that sent me, that every one which seeth the Son, and believeth on him, may have everlasting life: and I will raise him up at the last day **in the resurrection of the just**.

No man can come to me, except **he doeth the will of my Father who** hath sent me. **And this is the will of him who hath sent me, that ye receive the Son; for the Father beareth record of him; and he who receiveth the testimony, and doeth the will of him who

The Testimony of John

John 6:45 It is written in the prophets, And ~~they~~ shall ~~be~~ all taught of God. Every man therefore that hath heard, and hath learned of the Father, cometh unto me.

John 6:49 ~~Your fathers did eat manna in the wilderness, and are dead~~.

John 6:50 ~~This is the bread which cometh down from heaven, that a man may eat thereof, and not die.~~

John 6:51 I am the living bread which came down from heaven: if any man eat of this bread, he shall live for ever: and the bread that I will give is my flesh, which I will give for the life of the world.

John 6:54 Whoso eateth my flesh, and drinketh my blood, hath eternal life; and I will raise him up ~~at the last day~~.

John 6:65 And he said, Therefore said I unto you, that no man can come unto me, except ~~it were given unto him~~ of my Father.

John 7:3 His brethren therefore said unto him, Depart hence, and go into Judaea, that thy disciples also may see the works that thou doest.

John 7:4 For *there is* no man *that* doeth any thing in secret, ~~and~~ he himself seeketh to be known openly. If thou do these things, shew thyself to the world.

John 7:9 When he had said these words unto them, he ~~abode~~ *still* in Galilee.

sent me, I will raise up **in the resurrection of the just.**

For it is written in the prophets, And **these** shall all **be** taught of God. Every man therefore that hath heard, and hath learned of the Father, cometh unto me.

This is the bread which cometh down from heaven, that a man may eat thereof, and not die.

Your fathers did eat manna in the wilderness, and are dead.

But I am the living bread which came down from heaven: if any man eat of this bread, he shall live for ever: and the bread that I will give is my flesh, which I will give for the life of the world.

Whoso eateth my flesh, and drinketh my blood, hath eternal life; and I will raise him up **in the resurrection of the just.**

And he said, Therefore said I unto you, that no man can come unto me, except **he doeth the will** of my Father **who hath sent me.**

His brethren therefore said unto him, Depart hence, and go into Judea, that thy disciples **there** also may see the works that thou doest.

For there is no man that doeth any thing in secret, **but** he himself seeketh to be known openly. If thou do these things, shew thyself to the world.

When he had said these words unto them, he **continued** still in Galilee.

John 7:10 But ~~when~~ his brethren were gone up, then went he also up unto the feast, not openly, but as it were in secret.	But **after** his brethren were gone up, then went he also up unto the feast, not openly, but as it were in secret.
John 7:24 Judge not according to ~~the appearance~~, but judge righteous judgment.	Judge not according to **your traditions**, but judge righteous judgment.
John 7:33 Then said Jesus unto them, Yet a little while ~~am~~ I with you, and *then* I go unto him that sent me.	Then said Jesus unto them, Yet a little while I **am** with you, and then I go unto him that sent me.
John 7:39 (But this spake he of the Spirit, which they that believe on him should receive: for the Holy Ghost was ~~not yet given; because~~ that Jesus was ~~not yet~~ glorified.)	(But this spake he of the Spirit, which they that believe on him should receive: for the Holy Ghost was **promised unto them who believe after** that Jesus was glorified.)
John 8:1 Jesus went unto the mount of Olives.	**And** Jesus went unto the mount of Olives.
John 8:3 And the scribes and Pharisees brought unto him a woman taken in adultery; and when they had set her in the midst,	And the scribes and Pharisees brought unto him a woman taken in adultery; and when they had set her in the midst **of the people**,
John 8:6 This they said, tempting him, that they might have to accuse him. But Jesus stooped down, and with his finger wrote on the ground, ~~as though he heard them not~~.	This they said, tempting him, that they might have to accuse him. But Jesus stooped down, and with his finger wrote on the ground.
John 8:9 And they which heard *it*, being convicted by *their own* conscience, went out one by one, beginning at the eldest, *even* unto the last: and Jesus was left alone, and the woman standing in the midst.	And they which heard it, being convicted by their own conscience, went out one by one, beginning at the eldest, even unto the last: and Jesus was left alone, and the woman standing in the midst **of the temple**.
John 8:10 When Jesus had ~~lifted~~ up himself, and saw none ~~but~~ the woman, he said unto her, Woman, where are those thine accusers? hath no man condemned thee?	When Jesus had **raised** up himself, and saw none **of her accusers, and** the woman **standing**, he said unto her, Woman, where are those thine accusers? hath no man condemned thee?

The Testimony of John

John 8:11 She said, No man, Lord. And Jesus said unto her, Neither do I condemn thee: go, and sin no more.

John 8:43 Why do ye not understand my speech? *even* because ye cannot ~~hear~~ my word.

John 8:47 He that is of God heareth God's words: ye therefore ~~hear~~ *them* not, because ye are not of God.

John 9:4 I must work the works of him that sent me, while ~~it is day: the night~~ cometh, when ~~no man can~~ work.

John 9:13 They brought to the Pharisees ~~him that aforetime was blind~~.

John 9:17 They say unto the blind man again, What sayest thou of him, ~~that he~~ hath opened thine eyes? He said, He is a prophet.

John 9:27 He answered them, I have told you already, and ye did not ~~hear~~: wherefore would ~~ye hear it again? will ye also~~ be his disciples?

John 9:29 We know that God spake unto Moses: *as for* this ~~fellow~~, we know not from whence he is.

John 9:32 Since the world began was it not heard that any man opened the eyes of one that was born blind.

John 10:7 Then said Jesus unto them again, Verily, verily, I say unto you, I am the door of the ~~sheep~~.

She said, No man, Lord. And Jesus said unto her, Neither do I condemn thee: go, and sin no more. **And the woman glorified God from that hour, and believed on his name.**

Why do ye not understand my speech? even because ye cannot **bear** my word.

He that is of God heareth God's words: ye therefore **receive** them not, because ye are not of God.

I must work the works of him that sent me, while **I am with you; the time** cometh when **I shall have finished my work, then I go unto the Father.**

And they brought **him who had been blind,** to the Pharisees.

They say unto the blind man again, What sayest thou of him, **who** hath opened thine eyes? He said, He is a prophet.

He answered them, I have told you already, and ye did not **believe**: wherefore would **you believe if I should tell you again and would you** be his disciples?

We know that God spake unto Moses: as for this **man**, we know not from whence he is.

Since the world began was it not heard that any man opened the eyes of one that was born blind **except he be of God.**

Then said Jesus unto them again, Verily, verily, I say unto you, I am the door of the **sheepfold.**

John 10:8 All that ever came before me are thieves and robbers: but the sheep did not hear them.	All that ever came before me **who testified not of me** are thieves and robbers: but the sheep did not hear them.
John 10:11 I am the good shepherd: the good shepherd giveth his life for ~~the~~ sheep.	I am the good shepherd: the good shepherd giveth his life for **his** sheep.
John 10:12 ~~But he that is~~ an hireling, ~~and not the shepherd,~~ whose own the sheep are not, seeth the wolf coming, and leaveth the sheep, and fleeth: and the wolf catcheth ~~them~~, and scattereth ~~the sheep~~.	**And the shepherd is not as** a hireling, whose own the sheep are not, **who** seeth the wolf coming, and leaveth the sheep, and fleeth: and the wolf catcheth **the sheep**, and scattereth **them**.
John 10:13 ~~The hireling fleeth, because he is an hireling, and careth not for the sheep.~~	For I am the good shepherd, and know my sheep, and am known of mine.
John 10:14 ~~I am the good shepherd, and know my sheep, and am known of mine.~~	But he who is a hireling fleeth, because he is a hireling, and careth not for the sheep.
John 11:1 Now a certain *man* was sick, ~~named~~ Lazarus, of Bethany, ~~the town of~~ Mary ~~and~~ her sister Martha.	Now a certain man was sick, **whose name was** Lazarus, of **the town** of Bethany;
John 11:2 (~~It was that~~ Mary ~~which~~ anointed the Lord with ointment, and wiped his feet with her hair, whose brother Lazarus was sick.)	and Mary, **his sister, who** anointed the Lord with ointment and wiped his feet with her hair, **lived with her sister Martha, in** whose **house her** brother Lazarus was sick.
John 11:4 When Jesus heard ~~that~~, he said, This sickness is not unto death, but for the glory of God, that the Son of God might be glorified thereby.	**And** when Jesus heard **he was sick** he said, This sickness is not unto death, but for the glory of God, that the Son of God might be glorified thereby.
John 11:6 ~~When he had heard therefore that he was sick, he abode~~ two days ~~still in the same place where he was~~.	**And Jesus tarried** two days **after he heard that Lazarus was sick.**
John 11:7 ~~Then~~ after that saith ~~he to~~ *his* disciples, Let us go into Judaea again.	After that **he** saith **unto** his disciples, Let us go into Judea again.

The Testimony of John

John 11:8 *His* disciples ~~say~~ unto him, Master, the Jews of late sought to stone thee; and goest thou thither again?	**But** his disciples **said** unto him, Master, the Jews of late sought to stone thee; and goest thou thither again?
John 11:16 Then said Thomas, which is called Didymus, unto his fellow-disciples, Let us also go, that we may die with him.	Then said Thomas, which is called Didymus, unto his fellowdisciples, Let us also go, that we may die with him. **For they feared lest the Jews should take Jesus and put him to death, for as yet they did not understand the power of God.**
John 11:17 ~~Then~~ when Jesus came, ~~he found that he had~~ *lain* in the grave four days ~~already~~.	And when Jesus came **to Bethany, to Martha's house, Lazarus had already been** in the grave four days.
John 11:29 As soon as ~~she~~ heard *that*, she arose quickly, and came unto him.	As soon as **Mary** heard that **Jesus was come**, she arose quickly, and came unto him.
John 11:30 Now Jesus was not yet come into the town, but was in ~~that~~ place where Martha met him.	Now Jesus was not yet come into the town, but was in **the** place where Martha met him.
John 11:47 Then gathered the chief priests and the Pharisees a council, and said, What do ~~we~~? for this man doeth many miracles.	Then gathered the chief priests and the Pharisees a council, and said, What **shall we do**? for this man doeth many miracles.
John 11:56 Then sought they for Jesus, and spake among themselves, as they stood in the temple, What think ye, ~~that he~~ will not come to the feast?	Then sought they for Jesus, and spake among themselves, as they stood in the temple, What think ye **of Jesus**, will **he** not come to the feast?
John 11:57 Now both the chief priests and the Pharisees had given a commandment, that, if any man knew where he ~~were~~, he should shew ~~it~~, that they might take him.	Now both the chief priests and the Pharisees had given a commandment, that, if any man knew where he **was**, he should shew **them**, that they might take him.
John 12:7 Then said Jesus, Let her alone: ~~against the day of my burying hath~~ she ~~kept~~ this.	Then said Jesus, Let her alone: **for** she **hath preserved** this **ointment until now, that she might anoint me in token of my burial.**

John 12:14 And Jesus, when he had ~~found~~ a young ass, sat thereon; as it is written,

John 13:8 Peter saith unto him, Thou ~~shalt never~~ wash my feet. Jesus answered him, If I wash thee not, thou hast no part with me.

John 13:10 Jesus saith to him, He that ~~is~~ washed needeth not save to wash *his* feet, but is clean every whit: and ye are clean, but not all.

John 13:19 Now I tell you before it come, that, when it is come to pass, ye may believe that I am ~~he~~.

John 14:3 And ~~if~~ I go and prepare a place for you, ~~I will~~ come again, and receive you unto myself; that where I am, ~~there~~ ye may be also.

John 14:30 Hereafter I will not talk much with you: for the prince of this world cometh, ~~and~~ hath ~~nothing in~~ me.

John 14:31 ~~But that the world~~ may know that I love the Father; and as the Father gave me commandment, even so I do. Arise, let us go hence.

John 16:10 Of righteousness, because I go to my Father, and ~~ye~~ see me no more;

John 16:23 And in that day ye shall ask me nothing. Verily, verily, I say unto you, Whatsoever ye shall ask the Father in my name, he will give *it* you.

And Jesus, when he had **sent two of his disciples, and got** a young ass, sat thereon; as it is written,

Peter saith unto him, Thou **needest not to** wash my feet. Jesus answered him, If I wash thee not, thou hast no part with me.

Jesus saith to him, He that **has** washed **his hands and his head** needeth not save to wash his feet, but is clean every whit: and ye are clean, but not all. **Now this was the custom of the Jews under their law: wherefore, Jesus did this that the law might be fulfilled.**

Now I tell you before it come, that, when it is come to pass, ye may believe that I am **the Christ**.

And **when** I go **I will** prepare a place for you, **and** come again, and receive you unto myself; that where I am ye may be also.

Hereafter I will not talk much with you: for the **prince of darkness, who is of** this world cometh, **but** hath **no power over me, but he hath power over you.**

And I tell you these things, that ye may know that I love the Father; and as the Father gave me commandment, even so I do. Arise, let us go hence.

Of righteousness, because I go to my Father, and **they** see me no more;

And in that day ye shall ask me nothing **but it shall be done unto you.** Verily, verily, I say unto you, Whatsoever ye shall ask the Father in my name, he will give it you.

The Testimony of John

John 19:2 And the soldiers platted a crown of thorns, and put *it* on his head, and they put on him a purple robe,	And the soldiers platted a crown of thorns, and put it on his head, and they put on him a purple robe,
John 19:17 And he bearing his cross went forth into a place called *the place* of a ~~skull~~, which is called in the Hebrew Golgotha:	And he bearing his cross went forth into a place called the place of a **burial**, which is called in the Hebrew Golgotha:
John 19:29 Now there was ~~set~~ a vessel full of vinegar: and they filled a spunge with ~~vinegar~~, and put ~~it~~ upon hyssop, and put ~~it~~ to his mouth.	Now there was a vessel full of vinegar **mingled with gall**: and they filled a spunge with **it**, and put upon hyssop, and put [it] to his mouth.
John 20:1 The first *day* of the week cometh Mary Magdalene early, when it was yet dark, unto the sepulchre, and seeth the stone taken away from the sepulchre.	The first day of the week cometh Mary Magdalene early, when it was yet dark, unto the sepulchre, and seeth the stone taken away from the sepulchre, [and] **two angels sitting thereon.**
John 20:17 Jesus saith unto her, ~~Touch~~ me not; for I am not yet ascended to my Father: but go to my brethren, and say unto them, I ascend unto my Father, and your Father; and *to* my God, and your God.	Jesus saith unto her, **Hold** me not; for I am not yet ascended to my Father: but go to my brethren, and say unto them, I ascend unto my Father, and your Father; and to my God, and your God.

The Acts of the Apostles

King James Version

Acts 1:3 To whom also he shewed himself alive after his ~~passion~~ by many infallible proofs, being seen of them forty days, and speaking of the things pertaining to the kingdom of God:

Acts 1:4 And, being assembled together ~~with them~~, commanded them that they should not depart from Jerusalem, but wait for the promise of the Father, which, ~~saith he~~, ye have heard of me.

Acts 2:3 And there appeared unto them cloven tongues like as of fire, and it ~~sat~~ upon each of them.

Acts 2:27 Because thou wilt not leave my soul in ~~hell~~, neither wilt thou suffer thine Holy One to see corruption.

Acts 3:1 Now Peter and John went up together into the temple at the hour ~~of~~ prayer, ~~being the ninth hour~~.

Acts 3:4 And Peter, fastening ~~his~~ eyes upon him ~~with John~~, said, Look on us.

Acts 3:12 And when Peter saw *it*, he answered unto the people, Ye men of Israel, why marvel ye at this? or why look ye so earnestly on us, as though by our own power or holiness we had made this man to walk?

Acts 3:16 And ~~his name~~ through faith in his name hath made ~~this man~~ strong, whom ye see and know: yea, the faith which is ~~by~~ him hath given him this perfect soundness in the presence of you all.

Joseph Smith Translation

To whom also he shewed himself alive after his **sufferings** by many infallible proofs, being seen of them forty days, and speaking of the things pertaining to the kingdom of God:

And, being **with them when they were** assembled together, commanded them that they should not depart from Jerusalem, but wait for the promise of the Father, which ye have heard of me.

And there appeared unto them cloven tongues like as of fire, and it **rested** upon each of them.

Because thou wilt not leave my soul in **prison**, neither wilt thou suffer thine Holy One to see corruption.

Now Peter and John went up together into the temple at the **ninth** hour **for** prayer.

And Peter **and John**, fastening **their** eyes upon him, said, Look on us.

And when Peter saw **this**, he answered **and said** unto the people, Ye men of Israel, why marvel ye at this? or why look ye so earnestly on us, as though by our own power or holiness we had made this man to walk?

And **this man**, through faith in his name, hath **been** made strong, whom ye see and know: yea, the faith which is **in** him hath given him this perfect soundness in the presence of you all.

The Acts of the Apostles

Acts 3:17 And now, brethren, I ~~wot~~ that through ignorance ye ~~did it~~, as ~~did~~ also your rulers.

Acts 3:20 And he shall send Jesus Christ, which before was preached unto you:

Acts 3:21 Whom the ~~heaven~~ must receive until the times of restitution of all things, which God hath spoken by the mouth of all his holy prophets since the world began.

Acts 4:21 So when they had further threatened them, they let them go, finding nothing how they might punish them, because of the people: for ~~all men~~ glorified God for that which was done.

Acts 5:13 And of the ~~rest~~ durst no man join himself to them: but the people magnified them.

Acts 5:39 But if it be of God, ye cannot overthrow it; lest ~~haply~~ ye be found even to fight against God.

Acts 6:9 ~~Then~~ there arose certain of the synagogue, ~~which is~~ called ~~the synagogue of~~ the Libertines, and Cyrenians, and Alexandrians, and of them of Cilicia and of Asia, disputing with Stephen.

Acts 7:39 ~~To~~ whom our fathers would not obey, but thrust *him* from them, and in their hearts turned back again into Egypt.

Acts 7:40 Saying unto Aaron, Make us gods to go before us: for ~~as for~~ this Moses, which brought us out of the land of Egypt, we ~~wot~~ not what is become of him.

Acts 7:42 Then God ~~turned, and~~ gave them up to worship the host of

And now, brethren, I **know** that through ignorance ye **have done this**, as also your rulers.

And he shall send Jesus Christ, which before was preached unto you: **whom ye have crucified**

Whom the **heavens** must receive until the times of restitution of all things, which God hath spoken by the mouth of all his holy prophets since the world began.

So when they had further threatened them, they let them go, finding nothing how they might punish them, because of the people: for **many** glorified God for that which was done.

And of the **rulers** durst no man join himself to them: but the people magnified them.

But if it be of God, ye cannot overthrow it; **be careful therefore** lest ye be found even to fight against God.

And there arose certain of the synagogue, **who are** called Libertines, and **also** Cyrenians, and Alexandrians, and of them of Cilicia and of Asia, disputing with Stephen.

Whom our fathers would not obey, but thrust him from them, and in their hearts turned back again into Egypt.

Saying unto Aaron, Make us gods to go before us: for this Moses, which brought us out of the land of Egypt, we **know** not what is become of him.

Then God gave them up to worship the host of heaven; as it is written in

heaven; as it is written in the book of the prophets, O ye house of Israel, have ye offered to me slain beasts and sacrifices ~~by the space of~~ forty years in the wilderness?

Acts 7:44 Our fathers had the tabernacle of witness in the wilderness, as he had appointed, speaking unto Moses, that he should make it according to the ~~fashion~~ that he had seen.

Acts 7:59 And they stoned Stephen, calling upon *God,* ~~and saying~~, Lord Jesus, receive my spirit.

Acts 9:7 And ~~the men which journeyed~~ with him ~~stood speechless, hearing a~~ voice, ~~but seeing no man.~~

Acts 9:24 But their laying ~~await~~ was known of Saul. And they watched the gates day and night to kill him.

Acts 9:30 ~~Which~~ when the brethren knew, they brought him down to Caesarea, and sent him forth to Tarsus.

Acts 9:32 And it came to pass, as Peter passed throughout all ~~quarters~~, he came down also to the saints which dwelt at Lydda.

Acts 12:7 And, behold, the angel of the Lord came ~~upon~~ *him,* and a light shined in the prison: and he smote Peter on the side, and raised him up, saying, Arise up quickly. And his chains fell off from *his* hands.

Acts 13:36 For David, after he had served his own generation by the will of God, fell ~~on sleep~~, and was laid unto his fathers, and saw corruption:

the book of the prophets, O ye house of Israel, have ye offered to me slain beasts and sacrifices forty years in the wilderness?

Our fathers had the tabernacle of witness in the wilderness, as he had appointed, speaking unto Moses, that he should make it according to the **pattern** that he had seen.

And they stoned Stephen, **and he,** calling upon God, **said,** Lord Jesus, receive my spirit.

And **they who were journeying** with him **saw indeed the light, and were afraid; but they heard not the** voice **of him who spake to him.**

But their laying **in** wait was known of Saul. And they watched the gates day and night to kill him.

When the brethren knew **this,** they brought him down to Caesarea, and sent him forth to Tarsus.

And it came to pass, as Peter passed throughout all **these regions,** he came down also to the saints which dwelt at Lydda.

And, behold, the angel of the Lord came **unto** him, and a light shined in the prison: and he smote Peter on the side, and raised him up, saying, Arise up quickly. And his chains fell off from his hands.

For David, after he had served his own generation by the will of God, fell **asleep,** and was laid unto his fathers, and saw corruption:

The Acts of the Apostles

Acts 13:48 And when the Gentiles heard this, they were glad, and glorified the word of the Lord: and as many as were ordained to eternal life ~~believed~~.

Acts 14:14 *Which* when the apostles, Barnabas and Paul, heard *of,* they rent their clothes, and ran in among the people, crying out,

Acts 15:24 Forasmuch as we have heard, that certain which went out from us have troubled you with words, subverting your souls, saying, ~~Ye must~~ be circumcised, and keep the law: to whom we gave no ~~such~~ commandment:

Acts 16:13 And on the sabbath we went out of the city by a river side, where prayer ~~was wont~~ to be made; and we sat down, and spake unto the women which resorted *thither*.

Acts 17:19 And they took him, and brought him unto Areopagus, saying, May we know what this new doctrine, whereof thou speakest, *is?*

Acts 17:27 That they should seek the Lord, if ~~haply they might feel~~ after him, and find him, ~~though~~ he ~~be~~ not far from every one of us:

Acts 17:31 Because he hath appointed a day, in the which he will judge the world in righteousness by ~~that man~~ whom he hath ordained; ~~whereof~~ he hath given assurance unto all ~~men~~, in that he hath raised him from the dead.

Acts 20:21 Testifying both to the Jews, and also to the Greeks, repentance toward God, and faith toward our Lord Jesus Christ.

Acts 21:25 As touching the Gentiles which believe, we have written *and*

And when the Gentiles heard this, they were glad, and glorified the word of the Lord: and as many as **believed**, were ordained to eternal life.

When the apostles, Barnabas and Paul, heard **this**, they rent their clothes, and ran in among the people, crying out,

Forasmuch as we have heard, that certain **men** which went out from us have troubled you with words, subverting your souls, saying, Be circumcised, and keep the law: to whom we gave no commandment:

And on the sabbath we went out of the city by a river side, where **the people resorted for** prayer to be made; and we sat down, and spake unto the women which resorted thither.

And they took him, and brought him unto **the** Areopagus, saying, May we know what this new doctrine, whereof thou speakest, is?

That they should seek the Lord, if **they are willing to** find him, **for** he **is** not far from every one of us:

Because he hath appointed a day, in the which he will judge the world in righteousness by **him** whom he hath ordained; **and of this** he hath given assurance unto all, in that he hath raised him from the dead.

Testifying both to the Jews, and also to the Greeks, repentance toward God, and faith **on the name of** our Lord Jesus Christ.

As touching the Gentiles which believe, we have written and concluded that concluded that they observe no such thing, save only that they keep themselves from *things* offered to idols, and from blood, and from strangled, and from fornication.

Acts 22:29 Then straightway they departed from him which should have examined him: and the chief captain also was afraid, after he knew that he was a Roman, ~~and~~ because he had bound him.

Acts 22:30 On the morrow, because he would have known the certainty wherefore he was accused of the Jews, he ~~loosed him from *his* bands, and~~ commanded the chief priests and all their council to appear, and brought Paul down, and set him before them.

Acts 23:5 Then said Paul, I ~~wist~~ not, brethren, that he was the high priest: for it is written, Thou shalt not speak evil of the ruler of thy people.

Acts 23:15 Now therefore ye with the council signify to the chief captain that he bring him down unto you to morrow, as though ye would enquire something more perfectly concerning him: and we, ~~or ever~~ he come near, are ready to kill him.

Acts 23:27 This man was taken of the Jews, and ~~should~~ have been killed of them: then came I with an army, and rescued him, having understood that he was a Roman.

Acts 25:17 Therefore, when they were come hither, without any delay on the ~~morrow~~ I sat on the judgment seat, and commanded the man to be brought forth.

they observe no such thing, save only that they keep themselves from things offered to idols, and from blood, and from **things** strangled, and from fornication.

Then straightway they departed from him which should have examined him: and the chief captain also was afraid, after he knew that he was a Roman, because he had bound him, **and he loosed him from his bands**.

On the morrow, because he would have known the certainty wherefore he was accused of the Jews, he commanded the chief priests and all their council to appear, and brought Paul down, and set him before them.

Then said Paul, I **did** not **know**, brethren, that he was the high priest: for it is written, Thou shalt not speak evil of the ruler of thy people.

Now therefore ye with the council signify to the chief captain that he bring him down unto you to morrow, as though ye would enquire something more perfectly concerning him: and we, **before** he come near, are ready to kill him.

This man was taken of the Jews, and **would** have been killed of them: then came I with an army, and rescued him, having understood that he was a Roman.

Therefore, when they were come hither, without any delay on the **day following** I sat on the judgment seat, and commanded the man to be brought forth.

The Epistle to the Romans

King James Version

Romans 1:1 Paul, a servant of Jesus Christ, ~~called to be an apostle~~, separated ~~unto~~ the ~~gospel of God~~,

Romans 1:2 Which he had promised ~~afore~~ by his prophets in the holy scriptures,

Romans 1:3 Concerning his Son Jesus Christ our Lord, which was made ~~of~~ the seed of David according to the flesh;

Romans 1:4 And declared ~~to be~~ the Son of God with power, according to ~~the spirit of holiness, by~~ the resurrection from the dead:

Romans 1:5 By whom we have received grace and apostleship, ~~for~~ obedience ~~to the~~ faith among all nations, ~~for his name~~:

Romans 1:6 Among whom ~~are ye also~~ the called of Jesus Christ:

Romans 1:7 To all ~~that be~~ in Rome, beloved of God, called ~~to be~~ saints: Grace to you and peace from God our Father, and the Lord Jesus Christ.

Romans 1:8 First, I thank my God through Jesus Christ ~~for~~ you all~~, that~~ your faith is spoken of throughout the whole world.

Romans 1:9 For God is my witness, whom I serve ~~with my spirit in the gospel of his Son~~, that without ceasing

Joseph Smith Translation

Paul, **an apostle,** a servant of **God, called of** Jesus Christ, **and** separated **to preach** the gospel,

Which he had promised **before** by his prophets in the holy scriptures,

Concerning his Son Jesus Christ our Lord, which was made the seed of David according to the flesh;

And declared the Son of God, with power, **by the spirit,** according to the **truth, through** the resurrection from the dead:

By whom we have received grace and apostleship, **through** obedience, **and** faith **on his name, to preach the gospel** among all nations:

Among whom **ye also are** called of Jesus Christ:

Wherefore, I write to all **who are** in Rome, beloved of God, called saints: Grace to you and peace from God our Father, and the Lord Jesus Christ.

First, I thank my God through Jesus Christ **that** you **are** all **steadfast, and** your faith is spoken of throughout the whole world.

For God is my witness, whom I serve, that without ceasing I make mention of you always in my prayers, **that you may**

253

I make mention of you always in my prayers;

Romans 1:10 Making request, if by any means ~~now~~ at length I ~~might~~ have a prosperous journey by the will of God to come unto you.

Romans 1:11 For I long to see you, that I may impart unto you some spiritual gift, to the end ~~ye may be established~~;

Romans 1:12 ~~That is~~, that I may be comforted together with you by the mutual faith both of you and me.

Romans 1:13 Now I would not have you ignorant, brethren, that oftentimes I purposed to come unto you, (but was ~~let~~ hitherto,) that I might have some fruit among you also, even as among other Gentiles.

Romans 1:15 ~~So,~~ as much as in me is, I am ready to preach the gospel to you that are at Rome also.

Romans 1:17 For therein is the righteousness of God revealed ~~from~~ faith ~~to faith~~: as it is written, The just shall live by faith.

Romans 1:18 For the wrath of God is revealed from heaven against all ungodliness and unrighteousness of men, who ~~hold~~ the truth in unrighteousness;

Romans 1:19 ~~Because~~ that which may be known of God is manifest ~~in~~ them; for God hath ~~shewed it~~ unto them.

Romans 1:20 ~~For~~ the invisible things of him from the creation of the world are

be kept through the spirit, in the gospel of his Son.

Making request **of you to remember me in your prayers, I now write unto you, that you will ask him in faith,** that if by any means, at length, I **may serve you with my labors, and may** have a prosperous journey by the will of God to come unto you.

For I long to see you, that I may impart unto you some spiritual gift, **that it may be established in you** to the end;

That I may be comforted together with you by the mutual faith both of you and me.

Now I would not have you ignorant, brethren, that oftentimes I purposed to come unto you, (but was **hindered** hitherto,) that I might have some fruit among you also, even as among other Gentiles.

And as much as in me is, I am ready to preach the gospel to you that are at Rome also.

For therein is the righteousness of God revealed **through** faith **on his name**: as it is written, The just shall live by faith.

For the wrath of God is revealed from heaven against all ungodliness and unrighteousness of men, who **love not** the truth, **but remain** in unrighteousness;

After that which may be known of God is manifest **to** them; for God hath **revealed** unto them

The invisible things of him from the creation of the world, **which** are clearly

The Epistle to the Romans

clearly seen, being understood by the things that are made, ~~even~~ his eternal power and Godhead; so that they are without excuse:

Romans 1:21 Because that, when they knew God, they glorified *him* not as God, neither were thankful; but became vain in their imaginations, and their foolish ~~heart was~~ darkened.

Romans 1:28 And even as they did not like to retain God ~~in their~~ knowledge, God gave them over to a reprobate mind, to do those things which are not convenient;

Romans 1:32 Who knowing the judgment of God, that they which commit such things are worthy of death, not only do the same, but have pleasure in them that do them.

Romans 2:1 Therefore thou art inexcusable, O man, whosoever thou art that judgest: for wherein thou judgest another, thou condemnest thyself; for thou that judgest doest the same things.

Romans 2:16 In the day when God shall judge the secrets of men by Jesus Christ according to ~~my~~ gospel.

Romans 3:1 What advantage then hath the Jew? or what profit ~~is there~~ of circumcision?

Romans 3:2 Much every way: chiefly, because that unto them were committed the oracles of God.

Romans 3:5 But if our unrighteousness commend the righteousness of God, ~~what shall~~ we say? ~~Is~~ God unrighteous

seen; **things which are not seen** being understood by the things that are made **through** his eternal power and Godhead; so that they are without excuse:

Because that, when they knew God, they glorified him not as God, neither were **they** thankful; but became vain in their imaginations, and their foolish **hearts were** darkened.

And even as they did not like to retain God **according to some** knowledge, God gave them over to a reprobate mind, to do those things which are not convenient;

And some are inexcusable, who knowing the judgment of God, that they which commit such things are worthy of death, not only do the same, but have pleasure in them that do them.

Therefore thou art inexcusable, O man, whosoever thou art that **thus** judgest: for wherein thou judgest another, thou condemnest thyself; for thou that judgest doest the same things.

In the day when God shall judge the secrets of men by Jesus Christ according to **the** gospel.

What advantage then hath the Jew **over the Gentile**? or what profit of circumcision **who is not a Jew from the heart**?

But he who is a Jew from the heart, I say much every way: chiefly, because that unto them were committed the oracles of God.

But if **we remain in** our unrighteousness **and** commend the righteousness of God, **how dare** we say God **is**

who taketh vengeance? (I speak as a man)

Romans 3:7 For if the truth of God hath more abounded through my lie unto his glory; why yet am I also judged as a sinner?

Romans 3:8 And not ~~rather, (as~~ we ~~be~~ slanderously reported, and ~~as~~ some affirm that we say,~~)~~ Let us do evil, that good may come? ~~whose damnation is just~~.

Romans 3:9 What then~~?~~ are we better than they? No, in no wise: for we have ~~before~~ proved ~~both Jews~~ and Gentiles, ~~that they~~ are all under sin;

Romans 3:20 Therefore by the deeds of the law ~~there~~ shall no flesh be justified in his sight: ~~for by the law is the knowledge of sin~~.

Romans 3:24 Being justified ~~freely~~ by his grace through the redemption that is in Christ Jesus:

Romans 3:28 Therefore we conclude that a man is justified by faith without the deeds of the law.

Romans 3:30 Seeing ~~it is one~~ God, ~~which shall~~ justify the circumcision by faith, and uncircumcision through faith.

Romans 4:2 For if Abraham were justified by works, he hath ~~whereof~~ to glory; but not ~~before~~ God.

Romans 4:4 Now to him ~~that worketh~~ is the reward not reckoned of grace, but of debt.

Romans 4:5 But to him that ~~worketh~~ not, but believeth on him ~~that~~ justifieth

unrighteous who taketh vengeance? (I speak as a man **who fears God**.)

For if the truth of God hath more abounded through my lie (**as it is called of the Jews**) unto his glory; why yet am I also judged as a sinner?

And not **received because** we **are** slanderously reported? And some affirm that we say (**whose damnation is just**), Let us do evil, that good may come?

But this is false. If not so, what then are we better than they? No, in no wise: for we have proved **before that Jew** and Gentiles are all under sin;

For by the law is the knowledge of sin. Therefore by the deeds of the law shall no flesh be justified in his sight.

Therefore being justified **only** by his grace through the redemption that is in Christ Jesus:

Therefore we conclude that a man is justified **alone** by faith without the deeds of the law.

Seeing **that** God **will** justify the circumcision by faith, and uncircumcision through faith.

For if Abraham were justified by **the law of** works, he hath to glory **in himself**; but not **of** God.

Now to him **who is justified by the law of works** is the reward reckoned, **not** of grace, but of debt.

But to him that **seeketh** not **to be justified by the law of works**, but believeth

The Epistle to the Romans

the ungodly, his faith is counted for righteousness.

Romans 4:6 Even as David also describeth the blessedness of the man, unto whom God imputeth righteousness without works,

Romans 4:7 *Saying,* Blessed *are* they whose iniquities are forgiven, and whose sins are covered.

Romans 4:16 Therefore ~~it is~~ of faith, ~~that it might be~~ ~~by~~ grace; to the end the promise might be sure to all the seed; not to ~~that~~ only ~~which is~~ of the law, but to ~~that~~ also ~~which is~~ of the faith of Abraham; who is the father of us all,

Romans 5:3 And not only ~~so~~, but we glory in tribulations also: knowing that tribulation worketh patience;

Romans 5:13 (For ~~until~~ the law sin was in the world: ~~but~~ sin is not imputed ~~when there is~~ no law.

Romans 5:14 Nevertheless death reigned from Adam to Moses, even over them that had not sinned after the similitude of Adam's transgression, who is the figure of him that was to come.

Romans 5:15 But ~~not as~~ the offence, ~~so also~~ *is* the free gift. For if through the offence of one many be dead, much more the grace of God, and the gift by grace, ~~which is~~ by one man, Jesus Christ, ~~hath abounded~~ unto many.

Romans 5:16 And not ~~as it was~~ by one that sinned, ~~so~~ *is* the gift: for the judgment ~~was~~ by one to condemnation, but the free gift *is* of many offences unto justification.

on him **who** justifieth **not** the ungodly, his faith is counted for righteousness.

Even as David also describeth the blessedness of the man, unto whom God imputeth righteousness without **the law of** works,

Saying, Blessed are they whose iniquities are forgiven, and whose sins are covered **through faith**.

Therefore **ye are justified** of faith **and works, through** grace, to the end the promise might be sure to all the seed; not to **them** only **who are** of the law, but to **them** also **who are** of the faith of Abraham; who is the father of us all,

And not only **this**, but we glory in tribulations also: knowing that tribulation worketh patience;

(For **before** the law sin was in the world: **yet** sin is not imputed **to those who have** no law.

Nevertheless death reigned from Adam to Moses, even over them that had not sinned after the similitude of Adam's transgression, who is the figure of him that was to come. **For I say that through the offence death reigned over all.**

But the offence is **not as** the free gift, **for the gift aboundeth**. For if through the offence of one many be dead, much more the grace of God, and the gift by grace, **hath abounded** by one man, Jesus Christ, unto many.

And not by one that sinned is the gift: for the judgment **is** by one to condemnation, but the free gift is of many offences unto justification.

Romans 6:7 For he that is dead is freed from sin.	For he that is dead **to sin** is freed from sin.
Romans 6:14 For sin shall not have dominion over you: for ye are not under the law, but under grace.	For **in so doing** sin shall not have dominion over you: for ye are not under the law, but under grace.
Romans 6:17 But God be thanked, that ye ~~were~~ the servants of sin, ~~but~~ ye have obeyed from the heart that form of doctrine which was delivered you.	But God be thanked, that ye **are not** the servants of sin, **for** ye have obeyed from the heart that form of doctrine which was delivered you.
Romans 6:19 I speak after the manner of men because of the infirmity of your flesh: for as ye have yielded your members servants to uncleanness and to iniquity unto iniquity; even so now yield your members servants to righteousness unto holiness.	I speak after the manner of men because of the infirmity of your flesh: for as ye have yielded your members **in times past** servants to uncleanness and to iniquity unto iniquity; even so now yield your members servants to righteousness unto holiness.
Romans 7:1 Know ye not, brethren, (for I speak to them that know the law,) how that the law hath dominion over a man as long as he liveth?	Know ye not, brethren, (for I speak to them that know the law,) how that the law hath dominion over a man **only** as long as he liveth?
Romans 7:2 For the woman which hath an husband is bound by the law to *her* husband ~~so~~ long as he liveth; ~~but~~ if the husband be dead, she is loosed from the law of *her* husband.	For the woman which hath an husband is bound by the law to her husband **only as** long as he liveth; **for** if the husband be dead, she is loosed from the law of her husband.
Romans 7:5 For when we were in the flesh, the motions of sins, which were ~~by~~ the law, did work in our members to bring forth fruit unto death.	For when we were in the flesh, the motions of sins, which were **not according to** the law, did work in our members to bring forth fruit unto death.
Romans 7:6 But now we are delivered from the law, ~~that being dead~~ wherein we were held; that we should serve in newness of spirit, and not *in* the oldness of the letter.	But now we are delivered from the law wherein we were held, **being dead to the law**; that we should serve in newness of spirit, and not in the oldness of the letter.
Romans 7:9 For I was alive without the law ~~once~~: but when the commandment came, sin revived, and I died.	For **once** I was alive without **transgression of** the law: but when the commandment **of Christ** came, sin revived, and I died,

Romans 7:10 And the commandment, which *was ordained* to life, I found ~~to be~~ unto death.

Romans 7:11 For sin, taking occasion ~~by~~ the commandment, deceived me, and by it ~~slew me~~.

Romans 7:12 ~~Wherefore~~ the law *is* holy, and the commandment holy, and just, and good.

Romans 7:13 Was then that which is good made death unto me? God forbid. But sin, that it might appear sin, working death in me ~~by that which is good~~; that sin by the commandment might become exceeding sinful.

Romans 7:14 For we know that the ~~law~~ is spiritual: but I ~~am~~ carnal, sold under sin.

Romans 7:15 For that which I do I allow not: ~~for what I would, that do I not; but what I hate, that do I~~.

Romans 7:16 ~~If then I do that which~~ I would not, ~~I consent unto the law that it is~~ good.

Romans 7:17 ~~Now then it is no more I that do it, but sin that dwelleth in me~~.

Romans 7:18 For I know that in me ~~(that is, in my flesh,)~~ dwelleth no good thing: for to will is present with me; but ~~how~~ to perform that which is good I find not.

And **when I believed not** the commandment **of Christ which came**, which was ordained to life, I found **it condemned me** unto death.

For sin, taking occasion, **denied** the commandment, **and** deceived me, and by it **I was slain**.

Nevertheless I found the law **to be** holy, and the commandment **to be** holy, and just, and good.

Was then that which is good made death unto me? God forbid. But sin, that it might appear sin **by that which is good**, working death in me; that sin by the commandment might become exceeding sinful.

For we know that the **commandment** is spiritual: but **when I was under the law**, **I was yet** carnal, sold under sin.

But now I am spiritual, for that which **I am commanded to do**, I do: and that which **I am commanded not to allow**, I allow not.

For what **I know is not right** I would not **do, for that which is sin, I hate**.

If then I do not that which I would not allow, I consent unto the law, that it is good, **and I am not condemned**.

Now then, it is no more I that do **sin**; but **I seek to subdue that sin which dwelleth in me**. For I know that in me, that is, in my flesh, dwelleth no good thing: for to will is present with me; but to perform that which is good I find not, **only in Christ**.

Romans 7:19 For the good that I would I ~~do not: but the evil which I would not, that~~ I do.

Romans 7:20 ~~Now if I do that I would not, it is no more I that do it, but sin that dwelleth in me~~.

Romans 7:21 ~~I find then a law, that, when I would do good, evil is present with me~~.

Romans 7:22 For I delight in the law of God after the inward man:

Romans 7:23 ~~But~~ I see another law ~~in my members, warring against the law of~~ my mind, and bringing me into captivity to the law of sin which is in my members.

Romans 7:24 O wretched man that I am! who shall deliver me from the body of this death?

Romans 7:25 I thank God through Jesus Christ our Lord. ~~So~~ then with the mind I myself serve the law of God; but with the flesh the law of sin.

Romans 8:8 So then they that are ~~in~~ the flesh cannot please God.

Romans 8:9 But ye are not ~~in~~ the flesh, but ~~in~~ the Spirit, if so be that the Spirit of God dwell in you. Now if any man have not the Spirit of Christ, he is none of his.

For the good that I would **have done when under law,** I find not to be good; therefore I do it not.

But the evil which I would not do **under the law,** I find to be good; that I do.

Now if I do that, **through the assistance of Christ,** I would not do **under the law, I am not under the law;** and it is no more that **I seek to do wrong, but to subdue** sin that dwelleth in me.

I find then that under the law, that when I would do good, evil was present with me; for I delight in the law of God after the inward man.

And now I see another law, **even the commandment of Christ, and it is imprinted in** my mind. **But my members are warring against the law of my mind,** and bringing me into captivity to the law of sin which is in my members.

And if I subdue not the sin which is in me, but with the flesh serve the law of sin; O wretched man that I am! who shall deliver me from the body of this death?

I thank God through Jesus Christ our Lord then **that so** with the mind I myself serve the law of God.

So then they that are **after** the flesh cannot please God.

But ye are not **after** the flesh, but **after** the Spirit, if so be that the Spirit of God dwell in you. Now if any man have not the Spirit of Christ, he is none of his.

The Epistle to the Romans

Romans 8:10 And if Christ *be* in you, the body ~~is dead~~ because of sin; ~~but~~ the Spirit *is* life because of righteousness.	And if Christ be in you, though the body **shall die** because of sin, **yet** the Spirit is life because of righteousness.
Romans 8:11 ~~But~~ if the Spirit of him that raised up Jesus from the dead dwell in you, he that raised up Christ from the dead shall also quicken your mortal bodies by his Spirit that dwelleth in you.	**And** if the Spirit of him that raised up Jesus from the dead dwell in you, he that raised up Christ from the dead shall also quicken your mortal bodies by his Spirit that dwelleth in you.
Romans 8:13 For if ye live after the flesh, ye shall die: but if ye through the Spirit do mortify the deeds of the body, ye shall live.	For if ye live after the flesh, ye shall die **unto sin**: but if ye through the Spirit do mortify the deeds of the body, ye shall live **unto Christ**.
Romans 8:18 For I reckon that the sufferings of this present time *are* not worthy to be ~~compared~~ with the glory which shall be revealed in us.	For I reckon that the sufferings of this present time are not worthy to be **named** with the glory which shall be revealed in us.
Romans 8:20 For the creature was made subject to ~~vanity~~, not willingly, but by reason of him who hath subjected ~~the same~~ in hope,	For the creature was made subject to **tribulation**, not willingly, but by reason of him who hath subjected **it** in hope,
Romans 8:25 But if we hope for that we see not, *then* ~~do we~~ with patience wait for *it*.	But if we hope for that we see not, then **with patience we do** wait for it.
Romans 8:29 For whom he did foreknow, he also did predestinate *to be* conformed to ~~the~~ image ~~of his Son~~, that he might be the firstborn among many brethren.	For **him** whom he did foreknow, he also did predestinate to be conformed to **his own** image, that he might be the firstborn among many brethren.
Romans 8:30 Moreover whom he did predestinate, ~~them~~ he also called: and whom he called, ~~them~~ he also justified: and whom he ~~justified, them~~ he also ~~glorified~~.	Moreover **him** whom he did predestinate, **him** he also called: and **him** whom he called, **him** he also **sanctified**: and **him** whom he **sanctified**, **him** he also glorified.
Romans 8:31 What shall we then say to these things? If God *be* for us, who *can be* against us?	What shall we then say to these things? If God be for us, who can **prevail** against us?

Romans 9:3 For I could ~~wish~~ that myself were accursed from Christ for my brethren, my kinsmen according to the flesh:

Romans 9:4 Who are Israelites; ~~to~~ whom ~~pertaineth~~ the adoption, and the glory, and the covenants, and the giving of the law, and the service ~~of God~~, and the promises;

Romans 9:5 ~~Whose~~ *are* the fathers, and of whom as concerning the flesh Christ ~~came~~, who is over all, ~~God~~ blessed for ever. Amen.

Romans 9:7 Neither, because they are ~~the seed~~ of Abraham, *are they* ~~all children~~: but, In Isaac shall thy seed be called.

Romans 9:10 And not only ~~this~~; but when Rebecca also had conceived by one, ~~even~~ by our father Isaac;

Romans 9:23 And that he might make known the riches of his glory on the vessels of mercy, which he had ~~afore~~ prepared unto glory,

Romans 9:25 As he saith also in ~~Osee~~, I will call them my people, which were not my people; and her beloved, which was not beloved.

Romans 9:32 Wherefore? ~~Because they sought it~~ not by faith, but as it were by the works of the law. For they stumbled at that stumblingstone;

Romans 10:16 ~~But they have not all obeyed the gospel. For Esaias saith, Lord, who hath believed our report?~~

Romans 10:17 ~~So then faith *cometh* by hearing, and hearing by the word of God.~~

(For **once** I could **have wished** that myself were accursed from Christ) for my brethren, my kinsmen according to the flesh:

Who are Israelites; **of** whom **are** the adoption, and the glory, and the covenants, and the giving of the law, and the service, and the promises, **and**

Are **made unto** the fathers and of whom, as concerning the flesh, Christ **was**, who is **God** over all, blessed for ever. Amen.

Neither, because they are **all children** of Abraham, are they **the seed**: but, In Isaac shall thy seed be called.

And not only **Sarah**; but when Rebecca also had conceived by one, by our father Isaac;

And that he might make known the riches of his glory on the vessels of mercy, which he had **before** prepared unto glory,

As he saith also in **Hosea**, I will call them my people, which were not my people; and her beloved, which was not beloved.

Wherefore **they stumbled at that stumbling stone**, not by faith, but as it were by the works of the law.

So then faith cometh by hearing, and hearing by the word of God.

But I say, Have they not heard? Yes verily, their sound went into all the

Romans 10:18 ~~But I say, Have they not heard? Yes verily, their sound went into all the earth, and their words unto the ends of the world.~~

Romans 10:19 ~~But~~ I say, Did not Israel know? First Moses saith, I will provoke you to jealousy by *them that are* no people, *and* by a foolish nation I will anger you.

Romans 11:2 God hath not cast away his people which he foreknew. ~~Wot~~ ye not what the scripture saith of Elias? how he maketh ~~intercession~~ to God against Israel, saying,

Romans 11:7 What then? Israel hath not obtained that which ~~he seeketh~~ for; but the election hath obtained it, and the rest were blinded

Romans 11:12 Now if the fall of them ~~be~~ the riches of the world, and the diminishing of them the riches of the Gentiles; how much more their fulness?

Romans 11:15 For if the casting away of them ~~be~~ the reconciling of the world, what ~~shall~~ the ~~receiving of them be~~, but life from the dead?

Romans 11:16 For if the firstfruit ~~be~~ holy, the lump *is* also *holy:* and if the root *be* holy, so *are* the branches.

Romans 11:17 And if some of the branches be broken off, and thou, being a wild olive tree, ~~wert~~ graffed in among them, and with them partakest of the root and fatness of the olive tree;

earth, and their words unto the ends of the world.

But they have not all obeyed the gospel. For Esaias saith, Lord, who hath believed our report?

Now I say, Did not Israel know? First Moses saith, I will provoke you to jealousy by them that are no people, and by a foolish nation I will anger you.

God hath not cast away his people which he foreknew. **Know** ye not what the scripture saith of Elias? how he maketh **complaint** to God against Israel, saying,

What then? Israel hath not obtained that which **they seek** for; but the election hath obtained it, and the rest were blinded

Now if the fall of them **is** the riches of the world, and the diminishing of them the riches of the Gentiles; how much more their fulness?

For if the casting away of them **is** the reconciling of the world, what **is** the **restoring**, but life from the dead?

For if the firstfruit **is** holy, the lump is also holy: and if the root be holy, so are the branches.

And if some of the branches be broken off, and thou, being a wild olive tree, **wast** graffed in among them, and with them partakest of the root and fatness of the olive tree;

Romans 11:18 Boast not against the branches. ~~But if thou boast~~, thou bearest not the root, but the root thee.

Romans 11:19 Thou wilt say ~~then~~, The branches were broken off, that ~~I~~ might be ~~graffed~~ in.

Romans 11:24 For if thou ~~wert~~ cut out of the olive tree which is wild by nature, and ~~wert~~ graffed contrary to nature into a good olive tree: how much more shall these, which be the natural *branches,* be graffed into their own olive tree?

Romans 11:26 ~~And so~~ all Israel shall be saved: as it is written, There shall come out of Sion the Deliverer, and shall turn away ungodliness from Jacob:

Romans 12:2 And be not conformed to this world: but ~~be ye~~ transformed by the renewing of your mind, that ye may prove what *is* that good, and acceptable, and perfect, will of God.

Romans 12:9 ~~Let~~ love ~~be~~ without dissimulation. Abhor that which is evil; cleave to that which is good.

Romans 13:1 Let every soul be subject unto the higher powers. For there is no power but of God: the powers that be are ordained of God.

Romans 13:2 Whosoever therefore resisteth the power, resisteth the ordinance of God: and they that resist shall receive to themselves ~~damnation~~.

Romans 13:4 For he is the minister of God to thee for good. But if thou do that which is evil, be afraid; for he beareth not the ~~sword~~ in vain: for he is the minister of God, a revenger to *execute* wrath upon him that doeth evil.

Boast not against the branches, **for** thou bearest not the root, but the root thee.

For if thou boast, thou wilt say, The branches were broken off, that **we** might be **grafted** in.

For if thou **wast** cut out of the olive tree which is wild by nature, and **wast** graffed contrary to nature into a good olive tree: how much more shall these, which be the natural branches, be graffed into their own olive tree?

Then all Israel shall be saved: as it is written, There shall come out of Sion the Deliverer, and shall turn away ungodliness from Jacob:

And be not conformed to this world: but **is** transformed by the renewing of your mind, that ye may prove what is that good, and acceptable, and perfect, will of God.

And love without dissimulation. Abhor that which is evil; cleave to that which is good.

Let every soul be subject unto the higher powers. For there is no power **in the church** but of God: the powers that be are ordained of God.

Whosoever therefore resisteth the power, resisteth the ordinance of God: and they that resist shall receive to themselves **punishment**.

For he is the minister of God to thee for good. But if thou do that which is evil, be afraid; for he beareth not the **rod** in vain: for he is the minister of God, a revenger to execute wrath upon him that doeth evil.

The Epistle to the Romans

Romans 13:6 For for this cause pay ye ~~tribute~~ also: for they are God's ministers, attending continually upon this very thing.	For for this cause pay ye **your consecrations** also **unto them**: for they are God's ministers, attending continually upon this very thing.
Romans 13:7 Render ~~therefore~~ to all their dues: tribute to whom tribute ~~is due~~; custom to whom custom; fear to whom fear; honour to whom honour.	**But first** render to all their dues **according to custom**: tribute to whom tribute; custom to whom custom; **that your consecrations may be done in** fear **of him** to whom fear **belongs, and in** honour **of him** to whom honour **belongs**.
Romans 13:8 Owe no man any thing, but to love one another: for he that loveth another hath fulfilled the law.	**Therefore** owe no man any thing, but to love one another: for he that loveth another hath fulfilled the law.
Romans 13:14 But put ye on the Lord Jesus Christ, and make not provision for the flesh, to ~~fulfil~~ the lusts *thereof*.	But put ye on the Lord Jesus Christ, and make not provision for the flesh, to **gratify** the lusts thereof.
Romans 14:11 For ~~it is written, As~~ I live, saith the Lord, every knee shall bow to me, and every tongue shall ~~confess~~ to God.	For I live, saith the Lord, **and** every knee shall bow to me, and every tongue shall **swear** to God, **as it is written**.
Romans 14:15 But if thy brother be grieved with *thy* meat, ~~now~~ walkest ~~thou~~ not charitably. Destroy not him with thy meat, for whom Christ died.	But if thy brother be grieved with thy meat **thou** walkest not charitably **if thou eatest; therefore** destroy not him with thy meat for whom Christ died.
Romans 14:23 And he that doubteth is ~~damned~~ if he eat, because ~~he eateth~~ not of faith: for whatsoever *is* not of faith is sin.	And he that doubteth is **condemned** if he eat, because **it is** not of faith: for whatsoever is not of faith is sin.
Romans 15:5 Now the God of patience and consolation grant you to be likeminded one toward another ~~according to~~ Christ Jesus:	Now the God of patience and consolation grant you to be likeminded one toward another **as was** Christ Jesus:
Romans 15:15 Nevertheless, brethren, I have written the more boldly unto you ~~in some sort, as~~ putting you in mind, because of the grace that is given to me of God,	Nevertheless, brethren, I have written the more boldly unto you, putting you in mind, because of the grace that is given to me of God,

Romans 15:24 Whensoever I take my journey into Spain, I will come to you: for I trust to see you in my journey, and to be brought on my way thitherward by you, if first I be somewhat filled ~~with~~ your ~~company~~.	Whensoever I take my journey into Spain, I will come to you: for I trust to see you in my journey, and to be brought on my way thitherward by you, if first I be somewhat filled **through** your **prayers**.
Romans 16:10 Salute Apelles approved in Christ. Salute them which are of Aristobulus' ~~household~~.	Salute Apelles approved in Christ. Salute them which are of Aristobulus' **church**.
Romans 16:11 Salute Herodion my kinsman. Greet them that be of the ~~household~~ of Narcissus, which are in the Lord.	Salute Herodion my kinsman. Greet them that be of the **church** of Narcissus, which are in the Lord.
Romans 16:16 Salute one another with an holy ~~kiss~~. The churches of Christ salute you.	Salute one another with an holy **salutation**. The churches of Christ salute you.
Romans 16:25 Now to him that is of power to stablish you according to ~~my~~ gospel, and the preaching of Jesus Christ, according to the revelation of the mystery, which was kept secret since the world began,	Now to him that is of power to stablish you according to **the** gospel, and the preaching of Jesus Christ, according to the revelation of the mystery, which was kept secret since the world began,

The First Epistle to the Corinthians

King James Version

1 Corinthians 1:1 Paul, called ~~to be an apostle~~ of Jesus Christ through the will of God, and Sosthenes *our* brother,

1 Corinthians 1:4 I thank my God always on your behalf, for the grace of God which is given you ~~by~~ Jesus Christ;

1 Corinthians 1:5 That in every thing ye are enriched ~~by~~ him, in all utterance, and *in* all knowledge;

1 Corinthians 1:10 Now I beseech you, brethren, ~~by~~ the name of our Lord Jesus Christ, that ye all speak the same thing, and ~~that~~ there be no divisions among you; but ~~that~~ ye be perfectly joined together in the same mind and in the same judgment.

1 Corinthians 1:12 Now this I say, that ~~every one~~ of you saith, I am of Paul; and I of Apollos; and I of Cephas; and I of Christ.

1 Corinthians 1:24 But unto them ~~which are called~~, both Jews and Greeks, Christ the power of God, and the wisdom of God.

1 Corinthians 1:26 For ye see your calling, brethren, how that not many wise men after the flesh, not many mighty, not many noble, *are* ~~called~~:

1 Corinthians 1:27 ~~But~~ God hath chosen the foolish things of the world to confound the wise; and God hath

Joseph Smith Translation

Paul, **an apostle**, called of Jesus Christ through the will of God, and Sosthenes our brother,

I thank my God always on your behalf, for the grace of God which is given you **of** Jesus Christ;

That in every thing ye are enriched **of** him, in all utterance, and in all knowledge;

Now I beseech you, brethren, **in** the name of our Lord Jesus Christ, that ye all speak the same thing, and there be no divisions among you; but ye be perfectly joined together in the same mind and in the same judgment.

Now this I say, that **many** of you saith, I am of Paul; and I of Apollos; and I of Cephas; and I of Christ.

But unto them **who believe**, both Jews and Greeks, Christ the power of God, and the wisdom of God.

For ye see your calling, brethren, how that not many wise men after the flesh, not many mighty, not many noble, are **chosen**:

For God hath chosen the foolish things of the world to confound the wise; and God hath chosen the weak things of the

chosen the weak things of the world to confound the things which are mighty;

world to confound the things which are mighty;

1 Corinthians 1:28 And base things of the world, and things which are despised, hath God chosen, ~~yea,~~ and things which are not, to bring to nought things that are:

And base things of the world, and things which are despised, hath God chosen, and things which are not, to bring to nought things that are **mighty**:

1 Corinthians 2:11 For what man knoweth the things of a man, save the spirit of man which is in him? even so the things of God knoweth no man, ~~but~~ the Spirit of God.

For what man knoweth the things of a man, save the spirit of man which is in him? even so the things of God knoweth no man, **except he has** the Spirit of God.

1 Corinthians 3:2 I have fed you with milk, and not with meat: for hitherto ye were not able *to ~~bear~~ it,* neither yet now are ye able.

I have fed you with milk, and not with meat: for hitherto ye were not able to **receive** it, neither yet now are ye able.

1 Corinthians 3:15 If any man's work shall be burned, he shall suffer loss: but he himself ~~shall~~ be saved; yet so as by fire.

If any man's work shall be burned, he shall suffer loss: but he himself **may** be saved; yet so as by fire.

1 Corinthians 4:2 Moreover it is required ~~in~~ stewards, that a man be found faithful.

Moreover it is required **of** stewards, that a man be found faithful.

1 Corinthians 4:4 For I know nothing ~~by~~ myself; yet ~~am~~ I not hereby justified: but he ~~that~~ judgeth me is the Lord.

For **though** I know nothing **against** myself; yet I **am** not hereby justified: but he **who** judgeth me is the Lord.

1 Corinthians 4:5 Therefore judge nothing before the time, until the Lord come, who both will bring to light the hidden things of darkness, and will make manifest the counsels of the hearts: and then shall every man have praise of God.

Therefore **I** judge nothing before the time, until the Lord come, who both will bring to light the hidden things of darkness, and will make manifest the counsels of the hearts: and then shall every man have praise of God.

1 Corinthians 5:3 For ~~I~~ verily, as absent in body, but present in spirit, have judged already, ~~as though I were present, concerning~~ him ~~that~~ hath so done this deed,

For verily, as absent in body, but present in spirit, **I** have judged already, him **who** hath so done this deed, **as though I was present,**

The First Epistle to the Corinthians

1 Corinthians 5:4 In the name of our Lord Jesus Christ, when ye are gathered together, and ~~my~~ spirit, with the power of our Lord Jesus Christ,

1 Corinthians 5:12 For what have I to do to judge them also that are without? do not ~~ye~~ judge them that are within?

1 Corinthians 6:12 All things are lawful unto me, ~~but~~ all things are not expedient: all things are lawful for me, ~~but~~ I will not be brought under the power of any.

1 Corinthians 6:18 Flee fornication. Every sin that a man ~~doeth~~ is ~~without~~ the body; ~~but~~ he ~~that~~ committeth fornication sinneth against his own body.

1 Corinthians 7:1 Now concerning the things whereof ye wrote unto me: *It is good for a man not to touch a woman.*

1 Corinthians 7:2 Nevertheless, *to avoid* fornication, let every man have his own wife, and let every woman have her own husband.

1 Corinthians 7:5 ~~Defraud~~ ye not one the other, except *it be* with consent for a time, that ye may give yourselves to fasting and prayer; and come together again, that Satan tempt you not for your incontinency.

1 Corinthians 7:6 ~~But~~ I speak *this* by permission, *and* not ~~of~~ commandment.

1 Corinthians 7:9 But if they cannot ~~contain~~, let them marry: for it is better to marry than ~~to burn~~.

1 Corinthians 7:11 But ~~and~~ if she depart, let her remain unmarried, or be reconciled to *her* husband: and let not the husband put away *his* wife.

In the name of our Lord Jesus Christ, when ye are gathered together, and **have the** spirit, with the power of our Lord Jesus Christ,

For what have I to do to judge them also that are without? do not **they** judge them that are within?

All **these** things are **not** lawful unto me, **and** all **these** things are not expedient: all things are **not** lawful for me, **therefore** I will not be brought under the power of any.

Flee fornication. Every sin that a man **committeth** is **against** the body **of Christ; and** he **who** committeth fornication sinneth against his own body.

Now concerning the things whereof ye wrote unto me, **saying**: It is good for a man not to touch a woman.

Nevertheless, **I say** to avoid fornication, let every man have his own wife, and let every woman have her own husband.

Depart ye not one **from** the other, except it be with consent for a time, that ye may give yourselves to fasting and prayer; and come together again, that Satan tempt you not for your incontinency.

And now what I speak **is** by permission, and not **by** commandment.

But if they cannot **abide**, let them marry: for it is better to marry than **that any should commit sin.**

But if she depart, let her remain unmarried, or be reconciled to her husband: and let not the husband put away his wife.

1 Corinthians 7:26 I suppose therefore that this is good for the present distress, ~~I say, that it is~~ good ~~for a man so to be~~.

1 Corinthians 7:28 But and if thou marry, thou hast not sinned; and if a virgin marry, she hath not sinned. Nevertheless such shall have trouble in the flesh: ~~but~~ I spare you.

1 Corinthians 7:29 ~~But~~ this I say, brethren, the time *is* short: ~~it remaineth~~, that ~~both~~ they ~~that~~ have wives be as though they had none;

1 Corinthians 7:30 And ~~they that~~ weep, as though they wept not; and ~~they that~~ rejoice, as though they rejoiced not; and ~~they that~~ buy, as though they possessed not;

1 Corinthians 7:31 And ~~they that~~ use this world, as not ~~abusing~~ *it:* for the fashion of this world passeth away.

1 Corinthians 7:32 But I would have you without carefulness. He ~~that~~ is unmarried careth for the things that belong to the Lord, how he may please the Lord:

1 Corinthians 7:33 But he ~~that~~ is married careth for the things that are of the world, how he may please *his* wife.

1 Corinthians 7:34 There is difference *also* between a wife and a virgin. The unmarried woman careth for the things of the Lord, that she may be holy both in body and in spirit: but she that is

I suppose therefore that this is good for the present distress, **for a man so to remain, that he may do greater** good.

But if thou marry, thou hast not sinned; and if a virgin marry, she hath not sinned. Nevertheless such shall have trouble in the flesh: **for** I spare you **not**.

But I speak unto you, who are called unto the ministry, For this I say, brethren, the time **that remaineth** is **but** short: **that ye shall be sent forth unto the ministry. Even** they **who** have wives **shall** be as though they had none; **for ye are called and chosen to do the Lord's work.**

And **it shall be with them who** weep, as though they wept not; and **them who** rejoice, as though they rejoiced not; and **them who** buy, as though they possessed not;

And **them who** use this world, as not **using** it: for the fashion of this world passeth away.

But I would, **brethren, that ye magnify your calling. I would** have you without carefulness. **For he who** is unmarried careth for the things that belong to the Lord, how he may please the Lord: **therefore he prevaileth.**

But he **who** is married careth for the things that are of the world, how he may please his wife. **Therefore there is a difference, for he is hindered.**

There is **a** difference also between a wife and a virgin. The unmarried woman careth for the things of the Lord, that she may be holy both in body and in spirit: but she that is married careth for

The First Epistle to the Corinthians

married careth for the things of the world, how she may please *her* husband.

1 Corinthians 7:36 But if any man think that he behaveth himself uncomely toward his virgin, if she pass the flower of ~~her~~ age, and need so require, let him do what he ~~will~~, he sinneth not: let them marry.

1 Corinthians 7:38 So then he that giveth ~~her~~ in marriage doeth well; but he that giveth ~~her~~ not in marriage doeth better.

1 Corinthians 8:4 As concerning therefore the eating of those things ~~that~~ are offered in sacrifice unto idols, we know that an idol *is* nothing ~~in the world~~, and that *there is* none other God but one.

1 Corinthians 9:24 Know ye not that they which run in a race run ~~all~~, but one receiveth the prize? So run, that ye may obtain.

1 Corinthians 10:11 Now all these things happened unto them for ensamples: and they are written for our admonition, upon whom the ~~ends~~ of the world ~~are~~ come.

1 Corinthians 10:20 But ~~I say, that~~ the things which the Gentiles sacrifice, they sacrifice to devils, and not to God: and I would not that ye should have fellowship with devils.

1 Corinthians 10:23 All things are lawful for me, ~~but~~ all things are not expedient: all things are lawful ~~for me~~, ~~but~~ all things edify not.

1 Corinthians 10:24 Let no man seek his own, but every man another's ~~wealth~~.

the things of the world, how she may please her husband.

But if any man think that he behaveth himself uncomely toward his virgin **whom he hath espoused**, if she pass the flower of age, and need so require, let him do what he **hath promised**, he sinneth not: let them marry.

So then he that giveth **himself** in marriage doeth well; but he that giveth **himself** not in marriage doeth better.

As concerning therefore the eating of those things **which** are **in the world** offered in sacrifice unto idols, we know that an idol is nothing, and that there is none other God but one.

Know ye not that they which run in a race **all** run, but **only** one receiveth the prize? So run, that ye may obtain.

Now all these things happened unto them for ensamples: and they are written for our admonition **also, and for an admonition for those** upon whom the end of the world **shall** come.

But the things which the Gentiles sacrifice, they sacrifice to devils, and not to God: and I would not that ye should have fellowship with devils.

All things are **not** lawful for me, **for** all things are not expedient: all things are **not** lawful, **for** all things edify not.

Let no man seek **therefore** his own, but every man another's **good**.

1 Corinthians 10:27 If any of them that believe not bid you ~~to a feast~~, and ye be disposed to go; whatsoever is set before you, eat, asking no question for conscience sake.	If any of them that believe not bid you **eat**, and ye be disposed to go; whatsoever is set before you, eat, asking no question for conscience sake.
1 Corinthians 10:33 Even as I please all ~~men~~ in all *things*, not seeking mine own profit, but the ~~profit of~~ many, that they may be saved.	Even as I please all in all things, not seeking mine own profit, but **of** the many, that they may be saved.
1 Corinthians 11:10 For this cause ought the woman to have ~~power~~ on *her* head because of the angels.	For this cause ought the woman to have **a covering** on her head because of the angels.
1 Corinthians 11:19 For there must be also ~~heresies~~ among you, that they which are approved may be made manifest among you.	For there must be also **divisions** among you, that they which are approved may be made manifest among you.
1 Corinthians 11:20 When ye come together ~~therefore~~ into one place, ~~this~~ is not to eat the Lord's supper.	When ye come together into one place, is **it** not to eat the Lord's supper?
1 Corinthians 11:21 ~~For~~ in eating every one taketh before ~~other~~ his own supper: and one is hungry, and another is drunken.	**But** in eating every one taketh before his own supper: and one is hungry, and another is drunken.
1 Corinthians 11:29 For he that eateth and drinketh unworthily, eateth and drinketh ~~damnation~~ to himself, not discerning the Lord's body.	For he that eateth and drinketh unworthily, eateth and drinketh **condemnation** to himself, not discerning the Lord's body.
1 Corinthians 12:1 Now concerning spiritual ~~gifts~~, brethren, I would not have you ignorant.	Now concerning spiritual **things**, brethren, I would not have you ignorant.
1 Corinthians 12:31 ~~But~~ covet earnestly the best gifts: ~~and yet shew I unto you a more excellent way~~.	**I say unto you, nay; for I have shewn unto you a more excellent way, there**fore covet earnestly the best gifts.
1 Corinthians 14:2 For he that speaketh in ~~an unknown~~ tongue speaketh not unto men, but unto God: for no man understandeth *him*; howbeit in the spirit he speaketh mysteries.	For he that speaketh in **another** tongue speaketh not unto men, but unto God: for no man understandeth him; howbeit in the spirit he speaketh mysteries.

The First Epistle to the Corinthians

1 Corinthians 14:4 He that speaketh in ~~an unknown~~ tongue edifieth himself; but he that prophesieth edifieth the church.

1 Corinthians 14:13 Wherefore let him that speaketh in ~~an unknown~~ tongue pray that he may interpret.

1 Corinthians 14:14 For if I pray in ~~an unknown~~ tongue, my spirit prayeth, but my understanding is unfruitful.

1 Corinthians 14:19 Yet in the church I had rather speak five words with my understanding, that *by my voice* I might teach others also, than ten thousand words in ~~an unknown~~ tongue.

1 Corinthians 14:27 If any man speak in ~~an unknown~~ tongue, *let it be* by two, or at the most *by* three, and *that* by course; and let one interpret.

1 Corinthians 14:34 Let your women keep silence in the churches: for it is not permitted unto them to ~~speak~~; but *they are commanded* to be under obedience, as also saith the law.

1 Corinthians 14:35 And if they will learn any thing, let them ask their husbands at home: for it is a shame for women to ~~speak~~ in the church.

1 Corinthians 15:10 But by the grace of God I am what I am: and his grace which *was bestowed* upon me was not in vain; ~~but~~ I laboured more abundantly than they all: yet not I, but the grace of God which was with me.

1 Corinthians 15:24 ~~Then~~ *cometh* the end, when he shall have delivered up the kingdom to God, even the Father;

He that speaketh in **another** tongue edifieth himself; but he that prophesieth edifieth the church.

Wherefore let him that speaketh in **another** tongue pray that he may interpret.

For if I pray in **another** tongue, my spirit prayeth, but my understanding is unfruitful.

Yet in the church I had rather speak five words with my understanding, that by my voice I might teach others also, than ten thousand words in **another** tongue.

If any man speak in **another** tongue, let it be by two, or at the most by three, and that by course; and let one interpret.

Let your women keep silence in the churches: for it is not permitted unto them to **rule**; but they are commanded to be under obedience, as also saith the law.

And if they will learn any thing, let them ask their husbands at home: for it is a shame for women to **rule** in the church.

But by the grace of God I am what I am: and his grace which was bestowed upon me was not in vain; **for** I laboured more abundantly than they all: yet not I, but the grace of God which was with me.

Afterward cometh the end, when he shall have delivered up the kingdom to God, even the Father; when he shall when he shall have put down all rule and all authority and power.

1 Corinthians 15:26 The last enemy ~~that~~ shall be destroyed ~~is death~~.

1 Corinthians 15:27 For he hath put all things under his feet. ~~But when he saith~~ all things are put under ~~him, it is manifest that~~ he is ~~excepted, which~~ did put all things under him.

1 Corinthians 15:31 I protest ~~by your~~ rejoicing which I have in Christ Jesus our Lord, I die ~~daily~~.

1 Corinthians 15:37 And that which thou sowest, thou sowest not that body ~~that~~ shall be, but ~~bare~~ grain, it may ~~chance~~ of wheat, or of some other ~~grain~~:

1 Corinthians 15:40 ~~There are~~ also celestial bodies, and bodies terrestrial: but the glory of the celestial ~~is~~ one, and the ~~glory of the~~ terrestrial ~~is~~ another.

1 Corinthians 15:46 Howbeit that ~~was not first which~~ is spiritual, but ~~that which is natural; and afterward~~ that which is spiritual.

1 Corinthians 15:52 In a moment, in the twinkling of an eye, at the ~~last~~ trump: for the trumpet shall sound, and the dead shall be raised incorruptible, and we shall be changed.

1 Corinthians 16:9 For a great door and effectual is opened unto me, ~~and~~ there are many adversaries.

1 Corinthians 16:20 All the brethren greet you. Greet ye one another with an holy ~~kiss~~.

have put down all rule and all authority and power.

The last enemy, **death,** shall be destroyed.

For he **saith, when it is manifest that** he hath put all things under his feet, **and that** all things are put under, he is **accepted of the Father who** did put all things under him.

I protest **unto you the resurrection of the dead; and this is my** rejoicing which I have in Christ Jesus our Lord daily, **though** I die.

And that which thou sowest, thou sowest not that body **which** shall be, but grain, it may **be** of wheat, or of some other:

Also celestial bodies, and bodies terrestrial, **and bodies telestial**: but the glory of the celestial one, and the terrestrial another, **and the telestial another.**

Howbeit that **which is natural first, and not that which** is spiritual; but **afterwards,** that which is spiritual.

In a moment, in the twinkling of an eye, at the **sound of the** trump: for the trumpet shall sound, and the dead shall be raised incorruptible, and we shall be changed.

For a great door and effectual is opened unto me, **but** there are many adversaries.

All the brethren greet you. Greet ye one another with an holy **salutation.**

The Second Epistle to the Corinthians

King James Version	Joseph Smith Translation
2 Corinthians 3:4 And such trust have we through Christ ~~to~~ God~~-ward~~:	And such trust have we through Christ **toward** God:
2 Corinthians 3:16 Nevertheless when ~~it~~ shall turn to the Lord, the vail shall be taken away.	Nevertheless when **their heart** shall turn to the Lord, the vail shall be taken away.
2 Corinthians 4:12 So then ~~death~~ worketh ~~in~~ us, but life ~~in~~ you.	So then **it** worketh **death unto** us, but life **unto** you.
2 Corinthians 4:15 For all things ~~are~~ for your sakes, that the abundant grace might through the thanksgiving of many redound to the glory of God.	For **we bear** all things for your sakes, that the abundant grace might through the thanksgiving of many redound to the glory of God.
2 Corinthians 5:10 For we must all appear before the judgment seat of Christ; that every one may receive the ~~things~~ *done* in ~~his~~ body, according to ~~that~~ he hath done, whether ~~it be~~ good or bad.	For we must all appear before the judgment seat of Christ; that every one may receive **a reward of** the **deeds** done in the body, **things** according to **what** he hath done, whether good or bad.
2 Corinthians 5:13 For ~~whether~~ we ~~be~~ beside ourselves, *it is* to God: or whether we be sober, *it is* for your ~~cause~~.	For **we bear record that** we **are not** beside ourselves, **for whether we glory**, it is to God: or whether we be sober, it is for your **sakes**.
2 Corinthians 5:14 For the love of Christ constraineth us; because we thus judge, that if one died for all, then ~~were~~ all dead:	For the love of Christ constraineth us; because we thus judge, that if one died for all, then **are** all dead:
2 Corinthians 5:16 Wherefore henceforth ~~know~~ we no ~~man~~ after the flesh: yea, though we ~~have known Christ~~ after the flesh, yet now henceforth ~~know~~ we ~~him~~ no more.	Wherefore henceforth **live** we no **more** after the flesh: yea, though we **once lived** after the flesh, yet **since we have known Christ**, now henceforth **live** we no more **after the flesh**.

2 Corinthians 5:17 Therefore if any man ~~be~~ in Christ, *he is* a new creature: old things are passed away; behold, all things are become new.

2 Corinthians 5:18 And all things ~~are~~ of God, who hath reconciled us to himself by Jesus Christ, and hath given to us the ministry of reconciliation;

2 Corinthians 5:19 To wit, that God ~~was~~ in Christ, reconciling the world unto himself, not imputing their trespasses unto them; and hath committed unto us the word of reconciliation.

2 Corinthians 6:1 We then, ~~as~~ workers together *with him,* beseech *you* also that ye receive not the grace of God in vain.

2 Corinthians 8:1 Moreover, brethren, we ~~do~~ you to wit of the grace of God bestowed on the churches of Macedonia;

2 Corinthians 8:5 And ~~this they did~~, not as we ~~hoped~~, but first gave their own selves to the Lord, and unto us by the will of God.

2 Corinthians 8:22 And we have sent with them our brother, whom we have ~~oftentimes~~ proved diligent in many things, but now much more diligent, ~~upon~~ the great confidence which *I have* in you.

2 Corinthians 8:23 Whether ~~any do enquire~~ of Titus, ~~he is~~ my partner and fellow ~~helper concerning you~~: or our brethren ~~be enquired of, they are~~ the messengers of the churches, ~~and the glory of Christ~~.

Therefore if any man **live** in Christ, he is a new creature: old things are passed away; behold, all things are become new.

And **receiveth** all **the** things of God, who hath reconciled us to himself by Jesus Christ, and hath given to us the ministry of reconciliation;

To wit, that God **is** in Christ, reconciling the world unto himself, not imputing their trespasses unto them; and hath committed unto us the word of reconciliation.

We then, workers together with **Christ**, beseech you also that ye receive not the grace of God in vain.

Moreover, brethren, we **would have** you to **know** of the grace of God bestowed on the churches of Macedonia;

And not as we **required**, but first gave their own selves to the Lord, and unto us by the will of God.

And we have sent with them our brother, whom we have proved diligent in many things, but now much more diligent. **Therefore we send him unto you, in consequence of** the great confidence which **we have in you that you will receive the things concerning you to the glory of Christ,**

Whether **we send by the hand** of Titus my partner and fellow **labourer**, or our brethren the messengers of the churches.

The Second Epistle to the Corinthians

2 Corinthians 9:4 Lest ~~haply~~ if they of Macedonia come with me, and find you unprepared, we (that we say not, ye) should be ashamed in this same confident boasting.	Lest if they of Macedonia come with me, and find you unprepared, we (that we say not, ye) should be ashamed in this same confident boasting.
2 Corinthians 11:4 For if he that cometh preacheth another Jesus, whom we have not preached, or *if* ye receive another spirit, which ye have not received, or another gospel, which ye have not accepted, ye might well bear with ~~him~~.	For if he that cometh preacheth another Jesus, whom we have not preached, or if ye receive another spirit, which ye have not received, or another gospel, which ye have not accepted, ye might well bear with **me**.
2 Corinthians 11:23 Are they ministers of Christ? (I speak as a fool) I ~~am more~~; in labours more abundant, in stripes above measure, in prisons more frequent, in deaths oft.	Are they ministers of Christ? (I speak as a fool) **So am** I; in labours more abundant, in stripes above measure, in prisons more frequent, in deaths oft.
2 Corinthians 11:29 Who is weak, and I am not weak? who is offended, and I ~~burn~~ not?	Who is weak, and I am not weak? who is offended, and I **anger** not?
2 Corinthians 12:6 For though I would desire to glory, I shall not be a fool; for I will say the truth: but ~~now~~ I forbear, lest any man should think of me above that which he seeth me ~~to be~~, or ~~that~~ he heareth of me.	For though I would desire to glory, I shall not be a fool; for I will say the truth: but I forbear, lest any man should think of me above that which he seeth **of** me, or he heareth of me.
2 Corinthians 13:12 Greet one another with an holy ~~kiss~~.	Greet one another with an holy **salutation**.

The Epistle to the Galatians

King James Version	Joseph Smith Translation
Galatians 1:10 For do I now ~~persuade~~ men, or God? or do I seek to please men? for if I yet pleased men, I should not be the servant of Christ.	For do I now **please** men, or God? or do I seek to please men? for if I yet pleased men, I should not be the servant of Christ.
Galatians 1:24 And they glorified God ~~in~~ me.	And they glorified God **on account of** me.
Galatians 2:4 ~~And that because of~~ false brethren unawares ~~brought in~~, who came in privily to spy out our liberty which we have in Christ Jesus, that they might bring us into bondage:	**Notwithstanding there were some brought in by** false brethren unawares, who came in privily to spy out our liberty which we have in Christ Jesus, that they might bring us into bondage:
Galatians 2:14 But when I saw that they walked not uprightly according to the truth of the gospel, I said unto Peter before *them* all, If thou, being a Jew, livest after the manner of Gentiles, and not as do the Jews, why compellest thou the Gentiles to live as do the Jews?	But when I saw that they walked not uprightly according to the truth of the gospel, I said unto Peter before them all, If thou, being a Jew, livest after the manner of **the** Gentiles, and not as do the Jews, why compellest thou the Gentiles to live as do the Jews?
Galatians 3:14 That the blessing of Abraham might come on the Gentiles through Jesus Christ; that ~~we~~ might receive the promise of the Spirit through faith.	That the blessing of Abraham might come on the Gentiles through Jesus Christ; that **they** might receive the promise of the Spirit through faith.
Galatians 3:15 Brethren, I speak after the manner of men; Though ~~it be~~ but a man's covenant, yet ~~if it be~~ confirmed, no man disannulleth, or addeth thereto.	Brethren, I speak after the manner of men; Though but a man's covenant, yet **when** confirmed, no man disannulleth, or addeth thereto.
Galatians 3:18 For if the inheritance ~~be~~ of the law, ~~it is~~ no more of promise: but God gave *it* to Abraham by promise.	For if the inheritance **is** of the law, **then** no more of promise: but God gave it to Abraham by promise.
Galatians 3:19 Wherefore then ~~serveth~~ the law? ~~It~~ was added because of	Wherefore then **the law** was added because of transgressions, till the seed

transgressions, till the seed should come to whom the promise was made; ~~and it was~~ ordained by angels ~~in the hand of~~ a mediator.	should come to whom the promise was made **in the law given to Moses, who** was ordained by **the hand of** angels **to be a mediator of this first covenant (the law)**.
Galatians 3:20 Now ~~a~~ mediator ~~is~~ not *a mediator* of one, ~~but~~ God ~~is one~~.	Now **this** mediator **was** not a mediator **of the new covenant, but there is one mediator of the new covenant, who is Christ, as it is written in the law concerning the promises made to Abraham and his seed. Now Christ is the mediator of life; for this is the promise which** God **made unto Abraham**.
Galatians 3:24 Wherefore the law was our schoolmaster ~~to bring us unto~~ Christ, that we might be justified by faith.	Wherefore the law was our schoolmaster **until** Christ, that we might be justified by faith.
Galatians 3:29 And if ye ~~be~~ Christ's, then are ye Abraham's seed, and heirs according to the promise.	And if ye **are** Christ's, then are ye Abraham's seed, and heirs according to the promise.
Galatians 4:12 Brethren, I beseech you, be as I *am;* for I *am* as ye ~~are:~~ ye have not injured me at all.	Brethren, I beseech you **to be perfect** as I am **perfect**; for I am **persuaded** as ye **have a knowledge of me**, ye have not injured me at all **by your sayings**.

The Epistle to the Ephesians

King James Version	Joseph Smith Translation
Ephesians 2:8 For by grace are ye saved through faith; and that not of yourselves: ~~it is~~ the gift of God:	For by grace are ye saved through faith; and that not of yourselves: **but** the gift of God:
Ephesians 2:11 Wherefore remember, that ye ~~being~~ in time past Gentiles in the flesh, who are called Uncircumcision by that which is called the Circumcision in the flesh made by hands;	Wherefore remember, that ye **were** in time past Gentiles in the flesh, who are called Uncircumcision by that which is called the Circumcision in the flesh made by hands;
Ephesians 3:1 For this cause I Paul, the prisoner of Jesus Christ ~~for~~ you Gentiles,	For this cause, I Paul, **am** the prisoner of Jesus Christ **among** you Gentiles,
Ephesians 3:2 If ye have heard of the dispensation of the grace of God which is given me to you-ward:	**For** the dispensation of the grace of God which is given me to you-ward:
Ephesians 3:3 ~~How~~ that by revelation he made known unto me the mystery; {as I wrote ~~afore~~ in few words,	**As ye have heard** that by revelation he made known unto me the mystery **of Christ**; as I wrote **before** in few words,
Ephesians 3:18 May be able to comprehend with all saints ~~what is~~ the breadth, and length, and depth, and height;	May be able to comprehend with all saints the breadth, and length, and depth, and height;
Ephesians 4:4 ~~There is~~ one body, and one Spirit, even as ye are called in one hope of your calling;	**In** one body, and one Spirit, even as ye are called in one hope of your calling;
Ephesians 4:10 He ~~that~~ descended is the same also ~~that~~ ascended up ~~far above all heavens~~, that he might fill all things.}	He **who** descended is the same also **who** ascended up **into heaven, to glorify him who reigneth over all heavens**, that he might fill all things.
Ephesians 4:13 Till we ~~all come~~ in the unity of the faith, ~~and of~~ the knowledge of the Son of God, unto a perfect man,	Till we, in the unity of the faith, **all come to** the knowledge of the Son of God, unto a perfect man, unto the

The Epistle to the Ephesians

unto the measure of the stature of the fulness of Christ:	measure of the stature of the fulness of Christ:
Ephesians 4:21 If so be that ye have ~~heard~~ him, and have been taught by him, as the truth is in Jesus:	If so be that ye have **learned** [of] him, and have been taught by him, as the truth is in Jesus:
Ephesians 4:22 ~~That ye put off~~ concerning the former conversation the old man, which is corrupt according to the deceitful lusts;	**And now I speak unto you** concerning the former conversation, **by exhortation, that ye put off** the old man, which is corrupt according to the deceitful lusts;
Ephesians 4:23 And be renewed in the spirit ~~of your mind~~;	And be renewed in the **mind of the** spirit;
Ephesians 4:26 Be ~~ye~~ angry, and sin ~~not~~: let not the sun go down upon your wrath:	**Can ye** be angry and **not** sin? let not the sun go down upon your wrath:
Ephesians 4:28 Let him that stole steal no more: but rather let him labour, working with *his* hands the ~~thing~~ which ~~is~~ good, that he may have to give to him that needeth.	Let him that stole steal no more: but rather let him labour, working with his hands **for the things** which **are** good, that he may have to give to him that needeth.
Ephesians 5:17 Wherefore be ye not unwise, but understanding what the will of the Lord ~~is~~.	Wherefore be ye not unwise, but understanding what **is** the will of the Lord.

The Epistle to the Philippians

King James Version

Philippians 1:4 Always in every prayer of mine for you all making request with joy,

Philippians 1:21 ~~For to me to live *is* Christ, and to die *is* gain.~~

Philippians 1:22 ~~But if I live in the flesh, this *is* the fruit of my labour: yet what I shall choose I wot not.~~

Philippians 1:23 ~~For~~ I am in a strait betwixt two, having a desire to depart, and to be with Christ; which is far better:

Philippians 1:26 That your rejoicing may be more abundant in Jesus Christ for ~~me by~~ my coming to you again.

Philippians 1:27 ~~Only~~ let your conversation be as it becometh the gospel of Christ: that whether I come and see you, or else be absent, I may hear of your affairs, that ye stand fast in one spirit, with one mind striving together for the faith of the gospel;

Philippians 1:28 And in nothing terrified by your adversaries: which ~~is to them an evident token of perdition, but to you of~~ salvation, and that of God.

Philippians 1:30 Having the same conflict which ye saw in me, and now ~~hear to be~~ in me.

Joseph Smith Translation

Always in every prayer of mine for **the steadfastness of** you all making request with joy,

But if I live in the flesh, ye are the fruit of my labour; yet what I shall choose I know not.

For me to live is to do the will of Christ, and to die is my gain.

Now I am in a strait betwixt two, having a desire to depart, and to be with Christ; which is far better;

That your rejoicing **with me** may be more abundant in Jesus Christ, for my coming to you again.

Therefore let your conversation be as it becometh the gospel of Christ: that whether I come and see you, or else be absent, I may hear of your affairs, that ye stand fast in one spirit, with one mind striving together for the faith of the gospel;

And in nothing terrified by your adversaries: **who reject the gospel,** which **bringeth on them destruction; but you who receive the gospel,** salvation, and that of God.

Having the same conflict which ye saw in me, and now **know** to be in me.

Philippians 2:11 And ~~that~~ every tongue should confess ~~that~~ Jesus Christ *is* Lord, to the glory of God the Father.	And every tongue should confess Jesus Christ Lord, to the glory of God the Father.
Philippians 2:17 Yea, and if I be offered ~~upon the~~ sacrifice ~~and~~ service of your faith, I joy, and rejoice with you all.	Yea, and if I be offered **a** sacrifice **upon the** service of your faith, I joy, and rejoice with you all.
Philippians 3:1 Finally, my brethren, rejoice in the Lord. To write the same things to you, to me indeed *is* not grievous, ~~but~~ for you *it is* safe.	Finally, my brethren, rejoice in the Lord. To write the same things to you, to me indeed is not grievous, **and** for you it is safe.
Philippians 3:11 If by any means I might attain unto the resurrection of the ~~dead~~.	If by any means I might attain unto the resurrection of the **just**.
Philippians 3:18 (For many walk, of whom I have told you often, and now tell you even weeping, ~~that they are~~ the enemies of the cross of Christ:	(For many walk, of whom I have told you often, and now tell you even weeping, **as** the enemies of the cross of Christ:
Philippians 3:19 Whose end *is* destruction, whose God *is their* belly, and ~~whose~~ glory *is* in their shame, who mind earthly things.)	Whose end is destruction, whose God is their belly, and **who** glory in their shame, who mind earthly things.)
Philippians 4:6 Be ~~careful~~ for nothing; but in every thing by prayer and supplication with thanksgiving let your requests be made known unto God.	Be **afflicted** for nothing; but in every thing by prayer and supplication with thanksgiving let your requests be made known unto God.

The Epistle to the Colossians

King James Version	Joseph Smith Translation
Colossians 1:4 Since we heard of your faith in Christ Jesus, and of ~~the~~ love *which ye have* to all the saints,	Since we heard of your faith in Christ Jesus, and of **your** love which ye have to all the saints,
Colossians 1:6 Which is come unto you, as ~~it is~~ in all the world; and bringeth forth fruit, as ~~it doth~~ also in you, since the day ye heard ~~of it~~, and knew the grace of God in truth:	Which is come unto you, as in all **generations of** the world; and bringeth forth fruit, as also in you, since the day ye heard, and knew the grace of God in truth:
Colossians 2:2 That their hearts might be comforted, being knit together in love, and unto all riches of the full assurance of understanding, to the acknowledgement of the mystery of God, and of the Father, and of Christ;	That their hearts might be comforted, being knit together in love, and unto all riches of the full assurance of understanding, to the acknowledgement of the mystery of God, and of the Father, and of Christ, **who is of God, even the Father;**
Colossians 2:7 Rooted and built up in him, and ~~stablished~~ in the faith, as ye have been taught, abounding therein with thanksgiving.	Rooted and built up in him, and **established** in the faith, as ye have been taught, abounding therein with thanksgiving.
Colossians 2:20 Wherefore if ye be dead with Christ from the rudiments of the world, why, as though living in the world, are ye subject to ordinances,	Wherefore if ye be dead with Christ from the rudiments of the world, why, as though living in the world, are ye subject to ordinances, **which are after the doctrines and commandments of men,**
Colossians 2:21 ~~(~~Touch not; taste not; handle not:	who teach you to touch not; taste not; handle not;
Colossians 2:22 Which ~~all are~~ to perish with the using~~;) after the commandments and doctrines of men~~?	**All those things** which are to perish with the using?
Colossians 2:23 Which things have indeed a shew of wisdom in will	Which things have indeed a shew of wisdom in will worship, and humility,

worship, and humility, and neglecting ~~of~~ the body; ~~not in any honour~~ to the satisfying ~~of~~ the flesh.	and neglecting the body **as** to the satisfying the flesh, **not in any honor to God.**
Colossians 4:11 And Jesus, which is called Justus, who are of the circumcision. These only *are my* fellowworkers ~~unto~~ the kingdom of God, which have been a comfort unto me.	And Jesus, which is called Justus, who are of the circumcision. These only are my fellowworkers **in** the kingdom of God, which have been a comfort unto me.

The First Epistle to the Thessalonians

King James Version

1 Thessalonians 1:1 Paul, and Silvanus, and Timotheus, unto the church of the Thessalonians ~~which is~~ in ~~God the Father and~~ *in* ~~the Lord Jesus Christ~~: Grace *be* unto you, and peace, from God our Father, and the Lord Jesus Christ.

1 Thessalonians 1:2 We give thanks ~~to God~~ always ~~for you all~~, making mention of you in our prayers;

1 Thessalonians 1:8 For from you sounded out the word of the Lord not only in Macedonia and Achaia, but also in every place your faith ~~to~~ God-~~ward~~ is spread abroad; so that we need not to speak any thing.

1 Thessalonians 2:16 Forbidding us to speak to the Gentiles that they might be saved, to fill up their sins alway: for the wrath is ~~come~~ upon them to the uttermost.

1 Thessalonians 4:15 For this we say unto you by the word of the Lord, that ~~we which~~ are alive ~~and remain unto~~ the coming of the Lord shall not prevent them ~~which~~ are asleep.

1 Thessalonians 4:17 Then ~~we which~~ are alive ~~and remain~~ shall be caught up together ~~with them in~~ the clouds, to meet the Lord in the air: and so shall we ever ~~be~~ with the Lord.

Joseph Smith Translation

Paul, and Silvanus, and Timotheus, **servants of God the Father and the Lord Jesus Christ**, unto the church of the Thessalonians: Grace unto you, and peace, from God our Father, and the Lord Jesus Christ.

We give thanks always, making mention of you **all in our prayers to God for you**;

For from you sounded out the word of the Lord not only in Macedonia and Achaia, but also in every place your faith **toward** God is spread abroad; so that we need not to speak any thing.

Forbidding us to speak to the Gentiles that they might be saved, to fill up their sins alway: for the wrath is **coming** upon them to the uttermost.

For this we say unto you by the word of the Lord, that **they who** are alive **at the coming of the Lord shall not prevent them who remain unto the coming of the Lord, who** are asleep.

Then **they who** are alive shall be caught up together **into** the clouds **with them who remain**, to meet the Lord in the air: and so shall we **be** ever with the Lord.

| **1 Thessalonians 5:26** Greet all the brethren with an holy ~~kiss~~. | Greet all the brethren with an holy **salutation**. |

The Second Epistle to the Thessalonians

King James Version

2 Thessalonians 1:1 Paul, and Silvanus, and Timotheus, unto the church of the Thessalonians ~~in God our Father and the Lord Jesus Christ~~:

2 Thessalonians 1:9 Who shall be punished with ~~everlasting~~ destruction from the presence of the Lord, and from the glory of his power;

2 Thessalonians 2:2 That ye be not soon shaken in mind, or be troubled, ~~neither by spirit, nor by word, nor~~ by letter ~~as~~ from us, as that the day of Christ is at hand.

2 Thessalonians 2:3 Let no man deceive you by any means: for ~~that day shall not come, except~~ there come a falling away first, and that man of sin be revealed, the son of perdition;

2 Thessalonians 2:7 For the mystery of iniquity doth already work: ~~only he who now letteth will let~~, until he be taken out of the way.

2 Thessalonians 2:8 And then shall that Wicked be revealed, whom the Lord shall consume with the spirit of his mouth, and shall destroy with the brightness of his coming:

2 Thessalonians 2:9 *Even* ~~*him*~~, whose coming is after the working of Satan with all power and signs and lying wonders,

Joseph Smith Translation

Paul, and Silvanus, and Timotheus, **the servants of God the Father and our Lord Jesus Christ,** unto the church of the Thessalonians:

Who shall be punished with destruction from the presence of the Lord, and from the glory of his **everlasting** power;

That ye be not soon shaken in mind, or be troubled by letter, **except ye receive it** from us, **neither by spirit, or by word,** as that the day of Christ is at hand.

Let no man deceive you by any means: for there **shall** come a falling away first, and that man of sin be revealed, the son of perdition;

For the mystery of iniquity doth already work **and he it is who now worketh, and Christ suffereth him to work,** until **the time is fulfilled that** he **shall** be taken out of the way.

And then shall that wicked **one** be revealed, whom the Lord shall consume with the spirit of his mouth, and shall destroy with the brightness of his coming:

Yea, the Lord, even **Jesus,** whose coming is **not until** after **there cometh a falling away, by** the working of Satan with all power and signs and lying wonders,

The First Epistle to Timothy

King James Version | Joseph Smith Translation

1 Timothy 1:1 Paul, an apostle of Jesus Christ by the commandment of God ~~our Saviour~~, and Lord Jesus Christ, ~~which is~~ our hope;

Paul, an apostle of Jesus Christ by the commandment of God and **the** Lord Jesus Christ, **our Saviour and** our hope;

1 Timothy 2:4 Who ~~will~~ have all men ~~to be~~ saved, and ~~to~~ come unto the knowledge of the truth.

Who **is willing to** have all men saved, and come unto the knowledge of the truth, **which is in Christ Jesus, who is the only begotten Son of God,**

1 Timothy 2:5 ~~For there is one God~~, and ~~one~~ mediator between God and ~~men, the man Christ Jesus~~;

and **ordained to be a** mediator between God and **man, who is one God, and hath power over all men;**

1 Timothy 2:12 ~~But~~ I suffer not a woman to teach, nor to usurp authority over the man, but to be in silence.

For I suffer not a woman to teach, nor to usurp authority over the man, but to be in silence.

1 Timothy 2:15 Notwithstanding ~~she~~ shall be saved in childbearing, if they continue in faith and charity and holiness with sobriety.

Notwithstanding **they** shall be saved in childbearing, if they continue in faith and charity and holiness with sobriety.

1 Timothy 3:8 Likewise ~~must~~ the deacons ~~be~~ grave, not doubletongued, not given to much wine, not greedy of filthy lucre;

Likewise the deacons **must** be grave, not doubletongued, not given to much wine, not greedy of filthy lucre;

1 Timothy 3:15 But if I tarry long, that thou mayest know how thou oughtest to behave thyself in the house of God, which is the church of the living God, ~~the pillar and ground of the truth~~.

But if I tarry long, that thou mayest know how thou oughtest to behave thyself in the house of God, which is the church of the living God.

1 Timothy 3:16 And without controversy great is the mystery of godliness: God was manifest in the flesh, justified in the Spirit, seen of angels, preached

The pillar and ground of the truth is (and without controversy great is the mystery of godliness): God was manifest in the flesh, justified in the Spirit, seen

unto the Gentiles, believed on in the world, received up into glory.

1 Timothy 4:2 Speaking lies in hypocrisy; having their conscience seared with a hot iron;

1 Timothy 5:10 Well reported of for good works; if she have brought up children, if she have lodged strangers, if she have washed the saints' ~~feet~~, if she have relieved the afflicted, if she have diligently followed every good work.

1 Timothy 5:23 ~~Drink no longer water, but use a little wine for thy stomach's sake and thine often infirmities.~~

1 Timothy 5:24 ~~Some men's sins are open beforehand, going before to judgment; and some *men* they follow after.~~

1 Timothy 5:25 ~~Likewise also the good works *of some* are manifest beforehand; and they that are otherwise cannot be hid.~~

1 Timothy 6:15 Which in his times he shall shew, *who is* the blessed and only Potentate, the King of kings, and Lord of lords;

1 Timothy 6:16 ~~Who only hath immortality, dwelling in the light which~~ no man can approach ~~unto; whom no man hath seen, nor can see: to whom *be* honour and power everlasting~~. Amen.

of angels, preached unto the Gentiles, believed on in the world, received up into glory.

Speaking lies in hypocrisy; having their conscience seared **as** with a hot iron;

Well reported of for good works; if she have brought up children, if she have lodged strangers, if she have washed the saints' **clothes**, if she have relieved the afflicted, if she have diligently followed every good work.

Some men's sins are open beforehand, going before to judgment; and some men they follow after.

Likewise also the good works of some are manifest beforehand; and they that are otherwise cannot be hid.

Drink no longer water, but use a little wine for thy stomach's sake and thine often infirmities.

Which in his times he shall shew, who is the blessed and only Potentate, the King of kings, and Lord of lords, **to whom be honor and power everlasting;**

Whom no man hath seen, nor can see, unto whom no man can approach; **only he who hath the light, and the hope of immortality dwelling in him.** Amen.

The Second Epistle to Timothy

King James Version	Joseph Smith Translation
2 Timothy 1:2 To Timothy, ~~my~~ dearly beloved son: Grace, mercy, *and* peace, from God the Father and Christ Jesus our Lord.	To Timothy, dearly beloved son: Grace, mercy, and peace, from God the Father and Christ Jesus our Lord.
2 Timothy 1:9 Who hath saved us, and called *us* with ~~an~~ holy calling, not according to our works, but according to his own purpose and grace, which was given us in Christ Jesus before the world began,	Who hath saved us, and called us with **a** holy calling, not according to our works, but according to his own purpose and grace, which was given us in Christ Jesus before the world began,
2 Timothy 2:5 And if a man also strive for masteries, ~~yet~~ *is* ~~he~~ not crowned, except he strive lawfully.	And if a man also strive for masteries, **he** is not crowned, except he strive lawfully.
2 Timothy 2:8 Remember that Jesus Christ of the seed of David was raised from the dead according to ~~my~~ gospel:	Remember that Jesus Christ of the seed of David was raised from the dead according to **the** gospel:
2 Timothy 2:11 ~~It~~ *is* a faithful saying: ~~For~~ if we be dead with *him,* we shall also live with *him:*	**For this** is a faithful saying: If we be dead with him, we shall also live with him:
2 Timothy 3:13 ~~But~~ evil men and seducers shall wax worse and worse, deceiving, and being deceived.	**For** evil men and seducers shall wax worse and worse, deceiving, and being deceived.
2 Timothy 3:16 All scripture *is* given by inspiration of God, ~~and~~ *is* profitable for doctrine, for reproof, for correction, for instruction in righteousness:	**And** all scripture given by inspiration of God, is profitable for doctrine, for reproof, for correction, for instruction in righteousness:
2 Timothy 4:1 I charge *thee* therefore before God, and the Lord Jesus Christ, who shall judge the quick and the dead at his appearing ~~and~~ his kingdom;	I charge thee therefore before God, and the Lord Jesus Christ, who shall judge the quick and the dead at his appearing **in** his kingdom;

2 Timothy 4:2 Preach the word; be instant in season, out of season; reprove, rebuke, exhort with all longsuffering and doctrine.	Preach the word; be instant in season, [to] **those who are** out of season; reprove, rebuke, exhort with all longsuffering and doctrine.
2 Timothy 4:22 The Lord Jesus Christ *be* with ~~thy spirit~~. Grace *be* with you. Amen.	The Lord Jesus Christ be with **you, and grace** be with you **all**. Amen.

The Epistle to Titus

King James Version	Joseph Smith Translation
Titus 1:15 Unto the pure all things ~~are~~ pure: but unto them that are defiled and unbelieving ~~is~~ nothing pure; but even their mind and conscience is defiled.	Unto the pure **let** all things **be** pure: but unto them that are defiled and unbelieving nothing **is** pure; but even their mind and conscience is defiled.
Titus 2:11 For the grace of God ~~that~~ bringeth salvation ~~hath appeared~~ to all men,	For the grace of God, **which** bringeth salvation to all men, **hath appeared**,

The Epistle to the Hebrews

King James Version | Joseph Smith Translation

Hebrews 1:7 ~~And of the angels he saith,~~ Who maketh his ~~angels spirits, and his~~ ministers a flame of fire.

Who maketh his ministers **as a** flame of fire. **And of the angels he saith, Angels are ministering spirits.**

Hebrews 2:16 For verily he took not on him the ~~nature of~~ angels; but he took on him the seed of Abraham.

For verily he took not on him the **likeness** of angels; but he took on him the seed of Abraham.

Hebrews 3:3 For ~~this man~~ was counted worthy of more glory than Moses, inasmuch as he who hath builded the house hath more honour than the house.

For **he** was counted worthy of more glory than Moses, inasmuch as he who hath builded the house hath more honour than the house.

Hebrews 4:2 For unto us was the ~~gospel~~ preached, as well as unto them: but the word preached did not profit them, not being mixed with faith in them that heard *it*.

For unto us was the **rest** preached, as well as unto them: but the word preached did not profit them, not being mixed with faith in them that heard it.

Hebrews 4:3 For we ~~which~~ have believed do enter into rest, as he said, As I have sworn in my wrath, if they shall enter ~~into~~ my rest: although the works were finished from the foundation of the world.

For we **who** have believed do enter into rest, as he said, As I have sworn in my wrath, if they **harden their hearts they** shall **not** enter **unto** my rest: **also, I have sworn, If they will not harden their hearts, they shall enter into my rest;** although the works **of God** were **prepared, or** finished, from the foundation of the world.

Hebrews 4:5 And in this *place* again, If they shall enter into my rest.

And in this place again, If they **harden not their hearts they** shall enter into my rest.

Hebrews 4:12 For the word of God *is* quick, and powerful, and sharper than any two-edged sword, piercing even to the dividing asunder of ~~soul~~ and spirit, and of the joints and marrow, and *is* a

For the word of God is quick, and powerful, and sharper than any two-edged sword, piercing even to the dividing asunder of **body** and spirit, and of the joints and marrow, and is a discerner of

The Epistle to the Hebrews

discerner of the thoughts and intents of the heart.

Hebrews 5:7 Who in the days of his flesh, when he had offered up prayers and supplications with strong crying and tears unto him that was able to save him from death, and was heard in that he feared;

Hebrews 5:8 Though he were a Son, yet learned he obedience by the things which he suffered;

Hebrews 6:1 Therefore leaving the principles of the doctrine of Christ, let us go on unto perfection; not laying again the foundation of repentance from dead works, and of faith toward God,

Hebrews 6:2 Of the doctrine of baptisms, and of laying on of hands, and of resurrection of the dead, and of eternal judgment.

Hebrews 6:3 And ~~this~~ will ~~we do~~, if God permit.

Hebrews 6:4 For *it is* impossible for those who were once enlightened, and have tasted of the heavenly gift, and were made partakers of the Holy Ghost,

Hebrews 6:6 If they shall fall away, to ~~renew them~~ again unto repentance; seeing they crucify ~~to~~ themselves the Son of God afresh, and put *him* to an open shame.

Hebrews 6:7 For the earth which drinketh in the rain that cometh oft upon it, and bringeth forth herbs meet for them by whom it is dressed, receiveth ~~blessing~~ from God:

the thoughts and intents of the heart.

Note—The 7th and 8th verses of this chapter are a parenthesis alluding to Melchizedek and not to Christ.

Therefore **not** leaving the principles of the doctrine of Christ, let us go on unto perfection; not laying again the foundation of repentance from dead works, and of faith toward God,

Of the doctrine of baptisms, and of laying on of hands, and of **the** resurrection of the dead, and of eternal judgment.

And **we** will **go on unto perfection** if God permit.

For **he hath made** it impossible for those who were once enlightened, and have tasted of the heavenly gift, and were made partakers of the Holy Ghost,

If they shall fall away, to **be renewed** again unto repentance; seeing they crucify **unto** themselves the Son of God afresh, and put him to an open shame.

For the **day cometh that** the earth which drinketh in the rain that cometh oft upon it, and bringeth forth herbs meet for them **who dwelleth thereon**, by whom it is dressed, **who now**

Hebrews 6:8 ~~But~~ that which beareth thorns and briers *is* rejected, and *is* nigh unto cursing; ~~whose~~ end *is* to be burned.

Hebrews 6:9 But, beloved, we are persuaded better things of you, and things that accompany salvation, though we thus speak.

Hebrews 6:10 For God *is* not unrighteous ~~to~~ forget your work and labour of love, which ye have shewed toward his name, in that ye have ministered to the saints, and do minister.

Hebrews 7:3 Without father, without mother, without descent, having neither beginning of days, nor end of life; ~~but~~ made like unto the Son of God; ~~abideth~~ a priest continually.

Hebrews 7:19 For the law made nothing perfect, but the bringing in of a better hope ~~did;~~ by the which we draw nigh unto God.

Hebrews 7:20 And inasmuch as not without an oath ~~he was made priest:~~

Hebrews 7:21 ~~(For those priests were made without an oath; but this with an oath by him that said unto him, The Lord sware and will not repent, Thou art a priest for ever after the order of Melchisedec:)~~

receiveth **blessings** from God, **shall be cleansed with fire.**

For that which beareth thorns and briers is rejected, and is nigh unto cursing; **therefore they who bring not forth good fruits, shall be cast into the fire; for their** end is to be burned.

But, beloved, we are persuaded **of** better things of you, and things that accompany salvation, though we thus speak.

For God is not unrighteous, **therefore he will not** forget your work and labour of love, which ye have shewed toward his name, in that ye have ministered to the saints, and do minister.

For this Melchizedek was ordained a priest after the order of the Son of God, which order was without father, without mother, without descent, having neither beginning of days, nor end of life; **and all those who are ordained unto this priesthood are** made like unto the Son of God; **abiding** a priest continually.

For the law **was administered without an oath and** made nothing perfect, but **was only** the bringing in of a better hope by the which we draw nigh unto God.

Inasmuch as **this high priest was** not without an oath **by so much was Jesus made the surety of a better testament:**

By so much was Jesus made a surety of a better testament.

Hebrews 7:22 ~~By so much was Jesus made a surety of a better testament.~~	(For those priests were made without an oath; but this with an oath by him that said unto him, The Lord sware and will not repent, Thou art a priest for ever after the order of Melchisedec:)
Hebrews 7:26 For such an high priest became us, *who is* holy, harmless, undefiled, separate from sinners, and made ~~higher than~~ the heavens;	For such an high priest became us, who is holy, harmless, undefiled, separate from sinners, and made **ruler over** the heavens;
Hebrews 7:27 Who ~~needeth not~~ daily, ~~as those high priests, to offer up sacrifice~~, first for his own sins, ~~and then~~ for the ~~people's: for~~ this he did once, when he offered up himself.	**And not as those high priests** who **offered up sacrifice** daily, first **for their own sins, and then for the sins of the people; for he needeth not [to] offer sacrifice** for his own sins, **for he knew no sins; but for the sins of the people. And** this he did once when he offered up himself.
Hebrews 8:4 ~~For if~~ he ~~were~~ on earth, he ~~should not be a priest, seeing that there are priests that~~ offer gifts according to the law:	**Therefore while** he **was** on **the** earth, he **offered for a sacrifice his own life for the sins of the people. Now every priest under the law must needs** offer gifts, **or sacrifices**, according to the law:
Hebrews 8:5 Who serve unto the example and shadow of heavenly things, as Moses was admonished of God when he was about to make the tabernacle: for, See, saith he, ~~that~~ thou make all things according to the pattern shewed to thee in the mount.	Who serve unto the example and shadow of heavenly things, as Moses was admonished of God when he was about to make the tabernacle: for, See, saith he, thou make all things according to the pattern shewed to thee in the mount.
Hebrews 9:8 The Holy Ghost ~~this~~ signifying, that the way into the holiest of all was not yet made manifest, ~~while as~~ the first tabernacle was ~~yet~~ standing:	The Holy Ghost signifying **this,** that the way into the holiest of all was not yet made manifest, **yet** the first tabernacle was standing:
Hebrews 9:10 *Which* ~~stood~~ only in meats and drinks, and divers washings, and carnal ordinances, imposed ~~on them~~ until the time of reformation.	Which **consisted** only in meats and drinks, and divers washings, and carnal ordinances, imposed until the time of reformation.
Hebrews 9:15 And for this cause he is the mediator of the new ~~testament~~, that	And for this cause he is the mediator of the new **covenant**, that by means

by means of death, for the redemption of the transgressions ~~that were~~ under the first ~~testament~~, they which are called might receive the promise of eternal inheritance.

Hebrews 9:16 For where a ~~testament~~ *is*, there must also of necessity be the death of the ~~testator~~.

Hebrews 9:17 For a ~~testament~~ *is* of force after ~~men are~~ dead: otherwise it is of no strength at all while the ~~testator~~ liveth.

Hebrews 9:18 Whereupon neither the first ~~testament~~ was dedicated without blood.

Hebrews 9:20 Saying, This *is* the blood of the ~~testament~~ which God hath enjoined unto you.

Hebrews 9:26 For then must he often have suffered since the foundation of the world: but now once in the ~~end of the world~~ hath he appeared to put away sin by the sacrifice of himself.

Hebrews 9:28 So Christ was once offered to bear the sins of many; and ~~unto them that look for him shall~~ he appear the second time without sin unto salvation.

Hebrews 10:1 For the law having a shadow of good things to come, *and* not the very image of the things, can never with those sacrifices which they offered year by year ~~continually~~ make the comers thereunto perfect.

Hebrews 10:10 By ~~the~~ which will we are sanctified through the offering of the body of Jesus Christ ~~once~~ ~~*for all*~~.

of death, for the redemption of the transgressions under the first **covenant**, they which are called might receive the promise of eternal inheritance.

For where a **covenant** is, there must also of necessity be the death of the **victim**.

For a **covenant** is of force after **the victim is** dead: otherwise it is of no strength at all while the **victim** liveth.

Whereupon neither the first **covenant** was dedicated without blood.

Saying, This is the blood of the **covenant** which God hath enjoined unto you.

For then must he often have suffered since the foundation of the world: but now once in the **meridian of time** hath he appeared to put away sin by the sacrifice of himself.

So Christ was once offered to bear the sins of many; and he **shall** appear the second time without sin unto salvation **unto them that look for him**.

For the law having a shadow of good things to come, and not the very image of the things, can never with those sacrifices which they offered **continually** year by year make the comers thereunto perfect.

By which will we are sanctified through the offering **once** of the body of Jesus Christ.

Hebrews 10:13 From henceforth ~~expecting till~~ his enemies be made his footstool.	From henceforth **to reign until** his enemies be made his footstool.
Hebrews 10:21 And *having* an high priest over the house of God;	And having **such** an high priest over the house of God;
Hebrews 11:1 Now faith is the ~~substance~~ of things hoped for, the evidence of things not seen.	Now faith is the **assurance** of things hoped for, the evidence of things not seen.
Hebrews 11:12 Therefore sprang there even of one, and him as good as dead, ~~so~~ *many* as the stars of the sky in multitude, and as the sand which is by the sea shore innumerable.	Therefore sprang there even of one, and him as good as dead, **as** many as the stars of the sky in multitude, and as the sand which is by the sea shore innumerable.
Hebrews 11:21 By faith Jacob, when he was ~~a~~ dying, blessed both the sons of Joseph; and worshipped, ~~leaning~~ upon the top of his staff.	By faith Jacob, when he was dying, blessed both the sons of Joseph; and worshipped, [leaning] upon the top of his staff.
Hebrews 11:23 By faith Moses, when he was born, was hid three months of his parents, because they saw *he was* a ~~proper~~ child; and they were not afraid of the king's commandment.	By faith Moses, when he was born, was hid three months of his parents, because they saw **that** he was a **peculiar** child; and they were not afraid of the king's commandment.
Hebrews 11:24 By faith Moses, when he was come to years, refused to be called the son of Pharaoh's daughter;	By faith Moses, when he was come to years **of discretion**, refused to be called the son of Pharaoh's daughter;
Hebrews 11:32 And what shall I ~~more~~ say? for the time would fail me to tell of Gedeon, and ~~of~~ Barak, and ~~of~~ Samson, and ~~of~~ Jephthae; ~~of~~ David also, and Samuel, and ~~of~~ the prophets:	And what shall I say **more**? for the time would fail me to tell of Gedeon, and Barak, and Samson, and Jephthae; David also, and Samuel, and the prophets:
Hebrews 11:35 Women received their dead raised to life again: and others were tortured, not accepting deliverance; that they might obtain ~~a better~~ resurrection:	Women received their dead raised to life again: and others were tortured, not accepting deliverance; that they might obtain **the first** resurrection:
Hebrews 11:39 And these all, having obtained a good report through faith, received ~~not~~ the ~~promise~~:	And these all, having obtained a good report through faith, received the **promises**:

Hebrews 11:40 God having provided some better ~~thing~~ for ~~us, that they~~ without ~~us should~~ not be made perfect.	God having provided some better **things** for **them through their sufferings, for** without **sufferings they could** not be made perfect.
Hebrews 12:12 Wherefore lift up the hands which hang down, and the feeble knees;	Wherefore lift up the hands which hang down, and **strengthen** the feeble knees;
Hebrews 12:28 Wherefore we receiving a kingdom which cannot be moved, ~~let us~~ have grace, whereby we may serve God acceptably with reverence and godly fear:	Wherefore we receiving a kingdom which cannot be moved, **should** have grace, whereby we may serve God acceptably with reverence and godly fear:
Hebrews 13:3 Remember them that are in bonds, as bound with them; ~~and~~ them which suffer adversity, as being yourselves also in the body.	Remember them that are in bonds, as bound with them; **of** them which suffer adversity, as being yourselves also in the body.
Hebrews 13:5 *Let your* ~~conversation~~ *be* without covetousness; *and be* content with such things as ye have: for he hath said, I will never leave thee, nor forsake thee.	Let your **consecrations** be without covetousness; and be content with **giving** such things as ye have: for he hath said, I will never leave thee, nor forsake thee.

The Epistle of James

King James Version	Joseph Smith Translation
James 1:2 My brethren, count it all joy when ye fall into ~~divers temptations~~;	My brethren, count it all joy when ye fall into **many afflictions**;
James 1:4 But let patience have ~~her~~ perfect work, that ye may be perfect and entire, wanting nothing.	But let patience have **its** perfect work, that ye may be perfect and entire, wanting nothing.
James 1:12 Blessed *is* the man that ~~endureth~~ temptation: for when he is tried, he shall receive the crown of life, which the Lord hath promised to them that love him.	Blessed is the man that **resisteth** temptation: for when he is tried, he shall receive the crown of life, which the Lord hath promised to them that love him.
James 1:21 Wherefore lay ~~apart~~ all filthiness and superfluity of naughtiness, and receive with meekness the engrafted word, which is able to save your souls.	Wherefore lay **aside** all filthiness and superfluity of naughtiness, and receive with meekness the engrafted word, which is able to save your souls.
James 1:27 Pure religion and undefiled before God and the Father is this, To visit the fatherless and widows in their affliction, *and* to keep himself unspotted from the world.	Pure religion and undefiled before God and the Father is this, To visit the fatherless and widows in their affliction, and to keep himself unspotted from the **vices of** the world.
James 2:1 My brethren, have ~~not~~ the faith of our Lord Jesus Christ, *the Lord* of glory, ~~with~~ respect of persons.	My brethren, **ye cannot** have the faith of our Lord Jesus Christ, the Lord of glory, **and yet have** respect **to** persons.
James 2:2 ~~For~~ if there come unto your assembly a man with a gold ring, in goodly apparel, and there come in also a poor man in vile raiment;	**Now** if there come unto your assembly a man with a gold ring, in goodly apparel, and there come in also a poor man in vile raiment;
James 2:4 Are ye not then partial ~~in yourselves~~, and ~~are~~ become ~~judges of~~ evil thoughts?	Are ye not then **in yourselves** partial **judges**, and become evil **in your** thoughts?
James 2:7 Do not they blaspheme that worthy name by ~~the~~ which ye are called?	Do not they blaspheme that worthy name by which ye are called?

James 2:10 For whosoever shall ~~keep the whole law, and yet offend~~ in one *point*, he is guilty of all.

James 2:14 What ~~doth it~~ profit, my brethren, ~~though~~ a man say he hath faith, and ~~have~~ not works? can faith save him?

James 2:15 If a brother or sister be naked, and destitute ~~of daily food~~,

James 2:16 And one of you say ~~unto them~~, Depart in peace, be ~~ye~~ warmed and filled; notwithstanding ~~ye~~ give ~~them~~ not those things which are needful to the body; what ~~doth it~~ profit?

James 2:17 Even so faith, if it ~~hath~~ not works, is dead, being alone.

James 2:18 ~~Yea, a man may say, Thou hast faith, and I have works: shew me thy faith without thy works, and I will shew thee my faith by my works~~.

James 2:19 Thou believest ~~that~~ there is one God; thou doest well: the devils also believe, and tremble.

James 2:20 ~~But wilt thou know, O vain man, that faith without works is dead?~~

James 2:22 Seest thou how ~~faith~~ wrought with his ~~works~~, and by works was faith made perfect?

James 2:24 Ye see then ~~how~~ that by works a man is justified, and not by faith only.

James 2:25 Likewise also ~~was not~~ Rahab the harlot justified by works, when she

For whosoever shall, **save** in one point, **keep the whole law**, he is guilty of all.

What profit **is it**, my brethren, **for** a man to say he hath faith, and **hath** not works? can faith save him?

Yea, a man may say, I will shew thee I have faith without works; but I say, Shew me they faith without works, and I will shew thee my faith by my works. For if a brother or sister be naked, and destitute,

And one of you say, Depart in peace, be warmed and filled; notwithstanding **he** give not those things which are needful to the body; what profit **is your faith unto such?**

Even so faith, if it **have** not works, **it** is dead, being alone.

Therefore wilt thou know, O vain man, that faith without works is dead, and cannot save you?

Thou believest there is one God; thou doest well: the devils also believe, and tremble.

Thou hast made thyself like unto them, not being justified.

Seest thou how **works** wrought with his **faith**, and by works was faith made perfect?

Ye see then that by works a man is justified, and not by faith only.

Likewise also, Rahab the harlot **was** justified by works, when she had received

had received the messengers, and had sent *them* out another way?	the messengers, and had sent them out another way?
James 2:26 For as the body without the spirit is dead, so faith without works is dead ~~also~~.	For as the body without the spirit is dead, so faith without works is dead.
James 3:1 My brethren, ~~be not many masters~~, knowing that we shall receive the greater condemnation.	My brethren, **strive not for the mastery**, knowing that **in so doing** we shall receive the greater condemnation.
James 4:15 ~~For that~~ ye *ought* to say, If the Lord will, we shall live, and do this, or that.	Ye ought to say, If the Lord will, we shall live, and do this, or that.

The First Epistle of Peter

King James Version

1 Peter 1:9 Receiving the ~~end~~ of your faith, *even* the salvation of *your* souls.

1 Peter 1:10 ~~Of~~ which salvation the prophets ~~have enquired and searched diligently~~, who prophesied of the grace ~~that should come~~ unto you:

1 Peter 1:11 Searching what, ~~or~~ what manner of ~~time~~ the Spirit of Christ which was in them did signify, when it testified beforehand the sufferings of Christ, and the glory ~~that~~ should follow.

1 Peter 2:7 Unto you therefore ~~which~~ believe *he is* precious: but unto them ~~which be~~ disobedient, ~~the stone which the builders disallowed, the same is made the head of the corner~~,

1 Peter 2:8 ~~And~~ a stone of stumbling, and a rock of offence, ~~even to them which stumble at the word, being disobedient: whereunto also they were appointed~~.

1 Peter 2:12 Having your ~~conversation~~ honest among the Gentiles: that, whereas they speak against you as evildoers, they may by *your* good works, which they shall behold, glorify God in the day of visitation.

1 Peter 3:1 Likewise, ye wives, *be* in subjection to your own husbands; that, if any obey not the word, they also may without the word be won by the ~~conversation~~ of the wives;

Joseph Smith Translation

Receiving the **object** of your faith, even the salvation of your souls.

Concerning which salvation the prophets who prophesied of the grace **bestowed upon** you **inquired and searched diligently**:

Searching what **time, and** what manner of **salvation** the Spirit of Christ which was in them did signify, when it testified beforehand the sufferings of Christ, and the glory **which** should follow.

Unto you therefore **who** believe he is precious: but unto them **who are** disobedient, **who stumble at the word through disobedience whereunto they were appointed**,

A stone of stumbling, and a rock of offence, **for** the stone which the builders disallowed is **become** the head of the corner.

Having your **conduct** honest among the Gentiles: that, whereas they speak against you as evildoers, they may by your good works, which they shall behold, glorify God in the day of visitation.

Likewise, ye wives, be in subjection to your own husbands; that, if any obey not the word, they also may without the word be won by the **conduct** of the wives;

1 Peter 3:2 While they behold your chaste ~~conversation~~ *coupled* with fear.

1 Peter 3:3 ~~Whose~~ adorning ~~let it not~~ be that outward *adorning* of plaiting the hair, and ~~of~~ wearing of gold, or ~~of~~ putting on of apparel;

1 Peter 3:4 But ~~let it be~~ the hidden man of the heart, in that which is not corruptible, ~~even the ornament~~ of a meek and quiet spirit, which is in the sight of God of great price.

1 Peter 3:5 For after this manner in ~~the~~ old ~~time~~ the holy women ~~also~~, who trusted in God, adorned themselves, being in subjection unto their own husbands:

1 Peter 3:14 But ~~and~~ if ye suffer for righteousness' sake, happy *are ye:* and be not afraid of their terror, neither be troubled;

1 Peter 3:15 But sanctify the Lord God in your hearts: and *be* ready always to *give* an answer ~~to every man that asketh you a reason of the hope that is in you~~ with meekness and fear:

1 Peter 3:16 Having a good conscience; that, whereas they speak evil of you, as of evildoers, they may be ashamed that falsely accuse your good ~~conversation~~ in Christ.

1 Peter 3:18 For Christ also ~~hath~~ once suffered for sins, the just for the unjust, ~~that he might bring us to God~~, being put to death in the flesh, but quickened by the Spirit:

1 Peter 3:19 ~~By~~ which also he went and preached unto the spirits in prison;

While they behold your chaste **conduct** coupled with fear.

Let your adorning be **not** that outward adorning of plaiting the hair, and wearing of gold, or putting on of apparel;

But the hidden man of the heart, in that which is not corruptible, of a meek and quiet spirit, which is in the sight of God of great price.

For after this manner in old **times** the holy women, who trusted in God, adorned themselves, being in subjection unto their own husbands:

But if ye suffer for righteousness' sake, happy are ye: and be not afraid of their terror, neither be troubled;

But sanctify the Lord God in your hearts: and be ready always to give an answer with meekness and fear, **to every man that asketh of you a reason for the hope that is in you**:

Having a good conscience; that, whereas they speak evil of you, as of evildoers, they may be ashamed that falsely accuse your good **conduct** in Christ.

For Christ also once suffered for sins, the just for the unjust, being put to death in the flesh, but quickened by the Spirit, **that he might bring us to God**:

For which **cause** also he went and preached unto the spirits in prison;

1 Peter 3:20 ~~Which sometime~~ were disobedient, ~~when once the longsuffering of God waited~~ in the days of Noah, while the ark was ~~a~~ preparing, wherein few, that is, eight souls were saved by water.	**Some of whom** were disobedient in the days of Noah, **while the longsuffering of God waited**, while the ark was preparing, wherein few, that is, eight souls were saved by water.
1 Peter 4:1 Forasmuch then as Christ hath suffered for us in the flesh, arm yourselves likewise with the same mind: ~~for he that hath suffered in the flesh hath ceased from sin~~;	Forasmuch then as Christ hath suffered for us in the flesh, arm yourselves likewise with the same mind:
1 Peter 4:2 That ~~he~~ no longer ~~should live~~ the rest of ~~his~~ time in the flesh to the lusts of men, but to the will of God.	For **you who** hath suffered in the flesh **should cease** from sin; that **you** no longer the rest of **your** time in the flesh **should live** to the lusts of men, but to the will of God.
1 Peter 4:3 For the time past of ~~our~~ life may suffice ~~us~~ to have wrought the will of the Gentiles, when ~~we~~ walked in lasciviousness, lusts, excess of wine, revellings, banquetings, and abominable idolatries:	For the time past of life may suffice to have wrought the will of the Gentiles, when **ye** walked in lasciviousness, lusts, excess of wine, revellings, banquetings, and abominable idolatries:
1 Peter 4:4 Wherein they ~~think~~ it strange that ~~ye~~ run not with *them* to the same excess of riot, ~~speaking evil of you~~:	Wherein they **speak evil of you, thinking** it strange that **you** run not with them to the same excess of riot:
1 Peter 4:6 ~~For for~~ this ~~cause was~~ the gospel preached also to them ~~that~~ are dead, that they might be judged according to men in the flesh, but live according to God ~~in the spirit~~.	**Because of** this **is** the gospel preached to them **who** are dead, that they might be judged according to men in the flesh, but live **in the spirit** according to **the will of** God.
1 Peter 4:7 But the end of all things is at hand: be ye therefore sober, and watch unto prayer.	But **to you** the end of all things is at hand: be ye therefore sober, and watch unto prayer.
1 Peter 4:8 And above all things have fervent charity among yourselves: for charity ~~shall cover the~~ multitude of sins.	And above all things have fervent charity among yourselves: for charity **preventeth a** multitude of sins.
1 Peter 4:11 If any man speak, *let him speak* as ~~the oracles~~ of God; if any man	If any man speak, let him speak as **an oracle** of God; if any man minister, let

minister, *let him do it* as of the ability which God giveth: that God in all things may be glorified through Jesus Christ, to whom be praise and dominion for ever and ever. Amen.	him do it as of the ability which God giveth: that God in all things may be glorified through Jesus Christ, to whom be praise and dominion for ever and ever. Amen.
1 Peter 5:13 ~~The church that is~~ at Babylon, elected together with *you,* saluteth you; and ~~so doth~~ Marcus my son.	**They** at Babylon, elected together with you, saluteth you; and Marcus my son.

The Second Epistle of Peter

King James Version

2 Peter 1:10 Wherefore ~~the~~ rather, brethren, give diligence to make your calling and election sure: for if ye do these things, ye shall never fall:

2 Peter 1:19 We have ~~also~~ a more sure word of prophecy; ~~whereunto~~ ye do well that ye take heed, as unto a light ~~that~~ shineth in a dark place, until the day dawn, and the day star arise in your hearts:

2 Peter 1:20 Knowing this first, that no prophecy of the ~~scripture~~ is of any private ~~interpretation~~.

2 Peter 2:1 But there were false prophets also among the people, even as there shall be false teachers among you, who privily shall bring in ~~damnable~~ heresies, even denying the Lord that bought them, and bring upon themselves swift destruction.

2 Peter 2:3 And through covetousness shall they with feigned words make merchandise of you: whose judgment now of a long time lingereth not, and their ~~damnation~~ slumbereth not.

2 Peter 2:19 While they promise them liberty, they themselves are the servants of corruption: for of whom a man is overcome, of the same is he brought ~~in~~ bondage.

2 Peter 3:1 This second epistle, beloved,

Joseph Smith Translation

Wherefore rather, brethren, give diligence to make your calling and election sure: for if ye do these things, ye shall never fall:

We have **therefore** a more sure **knowledge of the** word of prophecy, **to which word of prophecy** ye do well that ye take heed, as unto a light **which** shineth in a dark place, until the day dawn, and the day star arise in your hearts:

Knowing this first, that no prophecy of the **scriptures** is **given** of any private **will of man**.

But there were false prophets also among the people, even as there shall be false teachers among you, who privily shall bring in **abominable** heresies, even denying the Lord that bought them, and bring upon themselves swift destruction.

And through covetousness shall they with feigned words make merchandise of you: whose judgment now of a long time lingereth not, and their **destruction** slumbereth not.

While they promise them liberty, they themselves are the servants of corruption: for of whom a man is overcome, of the same is he brought **into** bondage.

This second epistle, beloved, I now

The Second Epistle of Peter

I now write unto you; in ~~both~~ which I stir up your pure minds by way of remembrance:

2 Peter 3:2 That ye may be mindful of the words which were spoken before by the holy prophets, and of the ~~commandment~~ of us the apostles of the Lord and Saviour:

2 Peter 3:3 Knowing this first, that there shall come ~~in the last days~~ scoffers, walking after their own lusts,

2 Peter 3:4 And saying, Where is the promise of his coming? for since the fathers fell asleep, all things continue as *they* ~~were~~ from the beginning of the creation.

2 Peter 3:5 For this they willingly are ignorant of, that ~~by the word of God the heavens were~~ of old, and the earth standing ~~out of~~ the water and ~~in~~ the water:

2 Peter 3:6 ~~Whereby~~ the world that then was, being overflowed with water, perished:

2 Peter 3:7 But the heavens and the earth, which are now, ~~by the same word~~ are kept in store, reserved unto fire against the day of judgment and perdition of ungodly men.

2 Peter 3:8 But, beloved, ~~be not~~ ignorant of this one thing, that one day *is* with the Lord as a thousand years, and a thousand years as one day.

2 Peter 3:9 The Lord is not slack concerning his promise, as some men count slackness; but is longsuffering ~~to~~ us

write unto you; in which I stir up your pure minds by way of remembrance:

That ye may be mindful of the words which were spoken before by the holy prophets, and of the **commandments** of us the apostles of the Lord and Saviour:

Knowing this first, that **in the last days** there shall come scoffers, walking after their own lusts,

Denying the Lord Jesus Christ, and saying, Where is the promise of his coming? for since the fathers fell asleep, all things continue as they **are, and have continued as they are** from the beginning of the creation.

For this they willingly are ignorant of, that of old **the heavens**, and the earth standing **in** the water and **out of** the water, **were created by the word of God**:

And by the word of God, the world that then was, being overflowed with water, perished:

But the heavens and the earth, which are now, are kept in store **by the same word**, reserved unto fire against the day of judgment and perdition of ungodly men.

But **concerning the coming of the Lord**, beloved, **I would not have you** ignorant of this one thing, that one day is with the Lord as a thousand years, and a thousand years as one day.

The Lord is not slack concerning his promise **and coming**, as some men count slackness; but is longsuffering

~~ward~~, not willing that any should perish, but that all should come to repentance.

2 Peter 3:10 But the day of the Lord will come as a thief in the night; in the which the heavens shall pass away with a great noise, and the elements shall ~~melt~~ with fervent heat, the earth also and the works ~~that~~ are therein shall be burned up.

2 Peter 3:11 ~~Seeing~~ then ~~that~~ all these things shall be ~~dissolved~~, what manner *of persons* ought ye to be in ~~all~~ holy ~~conversation~~ and godliness,

2 Peter 3:12 Looking for ~~and hasting unto the coming of~~ the day of ~~God~~, wherein the heavens being on fire shall be dissolved, and the ~~elements~~ shall melt with fervent heat?

2 Peter 3:13 Nevertheless we, according to his promise, look for new heavens and a new earth, wherein dwelleth righteousness.

2 Peter 3:15 And account ~~that the longsuffering of our Lord is salvation~~; even as our beloved brother Paul also according to the wisdom given unto him hath written unto you;

2 Peter 3:16 As also in all *his* epistles, speaking in them of these things; in which are some things hard to be understood, which they ~~that~~ are unlearned and unstable wrest, as *they do* also the other scriptures, unto their own destruction.

toward us, not willing that any should perish, but that all should come to repentance.

But the day of the Lord will come as a thief in the night; in the which the heavens shall **shake and the earth also shall tremble, and the mountains shall melt and** pass away with a great noise, and the elements shall **be filled** with fervent heat, the earth also **shall be filled**, and the **corruptible** works **which** are therein shall be burned up.

If then all these things shall be **destroyed**, what manner of persons ought ye to be in holy **conduct** and godliness,

Looking **unto, and preparing** for the day of **the coming of the Lord,** wherein **the corruptible things of** the heavens being on fire shall be dissolved, and the **mountains** shall melt with fervent heat?

Nevertheless **if** we **shall endure, we shall be kept** according to his promise. **And we** look for a new heavens and a new earth, wherein dwelleth righteousness.

And account even as our beloved brother Paul also according to the wisdom given unto him hath written unto you, **the longsuffering and waiting of our Lord for salvation**;

As also in all his epistles, speaking in them of these things; in which are some things hard to be understood, which they **who** are unlearned and unstable wrest, as they do also the other scriptures, unto their own destruction.

2 Peter 3:17 Ye therefore, beloved, seeing ye know ~~these things~~ before, beware lest ye also, being led away with the error of the wicked, fall from your own stedfastness.	Ye therefore, beloved, seeing ye know, before **the things which are coming**, beware lest ye also, being led away with the error of the wicked, fall from your own stedfastness.
2 Peter 3:18 But grow in grace, and ~~in~~ the knowledge of our Lord and Saviour Jesus Christ. To him *be* glory both now and for ever. Amen.	But grow in grace, and the knowledge of our Lord and Saviour Jesus Christ. To him be glory both now and for ever. Amen.

The First Epistle General of John

King James Version

1 John 1:1 That which was from the beginning, which we have heard, which we have seen with our eyes, which we have looked upon, and our hands have handled, of the Word of life;

1 John 2:1 My little children, these things write I unto you, that ye sin not. ~~And~~ if any man sin, we have an advocate with the Father, Jesus Christ the righteous:

1 John 2:6 He that saith he abideth in him ought himself also ~~so~~ to walk, even as he walked.

1 John 2:7 Brethren, I write ~~no~~ new commandment unto you, but ~~an old~~ commandment which ye had from the beginning. The old commandment is the word which ye have heard from the beginning.

1 John 2:8 Again, a new commandment I write unto you, which thing is true in him and in you: because the darkness is past, and the true light now shineth.

1 John 2:15 Love not the world, neither the things ~~that are in~~ the world. If any man love the world, the love of the Father is not in him.

1 John 2:16 For all ~~that is~~ in the world, the ~~lust~~ of the flesh, and the lust of the

Joseph Smith Translation

Brethren, this is the testimony which we give of that which was from the beginning, which we have heard, which we have seen with our eyes, which we have looked upon, and our hands have handled, of the Word of life;

My little children, these things write I unto you, that ye sin not. **But** if any man sin **and repent**, we have an advocate with the Father, Jesus Christ the righteous:

He that saith he abideth in him ought himself also to walk, even as he walked.

Brethren, I write **a** new commandment unto you, but **it is the same** commandment which ye had from the beginning. The old commandment is the word which ye have heard from the beginning.

Again, a new commandment I write unto you, which thing **was of old ordained of God, and** is true in him and in you: because the darkness is past **in you**, and the true light now shineth.

Love not the world, neither the things **of** the world. If any man love the world, the love of the Father is not in him.

For all in the world **that is of** the **lusts** of the flesh, and the lust of the eyes, and

The First Epistle General of John

eyes, and the pride of life, is not of the Father, but is of the world.

1 John 2:23 Whosoever denieth the Son, the same hath not the Father: [but] he that acknowledgeth the Son hat the Father also.

1 John 3:6 Whosoever abideth in him sinneth not: whosoever ~~sinneth~~ hath not seen him, neither known him.

1 John 3:8 He that ~~committeth~~ sin is of the devil; for the devil sinneth from the beginning. For this purpose the Son of God was manifested, that he might destroy the works of the devil.

1 John 3:9 Whosoever is born of God doth not ~~commit~~ sin; for ~~his seed~~ remaineth in him: and he cannot sin, because he is born of God.

1 John 3:16 Hereby perceive we the love *of ~~God~~*, because he laid down his life for us: and we ought to lay down *our* lives for the brethren.

1 John 3:18 My little children, let us not love in word, neither in tongue; but in deed and in truth.

1 John 3:21 Beloved, if our heart condemn us not, *then* ~~have~~ we confidence toward God.

1 John 4:3 And every spirit that confesseth not that Jesus Christ is come in the flesh is not of God: and this is that *spirit* of antichrist, whereof ye have heard that it should come; and even now already ~~is~~ it in the world.

1 John 4:12 No man hath seen God at any time. If we love one another, God

the pride of life, is not of the Father, but is of the world.

Whosoever denieth the Son, the same hath not the Father.

Whosoever abideth in him sinneth not: whosoever **continueth in sin** hath not seen him, neither known him.

He that **continueth in** sin is of the devil; for the devil sinneth from the beginning. For this purpose the Son of God was manifested, that he might destroy the works of the devil.

Whosoever is born of God doth not **continue in** sin; for **the spirit of God** remaineth in him: and he cannot **continue in** sin, because he is born of God, **having received the holy spirit of promise.**

Hereby perceive we the love of **Christ**, because he laid down his life for us: and we ought to lay down our lives for the brethren.

My little children, let us not love in word, neither in tongue **only**; but in deed and in truth.

Beloved, if our heart condemn us not, then **we** have confidence toward God.

And every spirit that confesseth not that Jesus Christ is come in the flesh is not of God: and this is that spirit of antichrist, whereof ye have heard that it should come; and even now **it is already** in the world.

No man hath seen God at any time, **except them who believe.** If we love one

dwelleth in us, and his love is perfected in us.

1 John 5:13 These things have I written unto you that believe on the name of the Son of God; that ye may know that ye have eternal life, and that ye may believe on the name of the Son of God.

1 John 5:18 We know that whosoever is born of God ~~sinneth~~ not; but he that is begotten of God keepeth himself, and that wicked one ~~toucheth~~ him not.

another, God dwelleth in us, and his love is perfected in us.

These things have I written unto you that believe on the name of the Son of God; that ye may know that ye have eternal life, and that ye may **continue to** believe on the name of the Son of God.

We know that whosoever is born of God **continueth** not **in sin**; but he that is begotten of God, **and** keepeth himself, and that wicked one **overcometh** him not.

The Epistle of Jude

King James Version	Joseph Smith Translation
Jude 1:1 Jude, the servant of Jesus Christ, and brother of James, to them ~~that~~ are sanctified ~~by God~~ the Father, and preserved in Jesus Christ, ~~and called~~:	Jude, the servant of **God, called of** Jesus Christ, and brother of James, to them **who** are sanctified **of** the Father, and preserved in Jesus Christ:
Jude 1:11 Woe unto them! for they have gone in the way of Cain, and ran greedily after the error of Balaam for reward, and ~~perished~~ in the gainsaying of Core.	Woe unto them! for they have gone in the way of Cain, and ran greedily after the error of Balaam for reward, and **shall perish** in the gainsaying of Core.

The Revelation of John

King James Version

Revelation 1:1 The Revelation of Jesus Christ, ~~which God gave unto him~~, to shew unto his servants things which must shortly come to pass; ~~and~~ he sent and signified ~~it~~ by his angel unto his servant John:

Revelation 1:2 Who ~~bare~~ record of the word of God, and of the testimony of Jesus Christ, and of all things that he saw.

Revelation 1:3 Blessed ~~is he that readeth~~, and they ~~that~~ hear the words of this prophecy, and ~~keep~~ those things which are written therein: for the time ~~is at hand~~.

Revelation 1:4 John to the seven churches ~~which are~~ in Asia: Grace ~~be~~ unto you, and peace, from him ~~which~~ is, and ~~which~~ was, and ~~which~~ is to come; ~~and from the seven Spirits which are~~ before his throne;

Revelation 1:5 ~~And from Jesus Christ, who is~~ the faithful witness, ~~and~~ the first begotten of the dead, and the prince of the kings of the earth. Unto him ~~that~~ loved us, ~~and~~ washed us from our sins in his own blood,

Joseph Smith Translation

The Revelation of **John, a servant of God, which was given unto him of** Jesus Christ, to shew unto his servants things which must shortly come to pass; **that** he sent and signified by his angel unto his servant John:

Who **bore** record of the word of God, and of the testimony of Jesus Christ, and of all things that he saw.

Blessed **are they who read**, and they **who** hear **and understand** the words of this prophecy, and **keepeth** those things which are written therein: for the time **of the coming of the Lord draweth nigh**.

Now this is the testimony of John to the seven **servants who are over the seven** churches in Asia: Grace unto you, and peace, from him **who** is, and **who** was, and **who** is to come; **who hath sent forth his angel from** before his throne, **to testify unto those who are the seven servants over the seven churches;**

Therefore, I John, the faithful witness, **bear record of the things which were delivered me of the angel, and from Jesus Christ**, the first begotten of the dead, and the prince of the kings of the earth, **and** unto him **who** loved us, **be glory, who** washed us from our sins in his own blood,

The Revelation of John

Revelation 1:6 And hath made us kings and priests unto God ~~and~~ his Father; to him *be* glory and dominion for ever and ever. Amen.

Revelation 1:7 Behold, he cometh ~~with~~ clouds; and every eye shall see him, and they ~~also~~ ~~which~~ pierced him: and all kindreds of the earth shall wail because of him. Even so, Amen.

Revelation 1:8 I am Alpha and Omega, the beginning and the ending, ~~saith~~ the Lord, ~~which~~ is, and ~~which~~ was, and ~~which~~ is to come, the Almighty.

Revelation 1:12 And I turned to see the voice ~~that~~ spake ~~with~~ me. And being turned, I saw seven golden candlesticks;

Revelation 1:16 And he had in his right hand seven stars: and out of his mouth went a sharp twoedged sword: and his countenance *was* as the sun ~~shineth~~ in his strength.

Revelation 1:20 The mystery of the seven stars which thou sawest in my right hand, and the seven golden candlesticks. The seven stars are the ~~angels~~ of the seven churches: and the seven candlesticks which thou sawest are the seven churches.

Revelation 2:1 Unto the ~~angel~~ of the church of Ephesus write; These things saith he that holdeth the seven stars in his right hand, who walketh in the midst of the seven golden candlesticks;

Revelation 2:8 And unto the ~~angel~~ of the church in Smyrna write; These

And hath made us kings and priests unto God his Father; to him be glory and dominion for ever and ever. Amen.

For behold, he cometh **in the** clouds; **with ten thousands of his saints in the kingdom, clothed with the glory of his Father.** And every eye shall see him, and they **who** pierced him: and all kindreds of the earth shall wail because of him. Even so, Amen.

For he saith, I am Alpha and Omega, the beginning and the ending, the Lord **who** is, and **who** was, and **who** is to come, the Almighty.

And I turned to see **from whence** the voice **came which** spake **to** me. And being turned, I saw seven golden candlesticks;

And he had in his right hand seven stars: and out of his mouth went a sharp twoedged sword: and his countenance was as the sun **shining** in his strength.

This is the mystery of the seven stars which thou sawest in my right hand, and the seven golden candlesticks. The seven stars are the **servants** of the seven churches: and the seven candlesticks which thou sawest are the seven churches.

Unto the **servant** of the church of Ephesus write; These things saith he that holdeth the seven stars in his right hand, who walketh in the midst of the seven golden candlesticks;

And unto the **servant** of the church in Smyrna write; These things saith the

things saith the first and the last, which was dead, and is alive;

Revelation 2:12 And to the ~~angel~~ of the church in Pergamos write; These things saith he which hath the sharp sword with two edges;

Revelation 2:18 And unto the ~~angel~~ of the church in Thyatira write; These things saith the Son of God, who hath his eyes like unto a flame of fire, and his feet *are* like fine brass;

Revelation 2:19 I know thy works, and charity, and service, and faith, and thy patience, ~~and thy works~~; and the last *to be* more than the first.

Revelation 2:22 Behold, I will cast her into ~~a bed~~, and them that commit adultery with her into great tribulation, except they repent of their deeds.

Revelation 2:26 And ~~he that~~ overcometh, and keepeth my ~~works~~ unto the end, to him will I give power over ~~the nations~~:

Revelation 2:27 And he shall rule them with ~~a rod of iron~~; as the vessels of a potter ~~shall they be broken to shivers~~: even as I received of my Father.

Revelation 3:1 And unto the ~~angel~~ of the church in Sardis write; These things saith he ~~that~~ hath the seven ~~Spirits~~ of God, and the seven stars; I know thy works, that thou hast a name that thou livest, and art dead.

Revelation 3:2 Be watchful, and strengthen ~~the things which~~ remain,

first and the last, which was dead, and is alive;

And to the **servant** of the church in Pergamos write; These things saith he which hath the sharp sword with two edges;

And unto the **servant** of the church in Thyatira write; These things saith the Son of God, who hath his eyes like unto a flame of fire, and his feet are like fine brass;

I know thy works, and charity, and service, and faith, and thy patience; and the last to be more than the first.

Behold, I will cast her into **hell**, and them that commit adultery with her into great tribulation, except they repent of their deeds.

And **to him who** overcometh, and keepeth my **commandments** unto the end, will I give power over **many kingdoms**:

And he shall rule them with **the word of God; and they shall be in his hands** as the vessels of **clay in the hands of** a potter; **and he shall govern them by faith, with equity and justice**, even as I received of my Father,

And unto the **servant** of the church in Sardis write; These things saith he **who** hath the seven **stars, which are the servants** of God. I know thy works, that thou hast a name that thou livest, and art **not** dead.

Be watchful **therefore** and strengthen **those who** remain, **who** are ready to die:

~~that~~ are ready to die: for I have not found thy works perfect before God.

Revelation 3:5 He that overcometh, the same shall be clothed in white raiment; and I will not blot ~~out~~ his name out of the book of life, but I will confess his name before my Father, and before his angels.

Revelation 3:7 And to the ~~angel~~ of the church in Philadelphia write; These things saith he that is holy, he that is true, he that hath the key of David, he that openeth, and no man shutteth; and shutteth, and no man openeth;

Revelation 3:12 Him that overcometh will I make a pillar in the temple of my God, and he shall go no more out: and I will write upon him the name of my God, and the name of the city of my God, ~~which is~~ new Jerusalem, which cometh down out of heaven from my God: and ~~I will write upon him~~ my new name.

Revelation 3:14 And unto the ~~angel~~ of the church of the Laodiceans write; These things saith the Amen, the faithful and true witness, the beginning of the creation of God;

Revelation 4:1 After this I looked, and, behold, a door ~~was~~ opened ~~in~~ heaven: and the first voice which I heard ~~was~~ as it were of a trumpet talking with me; which said, Come up hither, and I will shew thee things which must be hereafter.

Revelation 4:4 And ~~round about~~ the throne *were* four and twenty seats: and upon the seats I saw four and twenty

for I have not found thy works perfect before God.

He that overcometh, the same shall be clothed in white raiment; and I will not blot his name out of the book of life, but I will confess his name before my Father, and before his angels.

And to the **servant** of the church in Philadelphia write; These things saith he that is holy, he that is true, he that hath the key of David, he that openeth, and no man shutteth; and shutteth, and no man openeth;

Him that overcometh will I make a pillar in the temple of my God, and he shall go no more out: and I will write upon him the name of my God, and the name of the city of my God, **this is** new Jerusalem, which cometh down out of heaven from my God: and **this is** my new name.

And unto the **servant** of the church of the Laodiceans write; These things saith the Amen, the faithful and true witness, the beginning of the creation of God;

After this I looked, and, behold, a door opened **into** heaven: and the first voice which I heard as it were of a trumpet talking with me; which said, Come up hither, and I will shew thee things which must be hereafter.

And **in the midst of** the throne were four and twenty seats: and upon the seats I saw four and twenty elders

elders sitting, clothed in white raiment; and they had on their heads crowns of gold.

Revelation 4:5 And out of the throne proceeded lightnings and thunderings and voices: and ~~there were~~ seven lamps of fire burning before the throne, which are the seven ~~Spirits~~ of God.

Revelation 4:6 And before the throne *there was* a sea of glass like unto crystal: and in the midst of the throne, and round about the throne, *were* four beasts full of eyes before and behind.

Revelation 4:9 And when those beasts give glory and honour and thanks to him that ~~sat~~ on the throne, who liveth for ever and ever,

Revelation 4:10 The four and twenty elders fall down before him that ~~sat~~ on the throne, and worship him that liveth for ever and ever, and cast their crowns before the throne, saying,

Revelation 5:1 And I saw in the right hand of him that ~~sat~~ on the throne a book written within and on the backside, sealed with seven seals.

Revelation 5:2 And I saw a strong angel proclaiming with a loud voice, Who is worthy to open the book, and ~~to~~ loose the seals thereof?

Revelation 5:6 And I beheld, and, lo, in the midst of the throne and of the four beasts, and in the midst of the elders, stood a Lamb as it had been slain, having ~~seven~~ horns and ~~seven~~ eyes, which are the ~~seven Spirits~~ of God sent forth into all the earth.

sitting, clothed in white raiment; and they had on their heads crowns of gold.

And out of the throne proceeded lightnings and thunderings and voices: and seven lamps of fire burning before the throne, which are the seven **servants** of God.

And before the throne there was a sea of glass like unto crystal: and in the midst of the throne **were the four and twenty elders:** and round about the throne, were four beasts full of eyes before and behind.

And when those beasts give glory and honour and thanks to him that **sits** on the throne, who liveth for ever and ever,

The four and twenty elders fall down before him that **sits** on the throne, and worship him that liveth for ever and ever, and cast their crowns before the throne, saying,

And I saw in the right hand of him that **sits** on the throne a book written within and on the backside, sealed with seven seals.

And I saw a strong angel **and heard him** proclaiming with a loud voice, Who is worthy to open the book, and loose the seals thereof?

And I beheld, and, lo, in the midst of the throne and of the four beasts, and in the midst of the elders, stood a Lamb as it had been slain, having **twelve** horns and **twelve** eyes, which are the **twelve servants** of God sent forth into all the earth.

Revelation 6:1 And I saw when the Lamb opened one of the seals, and I heard, as it were the noise of thunder, one of the four beasts saying, Come and see.	And I saw when the Lamb opened one of the seals, **one of the four beasts**, and I heard, as it were, the noise of thunder, saying, Come and see.
Revelation 6:6 And I heard a voice in the midst of the four beasts say, A measure of wheat for a penny, and three measures of barley for a penny; and ~~see thou~~ hurt not the oil and the wine.	And I heard a voice in the midst of the four beasts say, A measure of wheat for a penny, and three measures of barley for a penny; and hurt not **thou** the oil and the wine.
Revelation 6:14 And the ~~heaven departed~~ as a scroll when it is rolled together; and every mountain and island ~~were~~ moved out of ~~their places~~.	And the **heavens opened** as a scroll **is opened** when it is rolled together; and every mountain and island **was** moved out of **its place**.
Revelation 7:2 And I saw another angel ascending from the east, having the seal of the living God: and ~~he cried~~ with a loud voice to the four angels, to whom it was given to hurt the earth and the sea,	And I saw another angel ascending from the east, having the seal of the living God: and **I heard him cry** with a loud voice to the four angels, to whom it was given to hurt the earth and the sea,
Revelation 7:4 And ~~I heard~~ the number of them ~~which~~ were sealed: ~~and there were sealed~~ an hundred *and* forty *and* four thousand of all the tribes of the children of Israel.	And the number of them **who** were sealed were an hundred and forty and four thousand of all the tribes of the children of Israel.
Revelation 8:12 And the fourth angel sounded, and the third part of the sun was smitten, and the third part of the moon, and the third part of the stars; so ~~as~~ the third part of them was darkened, and the day shone not for a third part of it, and the night likewise.	And the fourth angel sounded, and the third part of the sun was smitten, and the third part of the moon, and the third part of the stars; so **that** the third part of them was darkened, and the day shone not for a third part of it, and the night likewise.
Revelation 9:1 And the fifth angel sounded, and I saw a star fall from heaven unto the earth: and to ~~him~~ was given the key of the bottomless pit.	And the fifth angel sounded, and I saw a star fall from heaven unto the earth: and to **the angel** was given the key of the bottomless pit.
Revelation 9:11 And they had a king over them, *which is* the angel of the bottomless pit, whose name in the Hebrew	And they had a king over them, which is the angel of the bottomless pit, whose name in the Hebrew tongue

tongue *is* Abaddon, but in the Greek tongue ~~hath *his* name~~ Apollyon.

Revelation 9:14 Saying to the sixth angel which had the trumpet, Loose the four angels which are bound in the ~~great river Euphrates~~.

Revelation 9:16 And the number of the army of the horsemen ~~were~~ two hundred thousand thousand: and I ~~heard~~ the number of them.

Revelation 10:4 And when the seven thunders had uttered their voices, I was about to write: and I heard a voice from heaven saying unto me, ~~Seal up~~ those things which the seven thunders uttered, and write them not.

Revelation 12:1 And there appeared a great ~~wonder~~ in heaven; a woman clothed with the sun, and the moon under her feet, and upon her head a crown of twelve stars:

Revelation 12:2 And ~~she~~ being with child cried, travailing in birth, and pained to be delivered.

Revelation 12:3 And there appeared another ~~wonder~~ in heaven; and behold a great red dragon, having seven heads and ten horns, and seven crowns upon his heads.

Revelation 12:4 And his tail drew the third part of the stars of heaven, and did cast them to the earth: and the dragon stood before the woman which was ~~ready to be~~ delivered, ~~for~~ to devour her child ~~as soon as~~ it was born.

is Abaddon, but in the Greek tongue Apollyon.

Saying to the sixth angel which had the trumpet, Loose the four angels which are bound in the **bottomless pit**.

And the number of the army of the horsemen two hundred thousand thousand: and I **saw** the number of them.

And when the seven thunders had uttered their voices, I was about to write: and I heard a voice from heaven saying unto me, Those things **are sealed up** which the seven thunders uttered, and write them not.

And there appeared a great **sign** in heaven, **in the likeness of things on the earth**; a woman clothed with the sun, and the moon under her feet, and upon her head a crown of twelve stars:

And **the woman** being with child cried, travailing in birth, and pained to be delivered. **And she brought forth a man child, who was to rule all nations with a rod of iron: and her child was caught up unto God and his throne.**

And there appeared another **sign** in heaven; and behold, a great red dragon, having seven heads and ten horns, and seven crowns upon his heads.

And his tail drew the third part of the stars of heaven, and did cast them to the earth: and the dragon stood before the woman which was delivered, **ready** to devour her child **after** it was born.

The Revelation of John

Revelation 12:5 ~~And she brought forth a man child, who was to rule all nations with a rod of iron: and her child was caught up unto God, and~~ *to* ~~his throne~~.

Revelation 12:6 And the woman fled into the wilderness, where she ~~hath~~ a place prepared of God, that they should feed her there a thousand two hundred *and* threescore ~~days~~.

And the woman fled into the wilderness, where she **had** a place prepared of God, that they should feed her there a thousand two hundred and threescore **years**.

Revelation 12:7 And there was war in heaven: Michael and his angels fought against the dragon; and the dragon fought ~~and his angels~~,

And there was war in heaven: Michael and his angels fought against the dragon; and the dragon **and his angels** fought **against Michael,**

Revelation 12:8 And prevailed not; neither ~~was their place found any more in heaven~~.

And **the dragon** prevailed not **against Michael**; neither **the child, nor the woman, which was the church of God, who had been delivered of her pains, and brought forth the kingdom of our God and his Christ.**

Revelation 12:9 ~~And~~ the great dragon was cast out, that old serpent, called the Devil, and Satan, which deceiveth the whole world: he was cast out into the earth, and his angels were cast out with him.

Neither was there place found in heaven for the great dragon **who** was cast out, that old serpent, called the Devil, and **also called** Satan, which deceiveth the whole world: he **who** was cast out into the earth, and his angels were cast out with him.

Revelation 12:11 ~~And~~ they ~~overcame~~ him by the blood of the Lamb, and by the word of their testimony; ~~and~~ they loved not their lives unto ~~the~~ death.

For they **have overcome** him by the blood of the Lamb, and by the word of their testimony; **for** they loved not their **own** lives, **but kept the testimony even** unto death.

Revelation 12:12 Therefore rejoice, ~~ye~~ heavens, and ye that dwell in them. Woe to the inhabiters of the earth and of the sea! for the devil is come down unto you, having great wrath, because he knoweth that he hath but a short time.

Therefore rejoice, O heavens, and ye that dwell in them. **And after these things I heard another voice, saying,** Woe to the inhabiters of the earth, **yea, and they who dwell upon the islands** of the sea! for the devil is come down unto you, having great wrath, because he knoweth that he hath but a short time.

Revelation 12:13 ~~And~~ when the dragon saw that he was cast unto the earth, he persecuted the woman which brought forth the man *child*.	**For** when the dragon saw that he was cast unto the earth, he persecuted the woman which brought forth the man child.
Revelation 12:14 ~~And~~ to the woman were given two wings of a great eagle, that she might ~~fly~~ into the wilderness, into her place, where she is nourished for a time, and times, and half a time, from the face of the serpent.	**Therefore** to the woman were given two wings of a great eagle, that she might **flee** into the wilderness, into her place, where she is nourished for a time, and times, and half a time, from the face of the serpent.
Revelation 12:15 And the serpent ~~cast~~ out of his mouth water as a flood after the woman, that he might cause her to be carried away of the flood.	And the serpent **casteth** out of his mouth water as a flood after the woman, that he might cause her to be carried away of the flood.
Revelation 12:16 And the earth ~~helped~~ the woman, and the earth ~~opened~~ her mouth, and ~~swallowed~~ up the flood which the dragon ~~cast~~ out of his mouth.	And the earth **helpeth** the woman, and the earth **openeth** her mouth, and **swalloweth** up the flood which the dragon **casteth** out of his mouth.
Revelation 12:17 ~~And~~ the dragon was wroth with the woman, and went to make war with the remnant of her seed, which keep the commandments of God, and have the testimony of Jesus Christ.	**Therefore** the dragon was wroth with the woman, and went to make war with the remnant of her seed, which keep the commandments of God, and have **also** the testimony of Jesus Christ.
Revelation 13:1 And I ~~stood upon the sand of the sea, and~~ saw a beast rise up out of the sea, having seven heads and ten horns, and upon his horns ten crowns, and upon his heads the name of blasphemy.	And I saw **another sign in the likeness of the kingdoms of the earth**, a beast rise up out of the sea, **and stood upon the sand of the sea**, having seven heads and ten horns, and upon his horns ten crowns, and upon his heads the name of blasphemy.
Revelation 16:7 And I heard another out ~~of~~ the altar ~~say~~, Even so, Lord God Almighty, true and righteous *are* thy judgments.	And I heard another **angel who came** out **from** the altar **saying**, Even so, Lord God Almighty, true and righteous are thy judgments.
Revelation 17:17 For God hath put in their hearts to fulfil his will, and to agree, and give their kingdom unto the beast, until the words of God ~~shall be~~ fulfilled.	For God hath put in their hearts to fulfil his will, and to agree, and give their kingdom unto the beast, until the words of God **are** fulfilled.

Revelation 19:2 For true and righteous *are* his judgments: for he hath judged the great whore, which did corrupt the earth with her fornication, and hath avenged the blood of his ~~servants~~ at her hand.

Revelation 19:5 And a voice came out of the throne, saying, Praise our God, all ye his ~~servants~~, and ye that fear him, both small and great.

Revelation 19:10 And I fell at his feet to worship him. And he said unto me, See ~~thou do it~~ not: I am thy fellowservant, and of thy brethren that have the testimony of Jesus: worship God: for the testimony of Jesus is the spirit of prophecy.

Revelation 19:11 And I saw heaven opened, and behold a white horse; and he that sat upon him ~~was~~ called Faithful and True, and in righteousness he doth judge and make war.

Revelation 19:12 His eyes ~~were~~ as a flame of fire, and on his head ~~were~~ many crowns; and he had a name written, that no man knew, but ~~he~~ himself.

Revelation 19:13 And he ~~was~~ clothed with a vesture dipped in blood: and his name is called The Word of God.

Revelation 19:15 And out of his mouth ~~goeth a sharp sword~~, ~~that~~ with it he ~~should~~ smite the nations: and he ~~shall~~ rule them with ~~a rod of iron~~: and he treadeth the winepress ~~of~~ the fierceness and wrath of Almighty God.

Revelation 19:16 And he hath on ~~his~~ vesture and on his thigh a name written, KING OF KINGS, AND LORD OF LORDS.

For true and righteous are his judgments: for he hath judged the great whore, which did corrupt the earth with her fornication, and hath avenged the blood of his **saints** at her hand.

And a voice came out of the throne, saying, Praise our God, all ye his **saints**, and ye that fear him, both small and great.

And I fell at his feet to worship him. And he said unto me, See **not that** I am thy fellowservant, and of thy brethren that have the testimony of Jesus: worship God: for the testimony of Jesus is the spirit of prophecy.

And I saw heaven opened, and behold a white horse; and he that sat upon him **is** called Faithful and True, and in righteousness he doth judge and make war.

His eyes [were] as a flame of fire, and **he had** on his head many crowns; and he had a name written, that no man knew, but himself.

And he **is** clothed with a vesture dipped in blood: and his name is called The Word of God.

And out of his mouth **proceedeth the word of God, and** with it he **will** smite the nations: and he **will** rule them with **the word of his mouth**: and he treadeth the winepress **in** the fierceness and wrath of Almighty God.

And he hath on **a** vesture and on his thigh a name written, KING OF KINGS, AND LORD OF LORDS.

Revelation 19:18 That ye may eat the flesh of kings, and the flesh of captains, and the flesh of mighty men, and the flesh of horses, and of them that sit on them, and the flesh of all ~~men~~, both ~~free~~ and ~~bond~~, both small and great.

Revelation 19:21 And the remnant were slain with the sword of him that sat upon the horse, which ~~sword~~ proceeded out of his mouth: and all the fowls were filled with their flesh.

Revelation 20:1 And I saw an angel come down ~~from~~ heaven, having the key of the bottomless pit and a great chain in his hand.

Revelation 20:6 Blessed and holy ~~is he that hath~~ part in the first resurrection: on such the second death hath no power, but they shall be priests of God and of Christ, and shall reign with him a thousand years.

Revelation 22:9 Then saith he unto me, See ~~thou do it~~ not: ~~for~~ I am thy fellowservant, and of thy brethren the prophets, and of them which keep the sayings of this book: worship God.

That ye may eat the flesh of kings, and the flesh of captains, and the flesh of mighty men, and the flesh of horses, and of them that sit on them, and the flesh of all **who fight against the Lamb**, both **bond** and **free**, both small and great.

And the remnant were slain with the sword of him that sat upon the horse, which **word** proceeded out of his mouth: and all the fowls were filled with their flesh.

And I saw an angel come down **out of** heaven, having the key of the bottomless pit and a great chain in his hand.

Blessed and holy **are they who have** part in the first resurrection: on such the second death hath no power, but they shall be priests of God and of Christ, and shall reign with him a thousand years.

Then saith he unto me, See **not that** I am thy fellowservant, and of thy brethren the prophets, and of them which keep the sayings of this book: worship God.